Chinese Pupils in Britain

Chinese Pupils in Britain

A Review of Research into the Education
of Pupils of Chinese Origin

Monica J. Taylor

NFER-NELSON

Published by the NFER-NELSON Publishing Company Ltd.
Darville House, 2 Oxford Road East,
Windsor, Berkshire SL4 1DF, England

and in the United States of America by
NFER-NELSON, 242 Cherry Street,
Philadelphia, PA 19106–1906.
Tel: (215) 238 0939. Telex: 244489.

First Published 1987
©National Foundation for Educational Research 1987

Library of Congress Cataloging in Publication data

Taylor, Monica Jean.
    Chinese pupils in Britain.

    Bibliography: p.
    Includes index.
    1. Chinese students—Education—Great Britain.
    2. Chinese—Great Britain—Social conditions.   I. Title.
    LC3085.G7T39   1986   371.8'2   86–17181
    ISBN 0–7005–1042–7

Phototypeset by David John Services Ltd., Maidenhead

Printed by Billing & Sons Limited, Worcester.

ISBN 0–7005–1042–7
Code 8240 021

CONTENTS

teaching materials; attainment; liaison with
parents; pupils' attitudes; extra-curricular
activities; supplementary schools; community
function of Chinese schools; English classes;
LEA support

TABLES IN THE TEXT

ACKNOWLEDGEMENTS

This is the third in a series of reviews of research, originally presented as a report to the Committee of Inquiry into the Education of Children from Ethnic Minority Groups (Swann Committee) in 1983. The work has been revised and updated in 1985–6 whilst I was in full-time employment on a research project, hence the delay in publication.

Although this review relates to pupils of Chinese origin, it does not deal explicitly with Vietnamese pupils, many of whom are also of Chinese ethnic origin. They, together with pupils of Cypriot, Italian and Ukrainian origin, Liverpool Blacks, and gypsies, will form the subject of a fourth review (Taylor with Hegarty, 1987).

It should, moreover, be noted that much of the material specifically relating to pupils of Chinese origin, particularly with respect to mother-tongue teaching and multicultural education, assumes consideration of the wider educational debate on these issues which was treated in more depth in the second review of research on pupils of South Asian origin, *The Best of Both Worlds . . . ?* (Taylor with Hegarty, 1985, NFER-NELSON).

Once again, obtaining material for review has drawn considerably on library facilities and I should like to thank the library and information staff for their ready help. Mavis Froud compiled the index, Tim Wright drew the map and Michael Halson facilitated the publishing arrangements. Once more, I should like to express my particular gratitude to Mary Dyer and Annie Cridge who typed the first draft of the manuscript and, above all, to Lynn Fardell, who single-handedly retyped a very ragged, revised draft with speed and fortitude. The inquiries of certain colleagues both within and outside the National Foundation for Educational Research (NFER) have also encouraged me to continue the work to publication.

In recent years there has been increasing interest in the Far East and, to some extent, the Chinese in Britain. This book is the only work to bring together all the extant research on the socioeconomic, cultural and educational position of pupils of Chinese origin and their families in the UK, and, it is hoped, therefore, that it will fill an important gap in the literature.

MJT

January 1986

Introduction

Pupils of Chinese origin form the third largest group of ethnic minority pupils in British schools. The majority of these pupils are second-generation, though there are some, in certain areas of Liverpool or London, who can claim to be third- or possibly even fourth-generation pupils with Chinese ancestry. But the Chinese population in the UK has received very little attention despite its growth over the last 15 years. Indeed, it has become a cliché that the Chinese are both little known and little understood. There have been few attempts to get beyond the stereotype: namely, that the Chinese are scattered, often isolated, economically and socially self-sufficient and law-abiding. In short, they have been perceived to maintain a distance and keep a low profile, hence living up to their traditional image as inscrutable.

Undoubtedly there have been cultural and linguistic barriers to more accurate perceptions. The peculiar social and economic position of the Chinese population – which may itself have been a shrewd response to inter-community perceptions, as well as a matter of economic survival – has not facilitated research into this dispersed group. Thus the perceived homogeneity of the Chinese has largely ignored successive phases of settlement, variations in social composition and differences in degree of orientation and adaptation to life in the UK, and especially changes over time. Only in the late 1970s and early 1980s with the emergence of a UK-born second generation and a small number of Chinese professionals who promote and serve the needs of their ethnic group, and together with increased awareness of political and economic links between the Far East and UK, has some interest in and concern about the Chinese in the UK been initiated. The stereotype of the Chinese has begun to be called into question, mainly by means of a number of national conferences sponsored by Chinese professionals and community groups: Community Relations Commission (CRC), 1975; Standing Committee of Scottish Community Relations Councils (SCSCRC), 1976; Chinese Action Group and Quaker Community Relations Committee (CAG & QCRC), 1979; and Quaker Community Relations Committee (QCRC), 1981 – and four national conferences on Chinese children in Britain: National Educational Research and

Development Trust (NERDT), 1977, 1978; and National Children's Centre (NCC), 1979, 1984, which have exposed some of the social and educational problems experienced by the Chinese, of which there has been considerable ignorance. This increased activity coincided with the reception and settlement of a number of Vietnamese refugees, a high proportion of whom are of Chinese ethnic origin. Their arrival may have provided an additional impetus to the disclosure and discovery of difficulties experienced by some Chinese adults and children living in the UK. Moreover, in the mid-1980s discussions and decisions on the future of Hong Kong and the likely expansion of economic and cultural contact with mainland China have further served to focus attention on the Chinese in Britain. Indeed, since this review was first undertaken the Home Affairs Committee of the House of Commons has investigated the position of the Chinese in Britain, through written and oral evidence and visits. The Committee's three-volume report (GB. P. H of C. HAC, 1985) recognizes the existence of problems in the Chinese community which have gone largely unnoticed. There is even some evidence that the existence of the inquiry itself has promoted greater awareness.

Thus, although a certain amount of evidence about the Chinese is gradually coming to light, there remains a serious gap in empirical research in the social sciences on this group in the UK. Methodologically work is sometimes unsound, often lacking a clear data base, with relevant information embedded in survey data covering other ethnic minority groups. This is particularly difficult to unravel, and when finally teased out, is sometimes subject to flat contradictions in interpretation, usually according to whether research has been undertaken by investigators of Chinese ethnic or British origin. This obtains with especial force in educational research, both with respect to ethnic minority pupils in general and pupils of Chinese origin* in particular. There have been few cogent attempts to consider the position of pupils of Chinese origin in the British school system; a lack of surveys and sample limitations make for restricted quantitative data so the emphasis is often qualitative at the level of description or anecdote interpretatively conveyed. Not surprisingly, language has been the pivotal focus of interest when investigations of any range and depth have been mounted either by Chinese community groups or British educationists. Apart from such data the uneven quality of much other work under review must be borne in mind when assessing its contribution and insights. Yet despite ambiguities in assessment, nevertheless there are trends. Even so it is difficult to avoid the view that in the field of multiethnic education attention has been almost exclusively focussed on pupils of Asian and West Indian origin, so that the as yet unrealized large and increasing number of pupils of Chinese origin have to date, with a few signal exceptions, failed to receive proper acknowledgement or to be shown due professional interest or concern.

Pupils of Chinese origin are dispersed around the country, rarely, it has been estimated, forming more than five per cent of any mainstream school population (Watson, 1977a). This presents a challenge for appropriate educational provision. But has the dispersal of pupils of Chinese origin (thereby lending an appearance of numerical insignificance) been allowed by default to become an excuse for not finding out more about their particular educational needs and taking steps to meet them? Conversely, to what extent is the cultural background of such pupils and their way of life and contribution to British society appreciated by teachers and other pupils in schools?

At present, according to recent estimates (OPCS, 1982a, 1984), there are approximately 30,000 pupils of Chinese ethnic origin in British schools, three-quarters (at least) are second generation, having been born in the UK. But where are they? How are they faring educationally? How are they perceived by teachers and other pupils? How do Chinese pupils and their parents see themselves within British society? This review attempts to bring together all the available evidence to assess the position and achievement of pupils of Chinese origin in British schools over the last 15 years or so. This educational assessment, which focusses on performance and attitudes, is set in the context of a wider examination of the social and economic background of pupils of Chinese origin in their country of origin and of their lifestyles in the UK.

---

* In this review it is proposed to use the term 'of Chinese origin' to describe the pupils who are its subject. This is a colloquial and shortened form which requires qualification if it is not to be misleading since it implies a certain homogeneity. Strictly the term 'of Chinese ethnic origin' would be more correct, though this would also include many of the more recently arrived Vietnamese pupils (who are the subjects of another review, see Hegarty in Taylor with Hegarty, 1987). Though most (yet by no means all) pupils of Chinese origin derive their cultural traditions from mainland China, they have forebears who came or have themselves come, directly from Hong Kong (or Singapore, Malaysia or Taiwan) and linguistically are more likely to be Cantonese speakers than speakers of the official Chinese Mandarin or other Chinese dialects. Even so three-quarters of the present school population of Chinese origin are UK-born, and some have mixed parentage. It is, moreover, important to draw attention to the significant distinction, which is always though often inexplicitly made between pupils of Chinese origin and other pupils with Asian backgrounds, having their origins in the Indian sub-continent (see Taylor with Hegarty, 1985). Pupils of Chinese origin are always perceived as of South East or Far East Asian origin, though this category may also include relatively small numbers of pupils of non-Chinese origin from that area.

Part One

The Hong Kong Background

By far the majority of pupils of Chinese origin in British schools have their roots in Hong Kong and the more rural New Territories. A minority have closer links with the People's Republic of China, though their parents will have emigrated via Hong Kong. Smaller numbers of Chinese pupils have connections with Taiwan, Singapore and Malaysia (see ILEA, 1975). Ninety-eight per cent of the population of Hong Kong are of Chinese ethnic origin (plus one per cent Westerners and 0.5 per cent non-Chinese Asians). But Singapore and Malaysia are much more ethnically pluralistic: Singapore's population is 76 per cent Chinese (Barnes, 1978) and Malaysia's 36 per cent Chinese (Clough and Quarmby, 1978). So it cannot be assumed that pupils with roots in such countries will share a common traditional Chinese cultural background. This review will therefore focus on the Hong Kong background, especially as this represents a modified form of traditional Chinese values and culture, even though there have been far-reaching social and economic changes since the Second World War, with spreading urbanization and industrialization, so that the more developed areas now encompass the traditions of both the East and West.

HISTORY

Hong Kong was eventually acquired as a British Crown Colony after a succession of attempts to expand trade with China. The East India Company was established in Canton early in the 18th century, but by the early 19th century strained relations developed between Britain and China on account of British encouragement to the Chinese to purchase opium and Chinese resistance to the development of British mercantile interests. Such tensions provoked the first Anglo-Chinese opium war (1832–42). At its conclusion Lord Palmerston demanded a small island where British merchants would be free to trade and Hong Kong (29 square miles) was ceded by the Treaty of Nanking in 1843. A second opium war took place in 1858–60. This was terminated by a treaty which also assigned to the British the 3¾ square miles of the Kowloon Peninsula and Stonecutters Island. Later, in 1898, under the Convention of Peking, an additional 365½ square miles north of Kowloon, known as the New Territories, was leased for 99 years and, after initial Chinese opposition, became an integral part of the Colony of Hong Kong. Following a series of land reclamations, Hong Kong now comprises an area of some 404 square miles and includes 236 islands (see Map 1, p.27).

PEOPLE

Although Hong Kong was just a barren rock at the end of the 19th century, it was nevertheless a strategic watering-place and soon became a growing centre of Chinese emigration and trade with the Chinese community abroad. Indeed, there has been a long tradition both of internal migration from north to south in China, and emigration to countries of South East Asia, America, the West Indies, Australia and New Zealand. There has been estimated to be at least 16 million Chinese abroad (Garvey and Jackson, 1975). In particular, after the end of the Second World War, with the defeat of the Kuomintang by the Communists in 1948, the removal of Chiang Kai Shek and his army to Taiwan, and the establishment of the People's Republic of China in 1949, there was a considerable movement of people over the border into the New Territories. This continued into the 1950s and early 1960s when numbers were estimated to be over one million. In Hong Kong as a whole the majority of the Chinese population are Cantonese in origin. The other main ethnic groups are Hakka, Sze Yap, Chiu Chow, Hokklo and Tan Ka, together with people from the Chinese midlands and the north, among whom people from Shanghai predominate. Until the post-war immigration from China there were three distinct ethnic groups in the New Territories, from which most of the Chinese immigrants to Britain come. The dominant Cantonese are thought to be descendants of Northern Chinese pioneers who were established in the flat and more fertile land by the end of the 10th century. The Hakka, of Mongolian race, arrived several centuries later and settled in the poorer hilly regions. Until relatively recently these two groups were fairly hostile and never intermarried. The third main ethnic group are Hokklo and Tan Ka boatmen and fishermen living and working aboard the junks and boats in the many harbours. These three ethnic groups comprise the indigenous population of the New Territories and would be roughly categorized as Southern Chinese, as distinct from the more recent northern immigrants.

POPULATION

These movements are reflected in the tremendous post-war growth in population. In 1945 this was estimated to be 600,000 but by the Census in 1961 it had increased to 3,133,131. By 1971 the population had reached nearly four million with 55 per cent of the urban population born in Hong Kong itself (Table 1).

Table 1: Population of Hong Kong, by area, 1971

	Number of persons	*% of total*
Hong Kong Island	996,183	25.3
Kowloon	716,272	18.2
New Kowloon	1,478,581	37.6
New Territories	665,700	16.9
Marine	79,894	2.0
Total	3,936,630	100.0

During the 1970s the population continued to grow, so that it was put at 4.5 million in mid-1977 and in 1983 was 5,344,400 after an influx of immigrants from China and Vietnamese refugees. Since 1961 there has been a movement in the population from Hong Kong Island inland to Kowloon, New Kowloon and the New Territories. In addition, there has been a dramatic decline in the boat-dwelling population and a trend to set up home on land and engage in factory work. Hence, whereas the 1971 figure for marine dwellers dropped by 50 per cent compared with the previous decade, the 1976 estimate registered a further decline to about 50,000. It is a predominantly young population, although the proportion is changing, for whereas in 1973 33.7 per cent of the population was under 15 in 1983 the figure was 23.9 per cent (HKG, 1984).

SOCIOECONOMIC DEVELOPMENT
With some 80 per cent of the population living in the urban areas of Hong Kong, Kowloon and New Kowloon, the density of population at 40,000 to the square mile makes this area one of the most densely populated in the world. Space is very cramped, land is at a premium and there has been much architectural reconstruction on compact rocky territory which has been difficult to develop. The post-1945 transformation of Hong Kong to a prosperous, international commercial and industrial centre has revolved around its fine 23-square-mile harbour. This international port is visited annually by some 11,000 vessels and loads and unloads 37,000,000 tonnes of cargo. Hong Kong is an international centre for communication by sea, by air and telecommunications. The rapid expansion of manufacturing industry, first, by developing the traditional textile industry, and later plastics, electrical goods and technological equipment, has continued to make Hong Kong a focus for export and re-export among the top 20 exporting nations. The industrial revolution from the mid-1960s to the mid-1970s is shown in Table 2. Hong Kong also functions as a centre for commerce, banking and insurance. For example, in 1983 there were 136 licensed banks, two – the Chartered founded in 1853, and the Hong Kong and Shanghai founded in 1885 – of international reputation.

The urban worker is generally reckoned to be prosperous by Asian standards, though families may depend on all their members, including older children, being in work. Although child labour is difficult to assess, 1971 Census figures show that there were more than 36,000 workers aged 10–14. However, legislation was introduced in 1976 to limit the hours worked by women and young people, so that no child under 15 may work in industry although children over 13 may work. Unemployment is said to be low. Increasing industrialization has, it is claimed, generally bettered working conditions and living standards. In 1983, 44 per cent of the population were living in public housing, both rented and owned.

These rapid changes have been paralleled in the more rural New

Table 2: Industrial undertakings, workers and domestic exports, Hong Kong, 1967 and 1977

	1967	*1977*
Industrial undertakings	11,232	37,568
Industrial workers	443,972	755,108
Domestic exports	$6,699m.	$35,004m.

Source: HKGO, n.d., p.17.

Territories, though to a lesser degree. In 1971 this area comprised 90 per cent of the land of the Colony but only 20 per cent of the population. Even then, figures already reflected a considerable growth in the land population with the extensive development of new towns and large public housing estates. Whereas in 1961 the Census recorded a land population of 409,945, by 1971 this had risen to 665,700. By contrast, the marine population had declined from 46,500 in 1961 to 28,215 in 1971.

Although the New Territories, a series of lowlands separated from one another and the urban areas by steep scrub-covered hills, were only 12 per cent arable, the traditional occupations of the village communities were farming and fishing. In the sub-tropical climate rice farming was the traditional labour-intensive occupation of the indigenous Cantonese and Hakka. Two crops of paddy per year were yielded by 25 per cent of all cultivated land, but this is now mainly limited to the remoter mountainous regions of the eastern mainland either on individual or communal land holdings. The Cantonese occupy most of the two principal plains in the north-west and own much of the most fertile valley land in the other areas. The Hakka occupy the more mountainous slopes and the poorer land. But in recent years, with the arrival of Hakka immigrants, the two ethnic groups have increasingly intermingled and intermarried. However, with the collapse of the agricultural economy in the 1950s there was a decline in rice cultivation, and where certain traditional farming areas are now closer to communications, much of the land has been rented out to Cantonese and Chiu Chow immigrants for market gardening. Thirty-five per cent of all cultivable land (only 9.1 per cent in 1983) now yields up to ten crops of vegetables a year. There has also been an increase in pig and poultry farming. By contrast, the fishing industry of the New Territories has declined and the rehousing of many boat-dwelling fishermen on land has been coupled with the movement of the fishing and agricultural population into industry. Before 1962, when industrial and housing developments in the New Territories began, many of the indigenous inhabitants were engaged in certain traditional industries linked with farming or fishing, such as the operation of salt pans, the preparation of salt fish, fish-paste, bean-curd, soya sauce and preserved fruits. It was as an alternative to changes in agricultural patterns or increasing industrialization that many of the Cantonese from this area came to Britain.

Over the last two decades there has been further expansion into the New Territories and the increasing change from an agrarian to an industrial society has had implications for traditional social structures, although the New Territories have a strong sense of cultural heritage. Instead of programmes of land reclamation engineering projects have focussed on the construction of reservoirs, desalination plants and facilitating communication by building a cross-harbour tunnel from Hong Kong Island to Kowloon and a mass-transit railway. Since 1982 this has extended to Tsuen Wan in the New Territories, one of the developed industrial areas where large textile mills are located. Although some of the small islands contain important centres of population and minor industries, development is concentrated on the mainland of the New Territories with the construction of large cities, such as Tuen Mun and Sha Tin, both of which will eventually house half a million people. It was anticipated that by 1980 some two million people would have been accommodated in the New Territories (Garvey and Jackson, 1975). This area has also provided scope for the development of leisure facilities for the urban population and an accompanying service industry. Tourism, too, is a major enterprise of the Hong Kong Colony. Thus it is clear that over the last decade traditional settlements and occupations have been eroded as the previously rural New Territories have increasingly been marked by pockets of urbanization and industrialization. Hong Kong has been characterized as a fiercely competitive status-conscious society and, to judge by the accounts of pupils of Chinese origin (Lee in ILEA English Centre, 1979; Fitchett, 1976), one which is increasingly violent and corrupt, though Ward (1977/8) has claimed crime rates are unusually low in view of the high density of population. Thus it is important to remember that whilst many descendants of Chinese immigrants now in British schools will have come from backgrounds rooted in the traditional social and economic organization of the New Territories, they will have become increasingly aware of and under the influence of developments in these areas. Indeed, the more recently arrived pupils of Chinese origin will have experienced these changes at first hand, either in an increasingly urbanized rural environment or in urban Hong Kong itself.

LANGUAGE

Although Hong Kong is officially bilingual – English and Cantonese – by far the majority of the population claim Cantonese as their first spoken language. Figures from the Hong Kong government for 1972 (quoted by Fitchett, 1976; and Ladlow, n.d. 1) show that 88.1 per cent of the population spoke Cantonese as their first language, 4.2 per cent Hokklo, 2.7 per cent

Hakka, 1.2 per cent Sze Yap and 2.3 per cent other Chinese dialects. Some 25 per cent of the population aged ten and over were said to understand English which is the internal language of official communication in the civil service and government and in many commercial companies. But within the Chinese community the spoken language is usually Cantonese or a mixture of English and Cantonese in which Cantonese is dominant (Gibbons, 1982). A recent British Council survey suggested that 30 per cent used English in written communications at work and made repeated reference to the importance of English to Hong Kong's economy. However, although a fluent command of English is seen as vital for personal, economic and social advancement, learning English is reportedly not regarded as an enjoyable exploration of another culture by most young Chinese.

Cantonese is the native speech of Hong Kong and Macao, and outside China is by far the most widely spoken form of the Chinese language – but it is only one dialect of Chinese. Within mainland China itself Cantonese is spoken by almost 40 million in the south-east province of Kwangtung, of which Canton is the capital. However, the principal dialect of Chinese is Mandarin, a form of northern Chinese and the main dialect of the capital, Peking. Some 70 per cent of the population of 800 million or so in the People's Republic of China speak Mandarin as their first language, and it is the basis of the official language, Modern Standard Chinese, of government, communication and education (Barnes, 1978; Wright, 1985). However, some 230 million Chinese, mostly in the coastal region of south-east China, speak dialects belonging to one of the seven other language groups which are not intelligible to Mandarin speakers (see CILT, 1986).

All dialects of Chinese are tone languages of the Sino-Tibetan family. In these languages a variation in the pitch of the voice gives a completely different meaning to an otherwise identical word. Tone languages are also normally monosyllabic. Dialects vary in having four to nine tones which are characterized both by the pitch of the voice and whether the tendency of the tone is steady, rising, descending or wavering. The written form of Chinese is particularly important as a means of communication between many different dialect speakers as it is represented by characters common to all dialects. Characters represent concepts rather than sounds and may be compared to internationally recognized mathematical symbols. Many Chinese characters are pictograms, simple concepts which during the evolution of the written language have been combined to form ideograms or more abstract ideas. Chinese education has traditionally emphasized calligraphy, which may rank as an art form, and memorization of written characters. Literacy in Chinese requires the memorization of thousands of characters. An everyday vocabulary is about 3,000 characters, though a working vocabulary adequate for reading newspapers is 7,000 characters (Clough and Quarmby, 1978). It has been suggested that 5,000 characters are commonly known, though a fully literate person might know 16,000. The characters have been in use over 2,000 years and have been continually modified. In 1956 a modified vocabulary of 3,000 characters was adopted for use in mainland China. Malaysia has also adopted a simplified form, but Hong Kong still uses the full form in books and newspapers.

The majority of Chinese immigrants to the UK are Cantonese speakers, though a significant minority have Hakka as their first language and others Mandarin. It cannot, therefore, be assumed in school that all pupils of Chinese ethnic origin will understand one another's speech, and sensitivity is required to the sociolinguistic connotations of different dialects, especially when making mother-tongue teaching provision. However, in its written form language serves to unite literate Chinese.

RELIGION

At least seven major religions are practised in Hong Kong. It is the blending of various religions or philosophies to interpret or order existence rather than adherence to a single ideology which is distinctively Chinese. Thus it is important to realize that Chinese culture is not mediated through any particular religious doctrine, as it may be for other Asian groups.

According to Ladlow (n.d. 2) many, especially from the New Territories, have believed in traditional Chinese religion. This is a mixture of ancestor worship, polytheism and superstition which have been both influenced by and influenced Confucianism, Taoism and Buddhism. Traditional Chinese religion is practised in Hong Kong today by worship at ancestral shrines and in the observance of annual festivals. Many New Territories villages, where traditional clan organizations persist, contain an ancestral temple or hall which forms the focus of religious and secular life. The temple commemorates the founding ancestors and their descendants, and emphasizes the individual's obligations both to his deceased ancestors and to his living clansmen. It is thought that the deceased members of the family continue to influence the living, who assist the dead by visiting the grave during the festival of Ching Ming, burning incense and offering sacrifice. As well as practising ancestor worship, many Chinese, especially in the rural areas, believe in a multitude of gods, goddesses and spirits. Spirits are associated with natural phenomena, so that when a village can be traced back over several hundred years, and there is a close affinity to the land, often a tree or rock may be associated with spirits and worshipped. In addition to animism, villagers may also subscribe to geomancy – the belief that the direction and configuration of local hills, rivers and other geographical features can influence human well-being. Thus auguries may be consulted to determine favourable building-sites for houses or propitious dates for marriage and other major decisions.

Religion, customs and festivals are closely interrelated in Chinese thinking and practice. For example, the belief in tutelary spirits as guardians of the home is expressed in the annual custom of posting strips of red paper with lucky gold characters on the doorposts at New Year. A link is made with Buddhism, especially in the form in which it developed in China, through the practice of visiting temples on the first and fifteenth days of the lunar month, thus upholding the traditional village custom of worshipping gods and spirits at these times. Taoism and Buddhism are the two most popular religions in Hong Kong and believers are likely to have an ancestral shrine in the home, although there are also over 360 Buddhist and Taoist temples. Taoism advocates submission to the course of nature, humility, compassion and the requiting of good for evil. Each temple is usually dedicated to one or sometimes two deities; however, images of many deities are to be found in most temples. Due to the traditional connection with the sea for fishing and trade, the most popular deities are those connected with the sea and weather. For example, the deity Tin Hau, the protector of seafarers, is said to be worshipped by 250,000 people (HKGIS, 1984a).

These beliefs and practices may be seen as representing the mystical and contemplative side of the Chinese character. But it is generally agreed that the secular philosophy and system of social ethics in the teachings of Confucius have been of most influence on Chinese culture. Confucianism is complementary to other belief systems, in that it is practical in orientation and linked to social action in everyday life. Confucius based his teaching on the concept of respectful attitudes towards ancestors and fellow men and influenced the establishment of a social structure with the family as the central force. Hence the significance of the five relationships in society between ruler and subject, father and son, older and younger brother, husband and wife, and friend and friend. The concept of filial duty was of paramount importance, starting with the son's respect for the father, grandfather and head of the clan. Confucius also propounded a three-class system and instituted public examinations which ensured that the bureaucracy, the first of the classes, survived despite changes in government. Although latterly in the People's Republic of China there has been ideological conflict about Confucian influences, this humanistic philosophy has been of undoubted significance, especially with respect to the importance of the family as a social unit. The Confucian practice of nepotism also survives in the influence which personal relationship plays in both social and business life.

The traditional festivals associated with the Chinese calendar provide occasions for family reunions as well as for cultural reaffirmation. The festivals are linked to the traditional Chinese lunar calendar which is shorter than the solar year. Years are named after the Chinese signs of the zodiac. At least five major festivals are regularly celebrated in Hong Kong: the lunar New Year, Ching Ming festival in spring, the Dragon Boat Festival, the Mid-autumn Festival and Chung Yeung. Ladlow (n.d.) gives a very clear account of the features of festivals, the different religions and the dimensions of traditional Chinese religion.

Hong Kong also has its Christian, Muslim, Hindu, Sikh and Jewish communities. Their spiritual centres also form the focus for many social and welfare activities, often spreading beyond their particular religious communities. In this way, from the early days of Hong Kong's development, Catholic and Protestant churches played an important role in providing educational and medical facilities, and many Chinese immigrants to Britain may have had contact with Christianity through attending church schools, clinics and hospitals. Christianity has become an increasingly middle-class religion with more adherents among the younger generation who have come into contact with it during their education. There are now nearly 600 churches and chapels in Hong Kong with 50 denominations. Roman Catholics and Protestants are estimated to be almost one-tenth of the population, with Roman Catholics (266,500) outnumbering Protestants (200,000). There are also estimated to be about 30,000 followers of Islam in Hong Kong, a 10,000-strong Hindu community, some 3,000 Sikhs and a Jewish community of about 1,000 people (HKG, 1984; HKGIS, 1984a).

FAMILY AND SOCIAL STRUCTURE

Despite British colonial rule for almost a century, the cultural and family traditions of the villages in the New Territories, which are shared with the inhabitants of Kwangtung, China's most southern province, have been maintained. In this region are to be found the largest and most complex lineage organizations in the world (Watson, 1977a). Towns and villages are built around lineages, or clans, or patrilineal descent. The lineages are based on exclusive land ownership which has typically been the property of one family expanding in numbers over many generations. The oldest villages may have been settled for up to 1,000 years and in some cases have populations of 3,000–4,000. Lineage members share a common surname, since it was the custom for sons to remain in the same village, and comprise representatives of nearly every social class (Watson, 1977a). The village of San Tin in a remote area of the New Territories, studied by Watson, is a good example of an élite kinship organization in a single lineage village and it is from such villages that many of the Cantonese-speaking Chinese in Britain have come. In 1970, during Watson's anthropological investigations, San Tin had a population of approximately 4,000 – including over 1,000 emigrants working in Europe. All the male members of the village shared the surname *Man* and traced their descent to an ancestor who had settled in the area six centuries earlier. The community was closed and self-contained. Membership of such a lineage conferred high status in the region, especially in politics, and the lineage traditionally served as an intermediary in establishing contacts outside the community.

Among the Chinese the importance of the family was stressed from the earliest times. Family consciousness was refined through a hierarchy of relationships based on Confucian philosophy and the concepts of filial piety, authority, obedience and respect. The most important concept of filial piety served to link the individual to his ancestors by obedience and duty to and respect for his parents. In the father–son relationship, the son was expected to obey, serve, show respect and always defer to his father. By extension the father–son relationship was the model for all family relationships: elder brother–younger brother, seniors and juniors of the same generation, husband–wife and all male–female relationships (Baker and Honey, 1981). Confucian thought urged the natural feeling of affection present in the family towards an attitude of duty which would support an authority structure, contribute to social control and provide a feeling of belonging for the individual. Such relationships and attitudes made the family and lineage a self-contained social entity, regulating its internal affairs and decision-making and providing the orientation for the individual's loyalty and sentiments. Indeed the senior–junior relationships continued to hold even when broken by death, as filial respect and service through ritual sacrifice and ancestor worship were still demanded. Thus the position of each individual in life and after life was rigidly stratified and subject to the welfare of the family unit as a whole. Though this made for security within the family, it minimized the individual's importance, freedom and initiative, demanding an absolute loyalty to kin.

Thus traditionally the family was seen as the strength of society (Baker in SCSCRC, 1976). Family loyalty took precedence over loyalty to the state and because of its predominant focus on the family Confucianism was often blamed for preventing the growth of national consciousness (O'Neill, 1972; QCRC, 1981). Historically the Hong Kong area was subject only to lax and distant central government control and local self-government evolved through mutual responsibility dependent upon the system of rights and duties in the family, clans and villages. This also strengthened the stress on kinship ties and the prime allegiance of the individual to the family. The principles of family organization – the superiority of age and the male – also applied to government of the clan village with the senior and older men forming an unelected village government. This mediated in disputes, administered communal funds and property and served as a judiciary issuing rewards and punishments. Thus the power of the village and the family over the individual was considerable. Intra-lineage conflicts between villages jealous of wealth, prestige or power were frequent. The larger and wealthier clans dominated, often by force of arms, and the better educated amongst their leaders were sometimes able to further clan interests in society at large by their prestige. Despite changes in the New Territories involving abandonment of agriculture, reliance on overseas earnings, a higher standard of living and education, and a considerable degree of sophistication and Westernization, much traditional family cohesiveness and self-reliance remains (Baker in SCSCRC, 1976). This may be seen, for example, in the attitude to social welfare provision which has prevailed (Lai, 1975). The tradition of voluntary social welfare, based on the family and lineage structures, has persisted and many find the concept of right to welfare alien, preferring to exhaust all personal family resources before applying for help. The voluntary sector remains important in all aspects of social welfare, complementing government provision (see HKGIS, 1982).

Traditionally in the New Territories families have lived together as an extended group, often three or more family relationships forming one household. Maintenance of a large family was seen as an indication of prosperity, and division of the household as a misfortune (O'Neill, 1972). The system of patrilineal descent excluded women from inheritance and, as it was customary for daughters to be married to families in other villages, girls were often seen as prospective daughters-in-law and sometimes regarded as a burden to the family. Parents chose marriage partners for their sons according to lineage rules, though arranged marriages have now declined in Hong Kong (O'Neill, 1972). Within the traditional authority structure of the family the daughter-in-law was subservient both to her husband and parents-in-law, the attention she gave to her parents-in-law being considered a very important virtue. Women were regarded as child-bearers and the domestic role fell to their lot, but they were usually industrious and recognized as a labour resource (Tsow in CAG & QCRC, 1979).

Just as the elderly were respected and cared for, so there was traditionally a general fondness for children, who were often looked after from day to day by their grandparents. The birth of a male child was seen as an addition to lineage membership and a cause for celebration, whereas females were not counted as lineage members and were regarded with less interest (Cheung, 1975). However, O'Neill (1972) suggested that female children had become more acceptable, with some Chinese parents preferring to have girls rather than boys, in contrast to the traditional wish for a large family of boys who would support their parents in their old age. Younger children would be treated leniently until about the age of 7 or 8 when it was deemed necessary for them to learn the meaning of reasonableness. However, the inculcation of discipline and values in the family may have become more difficult in recent years, especially in emigrant communities such as the villages of San Tin, where grandparents may indulge their grandchildren, and daughters-in-law – though experiencing strict control over their social lives – lack the disciplinary presence of their husbands (Watson, 1977a). Child care might not reside exclusively with the mother but be spread amongst extended family members, by whom children would be introduced to the principles of conduct and social behaviour such as the need to be highly circumspect in public. As Chann has put it,

> From a young age, we are taught to be modest, to respect and to obey our seniors, to be tolerant and try not to show our emotions. In dealing with

other people the question of face is very important. To apply these attitudes in everyday life, we are not to show-off, nor to argue with or question another person, especially when he is a senior in case we make them lose face. (Chann, 1976, p.7)
The concept of 'face', especially in a one-to-one relationship, is important in traditional Chinese social structure for, as Tsow (CAG & QCRC, 1979) has defined it, 'to "give face" to a person meant to take him into consideration as a human being to be honoured' (p.10). These examples illustrate the influence of both Confucianism with its emphasis on social man, and Taoism, stressing the need to give true value to the self, in the structure of Chinese social relationships. Self-reliance is another important concept which also receives early encouragement. The individual looks first to himself for help and, if this fails, to his immediate family, and only then to a more distant relation or friends. However, personal relationships play an important part in social life and the aim is to conduct such relationships with kindness, integrity, courtesy and wisdom. These basic values and attitudes have been transmitted orally within the family from generation to generation.

The traditional pattern of social relationships may be summed up as follows:

For the villager it was the family, the neighbours, the village and the market town which occupied the important places in his outward view. They comprise a more or less self-sufficient world within which was to be found all the companionship, entertainment, religious activity and livelihood he desired. In this 'cell' he was born and educated, was found a wife, played, prayed and sacrificed, and finally was buried. Within it were found uniform customs, manners, weights and measures, dress, architecture and language. (Baker and Honey, 1981, p.7)

This is the traditional family background and structure of social organization from which many Chinese in Britain will have come, though changes brought about by increasing urbanization and industrialization, and not least education outside the family itself, will have modified conventional patterns and outlooks. Young people and women have gained more freedom, and marriage is no longer regarded as in the service of the husband's ancestors and for the perpetuation of coming generations, but as a union of individuals. But though the family unit is becoming smaller and smaller, the Chinese family in the New Territories exhibits close relationships in which there is respect and care for its old and senior members, and a readiness to support clan members and provide for their needs (Chann, 1976). In recent years, however, Hong Kong has developed an expanding social welfare programme, especially for the elderly and child care (HKG, 1984).

EDUCATION

Traditionally Chinese – whether rich or poor, professional or working class – have greatly valued education. This high regard was reflected in the exalted and esteemed position held by teachers and scholars (CAG & QCRC, 1979). Education has been the only means for social and economic advancement. Even today in Hong Kong's competitive society, parents place a premium on education and often make personal sacrifices to ensure that their children of both sexes receive proper schooling (Chann, 1976; Watson, 1977a). Pupils are said to be keen to study and the majority have high expectations.

Until 1906 Chinese education was based on the classics and attempts at modernization proved difficult. The British colonialists inherited this system with the annexation of the New Territories. Schooling over the border in Kwangtung Province, as in other areas of China where there are a majority of native speakers of languages other than Mandarin, involves the acquisition of a competence in Mandarin. In Taiwan, too, Mandarin has been a prerequisite for education since 1946. Singapore, which is ethnically more pluralistic, has education in four official languages – Chinese, Malay, Tamil and English. The Chinese-medium schools operate in Mandarin but students are expected to obtain a proficiency in two languages. Hong Kong is therefore exceptional, in that Cantonese and English are the dominant languages of education, though Mandarin script is taught in the Chinese-medium schools. Barnes (1978) has suggested that Mandarin may assume a greater importance as its use in nearby countries increases. An independent commission, appointed in 1980 and which reported in 1982, recommended that a comprehensive language policy should be established for the education system moving from use of mother tongue in the formative years plus teaching of English as first foreign language leading to genuine bilingualism in the senior secondary years (HKG, 1984). As a result, the government instituted a retraining programme for primary teachers in 1982.

Education in Hong Kong, especially at secondary level, has been influenced by the idea of a liberal education as understood and developed in Britain. Provision has expanded considerably post-war, especially in the last decade, from an enrolment of less than 50,000, to 1.3 million. In the 1950s there was a focus on primary education provision, though this was not available to the majority, especially in rural areas. The contrast in urban–rural provision and take-up, is illustrated by illiteracy figures from the 1961 Census: urban areas, males 6 per cent, females 44 per cent; and New Territories, males 12 per cent, females 63 per cent (Cheung, 1975). The New Territories in fact had fewer educational facilities. Only in 1971 did primary education become free, and it was not until 1973 that six years of primary schooling became compulsory. Until 1978 secondary schooling was fee-paying, but in 1979 education up to 15 became free and compulsory, thus making general education nine years.

There are four levels of education in Hong Kong: pre-primary, primary, secondary and post-secondary. The private sector forms an important part of education in Hong Kong, so there are three main types of schools: those run by the government, those operated by voluntary bodies financially assisted by government and those run and financed by individuals or private institutions often associated with Christian organizations. In 1984 about 27 per cent of Hong Kong's population was at school (HKGIS, 1984b). Figures for the pre-primary, primary and secondary levels of schooling for 1975–84 may be compared in Table 3.

Table 3: School enrolment in Hong Kong, 1975–84

	1975	1984
Kindergarten	151,000	209,869
Primary	695,000	539,856
Secondary	380,000	451,528
Total	1,226,000	1,201,253

Source: Approximate figures for 1975 from Chann, 1976; and 1984 from HKGIS, 1984b.

Pre-primary schools or kindergartens cater for children aged three to five. All the 724 kindergartens in operation in 1984 were privately maintained but government supervised. They provided pre-school education for 88 per cent of children in this age group. Primary schooling starts at the age of six, but because of the number of pupils involved, most primary schools operate in two sessions, so that pupils attend either in the morning or in the afternoon. The aim of the six-year primary course is to provide a good general education appropriate to the age range and particular environment of the children. Ninety per cent of the primary schools use Chinese as the medium of instruction with English taught as a second language (Gibbons, 1982).

Since 1979 on completion of the primary course, a pupil is allocated a place in a government or government-aided private secondary school through a system based on internal school assessment, scaled by a centrally administered academic aptitude test, combined with parental choice. This provides free and compulsory access to junior secondary education (Form 1–3). Since 1981 there has been a further system of selection and allocation of subsidized school places for senior secondary education (Form 4–5), also based on scaled internal school assessments and parental choice. There are now four main types of secondary schools in Hong Kong: Anglo-Chinese secondary grammar schools, Chinese middle schools, secondary technical schools and pre-vocational schools. The medium of instruction, except in Chinese middle schools, is mainly English, although Chinese history and language are taught in Chinese. Anglo-Chinese schools, Chinese middle schools and secondary technical schools offer a five-year course in a broad range of academic subjects leading to the Hong Kong Certificate of Education examination. The pre-vocational schools, which aim to link experience with industrial training needs (see ILEA, 1975), provide a three-year secondary course of 50–60 per cent general education and 40–50 per cent technical education. Academically able pupils can also pursue a further two years of education with 30 per cent technical content up to Certificate of Education standard, leading to technical programmes in Hong Kong Polytechnic or the technical institutes.

Table 4: Types of secondary schools, number of students and number pursuing matriculation courses

Types of secondary schools	Number of students	Number of students pursuing matriculation courses
Government	30,304	2,841
Aided	249,695	19,347
Private	134,482	14,859

Source: HKGIS, 1984b.

In 1984, 97 per cent of children aged 12–14 and 76 per cent of the 15–16 age group were in receipt of full-time education. Those with suitable results in the Certificate of Education may enter a two-year course for Hong Kong A-level examinations or UK GCE O- and A-levels (Table 4). Five technical institutes and Hong Kong Polytechnic offer full- and part-time and evening courses at which over 3,000 pupils are enrolled. There are also two post-secondary colleges and three teacher training colleges. The latter offer three-year full-time courses in English and one college offers a three-year course in Chinese. The colleges are government maintained and students have to finance themselves by interest-free loans and maintenance grants. In 1984 enrolment on full-time courses was 2,519 students and 2,205 students on part-time, including in-service, courses. There has been a considerable expansion in higher education, for whilst there was keen competition and severe limitation on entry to university in the mid-1970s, necessitating emigration for higher education overseas (see the student's account in Fitchett, 1976, pp. 10–11), nowadays there are two universities in Hong

Kong and a polytechnic which is the largest single education institute. In all, these have about 36,000 enrolled students. Adult education covering a range of levels from literacy classes to secondary and post-secondary studies has an enrolment exceeding 100,000.

Although the Hong Kong education system has a certain affinity with the UK system, it has certain distinctive and distinguishing features. The large numbers involved and lack of space make for crowded facilities. Through the two-shifts per day primary schools may cater for about 1,000 children, each shift having about 12 classes of 40–45 children. More recently the pupil–teacher ratio may have been reduced to nearer 35–40 (Fitchett, 1976). Some have observed that classes are also poorly equipped (for example, Langton, 1979). But it is possible that with the new building programme in the New Territories facilities may have improved in recent years. The classroom atmosphere in Hong Kong schools is generally agreed to be very formal, and even in kindergartens children are seated formally. This arrangement characterizes the pupils' relationship with their teacher, which is generally one of respect. The traditional value of respect due to seniors and, by extension, honour to teachers, continues to have an influence in the teacher–pupil relationship (Chann, 1976). Learning is also highly disciplined with an emphasis on repetition and rote. In the strongly competitive ethos of education in Hong Kong, with its stress on academic examination-oriented learning, homework is expected from an early age. Thus pupils expect to work hard in a formal learning situation which does not provide much opportunity for informal social or cognitive learning through play, though sporting activities have been extended in the secondary curriculum.

The language of instruction is a matter of some difficulty and controversy. The two separate education systems, of English-medium or Chinese-medium schools, were established at the turn of the century (Gibbons, 1982). In the predominantly Chinese-medium primary schools a child is taught both Chinese and English from the age of six. Written Chinese is particularly difficult to learn as the construction of every character, based on Mandarin and not Cantonese, has to be committed to memory. But Chann (1976) has claimed that to learn English is doubly difficult 'since it is completely alien to the average child in Hong Kong' (p.11). It bears little relevance to his life outside the classroom and may not be taught by proficient teachers. Thus though a secondary school pupil should have a fair command of reading and writing in English, his spoken English is generally formal and the command quite poor due to lack of exposure to colloquial English and the opportunity to practise (Chann, 1976; Lai, 1976; and Lee in ILEA: English Centre, 1979). Yet the advantage of English for career opportunities is fully realized. Indeed, although educational consensus and government policy have promoted Chinese as the language of instruction in the first three years of secondary education, thereby providing continuity with the primary level, this has not been imposed – because of practical and political difficulties due to the perceived commercial value of English and parents' wishes – so that schools have been free to choose the medium of instruction. In fact Chinese language schools have declined, many reopening as English-medium schools, so that from 1960 to 1980 day pupils in Anglo-Chinese, English-medium schools increased by 30 per cent (Gibbons, 1982). The well-known correlation between proficiency in English and income appears to be the reason why parents wish their children to attend English-medium schools. But this presupposes that children are capable of receiving instruction in English and that there is a necessary link between English-medium education and the acquisition of English, especially as the English of many Hong Kong secondary school teachers is not of native-speaker standard. There is evidence that Chinese is a more effective medium of instruction simply because Chinese children, especially those of low ability, understand it better. English is virtually unusable as a medium of instruction with many children now in the first three years of compulsory secondary education. In fact there is a mixed use of language in both educational establishments: in the Chinese-medium schools some materials in English are used, so that speech and reading can be in both English and Chinese, whereas writing will normally be in Chinese; the English-medium schools make use of both languages, progressing steadily to sole use of English. Educational TV includes English-medium broadcasts which are closely linked with syllabuses and timetables.

In addition to language learning difficulties, the competitive educational system is not without its stress on children and parents (Langton, 1979). Unless a minimum mark has been achieved, pupils remain in the same class for a further year and there are several examination hurdles throughout the child's school life. Parental pressure is great – as they are aware that academic achievement is in the long-term interest of their child. Until recently financial pressures have also been a reason for the failure of thousands of children to complete more than one or two years of secondary schooling. Additional problems are experienced by children living in rural areas. In the New Territories educational facilities have generally been less well developed, pupils have started school later, they may have had to travel long distances to the few available secondary schools (Langton quotes five for the whole area) and their educational aspirations have normally been more modest (Lai, 1975). Many of the parents of pupils of Chinese origin in British schools will have had this kind of educational experience, though first-generation immigrant Chinese pupils themselves may well have received some schooling in more updated conditions.

EMIGRATION TO THE UK

There has been a long tradition of emigration from China since the 12th century. In the mid-19th century many thousands of poor peasants and artisans plus a few small merchant traders migrated from the areas of Kwangtung and Fukien in south China (Ng, 1968). Most went to South East Asian and Pacific countries and some as far as California and the Caribbean. The earliest Chinese emigrants to Britain were recruited from the villages of the New Territories to serve as sailors aboard European freighters (Watson, 1977a). Prior to the Second World War, such migrants came from traditional Chinese backgrounds (O'Neill, 1972). Several hundred jumped ship and established communities in the East End of London and the docklands of Liverpool and Cardiff. Numbers increased during the Second World War but many were subsequently repatriated. Those remaining formed the nucleus of, and the catalyst for, the much larger second-phase emigration from the New Territories which began in the 1950s. At this time also a small group of diplomats and intellectuals, refugees from the Kuomintang regime, decided to remain in London when the People's Republic of China was established (Ng, 1968).

The first seamen often had close ties with specific areas or villages in the New Territories, from which the post-war emigrants came. For example, many Chinese in London had strong links with the Sam Yap and Sze Yap districts of Canton (Jones, D., 1979) and nearly all the Chinese community in York hailed from the Sai Kung area of the New Territories, half from one particular village (Cheung, 1975) (see Map 1, p.27). Watson (1977a) has estimated that over 30 emigrant communities in the New Territories are dependent on remittances for more than half their income, from at least half of the men of working age who have emigrated internationally. The local-born New Territories emigrants held British passports and were able to enter Britain fairly freely until more restrictive immigration legislation in 1962 required employment vouchers or work permits. Emigration from Hong Kong in 1962 also included some 10,000 'stateless' Chinese, some of the thousands who had crossed the borders from the People's Republic into the New Territories during the 1950s and 1960s and who were issued with Certificates of Identity (Watson, 1977a). Many had lived for 10–15 years in New Territories villages mostly working as farmers before emigration (Lai, 1975; Cheung, 1975). Emigration to the UK was for them a second experience of migration. Culturally they had much in common with the New Territories villagers with a traditional Chinese lifestyle unadapted to urban living. Only in recent years has there been any emigration from the urban areas of Hong Kong to the UK, although later emigrants from the New Territories will have had some experience of an increasingly urbanized and industrial environment. Another group of emigrants were students from China or Hong Kong who subsequently settled (see Ng, 1968). Some emigrants have experienced a two-hop emigration, arriving in the UK after spending some time in other European or Commonwealth countries (Garvey and Jackson, 1975; O'Neill, 1972).

The reasons for emigration seem to have been both economic pressure and some previous connection overseas (see survey by Chen, 1939, and other cases quoted by Ng, 1968). The second phase of emigration in the early 1960s was largely due to the decline in the rice market because of competition from South Asia, as in the case of the San Tin villagers studied by Watson in 1969–71. The *Mans* were small-scale rice farmers in the largest single lineage village in rural Hong Kong who, unlike other New Territories villagers with more fertile land, were not able either to profit from the new market gardening opportunities in the 1960s or to rent out their land for cultivation by the refugees from China, as the brackish water of their paddy fields rendered them unsuitable for conversion into vegetable plots. As rice farming became unprofitable and the *Mans* were unwilling to work in urban Hong Kong, being qualified only for the most menial and low-paid industrial jobs, they chose to leave Hong Kong and seek employment in Europe. They were thus able to fully exploit the almost exactly contemporaneous opportunities which were opening up in the UK in the catering business (Watson, 1977b). The visibly increased standard of housing and living of those whose family members had emigrated and sent remittances convinced even the most conservative of families to allow their sons to emigrate (Watson, 1977a). The dream of emigration soon spread to other New Territories villages. But there was little thought of what life as an immigrant in the UK would be like – the overwhelming goal was of financial security and, if possible, economic prosperity (Cheung, 1975).

The *Mans* of San Tin, exhibited a classic pattern of emigration organization through chain migration, relying heavily on lineage ties at every stage. Lineage members from the first migration, already established in the UK restaurant trade, supervised immigration requirements, paid passage money and offered employment in some 80 per cent of the cases examined by Watson (1977a). Lineage leaders in Hong Kong arranged for passports and entry certificates. Thus 85–90 per cent of working-age men in San Tin were found work in Chinese restaurants in the UK and Europe (Watson, 1977b). Cheung (1975) also found that the *Tang* lineage with one-third of the catering business in York had a network related to one New Territories village, and Garvey and Jackson (1975) mention the business links of the *Fong* lineage in Sheffield, Leeds and Manchester. Chain migration was also based on shared dialect, common district of origin or extended family. The catering families studied by Lai (1975), in London, relied on established contacts, help from immediate family, other kin, friends and acquaintances. Financial arrangements for emigration were often a prime consideration: central funds and loan systems came into operation in certain emigrant villages as emigration became more organized and efficient (Ng, 1968).

The pattern of Chinese emigration was for single male workers to work abroad with great determination, to defer material gratification and make remittances to support their families. Early emigrants kept in touch with their home communities by means of formal associations and clubs, informal groups, correspondence, newspapers and return visits. Even though an emigrant might have returned only once in 20 years, his orientation was always towards the village with the intention of retiring there (Ng, 1968). Watson (1977a, 1977b) found that such attitudes were still largely held by the emigrants in San Tin and in London, in 1969. They made regular remittances, usually on an inflation-linked monthly basis, the lineage links in the UK being sufficient to evoke sanctions on any defaulters. San Tin villagers thus became precariously reliant on remittances for their basic standard of living. The orientation of the emigrants to their home community was also demonstrated by the construction of 'sterling' houses, constituting over a quarter of the residences, which transformed the appearance of the village. These served as a stake for personal security and future retirement in the village, though half were financed by emigrant workers in their twenties and thirties. Emigrants contributed on a generous scale to the construction of new public buildings and civic projects, which in San Tin included a new temple, a renovated ancestral hall, three new community halls and a school. Due to improved air communication, most emigrants returned for three-month trips, on average every three to five years. This facilitated communication between the community and its members in the UK, allowing them to exercise a direct, active and important influence on their home villages. Visits often coincided with festivals, usually New Year or the autumn moon festival, and were marked by enormous banquets which validated status and gave a right of re-entry to the village. Important family occasions such as marriage or the education of children and the division of property were made during these times.

The second phase of emigration until the mid-1970s strengthened the lineage as a social institution and increased the dependency of emigrant workers. In their quest for financial security, their emotional ties to the village had often deepened and become idealized, so that retiring emigrants often became enthusiastic proponents of traditional values. Watson suggested that despite some modernization, remittances had allowed San Tin to remain largely aloof from social and economic changes in the New Territories, whilst making it susceptible to European economic recession and immigration restrictions which disrupt kinship networks forming the basis of continuing ties to the village. During the 1970s the male emigrants' village orientation and intention to return were changing, not least on account of the third phase of emigration of wives and families to the UK. As a result, certain villages in the New Territories have become deserted (Baker and Honey, 1981). Other factors, including business investment in the UK and the emergence of a UK-born generation of Chinese, and the reclamation by China of Hong Kong by 1997, call into question the home orientation of the majority of these emigrants to the UK over the past 20 years or so. By now the dream of a prosperous return may well have faded, and some who have returned have failed to settle, so that the long-term position of the Chinese community in Britain deserves greater recognition.

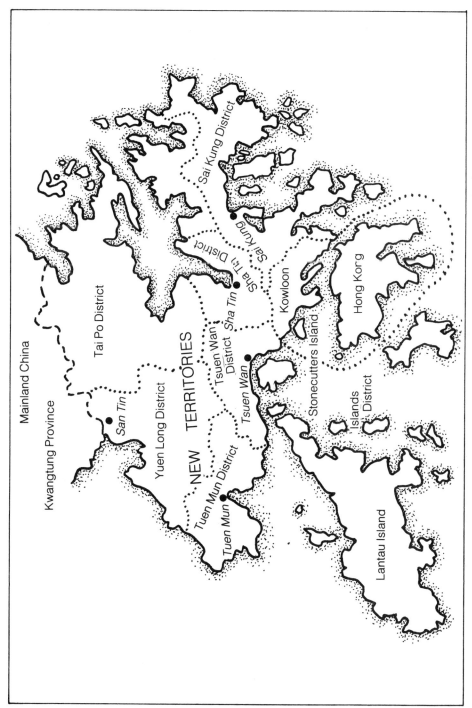

MAP 1   HONG KONG, KOWLOON AND THE NEW TERRITORIES

Part Two

The Chinese in the UK

Section 1
Settlement and Demography

The three phases of emigration, largely from the villages of the New Territories (pp.22–6), correspond to three phases of settlement of the Chinese in the UK. These can be distinguished as: a pre-war group of single men, who came to Britain as sailors; and two post-war groups, single men emigrating for work, and latterly their wives and children. This section examines the settlement of these groups in the UK, paying especial attention to the first phase of settlement and inter-community perceptions in so far as they formed the basis for later immigration. Post-war settlement is briefly outlined here and the socioeconomic conditions of family life affecting pupils of Chinese origin are examined in greater detail under the headings of Housing, Employment, Family Structure and Child Care and Community Perceptions in the following sections. Generally three groups of Chinese immigrants may be distinguished: seamen, students and catering workers, though the middle group overlaps with both the earlier and the later immigrants.

Neither the pre- nor the post-war settlement of the Chinese in Britain has been well documented by social historians. This section brings together evidence from the first days of immigration to present-day settlements to build up a more coherent picture of the social development of the Chinese in Britain, especially over the last two decades. Due to the lack of attention which the group has received, some of the sources are at variance, especially on early population numbers. Difficulty in interpreting the demographic trends of the ethnic Chinese has, however, largely remained. Census figures have not distinguished country of birth, country of emigration to the UK and ethnic group, focussing merely on the first category, although the overlaps of the three are significant. Particular difficulties associated with interpretation will be pointed out when figures are cited, and there is a larger than usual element of speculation about demographic trends and analysis. The general lack of attention which has been given to the meaningful collection of data on the Chinese in the UK tends to support frequently voiced claims on behalf of the Chinese in recent years, that they have existed as a largely unassertive and unnoticed group.

THE FIRST ARRIVALS: A SOCIOECONOMIC HISTORY

Consideration of the pre-war settlement of the Chinese in Britain focusses almost exclusively on the development of communities in London and Liverpool and draws upon two main sources, research by Broady (1952, 1955) in Liverpool and Ng (1968) in London, supplemented by further details from May (1978) and Jones, (D., 1979). In fact there have been Chinese in the UK since the 18th century when contact between China and Europe began to expand, Chinoiserie became fashionable and members of the Chinese aristocracy came to Britain as students (O'Neill, 1972). But there could not be a greater contrast between this intellectual élite and the illiterate peasants who were to emigrate from south-east China and later the New Territories of Hong Kong. As early as 1814 there were Chinese seamen in Britain, particularly in London (Ng, 1968). The practice of regularly employing Chinese seamen grew because of the increasing competition in the expansion of trade with China, following the East India Company's loss of the monopoly at Canton (1834), and later due to the establishment of the Treaty Ports after the British success in the opium war of 1842. Opportunities for additional trade required more ships and crews and Chinese could be cheaply and conveniently recruited.

With the establishment by 1865 of the first direct steamship service from Europe to China by Liverpool shipowners, the number of Chinese, though still very small, increased in Liverpool, London and Cardiff (Broady, 1952). By 1885 the first Chinese communities, both in London around Limehouse and Pennyfields, adjacent to the West Indian Docks, and in Liverpool around Pitt Street, began to develop. These communities serviced the needs of Chinese sailors and shore-gangmen, who in London originated mainly from Kwangtung Province, with a few from Chekiang, Malaya, Singapore and Fukien (Ng, 1968). The communities were led by Chinese boarding-house keepers, who often also acted as crew contractors and shopkeepers. The boarding-houses served as social centres for the seamen when they were ashore, providing facilities for gambling and opium smoking. By 1906, with the growth of the community, Chinese shops, a restaurant and even a temple had been set up in Liverpool (Broady, 1955). There was similar expansion in London with some 30 Chinese shops and restaurants in the Chinatown area by 1913 (Ng, 1968).

During the early years of the 20th century there was a growing awareness of the Chinese in Britain, largely on account of scares in the press about their increase in Australia, the USA and South Africa. This gave rise to some tension between Chinese residents and certain local communities in Britain, with some public demonstrations of anti-Chinese feeling, though there was generally no hostility, the Chinese being regarded with acceptance or indifference (May, 1978). The Aliens Act of 1905 exercised minimal control on the settlement of seamen who could be economically self-supporting. But some hostility towards Chinese was expressed during the 1906 election. By

1907 a welfare association had been established in London, with a branch in Liverpool, to protect its members from discrimination by the host society and to provide them with aid: adjudicating in quarrels between members, providing financial support for the sick, aid with travel expenses on return to China, overseeing appropriate burial rights and upholding certain traditional Chinese festivals (Ng, 1968). Concern began to be expressed about the social habits and behaviour of the Chinese in both London and Liverpool, which resulted in a series of inquiries about gambling, opium smoking, the conditions of boarding-houses and relationships with white women (May, 1978). But the Chinese were largely exonerated. Gambling was confined to their own ethnic group, as was limited violence after opium smoking, and they were generally found to be extremely law-abiding and indeed to have integrated to some extent by intermarriage with the white population.

Not surprisingly, the greatest opposition to the Chinese was in the economic sector. The seamen in Liverpool had established a union in 1906 (Broady, 1955) but there were growing protests by British seamen in the ensuing years about the increasing numbers of Chinese employed in British merchant ships, although their numbers were fewer than those of other Asian or European seamen. The British seamen complained that the Chinese were cheap labour and inferior seamen, but employers liked them for their discipline. To avoid the language test, the seamen claimed that they were from Hong Kong rather than China. But in 1908 Chinese seamen were on several occasions prevented from signing on at the East India Docks and required police protection from British seamen, who organized meetings demanding the implementation of the 1905 Act (Jones, D., 1979). As the communities became more established, starting in London and later growing, especially in Liverpool and Cardiff, the Chinese began to diversify into the laundry business. There was further opposition to the Chinese seamen who, in 1911, acted as strike-breakers between British and other foreign seamen and employers, and so frustrated were the British and foreign seamen at the protection of the Chinese by police in Cardiff that in one night of rioting they destroyed 30 Chinese laundries (May, 1978). Other ugly incidents were also reported in the north-east (Collins, 1957).

As Chinese seamen began to settle they increasingly intermarried with white women, and figures given by Ng (1968) show that in the first quarter of this century marriages between Chinese men and women must have been rare due to the imbalanced sex ratio. Ng cites several case studies of intermarriage: it seems generally to have been agreed that the Chinese made good fathers, although with traditional attitudes to women and the lack of free time on account of long working hours they often failed to provide companionship for their wives. Apart from some intermarriage, the Chinese remained a close community. The Aliens Restriction Act of 1914, still implemented at the end of the First World War, effectively curtailed the immigration of Chinese into British ports and many Chinese seamen were deported in 1920 for opium-taking and gambling (May, 1978). May maintains that the Chinese generally had cordial relations with the wider communities in which they lived and that opposition to them as seamen occurred not because of their numbers, but because of their predisposition to mobility between employers in order to obtain better terms. But a more recent commentator of Chinese origin (Lynn, 1982) has suggested that conflict arose because the Chinese were employed in an occupation which the host community regarded as their own, and that their response influenced the type of occupations in which the Chinese have subsequently been engaged.

Table 5: Chinese-born population of England and Wales, London and Liverpool, 1851–1931

Year	Nos born in China resident in England and Wales	Nos born in China resident in London	Liverpool (Merseyside)
1851	78	78	–
1861	147	78	–
1871	202	94	–
1881	665	109	15
1891	582	302	27
1901	387	120	76
1911	1,319	247	502
1921	2,419	711	571
1931	1,934	1,194	529*

*This figure includes British-born wives of Chinese men. The figures as a whole, especially in the latter years, may include some of British descent born in China.
Source: Adapted from Ng, 1968, Tables 2 and 3; and Broady, 1955, p.67.

Table 5 summarizes available data on the Chinese population in Britain and in the two main communities in London and Liverpool during 1851–1931. With severe restrictions on immigration, the Chinese population in London and Liverpool declined during the inter-war years and did not pick up again until the second phase of immigration in the 1950s. In the years after the First World War many Chinese entered the laundry business which gradually spread from Liverpool, London and Bristol to smaller towns, so that by the Census in 1931 there were over 500 Chinese laundries in the UK. It was during the 1920s, too, that the foundations of the Chinese catering business were established with restaurants in London's West End, open to a British clientele. Unlike the laundries, however, the restaurant trade survived the economic depression of the 1930s and the declining numbers of

Chinese in Britain. During this time the Chinese in both London and Liverpool were rehoused due to urban redevelopment. But the Second World War reversed the declining Chinese population as large numbers – Broady: 10,000; Jones, D.: 20,000 – of Chinese seamen mostly from Shanghai and Chekiang were recruited to man British merchant fleets from Liverpool. Many Chinese who married during the war were permitted to stay on in Liverpool subsequently, although large numbers returned home or were repatriated (Broady, 1955). The considerably augmented Liverpool Chinese community reintegrated around Nelson Street where, although many remained as seamen, others capitalized on the increased demand for Chinese food, in the catering business (Lynn, 1982). Thus by the late 1940s and early 1950s the successful economic adjustment of the Chinese was reflected in

> the development of a social class structure, which ranges from the humble level of laundry men, cooks, sailors and shore-gang workers, who live predominantly in the older parts of the town, to wealthy proprietors of restaurants and boarding-houses, many of whom have married Englishwomen and now live in middle- and upper-class residential districts, such as Crosby and Mossley Hill. (Broady, 1955, p. 67)

At that time the social centre of the Chinese community was still Nelson Street's eating-houses, gambling dens and clubs – political, social and masonic – though families had spread to settle in other wards of the city. But by the late 1960s O'Neill (1972) discovered that the extant social facilities were poorly supported and served little purpose for the majority of Chinese in Liverpool.

Similar changes occurred to the London Chinese community in the late 1940s and early 1950s. The East End Chinese community which had been badly blitzed was subsequently demolished. This coincided with the movement of Chinese to the Gerrard Street area of Soho where the restaurant trade was becoming brisk. There were two Chinese clubs in London at this time: one founded in 1920 to improve working conditions, look after welfare and latterly to provide recreational facilities; and a second dating from the late 1940s of a politically left-wing, pro-China nature. Until this time – effectively the end of the first phase of immigration and settlement – the Chinese had remained largely unobtrusive since their numbers were relatively small and only major ports had Chinese 'communities'. But they were in no way assimilated or integrated even though their social norms may have appeared superficially similar. They adapted to prevailing conditions, taking up economic opportunities and applying themselves through hard work, but their long-term orientation was towards the villages of their homeland and the traditional values of their Chinese backgrounds prevailed in their daily lives.

Apart from the seamen, there was a second very much smaller group of Chinese with very different social backgrounds in Britain during the early years of this century. These were the students, the intellectual élite of China who desired some Western education. In 1931 an inter-governmental agreement provided greater training opportunities for Chinese students in British industry and their numbers increased during the following decade. Students also arrived from Malaya and Hong Kong (Ng, 1968). After the Second World War and the Civil War in China (1946–9), a number of Chinese professionals and political refugees came to Britain (Tsow, 1977). Over the last 20 years a growing number of intellectuals and professionals, many of Chinese ethnic origin, especially students and nurses, have come from Hong Kong, Malaysia and Singapore and until 1980 many remained on completion of their studies or training, after five years becoming free of conditions on their residence (although their position under British nationality law is extremely complex, see Dummett in CAG & QCRC, 1979). Numbers in the groups are particularly difficult to estimate due partly to lack of congruence between country of origin and ethnic origin and also inadequate publicly available information (but see Ng, 1968; Chann, 1976; Watson, 1977a; Clough and Quarmby, 1978; Simsova and Chin, 1982; and Shang, 1984: 20,000–30,000). Though it is likely that numbers of professionals and students will have declined in recent years – 5,619 students from Hong Kong were admitted in 1983 (GB. P.H of C. HAC, 1985) – they constitute a small but significant minority of people of Chinese ethnic origin in the UK. As urban educated they have little in common with the earlier Chinese migrants or the more numerous post-war migration from the New Territories, but they are playing an increasingly important role in the development of the Chinese community in Britain.

POST-WAR ARRIVALS: THE SECOND AND THIRD PHASES

Relatively little is apparently known of the precise links between the first male migrants in the early 20th century and the second post-war phase of immigration and settlement. Watson (1977a, 1977b) has described certain connections. In general emigration from Hong Kong was largely an adaptive response to increased economic competition in agriculture and the influx of refugees from mainland China (see p.8). Young single male Chinese immigrants came to the UK in the 1950s and 1960s with the intention of earning enough money to support their families in their homeland and to retire there. Those born in Hong Kong were British subjects and held British passports; those from Hong Kong, but born in mainland China, or whose births were not registered, travelled on a Certificate of Identity. In the 1950s and early 1960s both groups were able to come to the UK without much restriction and were assisted by lineage, other kinship or village links with men from the first migration who were already in England, usually operating as restaurateurs. The Chinese traditionally employed relatives or friends in their businesses and kinship became increasingly important as immigration restrictions were strengthened. Due to this and other factors, having established themselves in the UK, these male migrants subsequently sent for their wives and families. This was the general pattern of the second and third phases of settlement, although it may have differed in certain respects for individuals and families with diverse backgrounds and in different localities (see, for example, the three families described by Shang, 1984).

Chann (in SCSCRC, 1976) has suggested that the pattern of immigration of Chinese from Hong Kong can be divided into four stages coinciding with the gradual tightening of immigration controls and the economic development of the Chinese community in the UK. From the late 1950s to mid-1960s the majority of Chinese immigrants were men, only a very small minority bringing their wives and families upon settlement or marrying girls already here. According to Chann, after this more men began to send for their wives and children to join them, but it was still more common to send for their adolescent sons and daughters to come to work, leaving wives at home to look after the younger children. But the immigration law in 1968 made it necessary for wives to accompany their children. Male immigrants were used to living in dormitory accommodation provided by their employers, but the advent of their families made other accommodation necessary, and at about the same time economic factors were conducive to the emergence of Chinese 'takeaway' shops ('carryout' in Scotland). For a relatively small capital outlay these provided independent living accommodation and employment. Chann has claimed that the fourth stage of immigration is to complete the family reunion by sending for aged parents, though it is doubtful due to immigration restrictions and social factors whether this will ever be achieved.

This general pattern can be exemplified in further detail. For example, Cheung (1975) claimed that in 1951 3,459 single male workers came from Hong Kong but by 1964 it was estimated that there were 30,000, mostly from the New Territories and employed in catering. With the introduction of the Commonwealth Immigration Act in 1962, it became more difficult for Hong Kong-born Chinese to enter Britain and immigration was controlled by the Work Voucher System, with admission mainly under Category A, where the migrant had a specific job to come to in the UK. Category C Vouchers, for unskilled workers without specific jobs, were not issued after September 1965. The Category A Voucher required an application by the employer rather than the employee, which necessitated sponsorship of the intending migrant by a relative or friend already in England and in a position to offer a job. Thus the kinship and village network system was a significant support but tended to restrict immigration to Hong Kong villages from which earlier settlers had come. Moreover, an overwhelming proportion of Category A Vouchers issued to applicants from Hong Kong were for the catering trade. In 1965 a ceiling of 300 Category A Vouchers per year was established for electing a wife (Freeberne, 1978), and for married men with families the lack of free state welfare or education provision might also have spurred family reunions (O'Neill, 1972). Other more personal and social considerations must also have played a part as Watson (1977a) has claimed that Chinese men over 35, who were least able to negotiate with British society in terms of language and knowledge about life in the UK, brought their families over. But Lynn (1982) maintained that the decision to send for wives and children was based primarily on economic grounds because the success of takeaways – which were beginning to be established at the end of the 1960s – relies heavily on family labour and commitment.

The arrival of women and children thus both occasioned and coincided with the spread of small businesses and the need for appropriate accommodation. The presence of Chinese women was in the 1970s seen to have the potential for strengthening and enforcing cultural traditions (O'Neill, 1972) but not necessarily to intensify a sense of community. Chinese wives often had a beneficial influence, increasing saving and inhibiting gambling (Lai, 1975; Cheung, 1975). But with the advent of women and children, migrants found themselves having to cope with problems which had not previously been encountered, such as housing, shopping, public transport, medical treatment, child care and schooling. Particular difficulties experienced with the upbringing of children have sometimes intensified contacts with traditional child-care agents – the grandparents in Hong Kong – thereby influencing the completion of both the third and fourth stages of immigration with children sometimes being brought up in Hong Kong or grandmothers brought to the UK. Figures from the Hong Kong Government Office (based on GB. Home Office, *Control of Immigration Statistics*) show that for 1971–81 14,219 Chinese dependants entered the UK for settlement on British (Hong Kong) passports and 5,542 on Certificates of Identity. In 1983, 1,487 applications, mostly from wives and children, were made in Hong Kong for UK settlement and almost all approved (GB. P. H of C. HAC, 1985).

DEMOGRAPHY AND SETTLEMENT

Whilst it is possible to provide such an outline of the stages of immigration and settlement of the Chinese population in Great Britain, their composition, time and means of arrival and settlement location are inadequately and unsystematically documented and therefore make further analysis difficult. A number of distinctions must be borne in mind when considering the Chinese in Britain: birthplace in China, Hong Kong or, in the case of children, in the UK; lineage or clan affiliations; region, town or village origins or emigration via another country to the UK; arrival time of the male family head in the UK; reunion of the family, nuclear or extended, or intermarriage in the UK; socioeconomic status of an individual or family – skilled working class, entrepreneurial as a restaurateur or independent

Hong Kong-born Chinese. Between 1968 and 1971, 87 per c
vouchers issued for that group were for Category A and 78 per c
migrants were under 45, the largest number aged 15–24 (Cheung,
this did not satisfy the need of the expanding catering business fc
labour, hence many restaurateurs drew upon a new pool of Chin
available in Hong Kong from among the China-born who, as al
not subject to the restrictions on Commonwealth immigration. C
claimed that they were several times more numerous than Hong F
Chinese up to 1970; possibly about 10,000 (Watson, 1977a). Afte
Immigration Act, both Hong Kong- and China-born immigr
admitted in restricted numbers on work permits. From 1971 to 1
holders of British (Hong Kong) passports were admitted on en
vouchers or work permits and 2,235 holders of Hong Kong Cer1
Identity were admitted to the UK on work permits. (Statistics st
HKGO, based on GB. Home Office, *Control of Immigration Stc*
relevant years.) The number of new workers remains low – 258 wo
were issued to workers from Hong Kong in 1983 (GB.P.H of
1985).

After the 1968 Commonwealth Immigration Act, which necess
wives accompany children, there was an increase in the n
dependants coming to the UK. Family reunions took place. Th
pattern is confirmed by two mid-1970s research studies: Cheu
illuminatingly investigated the Hong Kong Chinese community in
Lai (1975) studied 24 Chinese families in Camden, London. Che1
that wives had joined their husbands after some years in the UK
older – followed by younger – children were reunited with their p
second UK-born family was growing up, whilst some children ha
been brought over from Hong Kong, or had indeed been sent bacl
that as many children remained outside the family group as tl
within it. Lai (1975) found that the men in the families she in
mostly aged 30–40, had come to the UK first, most directly into em
prior to 1962. Their wives, who were younger, had mostly arrived a
and slightly over half of the 54 children who had been born in Hc
had been sent for in stages after a home had been prepared in Lonc
arriving between 1970 and 1973. The desire for family reunion wa
as the dominant reason.

The decision of many Chinese men to send for their wives unc
involved a mixture of economic, political and social considera
addition to immigration restrictions, Baker and Honey (19
suggested that riots and uncertainties provoked by the Chinese pi
cultural revolution gave added impetus to the trend to reunit
families, thus breaking away from more complex family structur
the land in Hong Kong. The increase in charter flights during the 19
return to Hong Kong easier, especially for the traditional pu

businessman or a professional; and settlement in one of the older Chinese communities in the seaports, in London or a small or large town where the numbers of Chinese may be in tens or hundreds. Owing to the significance of such distinctions, it is mistaken to consider the Chinese as a homogeneous group.

As to composition Watson (1977a) has suggested that approximately 70 per cent of the Chinese in Britain are Cantonese-speaking from the New Territories, 25 per cent are Hakka and the remainder are northern Chinese, mostly from Taiwan, and from Singapore. There are few Tan Ka or Hokklo, Hong Kong's boat people, in the UK. Watson has calculated that no more than one-third of the Cantonese speakers and few, if any, of the Hakka in Britain can claim élite lineage membership, tracing descent from a founding ancestor in the village of origin. Most Cantonese speakers come from multilineage villages and towns in the New Territories. From these emigrants – the seamen of the first pre-war migration and the catering workers of the subsequent mass migration – are to be distinguished the professionals, usually reared and educated in Hong Kong, few of whom trace their origins back to New Territories villages. According to Watson, these Chinese, doctors, solicitors, architects, teachers, university lecturers, bankers and business executives form 'a separate and distinct class', rarely identify with other Hong Kong migrants, interact more readily with their British counterparts and some may have effectively 'dropped out' of Chinese culture. Although there appears to be little research evidence about this section of the Chinese population, a number of Chinese professionals do seem to be taking an active part in promoting the interests of the Chinese community (see, for example, NCC, 1984). The overwhelming majority of Chinese in the UK have emigrated from Hong Kong but there are also a number of ethnic Chinese with origins in other Far East countries including those to which earlier emigrations from Hong Kong or China have been made. For example, the Chinese professionals at a conference on the Chinese in the UK (CAG & QCRC, 1979) hailed from backgrounds including India, Burma, Malaysia, West Indies, Taiwan, China and Hong Kong. The proportion of UK immigrants born in Singapore or Malaysia and of Chinese ethnic origin is difficult to calculate and, in any case, is likely to be less than half though their numbers may not be insignificant.

There are two main sources of information on the Chinese in the UK, the Census and the Labour Force Survey. However, complications with the data base of each means that it is only possible to estimate the size of the population of Chinese origin in Britain. Although the Census covers all households, it has not included a question on ethnic origin, but provides instead figures on country of birth – China, or the Far East Commonwealth (Hong Kong, Malaysia, Singapore). There are, however, a number of difficulties here. These Census figures do not include children of Chinese ethnic origin born in the UK, or distinguish persons of Chinese ethnic origin born elsewhere in the world now resident in the UK. On the other hand, birthplace in the Far East Commonwealth does not necessarily imply Chinese ethnic origin, for these figures misleadingly include children of white British parents, such as service personnel, born in Hong Kong, Singapore or Malaysia. Hence the Census data need careful interpretation and are likely to overstate the size of the Chinese population. Information from the 1981 Labour Force Survey (OPCS, 1983b) shows that only 43 per cent of those born in the Far East Commonwealth are of Chinese ethnic origin and 38 per cent are white – mostly service children (GB. P. H of C. HAC, 1985, Vol. 3, App. 14). In addition, the Census figures include a large number of nurses, students or other temporary visitors from the Far East Commonwealth. For example, it has been estimated that in 1971 there were 8,000 of Chinese ethnic origin from Malaysia and 20,000 from Singapore and that the total figures (see Table 6) included 15,000 nurses and students (Clough and Quarmby, 1978). By 1980 there were estimated to be 12,000 Malaysian students and 5,000 nurses (Simsova and Chin, 1982). The China- and Hong Kong-born population was estimated to include 6,000 full-time students and nurses in the mid-1970s (Watson, 1977a).

With these caveats in mind, Table 6 provides country of birth and UK-residence figures (1951, 1961, England and Wales only) which show that the second phase of post-war migration has been primarily of the Hong Kong- rather than the China-born population. Noting the increase in numbers over the thirty-year period the Hong Kong-born group in particular has doubled in the last decade. The second source of information on the Chinese population which complements the Census is the Labour Force Survey (LFS) conducted every second year by personal interviews from a nationally and regionally representative sample covering about half of one per cent of all households. The LFS usefully provides information on country of birth, ethnic origin and nationality and in addition, in 1983, parents' countries of birth and year of entry to UK. Though these data are highly reliable, as with

Table 6: Country of birth (China and Far East Commonwealth) and residence in Great Britain, 1951–81

| Year | Born in: | | | |
	China	Hong Kong	Malaysia	Singapore
1951	1,763	3,459	4,046	3,255 (est.)
1961	9,192	10,222	9,516	9,820
1971	13,495	29,520	25,680	27,335
1981	17,569	58,917	45,430	32,447

Sources: Census 1951, 1961, 1971, 1981; GRO, 1956, 1964; OPCS, 1974, 1983a.

any survey based on a sample care is needed in comparing results from different years, as small differences may be due to sampling error and response rates rather than real changes in the population. In addition, in considering data on ethnic origin it has to be remembered that the population of Chinese ethnic origin now includes Vietnamese refugees, a high proportion of whom are of Chinese ethnic origin, and also some persons of mixed ethnic origin. With these reservations, Table 7 shows the growth of the population of Chinese origin in the UK, according to LFS figures for 1979–83 which also distinguish birthplace within and outside the UK. The figures, indicating a current population of the order of 105,000 persons of Chinese ethnic origin in the UK, are confirmed by various estimates (for example, QCRC, 1981; GB. P. H of C. HAC, 1985). The LFS reveals that between a fifth and a quarter (1981, 27 per cent; 1983, 20 per cent) of the population of Chinese ethnic origin is UK-born and that their numbers almost doubled in the four years 1979–83.

Table 7: Population of Chinese ethnic origin, by birthplace, 1979, 1981, 1983 (thousands rounded up)

Birthplace	1979	1981	1983
All	80,000	91,000	105,000
UK	12,000	24,000	21,000
Outside UK	68,000	66,000	83,000
Far East Commonwealth	44,000	50,000	49,000
Other New Commonwealth	2,000		3,000
China, Vietnam, Rest of World	21,000	16,000	31,000

Sources: Labour Force Survey 1979, 1981, 1983; OPCS, 1982b, Table 5.7, 1983b, Tables 4 and 7, 1984, Table 7.

The 1981 LFS also revealed the sex and age range of the population of Chinese ethnic origin by birthplace as shown in Table 8. The data show that the population of Chinese ethnic origin is predominantly youthful, about 60 per cent being under 30. A particularly interesting educational statistic is also revealed in Table 8, namely, that three-quarters of the 0–15 year-olds in 1981, that is, the present school population of Chinese ethnic origin, are UK-born. This group numbers approximately 30,000 in total. Conversely, the 16-plus age group contains relatively few UK-born individuals. These figures are overwhelmingly borne out by the 1983 LFS (OPCS, 1984, Table 5), which also shows that of those born in the Far East Commonwealth resident in the UK, only 15 per cent are under 16 (OPCS, 1984, Table 2). By comparison, some 43 per cent of those born in the Far East Commonwealth

Table 8: Population of Chinese ethnic origin, by birthplace, age and sex, 1981 (thousands)

	Sex			*Age*				
Birthplace	All	m.	f.	0–15	16–29	30–44	45–59/64	60–65+
All	91	48	43	30	29	20	8	3
UK	24	14	11	23			2	
Outside UK	66	35	32	7	28	20	8	3

Source: Labour Force Survey 1981, adapted from OPCS, 1982a, Table 7.

were aged 16–29 and there was a particular imbalance in the sex ratio of this age group of 156 males to every 100 females; 1981 Census results suggest this may be due to the large number of single male students born in Malaysia and Hong Kong.

Information given for the first time in the 1983 LFS reveals that the 105,000 persons of Chinese ethnic origin were evenly divided between those with both parents born in the New Commonwealth and those with both parents born in the 'Rest of the World' (both 45 per cent), with seven per cent having one parent born in each. Only one per cent had parents who were both born in the UK (OPCS, 1984, Table 17). Table 9 shows the year of entry to the UK of the 83,000 persons of Chinese ethnic origin born outside the UK, almost half arriving in the last decade, thus confirming the trend indicated in the Census figures (see p.40).

Since it is difficult to enumerate the population of Chinese ethnic origin in the UK, it is even more difficult to provide a picture of their distribution by birthplace within or outside the UK (in China or the Far East Commonwealth) even on a regional or city basis, let alone to give a proper account of their well-known dispersal across Britain. Once again the main

Table 9: Year of entry of population of Chinese ethnic origin born outside UK (thousands)

Pre-1950	*1950–4*	*1955–9*	*1960–4*	*1965–9*	*1970–4*	*1975–9*	*1980–3*	*No reply*	*Total*
0	1	1	6	10	14	24	21	5	83

Source: Labour Force Survey, 1983, OPCS, 1984, Table 15.

sources of information are the Census and to a lesser extent the Labour Force Survey, though its sample is too small to give reliable statistics on the Chinese for smaller areas. Chann (1976) suggested that Hong Kong immigrants from the more rural New Territories have tended to settle in the provinces whereas those of urban origin, many born in China, have tended to settle in the Greater London area and are in a minority in the provinces and Scotland. But Simsova and Chin (1982) claimed that there is a higher proportion of China-born Mandarin speakers outside London. It is generally recognized that the Chinese have not usually settled in areas of high Asian or West Indian population. They are, nevertheless, represented in large numbers in conurbations, though they may not necessarily live in the same wards or streets as other ethnic minority groups. Such a detailed demographic analysis is missing and only hinted at in certain local studies, e.g. in Liverpool (Lynn, 1982) and London (Chin and Simsova, 1981). The complexities involved in data analysis on the Chinese in Britain (see pp.39–41) together with boundary changes between Censuses mean that it is often only possible to infer population trends, for example, across London boroughs, or estimate the comparative expansion and vitality of other centres of Chinese population in the conurbations of Manchester, Liverpool, Birmingham, Cardiff, Glasgow and Edinburgh (Watson, 1977a; Chin and Simsova, 1981). Yet a certain amount of evidence according to country of birth indicates the general pattern of distribution and population changes for the main locations of Chinese settlement.

Table 10 indicates the comparative growth of the China- and Hong Kong-born population in Greater London, the main centre of Chinese settlement over 30 years, from 1951 to 1981. Table 11 indicates the six locations with the largest Chinese populations in 1971 showing the pre-eminence of Greater London and Liverpool, the other area of older settlement with at least twice the numbers of other conurbations. Table 12 lists the London boroughs with populations of Chinese and Far East Commonwealth settlement in excess of

Table 10: China- and Hong Kong-born residents in (Greater) London, 1951–81

Year	China	Born in: Hong Kong	Hong Kong and China
1951	1,350	586	1,936
1961	2,981	2,834	5,815
1971	3,815	6,865	10,680
1981	4,965	14,536	19,501

Sources: Census 1951, 1961, 1971, 1981; GRO, 1964; OPCS, 1974, 1983a.

Table 11: Main centres of Hong Kong- and China-born population in the UK, 1971

| | *Born in:* | | |
	Hong Kong	*China*	*Hong Kong and China*
GLC	6,865	3,815	10,680
Liverpool	685	565	1,250
Glasgow	450	160	610
Birmingham	440	175	615
Manchester	395	175	570
Edinburgh	275	185	460

Source: Census 1971, adapted from Campbell-Platt, 1978, Table 15, p.15.

1,000 in 1971 (which may be compared with those for 1981 in Table 15, Footnotes 2 and 3).

A decade later the 1981 Census shows the growth in the UK resident population born in the Far East Commonwealth and China, bearing in mind that this is likely to overstate the population of Chinese ethnic origin (see p. 40). Table 13 demonstrates the distribution of the overseas-born Chinese by region of UK residence. On this analysis nearly half of both the Hong Kong- and China-born live in the south-east, mainly Greater London. These groups are also more numerous in the north-west and Scotland with the Hong Kong-born favouring the north and the China-born the south-west. Table 14, which indicates the regional distribution of the population of Chinese origin from the 1983 Labour Force Survey, confirms the south-east as the predominant area of residence, but also shows that a quarter of the Chinese are more widely dispersed, to a much greater extent than any other ethnic group.

Table 12: Population born in China, Hong Kong, Singapore and Malaysia numbering over 1,000 in GLC boroughs, 1971

GLC total	23,660
Westminster	2,245
Kensington	1,835
Camden	1,590
Barnet	1,425
Ealing	1,345
Brent	1,105

Source: Census 1971; adapted from CRE, 1978, Table 10, p.17.

Table 13: Population born in the Far East Commonwealth and China, by region of UK residence, 1981

Country of birth	Total	Wales	Scotland	North	Yorkshire & Humberside	East Midlands	East Anglia	Greater London	SE Outer Metropolitan	SE Outer SE	SW	West Midlands	NW
Hong Kong	58,917	2,092	4,907	4,713	3,637	3,030	1,536	14,536	6,939	5,719	3,864	3,632	6,543
Singapore	32,447	946	2,366	982	1,974	1,918	1,430	6,737	3,744	4,615	4,072	1,757	1,906
Malaysia	45,430	1,452	2,543	1,249	2,335	1,889	1,111	16,468	5,488	4,781	2,652	2,516	2,946
China (PR)	17,569	530	1,117	541	900	660	544	4,965	2,027	1,833	1,254	961	2,237

SE region combined totals (brace): Hong Kong 27,914; Singapore 15,096; Malaysia 26,739; China (PR) 8,825.

Source: Census 1981; OPCS, 1983a, Table 1.

Table 14: Selected areas of distribution of population of Chinese ethnic origin, 1983 (percentages)

Region	Sub-total %	Total %
Yorkshire and Humberside		2
South Yorkshire Metropolitan Co.	0	
West Yorkshire Metropolitan Co.	1	
Remainder	1	
East Midlands	7	7
South East		51
Outer Metropolitan	8	
Greater London:		
Inner London	16	
Outer London	17	
Remainder	10	
West Midlands		7
Metropolitan Co.	5	
Remainder	2	
North West		10
Greater Manchester Metropolitan Co.	5	
Remainder	5	
Rest of Great Britain		23

Source: Labour Force Survey 1983, OPCS, 1984, Table 6.

Finally Table 15 is derived from evidence submitted by the OPCS to the Home Affairs Committee inquiry on the *Chinese Community in Britain* for selected districts of major settlement. Table 15 reveals that compared with 1971 Census figures (Table 11), Manchester (as the second largest area), Birmingham, Glasgow, Edinburgh and their conurbations have overtaken Liverpool and Merseyside by 1981 as more numerous centres of Chinese population, although Merseyside continues to be the largest centre of China-born population outside Greater London. The other long-established Chinese community in Cardiff appears to be declining (see also Chin and Simsova, 1981). By comparison, there are an increasing number of inner and outer London boroughs with populations of over 1,000 born in the Far East Commonwealth (see nn. 2 and 3 in Table 15; CRE, 1985, also includes Tower Hamlets). However, the caveats concerning the Census data especially with respect to an overestimate of population of Chinese ethnic origin and exclusion of the UK-born, particularly those living in households with heads not born in the Far East Commonwealth (see p. 00), have to be remembered. Thus in its evidence to the Home Affairs Committee the Commission for Racial Equality (1985) suggested that the local estimates for

Table 15: Persons born in the Far East Commonwealth and People's Republic of China: persons in households with a head born in the Far East Commonwealth: Great Britain

	Far East CW[1]	People's Republic of China	Persons in households with head born in Far East CW		
			All persons	Born in the UK	Born elsewhere
Great Britain	136,794	17,569	120,123	39,742	80,381
Greater London	37,741	4,965	37,319	9,717	27,602
Inner London[2]	18,627	2,452	17,569	3,925	13,644
Outer London[3]	19,114	2,513	19,750	5,792	13,958
Greater Manchester	5,418	833	5,545	1,482	4,063
Manchester	2,380	300	2,408	416	1,992
Merseyside	3,153	966	3,518	1,383	2,135
Liverpool	1,692	521	2,085	818	1,267
West Midlands	4,337	498	4,592	1,428	3,164
Birmingham	2,304	282	2,353	636	1,717
Cardiff	1,008	98	922	197	725
Strathclyde	3,910	460	3,971	1,331	2,640
Glasgow City	1,972	201	2,045	575	1,470
Edinburgh City	1,406	243	1,239	402	837

[1] Hong Kong, Malaysia and Singapore.
[2] LBs in Inner London that have a population of more than 1,000 persons born in the Far East CW are Camden, Hackney, Hammersmith and Fulham, Haringey, Islington, Kensington and Chelsea, Lambeth, Newham, Wandsworth and City of Westminster.
[3] LBs in Outer London that have a population of more than 1,000 persons born in the Far East CW are Barnet, Brent, Croydon, Ealing, Hounslow and Redbridge.

Sources: Census 1981, OPCS, 1984; and GB. P.H. of C. HAC, 1985; Vol. 3, App.14, Table 4.

both Merseyside and Cardiff were at least double the 1981 Census figures because of the growing number of second- and third-generation Chinese.

THE FUTURE: THE UK OR RETURN?

Further data in relation to the family structure and household circumstances of pupils of Chinese ethnic origin are cited in the following section. But the main import of figures discussed in this section showing the dramatic change in numbers and the proportion of UK-born of Chinese ethnic origin in the last decade is clear. The focus of the Chinese community must now be on the second generation in this country.

By the early 1970s Watson (1977b) had noticed changes with regard to the orientation of the migrants from San Tin, though remittances were still sent regularly and return trips made every three to five years (see also Cheung, 1975). More recently Fong (1981), in a study of Chinese parents and children in Liverpool, discovered that even though 60 per cent of the parents born in Hong Kong or China had been in the UK for more than ten years and 25 per cent for more than 20 years, a quarter – mainly those who had houses and relatives in Hong Kong – intended to return home 'because of the traditional view that home is home'. Thirty per cent of the 31 children (one from each family) aged 11–18 were UK-born, 40 per cent had been in the UK for less than five years and 30 per cent had arrived within the previous year. Half, especially the recent arrivals, were eager to return because they experienced difficulties in adjustment, appreciated the lifestyle in Hong Kong and missed their relatives and friends. Those who did not wish to return permanently nevertheless enjoyed a return visit. Another study (Ng, 1982) concluded that although pupils of Chinese origin would not return to Hong Kong, they would not be culturally or linguistically assimilated in the third or fourth generations.

The ambivalence of long-term planning and of orientation, detected a decade or so ago by Watson, seems to remain. Baker and Honey (1981) have suggested that because of spreading urbanization, going 'home' no longer has the same deep meaning for Chinese in the UK, but they retain 'a sentimental attachment . . . to their magnetic and powerful cultural roots' (p.15). This has been demonstrated by the recent emergence of Chinese community projects and the rapid growth of interest groups, especially focussing on Chinese language and culture classes for the second generation. But there is also a pragmatic desire for economic success as shown by the movement of Chinese businesses into Western Europe using British status to maximize the opportunities opened up by EEC membership. This economic diversification results in further social fragmentation since some nuclear families are still divided between Hong Kong and the UK. The question is whether a comfortable compromise can be made between the economic success (and personal and social prestige) of the first generation with a traditional Hong Kong orientation, and the maintenance of a Chinese identity through awareness and appreciation of cultural roots in Hong Kong, by a second generation which is spending its influential youthful years in the UK. But it is clear that with the increasing numbers of UK-born children of Chinese ethnic origin another phase in the settlement of the Chinese in the UK has occurred.

Section 2
Housing

The housing of the Chinese in the UK has been inadequately documented and any research undertaken has usually been incidental to a larger investigation. For the most part, such material is very small scale and may be unrepresentative, though common trends suggest that, like other ethnic minority groups, the Chinese often experience very unsatisfactory housing and unfavourable living conditions. Due to the lack of data only a sketchy account can be given of the development of the post-war housing of the Chinese population covering type of accommodation for single men and families often in multi-occupation; tenure – private, owner-occupied and council housing; and housing facilities and furnishing. This information can be usefully augmented by contrasting evidence from three local studies in York (Cheung, 1975), London (Lai, 1975) and Liverpool (Lynn, 1982).

The decline of the Chinese population in the 1930s and the pre- and post-war demolition for urban redevelopment of centres of Chinese population in Liverpool and London led to the dispersal of the two largest Chinese communities into areas away from the original dockland sites of settlement (Jones, D., 1979; Ng, 1968). In London the Chinese community regrouped around Soho. In Liverpool by the early 1950s Broady (1955) reported that the Chinese community had begun to divide along social class lines with laundrymen, cooks, sailors and shoregang workers predominating in the older parts of the city whilst the wealthier restaurateurs and boarding-house owners lived in the middle- and upper-class residential districts. Some 20 years later O'Neill (1972) found that successful businessmen and those well qualified educationally were more likely to move out of the Chinese community, both physically and socially, and more recently Lynn (1982) observed that it was still the Chinese professionals or restaurant owners who lived in owner-occupied housing in the middle-class areas of Liverpool. Similarly, in Derby Fitchett (1976) noted that the more affluent restaurant owners had purchased houses or flats in the higher-class residential areas, and in York Cheung (1975) found that restaurant proprietors had their homes away from their businesses. However, this option is apparently only open to the relatively affluent in the catering trade or to Chinese professionals.

The post-war housing of the Chinese population is characterized by two main types of need-related provision: first, the accommodation of male workers, often unmarried, or without their families in dormitories owned by their employers; and secondly, on account of the arrival of women and children, accommodation more appropriate to a family's requirements, often privately owned and associated with the takeaway business. According to Cheung (1975), in the 1960s as the restaurants began to move out of London employers provided free accommodation as an incentive to work in the provinces. This was still the case in the mid-1970s for those working in food shops, the single and those living away from their homes elsewhere in the UK. However, this was unlikely in London due to lack of available space, and higher wages were given instead. Cheung claims that three-quarters of the Chinese catering population were housed up to 1968 in employer-related accommodation when more wives and older children began to arrive and Chinese takeaways were opened. Accommodation had then to be sought in the private market, either adjacent to or with the business, so that it should be both sufficient for the family and convenient to the business because of working hours.

In Cheung's in-depth study of three restaurants and six takeaways (approximately half of the Chinese catering trade in York in the early 70s) half the 73 adults lived in free accommodation provided with their job. The single men lived in very poor, spartan accommodation with little space and few possessions, usually a radio or a record player if anything. However, such accommodation was not a cause for complaint because it was known to be standard throughout the UK, and was always regarded as temporary. Although it provided little privacy (most of the employees' free time was spent at the shop), it reduced living expenses and avoided the need to seek accommodation outside the Chinese community. A major drawback, however, occurred when an employee gave notice or lost his job as it was then also necessary to seek alternative accommodation.

Multi-occupancy seems to have been a feature of the accommodation of the Chinese population, especially when families first arrived in the UK. This is shown, for example, by data from Brown's (1970) study of ethnic minorities in Bedford which also demonstrate that during 1968 the decline in the number living in multi-occupied housing coincided with the opening of takeaways. Multi-occupancy seems to have been a more permanent feature of the housing of the Chinese in London. Information from 13 community relations councils in London showed that it was often only health visitors who visited Chinese homes and reported that they were more likely to be multi-occupied and very crowded (Lai, 1975). One-third of the 24 families which Lai studied lived in multi-occupied housing. A Chinese family studied by Jackson (1979) in Huddersfield who lived adjacent to their takeaway also provided accommodation in their own home for two waiters. Indeed, data from the 1981 Labour Force Survey show that, compared with the general population, households of which the head is of Chinese origin are much more likely to be larger – almost a third of Chinese households comprise five or more persons compared with eleven per cent of all households (Table 16). Conversely, far fewer Chinese households are limited to one or two persons (36 compared with 54 per cent). Data from the Linguistic Minorities Project in three locations also confirm relatively large household size (see Table 23, p.131). Larger household size has implications for accommodation provision.

Table 16: Household size: Chinese households and others compared (percentages)

	Head of household of Chinese ethnic origin	All households
All households	100	100
One person	17	22
Two persons	19	32
Three persons	16	17
Four persons	17	18
Five persons	12	7
Six or more persons	20	4
Average household size	3.52	2.67

Source: Labour Force Survey 1981; GB.P. H of C. HAC, 1985.

Access to housing by Chinese families seems to have been characterized by a certain self-sufficiency within the community. For example, O'Neill found that half of the 30 families studied in the late 1960s in Liverpool had received help from relatives and friends in finding accommodation. They tended to seek property from other Chinese and move into property where other Chinese were already residing. The more prosperous Chinese also tended to move into areas where other Chinese had previously been accepted. This pattern was also confirmed by Lai's study in the Camden area of north-west London where accommodation was usually found through kin, and since access to work was a prime consideration location was restricted, so that in effect the Chinese families were competing amongst themselves. Similarly, a survey of the housing of 141 Chinese families in Liverpool in 1979 (Fru, 1980) discovered that the Chinese on arriving in the UK first lived with relatives or friends, upon whom they relied for information about available accommodation. As many as 29 out of the 35 Chinese families in private accommodation, 30 out of the 64 in owner-occupied premises, 11 of the 37 council tenants and four of the six families in housing association accommodation had learned of their accommodation from another Chinese. Contrary to expectation for owner-occupied accommodation, only 11 per cent had heard of their house from an estate agent. On the basis of this survey Lynn (1982) has claimed that the Chinese community have been largely deprived of access to information about housing because of language and lack of knowledge about housing rights.

Whether Chinese live in areas of high ethnic minority settlement may vary according to the age of the Chinese community, availability of suitable housing and the city or town. Thus, whilst Fru's (1980) survey revealed that most of the Chinese families lived in Liverpool 8, an area of high ethnic minority housing, and Freeberne (1978) reported that the Chinese in London lived in twilight housing zones, Fitchett (1976) discovered that the less affluent Chinese families in Derby, who settled there in the early 1970s, selected an area with easy access to their employment in the town centre but where the housing, though not too expensive, was of a better quality than that in the area occupied by most other ethnic minority families. The pattern of Chinese settlement was thus very different from that of Asian settlement in a specific area. In Sheffield although the Chinese population is scattered over the city, there are two main areas of settlement, one of students and the other of families (Mackillop, 1980).

In terms of housing tenure figures from the 1981 Labour Force Survey confirm that there is a much greater reliance amongst the Chinese population on privately rented accommodation – 29 per cent of households with a head of Chinese origin compared with eight per cent of all households. There are comparatively fewer Chinese households in owner occupation (39 compared with 54 per cent) and in accommodation rented from the Council or Local Authority (23 and 32 per cent). Data from the Linguistic Minorities Project show wide variations in the patterns of housing tenure across three locations – Bradford, Coventry and London (see Table 23, p.131).

Limited reports about the housing conditions of the Chinese, both in terms of property maintenance and living standards, vary but there is an indication that, especially in privately rented accommodation, standards may be inferior. Health visitors cited in Lai's study observed that the interiors of Chinese homes were clean and tidy despite the shabby exteriors. On the other hand, Garvey and Jackson (1975) claimed that there was often a contrast between the smart exterior of a Chinese takeaway with its outward indications of affluence – well-decorated shops with thick pile carpets, easy chairs and colour TV – and the interior living accommodation of the Chinese family which by West European standards was very poor. Many families lived in almost completely unfurnished accommodation without floor or wall coverings and with evident damp. Twenty-one out of the 24 families in Lai's survey lived in rented accommodation in very poor condition, ill-maintained and cramped. In 13 cases furnishing was provided, but of a very limited and inferior quality. Yet Jackson (1979, p.42) described a Chinese home in Huddersfield of mixed Chinese and British style in which, although the furniture was 'minimal and nondescript', the appurtenances and conveniences of a media and high-technology age were in evidence.

Subjective and impressionistic though some of these sources may be, the housing of the Chinese population, though varying in type and quality, is on the whole apparently not of a particularly high standard. Yet in a national CRE (1981) survey in 1980–1 using a quota sampling method, involving 1,073 whites and 1,057 of the ethnic minority population including 107 Chinese nearly half of whom were aged 25–39 and 45 per cent in the C1 socioeconomic category, found that only six per cent of the Chinese mentioned that lack of housing was a problem. In this the Chinese were more like Asians than other ethnic minorities. Evidence suggests that housing problems of the Chinese may be intensified in certain localities and according to local housing availability and conditions. Information from three researches in York, London and Liverpool may exemplify this.

In York Cheung (1975) found that the 200-strong Chinese community in 1974 was largely self-sufficient in terms of its accommodation. Half of a representative sample of 73 adults predominantly involved in catering were living in accommodation provided by employers, and almost all of the remainder dwelt in accommodation attached to business premises. Of the 20 proprietors, most lived in owner-occupied premises; the restaurateurs lived in homes away from their businesses, others at or adjacent to the takeaways. A negligible number of families were accommodated in council housing; most had either not lived in York long enough to qualify or did not know of its availability.

By contrast, it is unusual for Chinese families to be accommodated near business premises in central London. In a study of 24 couples, most aged 30–40, having between them 54 children, with an average family of 2.23 persons, Lai (1975) found that accommodation was a practical restraint on the reunion of families. Most of the women had arrived during the previous five years and were still of child-bearing age. Twenty-one families lived in private rented accommodation, only three in council flats. All except one family suffered overcrowding according to the usually accepted ratio of 1.5 persons per room. In the case of several families this was extremely severe; 11 families had only one room each and ten only had the use of two rooms. Apart from the families who lived in council accommodation, families shared facilities, especially toilet and bath, and half also shared cooking facilities. These facilities were very cramped and poorly maintained. The longer-established residents had cheaper tenancies. Ten families had occupied their accommodation for 2½–5 years, six families for longer. The accommodation's main advantage was its location near the husband's workplace, and in addition its proximity to Chinese entertainment and friends. The majority of families were not surprisingly dissatisfied with their accommodation, but thought it impossible to better the situation. They also exhibited a high tolerance of their living conditions because their expectations were conditioned by housing in Hong Kong, and because in the traditional Chinese way they did not wish to appear other than self-reliant, or to make a nuisance of themselves. Yet there was a feeling of general helplessness and opportunities for bettering their housing conditions were limited by lack of knowledge of housing rights and limited English. In fact 12 families were on the council waiting-list but had exercised little pressure to be rehoused. As Wilson (1977) characterized it, it was something of a Catch-22 situation: in some cases the couples did not qualify for rehousing because their children had remained in Hong Kong; and the children were not in the UK because there was nowhere for them to live.

It is possible, however, that in recent years the housing of the Chinese has improved. For example, Tan (1982) who studied the food habits of 50 Chinese families across London, found that they were mostly accommodated in council housing. The majority of fathers, almost all employed in the catering trade, had been in the UK over ten years, though 79 per cent of the mothers had been here for less. Some 68 per cent of families were living in council accommodation, 26 per cent in private accommodation, but only three per cent in owner-occupied premises.

But a survey in Liverpool in 1979 revealed the grim housing position of the Chinese population (Fru, 1980, quoted by Lynn, 1982). This study may have finally brought about the recognition of the Chinese community's particular housing difficulties and the need for further investigation (GB. P. H of C, 1981, p. xlvii). The survey involved 141 families, the majority having lived in Liverpool for less than 20 years. The sample was not random and may not have been representative, but nevertheless indicated that in both private and owner-occupied accommodation there is much sub-standard housing and inadequate facilities. Half of the 30 out of the 35 families living in private accommodation rented houses attached to their fish and chip shop businesses but had to use their bedrooms as dining-rooms (see also Fitchett, 1976). The families were overcrowded, with on average 1.4 persons in each room. About 40 per cent of these families lacked sole use of cooking facilities, and half shared a shower or bath, hot water, a lavatory and a passage with another household when moving from room to room. Indeed, 40 per cent shared rooms with another household. Although nearly two-thirds had central heating, the properties were in a poor state of repair, damp, lacking basic facilities, difficult to heat and with leaking roofs.

Some 64 out of the 141 families lived in owner-occupied accommodation, many in Liverpool 8, only three families in the traditional Chinatown area of Liverpool 1. The majority of the heads of these households were employed in or owned fish and chip shops. Fifty three per cent owned their property outright. Building society mortgages were more popular than local authority or bank finance, but 48 per cent of those in owner-occupation had paid cash for their property. Lynn, of Chinese background herself, interestingly suggests that the Chinese community might financially assist families who wished to settle in England to set up a business and acquire accommodation. Later when these families are in a position to do so, they assist others in their turn. Such financial backing may have been experienced by some of these outright purchasers in the survey. However, the cash purchases related to terraced houses in run-down areas and 14 out of the 36 outright owners had their businesses on the premises. All local authority and building society mortgages – 20 out of the 64 properties – were for dwellings only, and those with building society mortgages tended to be professional people or restaurant owners. Some 59 of the 64 families in owner-occupied property were unaware that the local authority might grant a mortgage. Although in owner-occupation the condition of these was often poor: eight had outside toilets, 20 leaking roofs, 15 defective inside walls, 11 faulty windows and four no bathrooms. Although many of these houses were in a housing action area, as 14 of the 64 with repair problems were also used for business they did not qualify for improvement grants. Yet it is likely that maintenance problems would eventually lead to the need for rehousing due to health risks or dangerous structures. Again there was evidence of lack of knowledge of improvement grants and difficulties with making applications because of inadequate English. Thus owner-occupation for these Chinese families meant a certain security of tenure but also very poor living conditions.

Lynn (1982) quotes from a survey by the Merseyside Area Profile Group in 1980, in which 28 per cent of Chinese were found to be in council housing. In Fru's survey 37 out of 141 families were council tenants and six lived in housing association property. Nearly two-thirds of the council tenants had lived in private rented accommodation previously. The survey revealed the need for a larger accommodation, for 29 of these families had council houses with three or more bedrooms. Yet local authority and housing association accommodation does not usually provide facilities for larger families. Indeed in 37 out of the 141 families in Fru's survey there were elderly grandparents, suggesting that a fair proportion of the Chinese families in Liverpool are of three generations. By contrast, the survey also showed that the Chinese elderly who did not live with their families were often excluded from sheltered housing, sometimes, Lynn has alleged, because of 'the need to maintain the social viability' of each sheltered group of accommodation. The Chinese community itself provided two houses in Chinatown for the elderly but the condition of the premises and their facilities were grim, as also in a Chinese-run hostel for six families in severe need who shared kitchen, bath and toilet facilities in an inadequate state of repair. These reports suggest that the Chinese community in Liverpool is not in a position to make suitable independent housing provision for its needs. Lynn argues that the Chinese are also at a disadvantage with respect to local authority provision because their housing policy constitutes a form of institutional racism since the provision was not intended to cater for the kinds of need which the Chinese have – accommodation for the elderly, for larger families, and for assistance with housing improvement on business premises. Local authorities need to take a more positive approach to assessing and catering for the needs of Chinese families (see also GB. P. H of C. HAC, 1985).

This substantial evidence from the survey of housing of the Chinese in Liverpool and the insights of other studies quoted amount to a situation of largely inadequate housing for the Chinese population – of overcrowded multi-occupancies, privately rented accommodation in poor condition and often with shared facilities, with the Chinese working class frequently in competition for sub-standard housing. Even owner-occupiers may have inadequate resources to keep properties in good repair or lack knowledge about or access to local authority grants or assistance with rehousing. Many inner city authorities are severely pressed for housing and may not have been sufficiently alert to the housing needs of Chinese families, but there may also have been a tendency to self-sufficiency on the part of the majority of the Chinese involved in catering as housing is often linked with business premises. But the housing situation revealed here must surely give cause for some concern, especially for the implications it has for the daily living conditions of the second generation.

Section 3
Employment

That the Chinese are largely employed in catering, in restaurants, takeaways and fish and chip shops is well known. How self-contained and exclusive is the Chinese catering business? Does concentration in this industry make for insularity or dependence, for ironically its very success requires a symbiotic interdependence between cook and consumer? Following a brief outline of the pre-war employment of Chinese male immigrants, as seamen, laundry workers and restaurateurs, this section focusses on the concentration of post-war Chinese workers in the catering trade. The reasons for this phenomenon, financial arrangements, recruitment and job-search methods, job mobility and dispersal, the growth of the takeaway business as an offshoot of the restaurant trade, conditions of work, unemployment, the diversification of Chinese workers into other businesses, and the involvement of Chinese women and children in work will be examined.

PRE-WAR EMPLOYMENT: SEAMEN, LAUNDRYMEN AND RESTAURATEURS
The first phase of Chinese immigration and settlement involved Chinese seamen who came to the UK as early as 1814 and up until the 1920s, and again during the Second World War. They were sailors on trading vessels to the East and also shore-gangmen in British ports. Ng (1968) cites Census figures for the occupation of Chinese men as seamen, laundrymen and restaurateurs and shopkeepers during the first pre-war phase of settlement (see Table 17).

In 1901 the occupations of the Chinese in London were varied but as many as 42 per cent were seamen, compared with 61 per cent nationally. By 1921 Chinese seamen in London had declined to 23 per cent, whereas 27 per cent of the Chinese workforce were employed in personal service such as laundrywork. Indeed the 1911 Census of seamen showed that 4,595 of Chinese origin were serving in the British merchant fleet, though their numbers were small compared with other seamen of Asian race (May, 1979). Moreover, Jones (D., 1979) records that in 1912 1,751 Chinese were engaged at Liverpool and 1,130 at various London docks. Although there were several outbreaks of hostility towards Chinese seamen during these years, May suggests that their employment in this capacity, which occurred as part of trade expansion with the East, was largely accepted and any opposition was mainly on account of the Chinese predisposition for mobility between employers in order to seek better terms. Generally, however, harmonious relations existed between the Chinese and the communities in which they lived at the seaports.

After the end of the Second World War in which 10,000 Chinese were employed as seafarers, largely operating from Liverpool, many were repatriated. But by 1953 Collins (1957) discovered that some 2,700 were employed by a Liverpool shipping firm. During the 50 years in which Chinese had been employees they had been integrated into the structure of the organization, so that in the early 1950s the 300 or so shore-based Chinese employees held a range of occupations from fitters, stewards, unskilled labourers to clerical or administrative work. Not all were employed at any one time, some being kept in reserve, and also since northern and southern Chinese preferred to work in separate groups, because of language and cultural differences. There was a feeling of security and general satisfaction amongst the Chinese workers who had developed a relationship of mutual confidence with the management and did not feel the need to be members of a trade union as they had benefited from successive pay increases and provision for sick benefit and gratuities. Due to the sponsorship of the shipping firm, the status and prestige of the Chinese workers had been raised above that of other ethnic minority groups in the town. Some of the Chinese also had their own businesses: about 30 cafés, restaurants, grocery shops and laundries were Chinese-owned.

The involvement of the Chinese in laundry work was first recorded in 1901 with the establishment of London's first Chinese laundry in Poplar (Jones, D., 1979). Although this met with initial opposition, it reopened, and during the next decade about 30 Chinese hand laundries were established in the East End of London, where Lee clansmen dominated the trade. The laundry business continued to expand, so that by 1907 there were 47 laundries in

Table 17: Employment of Chinese men in Britain, 1901–51

	Seamen		Laundrymen		Restaurateurs and shopkeepers
	No.	%	No.	%	No.
1901	237	61	27	15	–
1911	480	36	351	26	–
1921	455	19	547	22	26
1931	477	25	531	27	17
1951	551	–	20	–	36

Source: Census figures quoted by Ng, 1968, p.10.

Liverpool and by 1911 at least 30 in Cardiff. When the opportunities for trade had been exploited in the seaports, the Chinese moved out into the provinces setting up laundries in many smaller towns, so that in the 1920s and 1930s there were 500 Chinese laundries in Britain (Ng, 1968). However, with the advent of mechanization and self-service launderettes the Chinese laundries were gradually put out of business. Whereas after the war there were nearly 100 Chinese laundries in Liverpool, according to Cheung (1975) mainly run by Toishanese from Sze Yap, Lynn (1982) has claimed that only one Chinese laundry remains in Liverpool.

Prior to the 1940s, the Chinese restaurant business, which like the laundries was initially set up to serve the needs of the Chinese seafarers, was still largely concerned with providing authentic Chinese cuisine for the Chinese. The first recorded Chinese restaurant was set up, in London, in 1908 (Ng, 1968). In the inter-war period there were still only a few Chinese restaurants in the East End and two or three in the West End, where the Cheungs founded a group of successful restaurants to cater for the Soho theatre trade. During this time some seamen jumped ship to obtain jobs in Chinese restaurants. By 1951 there were known to be 36 restaurants and, according to Cheung (1975), by 1957 they had reached 50. This was the point of expansion for the restaurant trade, augmented by the labour of the second phase of Chinese immigrants, and building on the foundations gradually laid over the previous 30 years. Sources agree that these early restaurateurs displayed particular enterprise, industry and astuteness and were generally the wealthiest Chinese in their localities.

POST-WAR DEVELOPMENT OF THE CATERING TRADE

The second phase of Chinese male immigration, directly linked to the expansion of the catering trade, can be fairly precisely defined. In the 1950s and 1960s there was a considerable growth in Chinese restaurants (Watson dates this from 1956 to 1965), which peaked by 1970. Already in the 1960s as expansion reached its limits in Britain, Chinese restaurateurs were looking towards Western Europe (Ng, 1968) and there was further diversification within Britain with the establishment of takeaways to complement the restaurant trade. The takeaway trade diversified further in the 1970s when many Chinese took over fish and chip businesses to provide a variety of food. As with other ethnic minority groups, there is little evidence of the Chinese working in industry or in the public services. This has been attributed to lack of spoken English and because kinship links in the migration both facilitated and necessitated the involvement of the second phase of immigrants in the catering trade (Ng, 1968). Indeed, an estimated 90 per cent of the Chinese workforce is widely regarded as being employed in aspects of catering. (Of the 61,000 Chinese persons aged 16+ in 1981, 31,000 were economically active, of whom 29,000 were in employment. Of the economically inactive, 14,000 were students and 12,000 housewives:

GB. P. H of C. HAC, 1985, Vol. 3.) Lynn (1982) cites a survey in Merseyside, in 1977, which showed that more than 90 per cent of the 7,000 Chinese living there were employed in restaurants and takeaway shops. It is only possible to speculate to what extent the concentration of Chinese in self-employment was a response to some early tensions when Chinese seamen were employed with other British and foreign workers; a tendency of each ethnic group to develop its own working patterns and traditional family and lineage links, which for the Chinese (and some other ethnic minorities, notably the Cypriots) were reinforced by immigration rules; or a conscious choice to enhance their perceived image as independent and non-competitive in the wider labour market and the desire to be economically and socially self-sufficient, thereby gaining status in the Chinese community both in this country and Hong Kong.

According to Chann (in SCSCRC, 1976), overseas Chinese have tended to specialize in a certain line of business. He has suggested that their initial concentration in the laundry business and subsequently in catering was due to several factors. First, the post-war Chinese immigrants from the New Territories were generally unskilled, other than in farming or fishing, and spoke very little English. Both these factors restricted the occupations open to them. The immigrants, in turn, tended to keep to employment where enterprise and hard work could succeed. Secondly, the traditional regard for independence and self-reliance meant that it was natural for the ultimate goal to be to own a restaurant and to provide employment for relatives. Thirdly, the immigration system in operation in the mid-1960s, in which one of the conditions of admission was at the invitation of a specific employer to a particular job, coincided with the traditional Chinese preference for employing relatives. However, this confined the worker's experience to the restaurant trade which meant that, in turn, he was only able to continue independently in the same line of business. Fourthly, the Chinese restaurant business met a need for diversification in the British catering industry as tastes became more catholic and society more affluent. Until recently, at least, the profits and wages have been sufficiently attractive to keep the Chinese in catering, where considering their lack of sophisticated management techniques and market research, they have pioneered a remarkably successful development.

It was in some ways natural that the Chinese should excel in catering, for the love of cuisine – especially for the Cantonese – is an important part of life. Indeed, as Ladlow (n.d. 2) for example has described, the Chinese traditionally celebrate various festivals, especially New Year, with a family meal, and food is likely to be given as a present. The expansion of the catering trade was also closely associated with the post-war move to the West End of London following the blitzing and demolition of Chinatown. In the mid-1960s the Gerrard Street restaurants existed primarily for the Chinese, but by the time these properties were redeemed by a preservation order the restaurants were patronized by the British. Some trained chefs from Hong Kong and Kowloon were imported and the supporting Chinese business developed in what became a thriving community. Ng (1968) attributed the post-war popularity of Chinese food to several factors: the end of rationing and the proliferation of restaurants of all sorts; that a Chinese meal was more substantial and good value for money; a change in the eating habits of the English with more people eating out; and that service personnel, who had acquired a taste for Chinese food whilst stationed in the Far East during the war, began to frequent Chinese restaurants.

The Chinese were particularly skilful in adapting their menus to suit the British palate, especially when the catering trade expanded into provincial markets. In addition to the Chinese who set up catering businesses in the inter-war years, taking over from the Italians in the urban café trade (Jones, D., 1979), four main post-war groups of proprietors can be distinguished. Of these, by far the most numerous were the immigrants from the New Territories, but there were also non-Chinese proprietors and a group of restaurateurs from the Chinese People's Republic, marooned in London in 1950, as well as some Malayan Chinese proprietors, mainly from Singapore. There was hardly any co-operation or social interaction between the different Chinese groups who regarded each other with indifference, if not with dislike, as rivals. Among the Chinese community in Liverpool in the late 1960s O'Neill found that their concentration in catering led to competitiveness between businesses and families, which tended to inhibit co-operation within the community. Moreover, in York in the mid-1970s Cheung discovered that economic competition was so intense amongst the Chinese that it tended to inhibit social interaction and the establishment of a community as such. Three factors affected interaction: whether the shop was in direct competition; whether there were blood or marital ties; and whether the workers were from the same place of origin. Cheung discovered that restaurant proprietors could not visit another restaurant unless they had known the proprietors at some time previously, or were related otherwise their visit would be seen as a form of spying. Yet Garvey and Jackson (1975) have suggested that it was accepted as each worker's right to leave a restaurant to set up his own business even though it might be a direct rival. And Watson (1977a) has described a particular news-gathering system in the Soho restaurant trade whereby aspiring entrepreneurs and ordinary workers make a circuit of the restaurants of leading proprietors in order to receive and pass on news relating to the trade in this country, Hong Kong and the continent. These examples suggest that the rules of interaction on economic grounds are fairly explicitly defined and have implications for social intercourse.

62   Chinese Pupils in Britain

FINANCIAL ARRANGEMENTS

Ng (1968) found that, unlike the restaurant owners prior to the Second
World War, those from the New Territories usually owned their restaurants
in partnership. Indeed many of the proprietors were themselves cooks and
waiters in their own restaurants, and members of workers' clubs, by means
of which they kept in touch with other migrants and their villages. Cheung
also found all the restaurateurs in York except two had been given some
money by their families to enter into partnership, but apart from this they
had been virtually penniless, and by dint of hard work had gradually
expanded their businesses and managed to make generous remittances.
Entering the restaurant trade had been seen as the only possibility because
of their lack of English, for only restaurant managers communicated with
the customers. This was corroborated by Watson's (1977a) investigation of
125 medium-sized restaurants owned by the Mans from San Tin in suburban
and provincial areas of the London metropolitan region in 1970–1. Fewer
than 20 per cent of staff were able to hold a simple conversation with
customers, most waiters learning only enough to handle the menus; the
cooks and kitchen helpers had often never exchanged a single word with the
wider society. When a restaurant was to be opened, partners were recruited
from close relatives or friends with capital. Partnership could have a
cushioning effect if a new venture was being undertaken in an unfamiliar
neighbourhood or town, as bank loans, sought only in a minority of cases,
were only available after a business was established. In the mid-1960s
expansion the majority of restaurants were established as partnerships. In
this arrangement ownership was divided amongst the workers and the
resident manager according to a number of shares – up to a dozen each in the
smallest restaurants – so that, for example, a young waiter might own one
share, a cook two shares and the manager four. Watson noted a movement
towards individual ownership, as shares were sold by junior partners
requiring finance for their move in the takeaway trade. Such moves,
together with the imposition of VAT and SET, led to the emergence of
several restaurant chains. Moreover, through the growth into food markets,
the Chinese catering business became more fragmented.

One of the proprietors of a long-established and well-known group of
Chinese restaurants in London formed the Association of Chinese
Restaurateurs in 1961, largely with a view to maintaining the high standard
of Chinese cuisine and the good reputation enjoyed by the Chinese catering
business. These were causing some concern within the trade due to its
expansion. Members included individual takeaway and fish and chip shop
proprietors as well as laundry proprietors, suppliers and merchants. At one
stage the association played an important role in communicating between
the restaurant workers and their kinsmen at home (Ng, 1968). Apparently,
however, the dispersed nature of the restaurant trade made this and
organizations in general difficult, so that most of the trade associations and

some clubs formed over the years have generally had little long-term success. Watson (1977a) also reported the short-lived attempt to set up an association of the Chinese catering trade in Scotland early in the 1970s. According to Watson, these associations had little to offer the migrants in return for participation and support, neither was the position of their leaders particularly influential because of the undeveloped status hierarchy in Britain.

RECRUITMENT AND JOB-SEARCH METHODS

Not surprisingly, the catering trade has its own network for recruitment and job-search facilities. The traditional family links in work fitted well with the voucher system initiated in 1962 and work-permit quotas from 1971 onwards, but there has been a considerable decline especially in the last five years or so in the numbers of new workers who have been recruited directly from Hong Kong. The annual quota of 150 from Hong Kong and the level of skill required of chef or second chef continues to be criticized because of staff shortages experienced in restaurant kitchens (GB. P. H of C. HAC, 1985). Watson (1977a, 1977b) has described how in the early 1960s already established restaurant owners gave preferential treatment to their immediate kinsmen, and any new opening in trade became exclusively related to specific families or lineages. Immigration laws reinforced established kinship groups, so that it was almost impossible for emigrants to enter the catering trade without proper contacts. Restaurateurs tended to recruit by personal recommendation, preferring to employ men from the same village or district or speaking the same dialect, if not from kin or extended family. Cheung (1975) found that restaurateurs in York were linked to a Chinese seaman who had established himself in the restaurant trade in Stockton, in the 1920s. In the 1950s and 1960s recruitment methods became highly organized and efficient, especially with the increased facility in air communication. The Association of Chinese Restaurateurs, for example, set up a travel agency and organized recruiting missions. Some travel agencies and villages provided loan funds to finance the emigration, and in several case studies Ng (1968) showed the importance of family and kinship links as well as personal recommendation, often amounting to nepotism when it came to acquiring a job.

O'Neill's study in Liverpool (1972) also revealed the importance of relatives and friends in obtaining work, even when already in the UK. Of 66 Chinese interviewed, 29 out of 49 immigrants worked in the Chinese catering trade, four were professional and technical workers in English businesses and 16, mostly women, were unemployed. By contrast, out of 17 Liverpool-born Chinese five worked in the catering trade, nine in English businesses and three were unemployed. The overriding goal of many Chinese to own their own businesses was linked to their perception of catering as 'Chinese work'. Thirty immigrants gave the following reasons for being employed in the Chinese sector: language (18), family or friends offered work (24), immigration job permit (7), good money (7), valued own business (21), only Chinese work available (20) and other reasons (3). O'Neill claimed that the business was largely restricted to family members in order to establish a bond of trust, and whilst this imposed a certain obligation it was not generally regarded as exploitation. Few Chinese aspired to move out of the business, even when they spoke English and were not restrained by kinship ties, largely because they wanted to work in catering and considered it the only type of work available. Though younger workers would have preferred more free time, older workers valued the opportunity to gain more personally through hard work and flexibility. O'Neill suggested that the Chinese kept to catering in order to forestall perceived incipient discrimination, as in their own businesses they were not directly in competition with other workers. Though this seemed to indicate a certain conservatism amongst the Chinese, they had demonstrated flexibility in changing from laundry work to catering, so that although certain types of work had come to be seen as 'Chinese work', its definition may have changed over time. O'Neill reported that in Liverpool the Chinese were not regarded as a work threat, they were accepted as business competitors, providing a wider range of food, of a higher quality, and with smaller profit margins, but would not have been so accepted in the wider job market. Their position also suited the Chinese need for independence. But catering provided few opportunities for the better educated who tended to move into the English labour market.

Yet it is curious that the Chinese involvement in catering should have been so accepted when previous experience in this trade has, for the most part, not been a necessary qualification. For example, Lai (1975) discovered that all but two of the men in the 24 families whom she studied were involved in the catering trade in London, 16 as cooks, two as waiters, two as English cooks, one as part owner of a restaurant and one who worked in a beansprout workshop. All the men had begun working in England as cooks or kitchen-hands and only three had been specially recruited as skilled workers. Most had received considerable help from kin and acquaintances in finding a job: four from immediate family, nine from relatives, two from clansmen and six from friends who introduced them to their first jobs, all contacts having been established prior to emigration. Similarly, Cheung discovered that only one of a sample of catering workers in York had trained in catering prior to emigration.

JOB MOBILITY AND DISPERSAL

Undoubtedly, part of the remarkable success of the Chinese in catering has been their policy of taking up opportunities for expansion of trade, following the same principle of saturation and dispersal initiated by the laundrymen. London was the training-ground for new arrivals from Hong Kong. There the uninitiated and unskilled learned their trade, and from there many – assisted by family and kinship ties and personal recommendation – would go further afield to seek their fortunes. The goal was always independent proprietorship because the rationale of employment was financial and this, in turn, was perceived as providing social, emotional and cultural security. Sometimes it was possible to set up a business two or three years after arrival. But expansion was not restricted to the UK, for as early as 1960 Chinese restaurateurs were turning their attention to Western Europe, particularly Belgium, Holland and West Germany. Watson has suggested that economic stagnation was the principal reason for the migration to Europe. By 1975, of the 1,000 or so San Tin emigrants living in Europe, Watson (1977b) estimated that 600 worked in the UK, 350 in Holland and 50 in Belgium and West Germany, mostly in Chinese restaurants owned and operated by fellow lineage members. In another article (Watson, 1977a) he further suggested that 10,000 Hong Kong Chinese were working in the restaurant trade in Holland and that despite stricter regulations in Germany and Belgium, some 4,000 and 2,000 Chinese were to be found in those countries. Indeed it is likely that with Britain's membership of the EEC the movement to the continent will have increased, as after five years of residence in Britain 'right of abode' in the UK admits workers to other EEC member countries. As Watson suggests, therefore, the Chinese community in Britain cannot be understood in isolation from its extensions on the continent as this has become the territory for further expansion.

GROWTH OF TAKEAWAYS

Within Britain movement away from the larger cities to provincial towns was also accompanied by the provision of a wider range of food and different types of food outlet, including takeaways and fish and chip shops as well as restaurants. The development of Chinese takeaways occurred in the late 1960s and early 1970s when there was further expansion into the fish and chip trade. These changes coincided with the arrival of women and older children due to alterations in the immigration rules, and therefore the attendant requirement for different accommodation which, together with the increase in available manpower, provided the incentive to attain greater independence in business. It so happened that the restaurant trade was declining slightly due to the imposition of VAT and SET, and the establishment of takeaways rendered the restaurant trade relatively uneconomic in the early 1970s. Thus Brown (1970) recorded the opening of Chinese takeaways in Bedford in the late 1960s, with the advent of additional family labour, and the arrival of Chinese children into schools in Derby monitored by Fitchett (1976) showed that there was still a movement of Chinese labour out of London and from different provincial towns in the mid-1970s.

The growth in Chinese catering outlets has been variously estimated over the years. Cheung (1975) suggested there were 50 Chinese restaurants in the UK in 1957, and by 1963–4 Ng (1968) suggested 1,000. In 1970 Watson (1977a) proposed 1,400, but by 1971 restaurants and takeaways were estimated at 4,000 (Cheung, 1975; Harris, 1980) and in the late 1970s the figure was put as high as 6,500 (CAG & QCRC, 1979). Estimates for different localities are hard to come by: in London Ng (1968) suggested 150–200 Chinese restaurants in the early 1960s, although Cheung (1975) put this as high as 300 and Watson (1977a) estimated 200 restaurants. There are apparently over 184 fish and chip shops run by the Chinese in Liverpool (Jones, D., 1979; Lynn, 1982) and almost 100 Chinese fish and chip shops, seven restaurants and two grocery shops run by Chinese in Sheffield (Mackillop, 1980).

The continuity of Chinese personnel in catering may be similarly traced. The 1966 sample Census figures (quoted by Clough and Quarmby, 1978) showed that 4,210 out of 6,320 Chinese men and 460 out of 1,530 women were employed in service industries including catering, and 700 males and 80 females were self-employed. A Commission for Racial Equality (CRE) survey in 1981, which included a nationally representative sample of 107 Chinese, discovered that 34 per cent (more than Asians, but fewer than Cypriots) were self-employed. The general estimate of 90 per cent of Chinese involved in catering of which 60 per cent work in takeaways (GB. P. H of C. HAC, 1985) is also borne out by two small-scale researches. Tan (1982), who studied 50 families in London, discovered that all but one of the fathers were engaged in catering, 46 per cent as cooks, 30 per cent as waiters and 18 per cent as proprietors of shops or restaurants. Four per cent engaged in meat distribution for the restaurants. Only one of the Chinese worked in a factory (see also Lai, 1975). Similarly, of 31 families studied in Liverpool (Fong, 1981), nearly all the parents worked in restaurants and fish and chip shops, 14 being chefs.

CONDITIONS OF WORK

As well as offering a wider range of food than any of their competitors, the success of the Chinese has also been due in large part to their willingness to work longer hours than other caterers (see, for example, Watson 1977a). Although this may not necessarily lead to the picture of social isolation, cultural estrangement and unremitting toil painted by Garvey and Jackson (1975), there is little doubt that persistent hard work for long and often irregular hours by many Chinese workers has considerable implications for family and social life (see p.82). Working hours in catering, on average ten a day, are spread from morning till midnight, typically from 10 or 10.30 am or 11 am to 11.30 pm or 12 pm with three-to-four-hour breaks during the afternoon, usually 2–5 pm or 5–9 pm (Lai, 1975; Cheung, 1975; Fong, 1981; Tan, 1982). The number of working days per week might vary according to whether the worker was employed in a takeaway, in which case he would be likely to work seven days a week, or in a restaurant from which he would usually be permitted a one-day or even one-and-a-half-day break per week (Lai, 1975; Tan, 1982), although this was often discouraged (Cheung, 1975). According to Cheung, holidays usually accumulated over a six-month or even yearly period might also be discouraged. The need for time off to enable workers to seek help and for more attention to labour relations and conditions and hours of work amongst Chinese caterers was advocated by a conference on the Chinese (CAG & QCRC, 1979). The worker usually receives a net wage from his employer who is responsible for paying income tax and National Insurance contributions (Lai, 1975; Cheung, 1975). Tan (1982) found that the income of men involved in the catering trade was greater than the national average. In addition to accommodation being provided for single workers, especially out of London, a significant feature of the working arrangement is the provision of meals by employers and this has had an impact on the family eating pattern in the UK.

Despite what might seem onerous conditions of work, Cheung (1975) reported that half of the workers whom he studied liked their work, a quarter accepted it and a quarter disliked it. Those who claimed to be satisfied only liked the relatively good pay compared with that of their previous jobs in the UK or with what they would earn if they were in Hong Kong. Though few were thinking or had ever thought of leaving the catering trade for another, there were frequent job changes – more than half had worked in their present employment for less than a year and an average period of work was six to nine months. The reason given for changing jobs was 'to see more and experience more'. Similarly, O'Neill (1972) found that there was a higher degree of mobility, especially of single workers, to and from Liverpool, and between jobs.

To what extent have the Chinese employed workers of other ethnic origins? The preference for employing kin, other villagers or workers by personal recommendation has been noted. However, a labour shortage created by restrictions on Commonwealth immigration in the early 1960s and the coincidental influx of workers from China to Hong Kong, who due to a loophole in the immigration rules were able to travel to the UK, meant that many of the larger Chinese restaurant chains drew on this alternative labourforce. Watson (1977a) also reported that in the provinces the acute labour shortage which was not met by indigenous workers led to some Chinese restaurateurs employing Spanish waiters. Harris (1980) recorded the employment of non-Chinese waiters, although Cheung (1975) observed that despite a staff shortage English workers were not employed, as it was important to the Chinese workers in York that they could all communicate in Cantonese and they wished to preserve their job security. Yet interestingly, Collins (1957) reported that Anglo-Chinese as well as British waiters, waitresses, cooks and domestics were also employed in the Chinese businesses in Liverpool.

At that time these businesses and the shipping company in which the Chinese were largely employed (see p.58) provided adequate employment for all. But a decade or so later O'Neill (1972) claimed that the Chinese in Liverpool were underrepresented in employment exchange records, although they were generally unemployed for shorter periods than average in the area. In London Lai (1975) found that unemployment benefit was not necessarily claimed, partly because of language difficulties and baffling procedures, but also because of the Chinese attitude to 'state charity'. They were highly suspicious that receipt of such money might be held against them if they subsequently wished to improve a business and also concerned about their own loss of face within the community and that their reputation would be tarnished. Thus both traditional Chinese attitudes and negative perceptions due to lack of information about social services, have influenced take-up of welfare benefits by the Chinese. Until recently the Chinese catering trade, despite some decline during the recession, appears to have absorbed the Chinese workforce. But increasing unemployment amongst the Chinese was noted at a National Children's Centre conference in 1982 (NCC, 1984) with particular difficulties experienced by those who immigrated in the 1950s, had ill-health or small businesses which were no longer economically viable, but who were not otherwise employable and unable to claim pensions because they were between 50 and 55 years of age. Doubts have also been expressed about whether the catering trade can continue to absorb the increasing numbers of Chinese pupils leaving school (GB. P. H of C. HAC, 1985). In such cases employment may mask virtual unemployment.

DIVERSIFICATION
Although the Chinese workforce has been predominantly concentrated in catering as such, over the years there has been a considerable growth in a supporting network of Chinese businesses which has developed its own internal economy. Thus in the early 1960s Ng (1968) reported that there were several Chinese merchandise shops in both London and Liverpool, usually run by sophisticated Hong Kong merchants, catering for the needs of Chinese restaurants, students, workers and non-Chinese. Other Chinese businesses such as barber's shops and specialists in Chinese restaurant décor have also developed in London to provide services to the Chinese catering workers (Jones, D., 1979). Watson (1977a) also reported some expansion into travel agencies, hire cars, gambling halls, specialized grocery shops, food processing and distribution, and cinemas. He suggested that the Chinese had restricted themselves to these economic niches in response to intense competition from other ethnic minority workers, for although the Chinese compete vigorously in the catering trade, especially with Cypriots and Bengalis, they have not appeared to extend their entrepreneurial activities into wider society. This has tended to result in a gradual insulation

of the New Territories immigrants from social contact with members of the host society except within a symbiotic customer–waiter relationship.

However, it is possible that during the last decade there has been increasing entrepreneurial diversification. Harris (1980) noted the expansion into property and air travel by some of the early Mans immigrants. Other Chinese, in addition to oriental food retailing or processing, run Chinese bookshops, tape cassette and record shops, and a whole range of cultural services which now have an appeal beyond the Chinese community. The handbook for the Chinese community in Britain, in 1980 (Sing Tao, 1980, quoted by Simsova and Chin, 1982), lists some 247 addresses of Chinese businesses in the country outside catering. It is also important to note the growing number of Chinese professionals working in this country, estimated at two per cent of the Chinese population (GB. P. H of C. HAC, 1985), who include doctors, solicitors, architects, bankers, stockbrokers, business executives, teachers and university lecturers. However, most of these professionals have urban-educated origins in Hong Kong and few come from the New Territories villages (Watson, 1977a). Little is known about the employment of this group of Chinese and the likelihood of the satisfaction of the aspirations of many pupils of Chinese origin to join their ranks cannot be assessed. However, Lynn (1982) for example reports that even in Liverpool there is little evidence of the Chinese being employed in shops, offices or local government. Data from the Linguistic Minorities Project suggest wide variations across three locations in men and women at work outside the home or family business (see Table 23, p.131). It remains the case that the majority of Chinese are employed in catering, and that even if there is increasing employment of Chinese in insurance, in the motor trade, as fashion designers and with computers as some Chinese have claimed (see Wong in NCC, 1984; Tsow, personal communication), these Chinese are in a minority.

WOMEN IN WORK

Relatively little is known about Chinese women in work, though it appears that a fair proportion are employed, most often in association with the family takeaway, fish and chip shop or other jobs linked with the catering trade, in addition to their tasks as housewives. Unlike for some other ethnic minority women, there is no traditional reservation against the employment of Chinese women – indeed in Hong Kong many women are actively employed and even in village communities often take a leading role in labouring tasks. Perhaps one of the best insights into the employment of Chinese women and their involvement in the family business, and its effect on family life, can be gained from Timothy Mo's (1982) novel, *Sour Sweet*. Although the arrival of women and children necessitated the provision of other accommodation for Chinese catering workers, the availability of family labour, which avoided the need to pay wages and overtime, in many ways facilitated the goal of independent proprietorship for enterprising Chinese. As O'Neill's study (1972) showed, the involvement of wives was an important part of the business arrangement which, because of its operation on small profit margins, was dependent on the wife's labour to make it profitable. In a sample of 33 wives of Chinese, three of whom were English and six of whom were in full-time education, O'Neill found that half of the immigrant Chinese wives, compared with a third of the Liverpool-born Chinese wives, were involved in catering. O'Neill observed that though some husbands might expect their wives to stay at home, most worked part-time and sometimes for very long hours in the family businesses. Most disliked this work though they thought it was necessary for the family to be self-supporting, although others alleged that the hard work of some of the Chinese women in England was self-imposed and unnecessary. In York Cheung (1975) also found that most Chinese wives, even those of restaurant proprietors, worked. He established a close interrelation between the arrival of Chinese women and the development of the takeaway trade.

By contrast, in London Lai (1975) discovered that out of 24 families, only seven wives had full-time jobs outside the home, five in the restaurant trade in which they worked the same hours as their husbands. Another nine wives took in sewing at home, which gave them greater domestic flexibility but meant that they were often working under pressure to obtain any real income at piece-rates. Tan (1982) also discovered that over half of the 50 mothers whom she interviewed were full-time housewives and the remainder had part-time employment. As all the mothers had children under five years old, home sewing was the most popular part-time occupation, although three worked in catering. Though work at home may facilitate child care, give wives access to some money of their own or to augment the family income, such work is often undertaken in extremely cramped housing conditions with poor facilities and may serve to reinforce the social isolation of some Chinese women. However, the evidence from these studies is incidental and possibly unrepresentative; it suggests trends but without further evidence it is not possible to generalize about the employment of Chinese women.

CHILDREN WORKING

Traditionally child labour or the employment of young adolescents in Hong Kong has been important, especially amongst farming and fishing communities. The tendency also for children in urban areas to be employed in factories was to some extent linked with the lack of opportunity for many children to continue their schooling after the age of 12, as until the late 1970s education at that level was neither free nor compulsory.

Disquiet was expressed in British educational circles about the employment of Chinese schoolchildren in their parents' businesses after a somewhat exaggerated and culturally biased report of a three-month study of various Chinese families across Britain (Jackson and Garvey, 1974; Garvey and Jackson, 1975). The researchers described the involvement of some Chinese children from a very early age and late at night in their parents' takeaways, which may result in late attendance at school, tiredness, lack of time for homework and to study for examinations, physical exhaustion, curtailment of further education in order to support business commitments, and even lack of registration of children for schooling and their removal to other areas for employment if inquiries are made. Garvey and Jackson claimed that each of the Chinese children they interviewed worked on average three-and-a-half hours every evening in the family business, often on a shift system with other siblings. Whilst this position may still obtain in families struggling to be self-supporting, it may by no means obtain for all pupils of Chinese origin. More recently, for example, Fong (1981) discovered that out of 31 families interviewed in Liverpool, the secondary age children of seven families helped out in their fish and chip shops until late at night. Children whose parents worked in restaurants took care of themselves, preparing meals and cleaning the house.

Yet in another study of Chinese classes (Tsow, 1984) only 4.3 per cent of 138 Chinese mothers, mainly middle class and living in London, claimed that their children, who were predominantly under 11 years, spent some time helping in a shop or supermarket. It is possible, however, that this particular sample, the children's ages and the inclusion of the question under the heading 'Pastimes' may explain this low figure. At a conference in Scotland, in 1976 (SCSCRC, 1976), it was said that Chinese pupils only worked at the weekends. Garvey and Jackson (1975) also reported that Chinese students in further and higher education supplemented their parental allowance by working in takeaways. Langton (1979) has claimed that Chinese parents and children consider it normal for all but the youngest family members to contribute some time to the family livelihood, and that the great majority of Chinese parents are careful not to exploit their children who may gain by making a useful contribution, and may thereby be building confidence in their own linguistic and arithmetical abilities. Contributors to a Quaker Community Relations Committee conference (1981) also stressed that to take teenage children into care, in order to prevent them working in the family business, was a misunderstanding of Chinese family life. More recently the Merseyside Chinese Youth Association claimed that most members helped their parents in their business for an hour or so daily. There was some concern that girls were expected to work longer hours and to leave school early to help full-time. Children tended to act as interpreters in relating to tax inspectors (GB. P. H of C. HAC, 1985).

Though only an impression can be gained from the scant literature on this subject, there is a suggestion that the involvement of Chinese children in family businesses may have declined in recent years, as parents have come to be better informed about legal restrictions and their aspirations for their children focus on the education system. But parents' views about the long-term employment of their children are likely to be an influential factor; these are influenced by traditional patterns of work, the desire for their children to be in employment and the belief that it is good if the family business can provide employment, even though they might want the child to break out of the cycle of employment in the catering trade. Meanwhile some teachers have been concerned about the involvement of some pupils of Chinese origin in their family businesses because of the effect this may have on their ability to profit from schooling (see pp.285–6).

In tracing the employment of the Chinese since their earliest arrival in the UK their considerable enterprise and talent in exploiting the potential of the laundry trade, and in catering subsequently in the post-war years, has been demonstrated. Indeed so exclusive has been their concentration in this type of business (although other ethnic minorities are also involved in catering), which has been assisted by kinship links, lack of knowledge of English and the immigration system itself, that little is known of the employment of the Chinese *not* working in catering, both Chinese professionals and those in businesses supporting catering. So successful have the Chinese been in catering that, with the possible exception of the fish and chip trade, they have not been seen as competitors in work and have in addition effectively insulated themselves by confining their interaction with the wider community to a customer–service relationship. As Watson has put it: 'The restaurants are virtual islands of Chinese culture in the larger British society – isolated pockets where the emigrants can interact with the alien outside world on their own terms' (1977b, p.345).

Yet interaction with wider society may have increased perforce as the second generation of Chinese, largely UK-born, participate in the British educational system. The extent to which this second generation, if they and their parents so wish, and in so far as an economic recession may permit, may be able to diversify their employment prospects and opportunities away from the present concentration in the catering trade will undoubtedly depend greatly on their educational achievements.

Section 4
Family Structure
and Organization

In the traditional Chinese rural background, from which most of the New Territories immigrants to the UK have come, the family is the primary and central unit of social organization. As has been shown, the lineage and kinship systems have formed a network for emigration and subsequent employment in the UK. The role of the family and its importance in the life of Chinese in this country will be considered through research data on their marital status, the structure and organization of Chinese families, relationships, separated families, the position of women, the elderly and social activities in a family context. This section focusses on the second phase of Chinese settlement since the Second World War and the nature of the family in which both of the married partners are of Chinese ethnic origin.

EARLY CHINESE FAMILIES IN THE UK

Due to the absence of Chinese women in the pre-war emigration because of restrictions on admission by the Aliens Act, Chinese families in which both married partners were of Chinese ethnic origin were very rare during the first phase of settlement. Many of the early seamen and laundrymen married or set up home with working-class English women. According to Ng (1968), who described some Chinese families, no figures are available on mixed marriages or Chinese marriages during the earlier decades of this century. However, May (1978) records that within the first decade the Chinese in Liverpool and Cardiff had intermarried with white women and were reported to be considerate and very industrious. This view was confirmed by a report, in the 1930s, in Liverpool (cited by Broady, 1955) which noted widespread intermarriage and cohabitation with white women and that the Chinese appeared to make excellent husbands and provided for their families. Moreover, their children were said to find no difficulty in obtaining work or marrying into the local white population.

Indeed, after the war, intermarriage was almost a prerequisite for securing permission for permanent residence (Broady, 1955). Collins (1957) indicated that there were about 400 Chinese families in Liverpool in 1954, compared with 70 in 1939. If a Chinese wished to find a wife, he usually arranged for a friend to introduce him to an Englishwoman since traditional attitudes to women were retained. According to Broady, on the basis of fieldwork in 1951 with ten families (nine Anglo-Chinese), the Chinese made jealous husbands and did not provide the kind of companionship expected of an English husband, preferring instead to go alone to the clubs, cafés and gambling-houses in Chinatown for entertainment. Yet the Chinese were reported to be conscientious fathers taking care physically of their children and sharing in household activities, including cooking and washing-up. Many of the wives considered that the children were spoilt by their fathers who gave them too much money. Though there was some emotional maladjustment between some spouses because of differences in attitude and behaviour, this was largely counter-balanced by the husband's acknowledged responsibility in providing for the family and in looking after the children. A few Chinese seamen in Liverpool supported English women and their children, deserted by their fathers, even though they maintained their obligations to their first wives in China, regardless of infrequent contact. Neither separation nor intermarriage seemed to affect consciousness of responsibility towards the family in China and the binding morality of a family member. This orientation may have been due to the belief in eventual return to retire in the homeland. Yet as Broady (1955) points out, intermarriage did not mean assimilation, for interaction with wider English society was not increased. Owing to the general disapproval of intermarriage, by both the Chinese and the British, except in the case of practical necessity for the Chinese, it is possible that mixed families experienced a certain social rejection from both communities and even estrangement from family and friends. Collins (1957) also suggests that Chinese fathers preferred their children to marry within the Chinese community rather than Anglo-Chinese. Unfortunately, there appears to be no further research evidence about the status and development of the second and third generations resulting from these early mixed marriages.

MARITAL STATUS

The family life of the post-war Chinese immigrants is to some extent better documented. General trends in marital status can be observed from the Census figures for 1971 (Table 18) and 1981 (Table 19). From Table 18 it can

Table 18: Marital status of population born in Hong Kong and China usually resident in UK, 1971

	Total	Single	Married	Widowed	Divorced
Male	5,875	2,680	3,095	60	40
Female	4,805	2,210	2,250	280	85

Source: Census 1971, OPCS, 1974.

Table 19: Population usually resident, by country of birth, marital status and sex, 1981

Country of birth	Sex	Total	Single	Married	Widowed	Divorced
Hong Kong	male	31,689	17,882	13,389	156	262
(58,917)	female	27,228	13,010	12,922	932	364
Singapore	male	15,965	11,752	3,935	61	217
(32,447)	female	16,482	10,538	5,217	324	403
Malaysia	male	22,998	15,216	7,480	91	211
(45,430)	female	22,432	11,723	9,766	477	466
China (PR)	male	8,492	1,506	6,634	191	161
(17,569)	female	9,077	1,393	6,097	1,283	304

Note: Figures may include some of non-Chinese ethnic origin born abroad to service personnel; people from Malaysia and Singapore are not necessarily of Chinese ethnic origin (see p.6).
Source: Census 1981, adapted from OPCS, 1983a, Table 1.

be seen that there was a slight imbalance in the sex ratio with men predominating in the Chinese ethnic population in the UK in 1971, but with just over half of the men and just under half of the women married. Whilst it is likely that almost all of the women would be married to another Chinese in this country, the Chinese married men might have white spouses in this country, or spouses in their country of origin. There was little indication of divorce. The 1981 figures suggest differences between the Hong Kong-born and China-born population. Whereas the Hong Kong-born population contains a high proportion of unmarried persons, suggesting a predominantly youthful population, and there is comparatively little evidence of divorce, the China-born population is predominantly married, but there are an increasing number of widows, which suggests an older age group. Moreover the 1983 Labour Force Survey (OPCS, 1984) demonstrated a sex imbalance for persons born in the Far East Commonwealth, especially in the 16–29 age group where the ratio was 156 males to 100 females, largely due to the presence of a large number of male students born in Malaysia and Hong Kong.

FAMILY STRUCTURE

Data from the 1983 Labour Force Survey (OPCS, 1984, Table 8) show that there are 31,000 heads of households of Chinese ethnic origin, of whom 19,000 were born in the Far East Commonwealth (Hong Kong, Singapore, Malaysia) and 10,000 in the rest of the world (i.e. mainly China). Only about one per cent of heads of household of Chinese ethnic origin were UK-born. Data from the 1981 Census (OPCS, 1983a, Table 6) show that a fair proportion of households of which the head was born in the Far East are non-nuclear.

The traditional Chinese family was one of close and strong ties, a particular system of relationships, of which the economic relationship was one that served to support a system of social relationships. The kind of family organization from which many of the New Territories immigrants came was usually one where joint families of three generations formed one household in which individual family members had specific rights and duties, where the authority structure was strong and the Confucian ideals of filial piety, self-sufficiency, loyalty and family pride informed daily behaviour. The family's orientation was to a pre-revolutionary Chinese culture, not to an urban Hong Kong influenced by the West.

To what extent has an attempt been made to put into practice some of the traditional concepts of the Chinese family in this country? O'Neill (1972), in a participant observation study of 30 Chinese families and other Chinese in Liverpool in the 1960s, found that the orientation of the family had an important influence on the attitude to life in this country. If the break from Hong Kong was seen as final, then it was more likely for the family to be nuclear and that it would look to the 'community' for support. Some of the nuclear families in Liverpool, in which there tended to be a preference for two children, bemoaned the loss of closeness of the extended family, whereas others valued the greater freedom. O'Neill also observed that it was not always possible for the immigrant family to survive as a unit as older children often moved away to start their own businesses and households. Yet separate provision and economic division might aid family unity. She suggested that many of the siblings experienced the same sense of spiritual and mutual help as in a joint family and that there were continued family ties through physical dispersal. Other writers (for example, Wang, 1981) have pointed to the closeness of the Chinese family in Britain, that fear of bringing dishonour to the family is strong, although the family circle and social contacts are often limited. An article by Tsang (1983) reinforces this view, but also points to certain ways in which a fairly typical Chinese family has effected a compromise between a traditional and Western orientation in its structure and lifestyle. Indeed the traditional family ideal had already come under attack, both as an ideology in China and on account of industrialization in Hong Kong, before the second phase of settlement in this country.

As a result of her research, O'Neill (1972) realized that there was no one family structure which could be called 'the Chinese family' in the UK. She suggested a threefold typology: the traditional family; the modern Chinese family; and the Anglicized family. The traditional Chinese family, of which there were seven in her sample, was characterized above all by internal family loyalty. These families tended to be early settlers, and although they lived in separate family units, there was a strong father–son relationship which was important both in living and working arrangements. Marriage was usually semi-arranged to a Chinese spouse, and wives only worked occasionally in the family business. Family meetings always took place at traditional festival times. The modern Chinese family, which was dominant in Liverpool, was an adaptation of the traditional structure to new living conditions. It retained certain traditional features in the obligation of children to parents but differed in its degree of attachment. In these families there was a sense of belonging to the residential unit, which was usually nuclear, relatives were peripheral and friends more important. There was no authority hierarchy within the family and the father–son relationship had lost its significance with a new emphasis on the husband–wife relationship, although parental consent to marriage was still considered important. Men were more likely to take part in household activities. The Anglicized family emphasized the individuality of family members and again differed in degree. There was no family hierarchy, a greater independence for children, especially in the freedom to choose their own marriage partners, and wives worked outside the home. The families included almost all those who were locally born Chinese and brought up in Liverpool. Often Chinese women married Englishmen and were drawn into wider society through marriage. This was also the case for those Chinese men who wanted to take a greater part in an English way of life and leave the Chinese community. O'Neill found that the adoption of a particular family pattern was not related to the length of time that the family members had been resident in the UK, but rather reflected the varying experiences of rapid changes in lifestyles in Hong Kong and different influences in England. She suggested that the predominance of the modern Chinese family, which was generally more acceptable than the full transition to the Anglicized family form, would not be able to give rise to the formation of a Chinese community.

FAMILY RELATIONSHIPS

Chinese family life in this country can also be considered by means of information on types of marriage and relationships between husband and wife, siblings and parent and child (of the first generation). As Watson (1977a, 1977b) has described, it was customary for the first male migrants to return home to Hong Kong to select a bride. This was an expensive process as a bride price had often to be paid and a wedding feast given, often amounting to over £1,000. New wives sometimes returned with their husbands, or were otherwise sent for later. In her study in Liverpool O'Neill (1972) discovered four types of arranged marriage: in nine of the families the married partners had experienced a marriage arranged by their parents in Hong Kong, five had experienced a semi-arranged marriage, four a 'photo' marriage – an extension of an arranged marriage – and 15 had made lone matches, although these often had an arranged element through the involvement of parents or relatives. Living in Britain away from the extended family had brought about a reorientation of roles with the married partners seeing themselves much more as husband and wife rather than as son and daughter-in-law. The reorientation away from the authority of the parents and the family in the village of origin proved most difficult. Although the moral stigma of leaving parents had usually vanished with the economic necessity to migrate, the relationship with the parents was nevertheless maintained by means of financial support through remittances. But some sons still regarded loyalty to their parents as paramount, and remained in the family home after marriage. On the whole, however, there was a closer husband and wife relationship and the man was the head of the household. The extent to which the household was organized according to an authoritarian or *laissez-faire* style varied as much according to the personality of the couple as to their traditional or modern orientation.

In this context it is interesting to consider the division of responsibilities in the Chinese household. For example, Ladlow (1980) points out that even the most trivial decisions may need to be referred to the father for his approval. Some indication of the attitudes of Chinese men can also be gained from researchers' comments whilst conducting interviews at home. For example, Cheung (1975) found that although he tried to interview both the male and female partner, the husbands preferred speaking for their wives; and Tan (1982) reported that even though her study was specifically concerned with Chinese women's views of family diet and child care, when their menfolk were present during the interview they were more talkative and tried to convince the researcher that they knew more about this than their wives. On the other hand, Tsow (in CAG & QCRC, 1979; 1984) has maintained that women have overall responsibility in domestic matters, and even in traditional family structures they play a significant part in making decisions concerning their children's education. Indeed O'Neill found that wives generally had greater control over household affairs, particularly in the families where the women did not work. Moreover, the important role of women in Chinese family businesses must not be overlooked (see pp.69–70). Sibling relationships, as many observers have commented (see for example, Lobo, 1978), are usually very close, and are enhanced by the responsibility which the older often take for the younger since in Chinese families, from an early age, many children are given adult roles which involve domestic tasks and caring for other family members (Garvey and Jackson, 1975). Such closeness may provide great support in times of stress, and deeper loyalties may develop amongst siblings rather than to parents as the children experience more of Western ways through schooling and language and from which their parents are largely excluded (see ILEA, 1975).

SEPARATED FAMILIES

In some Chinese families, however, relationships may be complicated by separation as many have only been reunited in recent years and some are still in the process of effecting a reunion. Ng (1968) found that in the early 1960s, in London, Chinese workers' wives and any children were generally still resident in Hong Kong, and there was a tendency to maintain ties with the homeland by sending children back for education or, if both parents were working and had no time to care for babies or small children, they were often consigned to the care of their grandparents in Hong Kong. Garvey and Jackson (1975) claimed that some Chinese parents, concerned that their children should maintain their Chinese heritage and not become too Anglicized, had sent their children back to Hong Kong in order to ensure that they received a Chinese education. But this may be too simplified a view. O'Neill noted that it was only the rich Chinese who could afford to send their children back to Hong Kong for their entire education or to complete it. These parents thought that a Chinese education was important not just for academic learning, but for the teaching of attitudes in support of the social structure. O'Neill claimed that most of these Chinese parents wanted their children to identify completely with the Chinese way of life, which was often epitomized by their concern that they should be looked after in their old age. There is little evidence about the effects on children of changes in lifestyle or of separation from their parents, though Watson (1977a) who during the early phase of his research in San Tin (1969–70) observed that two-thirds of the *Man* children born in Europe were returned to their paternal grandmothers to be brought up, records that this grandparent socialization was likely to have profound implications for behaviour, because the children were treated in a very lenient manner and with very little discipline. Instead the focus of concern has been on the reunion subsequently of children with their parents in the UK. Generally children were not brought over from Hong Kong unless adequate provision had been made by their parents for their accommodation and care (Garvey and Jackson, 1975). For example, in Lai's (1975) study in London nearly half the children in 24 families had arrived in the early 1970s, although there were often tensions between parents, especially mothers and the Hong Kong-based grandparents as to where the child should stay. Although parents appreciated the value of a Chinese education in Hong Kong, the fact that the child was with the grandparents ensured the continuation of remittances to the family of origin. Thus the children served to focus the orientation towards Hong Kong and to the perpetuation of Chinese values with respect to the elderly as well as developing their awareness and appreciation of Chinese culture. The same pattern was exemplified by the families in York studied by Cheung (1975). Only half of their children lived with them in York, mostly those born there. A third of the others were elsewhere in the UK with their mothers, but some two-thirds were abroad. Children were sometimes sent back to Hong Kong, or left with their grandparents, both for education and to fulfil the son's duty to his parent. Indeed sometimes the grandparents arrived in this country together with the youngest child, thus completing the fourth stage of emigration (Chann, 1976).

This research evidence suggests that the decision to leave or send children back to Hong Kong has not been on educational grounds alone, but reflected an ambivalence of orientation and provided a means whereby duties towards parents could be seen to be maintained. Moreover, Chinese families may not only be divided between Hong Kong and the UK, but nuclear families may also be separated within Britain. In a study of 31 secondary age Chinese children and their families in Liverpool Fong (1981) discovered that 30 per cent of the children lived with one parent only, the other parent being dead, and that two of the children lived with their grandmothers because their parents were working in other parts of the country. Since 30 per cent of these children were UK-born, 40 per cent had been resident for fewer than five years and 30 per cent were recent immigrants, it is clear that although it is generally claimed that the Chinese family is close-knit, there is obviously a considerable variation in the life experience and continuity of family relationships experienced by Chinese children. Whilst the psychological tensions of children being reunited with their families – often as adolescents – has received a certain amount of comment, if not serious attention (though more often in connection with children of West Indian or Asian origin), a number of family-centred problems experienced by the Chinese, but generally kept to themselves, including the elderly, single-parent families, children in care, teenage children in work, disabled children and adults, and gambling, have been noted (QCRC, 1981). In the context of the family it is appropriate to consider two of these: what has widely been perceived as the isolation of many Chinese women, and the position of the elderly.

POSITION OF WOMEN

Traditionally Chinese women enjoyed close friendship and companionship with other women (Tsow, 1977), but it appears that the dispersed nature of the Chinese population in this country, and economic factors such as women working in family businesses, or competition between businesses, have minimized opportunities for socialization between women. Indeed Watson (1977a) suggested that Chinese mothers found it extremely difficult to adjust from their village orientation to life in an urban environment in Britain, and since they rarely made an effort to learn English and were rather unhappy with life here, they might in the long term constitute a social problem within the Chinese community. Lai's (1975) research (commented upon by Wilson, 1977; and Lobo, 1978) revealed the plight of some Chinese women in London. She discovered that many were living in very poor housing, unable to talk to their neighbours because they had very limited English, were frightened to go out of the home, or certainly not beyond Soho, and were confined in cramped conditions with their children, sometimes attempting to do piece-work, but often waiting for their husbands for any meaningful communication and in order to go out, even for shopping. Yet this isolation, largely through lack of English (Lee in ILEA: English Centre, 1979), was rarely a cause of complaint. Indeed, since few knew of British welfare services and found any interaction with the wider community such as visits to the doctor or dentist, use of public transport or shopping out of Chinatown extremely stressful, the social isolation of such women had until the mid-1970s gone largely unnoticed, and may continue to do so. Though there is always a danger in interpreting such situations through cultural blinkers, it is difficult in view of Lai's description to regard some of these women's lives, with their loss of traditional family support, as anything but impoverished, even if the Chinese reliance on self-sufficiency and independence is taken into account. Moreover, several members of the Chinese community have drawn attention to the social problems of such Chinese women, and although it has often been agreed that there are a lack of facilities for them to meet (e.g. CRC, 1975) and that it is difficult to establish and maintain contact (SCSCRC, 1976), some initiatives such as that in which a women's self-help group provided contact and companionship, especially for the elderly, have been reported (CAG & QCRC, 1979). Such groups provide an opportunity for building on the Chinese tradition of self-help. The establishment of Chinese language and culture classes for Chinese children has also had a beneficial side-effect in making an occasion for Chinese parents, especially mothers, to meet. Although the lives of some Chinese women who stay at home may be socially restricted, by comparison an increasing number of women involved in family businesses may experience very different lifestyles. Simsova and Chin (1982), for example, contest Watson's view that many Chinese women are lonely and disorientated and claim that they experience greater social interaction because of their involvement in family businesses. But although an obvious interaction is taking place within the context of the supply and demand of the caterer–customer relationship, this may be entirely superficial, for the quality of the interaction will depend both on the extent to which it is seen as an opportunity for involvement with the wider community and the extent to which there is a realistic chance of communicating meaningfully. Cheung (1975), for example, observed the social isolation of Chinese women who worked in small town businesses. The recent parliamentary inquiry on the Chinese community in Britain (GB. P. H of C. HAC, 1985) also drew attention to the financial dependence of many Chinese women, some of whom are bringing up children on their own while their husbands work in other cities or towns.

THE ELDERLY

There also seem to be conflicting views on the position of Chinese elderly in the UK. Tsow (in CAG & QCRC, 1979) opined that older people are largely respected and cared for by their families, and Lynn (1982) (quoting from a survey by Fru, 1980) reported that 26 per cent of 141 Chinese families interviewed in Liverpool in 1979 had one or both of their retired parents living with them. Earlier, however, O'Neill (1972) found that in some cases resp'ect for and obedience to parents had been undermined by the experience of migration, so that when elderly parents were reunited with their families traditional family concepts such as filial piety and the superior–inferior relationship were no longer accepted. Simsova and Chin (1982) also reported conflicts between mothers and grandmothers because of expected obedience and adherence to social customs, but that differences might be masked to those outside the extended family. At the QCRC Conference (1981) it was noted that the elderly sometimes became rejected, lonely and isolated as a result of family conflicts. The plight of such old people and the difficulty of helping them were examined by Lai (1972).

SOCIAL ACTIVITIES

Though this section has tended to focus on certain problematic aspects of Chinese family life (see pp.248–56 for an examination of parent–child relationships with the second generation), it is also important to record the way in which families spend time together thereby confirming their loyalty and identity (see also pp.106–7). O'Neill (1972) found that although a number of Chinese kept in close contact with their kin, family relationships beyond the nuclear family might be of less significance than relationships with friends. Nearly two-thirds of the immigrant families and almost all of the locally born Chinese in Liverpool at the end of the 1960s tended to associate with friends socially. From within the restaurant trade in York Cheung (1975) distinguished the socialization practices of single Chinese men and those with families. Whilst the single spent most of their spare time, especially during their afternoon off, with their colleagues at the restaurant chatting or gambling, those with families were more likely to spend their break-time at home doing chores and having a rest. About half of those with a day off during the week spent it out of York, especially if their families were outside the town, seeing relatives and friends. Such meetings were considered important for personal security, to renew cultural traditions and to provide entertainment, such as mahjong and gambling. As a substantial proportion of Cheung's sample had cars, many attended Chinese film-shows in the early hours of the morning after the closure of their businesses on the busy days of the week. Other researches (Garvey and Jackson, 1975; Simsova and Chin, 1982) have also pointed to the popularity of the cinema and Kung Fu films appear to be favoured by the second generation (Lee in ILEA:English Centre, 1979).

Cheung discovered that social activities were almost always confined to the immediate family and there was very little social interaction with the wider Chinese community. Among the 31 families studied in Liverpool Fong (1981) found that family outings were rare since a fifth of the parents worked throughout the week and others had holidays on weekdays when the children were at school. Although some visited relatives and friends, many of their activities were home-based and, as almost two-thirds of the Chinese families had no contact with English or foreign families, the Chinese children had limited opportunities to meet other people. On the other hand, some (e.g. Tsow, personal communication) have suggested that the Chinese have similar spending patterns to the British, and similar forms of entertainment. There is little social demarcation, so that families have friends from different social groupings. Special treats for Chinese families would usually involve trips to London's Soho, especially at festival times, and revolve around eating out. But in general any spare-time family activities may be severely limited, in practice, by the constraints of a family business, will be home-based and may include a particular interest in Chinese music (Simsova and Chin, 1982; Lee in ILEA: English Centre, 1979). Moreover, Chinese children appear to have largely home-based domestic interests, as a number of case studies quoted by Fitchett (1976) show: time spent at home during the evening would include helping parents with housework or childminding, sewing, watching TV, playing with siblings, reading books, doing homework and various sporting activities (see also Fong, 1981). Commenting on the spare-time activities of their children, 138 mothers whose children did not attend Chinese language classes claimed that a third did 'nothing specific', although sports were most popular and other activities included watching TV (19.6 per cent), playing with friends or going on outings (18 per cent), reading, writing and painting (16.7 per cent), music (10 per cent) and helping in the shop or supermarket (4.3 per cent) (Tsow, 1984).

It would appear from the evidence brought together in this section that the family is an important social force in the lives of Chinese in the UK. However, there has been an adjustment to the traditional patterns of family life due to the changed economic, social and cultural conditions in which Chinese families find themselves living in the UK. Many families are therefore in a state of transition to a family structure which accommodates to the demands of urban living in which the need for the family to be supported economically is paramount. This condition essentially dictates the quality of life enjoyed by family members and has obvious implications for spare-time activities. Though their spare-time activities may seem to be superficially in line with those of the wider community, there are indications of a different philosophy of life through the observance of some Chinese traditions, especially the values inherent in family life and the desire for the second generation to learn Chinese language and culture (see pp. 00–0). But the presence of women and children as well as elderly Chinese in this country has in some cases given rise to a number of social problems, often isolation, despite traditional self-sufficiency and independence of the family unit. The focus on the family as the social unit, the dispersal of the Chinese population and the lack of 'community' are influential factors in the changing patterns of family life amongst the Chinese in Britain. The evidence available provides some insights and variations in interpretation, and suggests a range of family lifestyles. The significance of the Chinese family, the adaptability and flexibility of its structure, shown in the emigration and its reorientation to life in the UK through the second generation born here, is continually subjected to the influence of other cultural values in a Western context. Further study of contemporary Chinese family life is required in order that the processes of transition may be observed and interpreted.

Health
For the Chinese health is particularly closely linked with diet. The Chinese orientation towards health is quite different from the Western concept of health care, and in Hong Kong the Chinese have access to both health systems although hospitals are exclusively Western in practice. On migration to Britain Chinese families experienced several changes with respect to health care: on the one hand there was a greater range of Western medicine which became available almost free of charge, whilst on the other traditional Chinese health care advice became less available, as did the range of available fresh foods and nutritional substances to which they were accustomed. The position of a dispersed minority group is neatly demonstrated by the existence of Chinese practices with regard to health care in the UK context where the orientation in this field is overwhelmingly Western.

As with other aspects of the lifestyles of the Chinese in the UK, there is relatively little empirical data on the patterns of health care and nutrition of the Chinese. So Tan's (1982) study of the food ideology and habits of Chinese immigrants in London and the growth of their children is an illuminating source which incidentally also supplies socioeconomic and educational data. This work augments that of Chan (1981), who studied the height, weight, diet and daily nutrition of 6–16-year-old Chinese schoolchildren in London. Tan's research involved 50 families contacted through attending clinics for the under-fives in hospitals, using other voluntary services, or known to social workers. They were visited five times at four-monthly intervals during 1980–1, though at the end of the study only 20 families were still involved. Some of the families contacted initially were suspicious of the project's intentions and unwilling to co-operate, although others were very co-operative and friendly, being pleased to help with a study that would promote understanding between them and the host community. Even though the intentions of the project were fully explained and all the interviews were conducted in Cantonese, Tan claimed that most mothers did not fully understand. Their average age was 29, that of the fathers 35, and more of the mothers (79 per cent) had been in the UK for less than ten years (48 per cent of the fathers). All but one of the fathers were engaged in catering activities and half of the mothers were full-time housewives. Nearly all the families lived in rented accommodation, two-thirds as council tenants. The families had 74 children aged five years and under.

Tan (1982) found that the children's mothers perceived health as the maintenance of sound bodily and mental condition, not just the absence of disease. They saw keeping healthy as a complex procedure whereby the body has to be maintained in a state of equilibrium between two extremes, 'cold' and 'hot'. Each person's body base is in a different state of equilibrium and this changes at each stage of life, so that health is an active process of continued readjustment and the correction of imbalances. It is affected by the degree of tolerance of any hot or cold input, from foods, herbs or the weather. Foods, variously categorized according to the effects of ingredients and cooking methods, are considered to be the means by which an equilibrium can be maintained and hence a person kept in good health. As Lobo (1978) has observed, the Chinese eat many varieties of vegetables which are very lightly cooked, thereby preserving their vitamin content, and also favour white meat and many varieties of fish. In keeping with their ideology about food Tan discovered that the Chinese mothers knew of – and to varying degrees observed – specific practices with regard to the preparation and eating of foods, some of which were thought to have particular significance. 'Bo', usually a preparation of meat with medicinal materials, including herbs, but sometimes also dried fruits, nuts or grain, is thought to be particularly important in restoring a body to equilibrium, and of especial assistance in convalescence for the elderly, and after giving birth. By contrast, tea, rice, oil and salt are considered basic and essential. For example, rice, regarded as strength-giving, is given to babies in the form of congee as soon as the mother believes the infant's digestive system is ready. Moreover, the mothers claimed that their children were very susceptible to becoming 'hot', so fatty and oily foods were avoided.

Tan (1982) discovered that by and large the mothers had maintained their food beliefs and practices. However, in certain circumstances such as hospitalization and especially for a birth which is associated with many specific Chinese beliefs and practices, they were increasingly forced to compromise with or modify their traditional views and behaviours. Although Tan's study showed that the mothers varied considerably in their adherence to the positive Chinese approach to health, for example, in the extent to which they introduced English food types into the family diet (see p.241), they were unconvinced of the superior value of the British or Western system of health care, and because the families were not in financial difficulties and Chinese characteristically spend generously on food, they were largely able to invest in the kinds of food they desired. Though the mothers were on the whole not changing their ideas about health and diet, there was some evidence from a sub-study of 36 Chinese teenagers in British schools that the second generation, exposed to Western ideas through education, the media and school meals, had a better understanding than the mothers of Western ways of classifying nutrients. They also demonstrated by comparison a greater liking of English food, though overall the preference for Chinese food, largely for cultural rather than health reasons, prevailed (see pp. 275–6). Other evidence collected by Tan from food recalls over a three-day period prior to each of the first three visits, questions about infant feeding practices and various measurements of the young children showed that the diet and health care given by Chinese mothers resulted in healthy well-grown children (see p.96). It was when they encountered the health service and school meals part of the educational system that their perceptions of their needs with respect to health care and diet were not met, and rather than demanding preferential treatment the mothers attempted themselves to make up what they saw as the deficiencies. Tan's study is important in documenting an area which touches significantly upon an aspect of the provision of education for pupils of Chinese origin through the school meals service and also more generally in its implications for the health service and other types of social welfare provision. Moreover, the data which it provides help to form a context into which some of the more general observations made by other commentators in the area of health can be located.

Using the National Health Service (NHS), when illness or imbalance in health has reached a point where it cannot be treated by dietary provision, presents particular difficulties for the Chinese, not least because of the need to communicate in English in such a situation. The recent parliamentary inquiry on the Chinese in Britain (GB. P. H of C. HAC, 1985) noted indications that the Chinese made less than average use of the NHS, but that demand increased as soon as Chinese intermediaries were available. Many Chinese families in catering try to use Chinese doctors who practise within the public health service, especially in Soho (Watson, 1977a; GB. P. H of C. HAC, 1985). Both Watson and Lai (1975) mention one Chinese-speaking Indian doctor, with whom 17 out of the 24 families studied by Lai were registered, continuing to consult him even when he moved his practice to south London. A few of the families in Lai's study also regularly used Chinese herbalists, and Garvey and Jackson (1975) also make reference to herbal remedies in the home. A conference on the Chinese in the latter 1970s (CAG & QCRC, 1979), recognizing the Chinese preference for traditional Chinese medicine, pointed to the need to identify Chinese doctors with such practices. However, as Watson (1977a) observed, the increasing number of Chinese nurses, from Hong Kong or Malaysia, may ease an experience of hospitalization and counteract traditionally negative expectations. Lynn (1982) refers to Chinese doctors working in hospitals in Liverpool, although there is no official system to contact these doctors to help Chinese patients who cannot speak English. Despite the preference for Chinese medicine, Lai (1975) for example records that the Chinese families did appreciate NHS care. They welcomed health visitors, who were often the only British and social service workers to visit their home, though they sometimes experienced problems of communication and a mismatch in understanding. For example, although the health visitors saw that the babies were well cared for they regarded them as over-fed, not appreciating that the Chinese mother's concept of a healthy baby is that it should be chubby and that fatness is equated with 'prosperous' growth (Tan, 1982; CAG & QCRC, 1979).

Despite relatively low take-up, it appears that the Chinese do use the NHS more than other social services. Tan (1982), for example, found that the Chinese families used the NHS freely in pregnancy and childbirth and when the children developed a recognizable illness. Chinese workers in York had experienced most contact with the NHS and had found it very satisfactory and were encouraged to utilize it, notwithstanding their linguistic difficulties (Cheung, 1975). In fact contact had been increased through the arrival of family members. Most were registered with a doctor, with the assistance of their employer or relatives, and tended to maintain their registration through their original place of work despite several subsequent changes. Wives tended to be accompanied by their husbands on visits to the doctor, and one-quarter of the sample had been hospitalized for some reason or another, though many fewer had received any form of dental treatment. Almost all spoke highly of the NHS compared with that in Hong Kong, not only because it is free, but also because of the quality of the treatment received. However, the need to be accompanied by an interpreter often led to visits to the doctor being deferred and, as it was customary for only one week's sick leave to be allowed before a worker in the catering trade was replaced, which also meant a loss of accommodation, the catering trade, with its long hours of work, often in cramped conditions, was only for the healthy.

Other observers (for example, CAG & QCRC, 1979; Lynn, 1982) have pointed to the disadvantages suffered by the Chinese in terms of access to health care, preventative health measures, diagnosis, treatment and rehabilitation. Through several case studies Lynn draws attention to the mismatch which can occur between doctor and patient in diagnosis and treatment on account of difficulties in linguistic and cultural understanding. In Liverpool many Chinese apparently rely on self-administered forms of Chinese medicine rather than seeking professional attention, particularly as there is no Chinese general practitioner despite the size and long-established nature of the Chinese community. In attempting to communicate with a non-Chinese-speaking doctor there are difficulties in explaining symptoms, understanding what the doctor requires and interpreting medication. Even when interpreters accompany Chinese to hospital, they may only be able to act as translators and may not be in a position to make medical explanations or to allay fears and suspicions, so that a more trusting patient–doctor relationship might be established. In some cases of dissatisfaction the

Chinese may completely withdraw from the use of Western medication.

As Lynn points out, doctors and others involved in the health services need to know more about the diseases and illnesses characteristic of ethnic minority groups. The particular health problems of the Chinese can be divided into those which are primarily physical and others which relate to aspects of mental health. Difficulties experienced by Chinese migrants in adjusting to the British climate have been frequently noted (Cheung, 1975; Watson, 1977a; and CAG & QCRC, 1979). Apparently there is a higher incidence of rubella amongst Chinese mothers than amongst mothers in any other ethnic minority groups (GB. P. H of C. HAC, 1985). Chinese babies are smaller at birth than their British peers, tend to become more jaundiced and may need transfusions (Lobo, 1978). Tan's study (1982) showed that Chinese mothers placed particular importance on the feeding of their young infant. But two-thirds of the mothers who had previous experience of breast-feeding in Hong Kong had given up the practice after coming to the UK, so that 24 per cent of those who were born in the UK were breast-fed compared with 83 per cent of the babies born in Hong Kong. This change was for convenience and because the mothers thought that the babies would put on more weight if bottle-fed and introduced to Western-type solid foods a little earlier. In changing traditional habits of infant feeding they were demonstrating the improvement in their economic position, and hoped that the chubbiness of their offspring would be regarded as healthy growth and good child care by other Chinese family members. Thus, whilst the Chinese babies were born slightly smaller than the UK average, they rapidly increased in weight in the first six months. There was a gradual decline in their weight after their first year, but they grew more than Hong Kong-born children because of an improved standard of living. Although older children in the sample were not as tall or as heavy as the white UK children, their weight for height was comparable and suggested that they might be taller than their parents. As Lobo and Lynn have both remarked, it is characteristic of some babies and infants of Chinese – and also of Asian and Negro origin – to have patches of pigment known as 'Mongolian spot' on their skin, which may last into adolescence. But it is important that these patches should not be confused with bruises or arouse suspicion of mistreatment, as Lynn instances. It has been suggested that Chinese children usually have bad teeth and that there is a need for dental education. Lynn also cites other health problems to which the Chinese are prone: hay fever, low blood pressure and a form of cancer which affects the ears and nose.

Considering aspects of the mental health of the Chinese, there are conflicting views as to whether the Chinese, as a minority group, suffer particularly in adjusting to a new mode of life in this country. Cheung (1975), for example, claimed that the Chinese in catering in York were not suffering particular psychological stress because cultural conflicts were reduced as their living and working arrangements were so self-contained. Yet others (Watson, 1977a; Lai, 1975; and Wilson, 1977) have suggested that the constant stress of life under very changed conditions contributes to a high level of psychosomatic illness amongst Chinese adults, especially women. Reference has already been made to the social isolation which some Chinese women may experience (pp. 80–1), either because they are bound to the home in an urban environment or because theirs may be the only Chinese family in the area, but there are no clear indications as to how often such conditions promote pathological symptoms. Littlewood and Lipsedge (1982) claim that the Chinese community in Britain does not have a particularly high level of psychological illness. However, there seems to be a lack of empirical evidence on this question.

There are clearly difficulties for the Chinese population in the UK as regards access to health service facilities and particularly during hospitalization when linguistic and cultural differences are heightened and emotional distress may retard the patient's resistance and recovery, especially in the case of the elderly. In the absence of a co-ordinated national policy for the planning and provision of health service facilities specific to the needs of ethnic minority populations, Lynn has argued that health authorities with ethnic minority populations should give special attention to differences in cultural attitudes to health and health care, barriers imposed by language and an experience of different lifestyles, social and psychological stresses of adaptation, attitudes of those providing health care for ethnic minorities and the lack of trust felt by some members of those groups towards the health service. With respect to the Chinese population, as Tan (1982) has argued, more attention should be given to Chinese preferences for certain patterns of food preparation and choice when undergoing hospitalization, especially as these preferences are not held on moral or religious grounds and cannot be justified in terms of Western scientific practices. Both Tan and Lynn argue that the Chinese have rights to health care which is more appropriate to their traditional cultural patterns and that they need access to medical advice centres where they can receive advice and information in their own language, and which is expressed with the conceptual framework of the traditional Chinese system of health care. Information about the facilities available in the health service is also required, such as the Health Education Council's leaflet *Your Right to Health* in Chinese, and several commentators have pointed to the need for health education ranging over such topics as child development, child care, the elderly and specific medical conditions – as provided in Edinburgh (SCSRC, 1976) and by some Chinese community centres (GB. P. H of C. HAC, 1985) – in order that the Chinese population may be more aware of the range of health-care provision open to them.

Social services

Access to health-care services, attitudes to provision, the extent of and the reasons for use or non-use may be seen as one instance of the relationship of Chinese families to the type of welfare provision extended by the British social services system. Together with aspects of education, access to the social services has consistently been identified throughout the literature on the Chinese in the UK as most problematic. This section assesses the attitude of the Chinese to the social services and the extent to which they have availed themselves of provision in such areas as housing, unemployment benefit and library facilities. The extent of specific provision for the Chinese and the distinctive contribution in recent years of Chinese community organizations will also be considered.

The attitudes of the Chinese in Britain to the welfare state have largely been conditioned by traditional attitudes of distrust towards governmental authority. As Tsow (in CAG & QCRC, 1979) records, the lack of stable government in China from the beginning of this century until 1949 promoted suspicion of governmental affairs which led to an intensification of family allegiance and mutual help. Watson (1977a) has also indicated that the attitudes of the New Territories emigrants closely parallel those of their relatives at home since, at an early age, the villagers learn to avoid contact with authority of any kind. There was in any case a strong tradition of self-help in the Chinese extended family, clans and lineages and any requests for help from those outside these groups would usually mean considerable loss of face and have serious implications for family loyalty and pride.

There was in addition a traditional dislike of bothering those outside these groups with problems as epitomized in the old Chinese saying 'As long as you have a roof over your head, keep your troubles under it' (ILEA, 1975). These various factors, which combine to make culturally distinctive attitudes and traits in behaviour have been transmitted through the generations into a desire to avoid contact with officialdom – a predisposition which seems to have been transferred to this country. In this way many stereotypes have emerged about the Chinese who, when they are noticed at all, are generally perceived as self-sufficient, independent and self-contained. Moreover, it is assumed that because they make few demands on social services provision there are in fact no problems amongst the Chinese. However Lynn (1982), herself second-generation Chinese, has claimed that 'the Chinese community, despite appearing to be a quiet and self-sufficient one, is in fact rife with all sorts of social problems' (pp.49–50).

That the Chinese might not be availing themselves of social services provision does not seem to have caused much concern until the mid-1970s when, for example, a meeting of representatives of the Chinese community in the UK (CRC, 1975) reported that many Chinese were reluctant to approach government organizations for assistance and advice, and there was a general lack of knowledge about where such help could be obtained.

About this time, too, Lai (1975) reported that, on the basis of 13 replies received from 26 Community Relations Councils in London to questionnaires to discover the perceptions of social agencies and members of the helping professions towards the Chinese, most said contact was difficult to establish without Chinese-speaking staff, and that the Chinese themselves had not requested contact. Nevertheless, there was a suspicion that the community might have needs which were not known, for example, overcrowded housing or exploitation in employment. In Liverpool it was claimed that the internal self-reliance of the Chinese community could be restrictive because little use was made of the services available (Hopkins, 1977) and there had been an attempt to identify reasons for the non-use of the social services by the Chinese community (Chow, 1974, quoted by Lai, 1975). Limitation on access to welfare agencies due to linguistic difficulties was identified by Cheung (1975), whose wife was a Chinese social worker, as one of the main problems of the Chinese community in York. This group had experienced little contact with Citizens Advice Bureaux (CABs), social services, the Department of the Environment, Chinese agencies or the Department of Health and Social Security. They tended to prefer the help of a friend, solicitor or accountant, whom they could pay to help with problems of housing, immigration and health. Cheung quoted cases of hardship but suggested that a number of factors, including lack of knowledge of social services, diffidence in approaching such authorities for help, the view that it was time wasted or too troublesome, fear of intrusiveness and the questions that would be asked, and feelings of shame and inadequacy, especially *vis-à-vis* other members of the Chinese community, meant that family allowance and unemployment benefits were often not claimed.

By contrast, however, Lai's (1975) research in London at about the same time indicated that many of the families knew of the social services, though they did not necessarily use them. All of the mothers had heard of family allowances and maternity grants as they had received this information in hospital and half of them took up these benefits as they were not means-tested and accepted for the sake of the children, hence no stigma was felt in making a claim. Yet, only one-third of the families had heard of family income supplement, rent and rate rebates or welfare food, and very few had claimed these benefits. There seemed to be a reluctance to make an application as the Chinese did not want their family's circumstances investigated. Few understood their rights and entitlements. They could not distinguish personal social services from social security, only two families having received such benefits (see also Fong, 1981). CRCs, CABs, housing aid centres and the probation service were all agencies which were unknown to Chinese families. Thus they seemed to have a poor general knowledge of the social services and, with the exception of family allowance, maternity benefit and applications for council housing (see p.54), they seemed to have made few demands. Such findings have also been corroborated by

Watson (1977a) and Tan (1982), who stress the Chinese lack of patience with the official welfare system and the dislike of what they perceive as charity, though both these commentators consider that the Chinese are generally aware of their welfare rights. Examples quoted by Watson show that personal networks are still considered important, but there are obviously popular misconceptions and myths amongst the Chinese community about sanctions attached to receipt of welfare benefits. It seems likely that views will be family and location specific and also vary over time according to the particular pressures which the Chinese family in transition experiences.

Another aspect of social services provision concerns a particular group, the elderly. Lynn (1982) suggests that Chinese families to date have been vary caring for their elderly, but it is likely that there will be an increasing number of Chinese elderly without anyone available to care for them. Yet she quotes figures from Liverpool to show that Chinese elderly have made practically no demand on the social services (see also GB. P. H of C. HAC, 1985). They do not receive mobile meals since Chinese food is not provided, neither do they avail themselves of any day-care or residential facilities, from which they are isolated by both language and culture. There is an evident preference for the grossly inadequate facilities provided by the Chinese community itself, but the very fact that even this provision exists may be unique to the longer-established community of Liverpool.

An interesting parallel to social services provision concerns the use of library facilities by the Chinese which was researched in London by Simsova and Chin (1982). Although their sample was large (499 of Chinese ethnic origin) and predominantly from Hong Kong (41 per cent) and Malaysia (37 per cent), they cannot be considered as a representative sample of the Chinese population since they included a far greater than average proportion of professionals, especially students from Hong Kong and Malaysia and nurses from Malaysia, and 58 per cent of the sample were interviewed in English. A high proportion (76 per cent of students and 38 per cent of non-students) were also members of non-public libraries. But in any case Simsova and Chin suggested that library access left something to be desired since those who belonged to one or more libraries wanted more books, and those who were non-members (18 per cent) were not aware what they were missing. All wanted more books in Chinese, greater access to newspapers, books on Chinese culture, music and materials from which to learn English. Half of the members and 30 per cent of the non-members used the library as an information source. Forty per cent also used their place of work, college or school; 38 per cent friends and relatives; 14 per cent government departments; 11 per cent the media; two per cent the CAB; two per cent Chinese centres; two per cent books; and one per cent an accountant. The needs of those who used Chinese mainly in their work were noticeably less likely to be well served. The Chinese readers' comments on the public library service were similar to those voiced by English readers, plus their need for additional material in their own language. But interestingly, although they were critical of the shortcomings of the library facilities, they did not make these known to the librarian, rather they ceased to use the library.

The problems in making provision for adequate library facilities for the Chinese are similar to those for social welfare and education since these focus largely on the dispersal of the Chinese communities. Simsova and Chin (1982) also suggested that it would be helpful to make access available at different hours at weekends and proposed a collaborative model using a library with a largish selection of Chinese books, professionally administered, with assistance from the Chinese community who would have an influence over book acquisition and distribution. Like Tan's (1982) view with respect to the satisfaction of dietary needs when the Chinese are hospitalized, Simsova and Chin's concern arose from the realization that the reading and other library needs of the Chinese were not being satisfied despite their rights as ratepayers. They saw a tension between the requirement on the library to provide an efficient service within limited means and the provision of a variety of types of reading matter for a diverse readership, and they thought this was unlikely to be possible in both Cantonese and Mandarin. They concluded that the Chinese were a group who were particularly difficult to serve: linguistically because of the difficulty of finding experts among existing public library staff, and socially because the Chinese themselves were reticent about making their needs known. Yet some local authorities are recognizing the library needs of their Chinese population; for example, Tameside in Greater Manchester, Westminster in London, and Glasgow. This facility would be particularly useful where Chinese is taught locally (see also p.195).

Over the years many suggestions have been made to facilitate and increase the take-up of social services provision by the Chinese. Lai (1975), for example, suggested that the Chinese community should be consulted to a much greater extent as their natural passivity and the very reasons which prevented them from availing themselves of welfare benefits also caused difficulties in setting up an institutional framework to exchange perceptions and negotiate standards. There have consistently been suggestions that more Chinese personnel should be employed at all levels of the social services, from Chinese home-helps to social workers acting in advisory and liaison capacities (Lynn, 1982) as well as the need for more information, for example, about DHSS benefits in Chinese (Chan, A., private communication). Since the mid-1970s when the needs of the Chinese community began to be exposed, three Chinese social workers and a housing adviser have been appointed in Camden (Wilson, 1977; GB. P. H of C, 1985), and more recently three social workers for the Chinese community in Liverpool (Lynn, 1982), a community adviser in Manchester to help with social problems and to act as an escort service and interpreter in for example hospital cases (Powell, 1982), a community worker in Birmingham (NCC, 1984) and a librarian in Westminster (GB. P. H of C. HAC, 1985). These developments, together with the recent provision of Chinese community centres in Liverpool and Westminster, have been made possible through Urban Aid (Section 11) funding, but such funding may not be available to satisfy the needs of ethnic minority communities in Scotland (Chan, A., private communication). Indeed a recent parliamentary report (GB.P.H of C. HAC, 1985) indicated that LEAs' lack of knowledge of their Chinese populations had led to them receiving low priority, and that the size and needs of the Chinese population appeared to justify a larger share in Section 11 funding as they only received £90,000 out of £3 million from the Urban Aid Programme in 1984–5.

But this specific provision apart there is, as Lynn has argued, a need for a more fundamental reassessment within the social services, so that client groups are not merely perceived in terms of traditional definitions such as 'the elderly' or 'the handicapped', but so that there is a positive recognition that there are disadvantages experienced by ethnic groups which arise from their experiences as a group, through immigration, racial discrimination and cultural differences, and not merely on account of personal handicap. So, in the case of the mismatch in cultural practices whereby the Chinese family expect the child to work in the family business whereas the law in Britain stipulates the non-employment of children, which may lead to considerations of child abuse, it is important in the training of social workers that they should be sensitive to this as a cultural difference and not a deliberate flouting of the law (Lynn, 1982). Moreover, as in many educational respects, so in the social services there is a need both for the employment of ethnic minority personnel in positions of influence and direct assistance and also a much greater mutual exchange of knowledge, perceptions and expectations on the part of the minority and the majority community in order to enhance awareness of need and appreciation of difficulty, for both parties. In the case of the Chinese community such an exchange is only just beginning as for so long the stereotypical perceptions of exclusivity and self-sufficiency have combined with an awareness of the problematic provision for the Chinese as a dispersed community to prevent either a proper assessment of need or a positive appreciation of community strengths in self-reliance.

Child care
It is widely held that the Chinese have a general fondness for children and love and treasure them (e.g. Tsow in CAG & QCRC, 1979; Lai, 1975). Traditionally girls were not so prized as boys – not for any religious reasons, but mainly because of the marriage system whereby girls would become members of another family and remove to the homes of their parents-in-law. Although it has traditionally been thought that the Chinese like to have

several boys in their family, O'Neill (1972) suggested that in Liverpool the ideal of three sons and two daughters had given way to a preference of most families for two children. Indeed some parents were expressing a preference for girls. However, the families in York studied by Cheung (1975) seemed to display more traditional attitudes as with only a few exceptions they regarded their sons as more important than their daughters. A few were strongly against their sons marrying non-Chinese, but were not concerned about their daughters marrying out of the community (unlike Asian parents). In other cases of male preference, out of a family of three siblings up for adoption, most Chinese families only wanted to adopt the boy and a full-month birthday party was given for a baby son, but this would not have been held had the baby been a daughter.

Traditionally grandparents and other members of the extended family helped with child care, especially as the mothers were often working. In the UK it appears that practices may depend on whether the mother is involved in the running of the family business. In London both Lai (1975) and Tan (1982) found that most mothers whose husbands worked in catering were at home looking after their young children. The extent of contact which fathers have with their young children varies according to whether the father works at home or for long hours away from the home. In post-war years, in Liverpool, Broady (1955) reported that many Chinese fathers who had married into the white community often shared in the physical care of their children and were clearly kind and indulgent fathers. Some 20 years later O'Neill noticed that when the wife did not work she was much more likely to have greater control over household affairs and be entirely responsible for child care. When the husband was working away in the restaurant trade, the child experienced little contact with his father. Grandparents might take complete care of the child if both parents are engaged in business or working in other parts of the country (O'Neill, 1972; Fong, 1981). According to Cheung (1975) and Khan (1976), some Chinese children in York and Huddersfield were attending childminding centres, especially if their mothers were working, but there does not appear to be any further information on this. In Lai's (1975) study in London 18 out of the 42 children in the 24 families interviewed who were under five were all looked after by their mothers, who were mainly full-time housewives at home. But three of the children attended a nursery school, which was well known to the Chinese families and liked, and a further five families were awaiting enrolment.

Chan (1983) has stressed the materialism of many Chinese families, which may be particularly displayed with respect to children. The desire to provide as well as possible for their children seems to have justified some Chinese families' acceptance of family allowances when other social welfare entitlements have not been claimed (Lai, 1975, see pp.91–2). There is some concern about being able to give pocket-money to older children (Broady, 1955; Garvey and Jackson, 1975; and Chan, 1983). But much of the focus on caring for younger children is directed towards providing plentiful and good-quality nourishment (Tan, 1982). This is understandable since food has assumed an important place in Chinese culture and, in Hong Kong, the ability of parents to care for their young child would be very much judged by the chubbiness of the infant.

Tan's study revealed that the Chinese babies in London were well fed, so that although they were often small at birth during the first six months they grew rapidly and by school age had similar weight–height ratios as white British children, and were in fact larger than their Hong Kong peers. Interestingly, Tan observed that after the toddler stage the mothers did not seem to pay so much attention to the growth of their children, partly because by then another new baby had often arrived, or because the vulnerable period was considered to be over and they were more concerned with preventing the child from becoming ill. Tan's study is also illuminating, in that through the method of dietary recall over a period of three days prior to each of three visits, it demonstrates how Chinese dietary patterns in the UK have changed, particularly with respect to young and school-age children. Although the primary school children had some form of breakfast, some secondary school children often went to school without breakfast. Breakfast has become simplified to suit the parents' different lifestyle, allowing both older and younger children to help themselves to food, so that mothers who had a late night because of their husband's work schedule could be left undisturbed. Most school-aged children ate school meals (see p.240). Mothers with pre-school children had quick meals at home. By contrast, dinner was a traditional meal with rice as the main staple food and a meat and/or a fish dish and vegetable dish, although sometimes potatoes and Western foods were consumed. The children's bedtime was about 9 pm, one to two hours after dinner. There was an interesting innovation in the family food pattern in the adoption of 'teatime' around 4 pm when children returned from school. As well as tea, 'cooling' drinks, milky or fruit-based beverages and a variety of teatime foods are consumed. The meal had been created as a supplement because mothers felt that school lunches were insufficiently filling, but it had also become incorporated into the eating pattern of weekends and vacations.

Tan's carefully researched account contrasts markedly in some respects with the more anecdotal descriptions provided by Garvey and Jackson (1975), who claimed that there are no special child-care regimes regarding mealtimes or bedtimes, and that Chinese children are often left to help themselves when hungry or to sleep when tired. They also implied a possible dietary imbalance for some children left to help themselves to meals from their parents' takeaways. On the other hand, two-thirds of the Chinese children in Fong's (1981) sample always ate their meals as a family group and all, except one of the remainder, sometimes did. In a case study of one Chinese family Jackson (1979) showed that both Western and Chinese food was eaten, as did Tan. However, Tan thought that the types of food consumed were mainly similar to what would be eaten in Hong Kong, largely because in London most of the ingredients were readily available in Chinese supermarkets and they could afford to purchase such foodstuffs because of their sound economic position. Moreover, the language barrier deterred them from purchasing and learning about preparation of Western food, so that they opted for processed foods which only required quick preparation. In addition to a preference for the taste of their traditional dishes, they were considered important for health reasons. Although most mothers claimed that they did not mind if their children wanted to follow a Western pattern of eating, as they regarded language and social customs especially those relating to the cultivation of good manners as far more important, the mothers nevertheless felt personally responsible for the well-being of their families, especially in the provision of food, which is seen as playing an important role in health maintenance. When shopping, a mother would have the needs of her children and their 'hot–cold' status (see p.85) in mind, so that appropriate foodstuffs could be purchased and prepared as necessary. Generally feelings of responsibility for producing and rearing healthy children and for maintaining the family's health were assuaged by following the Chinese system.

Several writers (for example, Lai, Garvey and Jackson) have commentated on the permissive upbringing of young Chinese children who are frequently the centre of attention and involved in all the family's activities. However, at a certain age (Garvey and Jackson put it at four or five, Lai at seven) stricter training methods are adopted and children learn positions of deference and humility within the family. Children are expected to respect their elders, to be obedient without question, to show strong loyalty to the family, to be modest and tolerant, not to show their emotions and to become self-reliant (Garvey and Jackson, and Tan; and Tsow in CAG & QCRC, 1979). The inculcation of these traditional virtues in Chinese upbringing is aimed at developing good conduct and social cohesion, emphasizing the individual's responsibility and also the importance of personal relationships and family ties. Although strict demands are sometimes made on children, in many respects they are treated as adults and expected to adjust to an adult world, being involved in the affairs of the family and all its social activities.

It is difficult to assess the extent to which the traditional virtues are learnt within the Chinese family in the UK, but observational studies tend to suggest a possibly stricter upbringing than that which a white British child would experience (see also Lau, 1964). Whereas mothers are seen as indulgent and careful (Tan, 1982), fathers are perceived as disciplinarians and especially important in the socialization of sons (Lai, 1975). Physical punishments are reportedly common (Garvey and Jackson, 1975; Wang, 1981). Despite the generally caring attitude of Chinese parents which is revealed in the studies, some researchers (e.g. Cheung, Fong) have suggested that some Chinese children in families operating their own businesses may be deprived of proper attention, especially if mothers are working. Indeed when the whole family is involved in running the business, children themselves may suffer directly from the expectations placed upon them to contribute, sometimes to the extent of having interrupted sleep patterns (Garvey and Jackson). Lack of adequate parental care may not only mean a loss of attention to younger children, lack of socialization and family outings (see p.82), but may also lead to a poor relationship between adolescents and their parents (see p.252). Thus there seems to be a contrast between those families in which the child may not only be neglected but also expected to help in the family business rather than play (Fong, 1981; Lynn, 1982), and those who are well provided for materially (Tan, 1982). Tsow (1977) has also claimed that Chinese families would expect to buy toys and books for their children and would not necessarily be used to the idea of borrowing these from the library. Jackson's (1979) case study also shows that the Chinese home may include many toys, and Chinese books ordered from the homeland, though these may be 'a bizarre mix of western and oriental visual styles' (p.46). However, by all accounts the ever-present TV seems to be influential from an early age (see pp.83 and 245–6).

Due to the particular problems of conducting research on family life and in the especially sensitive area of child care, where assessment criteria may be particularly subjective, it is difficult to gauge the extent to which traditional family lifestyles and patterns of child care have been modified in the context of urban living in the UK. Whilst it would seem that a certain emphasis is still placed upon the learning of the traditional virtues, the exigencies of everyday life, especially when parents are running their own businesses adjacent to the home, may take priority with some consequential deprivation of attention to children. On the other hand, there is sound evidence that many children are physically and materially well cared for, probably more in the Chinese than the British style.

Religion
Traditionally and to a large extent in contemporary practice in Hong Kong (see pp.12–14) the Chinese approach to religion has often been to blend several different religious beliefs, especially stemming from Buddhism and Taoism, with certain superstitious practices and ancestor worship, and more practical philosophies of life, particularly influenced by Confucianism. Moreover, with the increasing British influence in Hong Kong the number of those who adhere to Christian beliefs and practices has grown. Though the religious aspect of the lifestyle of the Chinese in the UK does not appear to have received special attention, it is nevertheless possible to build up a picture of certain features from incidental information contained in some studies.

Broady (1955) reported that a room in Pitt Street, Liverpool had been used as a temple but had fallen into disuse and ancestor or spirit worship no longer appeared to be practised by the local Chinese. Although certain ritualistic practices, especially associated with honouring the dead, were observed by some Chinese families and several Chinese associations, marriages and the celebration of the first month after a child's birth were secularized (see also Garvey and Jackson, 1975). Adherence to the traditional beliefs behind such occasions had disappeared, but their social function, as evidenced by conspicuous expenditure, still revealed a desire to demonstrate or acquire social prestige. These changes, which reflected those within China and Hong Kong as well as adjustment to life in Liverpool, tended to minimize behaviour which made the Chinese obviously different from the wider society. Some years later, O'Neill (1972) discovered that there was a small but growing attendance at two Chinese churches, though generally O'Neill felt that the Chinese religious philosophy was more concerned with practical family life.

In the early 1960s, in London, Ng (1968) asserted that, if they subscribed to any religion at all, the Chinese were usually Buddhists. However, they lacked a specifically Chinese Buddhist temple, which Ng suggested was because there was no concentrated 'Chinatown', the absence of Chinese women, who were traditionally more religious, and the impression that the Chinese emigrants were less 'superstitious'. The religious observances described by Ng were limited to perfunctory rituals, mainly associated with honouring the dead. However, there was a trend towards Christianity, mostly amongst students from Hong Kong and Malaysia, and even a certain amount of evangelical work, possibly to compensate for the lack of opportunity in the People's Republic. One Chinese church, founded in the West End in 1951, had by the early 1960s a congregation of 150–200, mainly Chinese students. Since the service was conducted in Mandarin and interpreted in English, it effectively debarred the workers. In 1958 the Chinese Mission Centre was opened in the East End for the spiritual welfare of Chinese seamen coming into the Port of London for short shore leaves, and the Council of Service for Chinese Workers was inaugurated in 1964 to serve a similar function for catering workers. Though it is not clear how this body has subsequently fared, it is interesting to note that Clough and Quarmby (1978) confirmed the existence of the first two institutions in 1975, though Lai (1975) observed that Chinese clergymen in London did not have any responsibility for social welfare. At that time representatives of the Chinese community (CRC, 1975) suggested that some 50 per cent of the Chinese might be Christian, with many agnostics, some Buddhists and some Taoists. But more recently in London Simsova and Chin (1982) discovered that only five per cent of a sample of 499, including a high proportion of students and professionals, belonged to religious groups – all Christian.

It would appear therefore that there has been a decline in religious practices associated with traditional Chinese religion and that the Chinese who do have religious beliefs are likely to be associated with the Christian church, usually an evangelical denomination. The rise of the influence of Christianity runs parallel to the increasing number of Christians in Hong Kong and emigrants may well have had some previous contact with Christian groups. It is, however, predominantly students and nurses of Chinese origin who belong to various Christian denominations. For example, Ladlow (n.d. 2) has reported the existence of a thriving Chinese evangelical church in Liverpool and that about 500 recent Chinese immigrants belong to the True Jesus Church in the north of England and Scotland, as well as a large membership of Chinese students and nurses in churches of several denominations in London. According to Ladlow, the Chinese Overseas Christian Mission has about 30 fellowships in cities throughout Britain. The work of the fellowship in Sheffield is described in Mackillop (1980). The Association is interdenominational and related to wider society, for in addition to Bible study and prayer meetings they have assisted with ethnic Chinese refugees from South Vietnam, and provided interpretation facilities for Vietnamese children in Sheffield. Although the members of this fellowship are primarily Chinese nurses, students and lecturers, Mackillop records that a number of catering workers and their families join them for worship and that the group organizes classes in reading and writing Chinese.

Further evidence of the involvement of Chinese Christian organizations in the running of Chinese language schools is provided in the survey conducted by Tsow (1983a, 1984) and information available from the Hong Kong Government Office (1984). In a survey of 312 Chinese children aged 8–14 attending Chinese language classes in London, Liverpool and Manchester Tsow (1984) discovered that three-fifths of the children attended classes on Sundays, some of which were religiously based and included some religious teaching such as catechism or Bible study. Children who attended the Sunday classes were more likely to have been born in Hong Kong (65 per cent compared with 55 per cent), to have come from the lower social classes (70 per cent from D or E) and to attend classes outside London (73 per cent). Apparently local Christian groups were responsible for establishing classes (Tsow, 1984) which used the same kind of written Chinese and spoken Cantonese or Mandarin as in the secular Chinese language classes, but instead of the ordinary text taught using the Chinese Bible or catechism (Tsow, 1983a). The Hong Kong Government Office list of Chinese schools and classes in the UK (1984) shows, moreover, that some 224 pupils attended classes in Newcastle associated with the True Jesus Church and that there are at least 23 other Chinese language schools associated with various Christian denominations throughout Scotland, Eire, England and Wales – in Aberdeen, Edinburgh, Glasgow, Coventry, Preston, Liverpool, Leicester, Manchester, Dublin, Sheffield, Birmingham, Bolton, Leeds, the East End of London, Finsbury Park, west central London, north-west

London, Brighton, Devon and Cornwall, Worthing, Oxford, Cardiff and Southampton. These comprise over a quarter of the Chinese schools known to the HKGO, thus the newly formed religious groupings of some Chinese professionals appear to be having a distinctive influence in providing Chinese language and culture classes for the second generation combined with teaching about Christianity.

Jones (I., 1979), however, has warned that in mainstream schools it should not be assumed that Chinese children are Christian, therefore the broad-minded approach of the Chinese to a combination of religious philosophies with a practical emphasis should be respected through the opportunities which should be made for studying comparative religion in schools. There is little evidence about the beliefs of second-generation Chinese, although Fong (1981) discovered that 23 out of 31 Chinese secondary pupils professed no religion, four claimed to be Buddhists and four Christians. Moreover, Ladlow (n.d. 2) has noted the difficulty of discussing religion or mythology with Chinese children, despite their enthusiastic response to Chinese stories, film-strips on Chinese religion or the celebration of a festival. Thus, whilst there is evidence that many Chinese families observe a number of the traditional Chinese festivals associated with religious practices in the broadest sense, nevertheless apart from specific Chinese Christian groups, often appealing to the professional and more temporary members of the Chinese community in Britain, there seems to be little specifically religious in the lifestyles of the Chinese family involved in catering. Rather their philosophy of life would be based on a system of social ethics in the Confucian tradition.

Other aspects of the lifestyle of the Chinese in the UK, concerning the education of Chinese parents and language are considered in Parts 3 and 4 as they have a particular and obvious bearing on the education of pupils of Chinese origin (see pp.228–9 and pp.127–200).

Section 5
Community Perceptions

Having reviewed the socioeconomic circumstances and settlement of the Chinese in the UK, it is important to examine the nature of the Chinese 'community' and its development over the last 20 years and perceptions of the relationship between the Chinese and British. 'Community' is a difficult sociological concept, which may be defined as 'a cohesive and self-conscious social group' (Watson, 1977a); it is especially difficult to define and apply in the case of the Chinese, for apart from one or two areas in London and Liverpool there are no identifiable settlements as the Chinese are dispersed across the country. Moreover, researchers' interpretations of trends in behaviour may prove to be particularly subjective, varying according to time and location as well as the particular sub-groups involved in the research, and whether the writer is himself of Chinese or British origin. Given these caveats, the following section addresses such questions as: in what sense do the Chinese see themselves as a community? How and for what purposes have they attempted to organize themselves to promote their own cultural activities? How do the Chinese perceive the British and other ethnic groups in the UK, including recent Vietnamese refugees? And finally, how are the Chinese seen by the British?

CHINESE SELF-PERCEPTIONS OF A COMMUNITY

Although the Chinese in the UK may be perceived as an homogeneous group by the British, it is important in considering whether the Chinese constitute a community as such to explore the extent to which ethnic lineage, clan, district, village and linguistic differences which count in the country of origin are perceived as significant by the Chinese in the UK. There were two main ethnic groups in the second phase of emigration from Hong Kong, namely the Cantonese Punti and the Hakka, whereas the earlier migrants were nearly all from mainland China (see p.31). Initially these divisions were apparently recognized in the UK. For example, O'Neill (1972) found that in Liverpool the first Chinese settlers saw the new Hakka as 'flighty and unreliable and not showing due respect', whereas the settlers were perceived as very 'old-fashioned'. In London Ng (1968) also reported that the older Chinese immigrants had an antagonistic attitude towards the new immigrants who aroused envy and jealousy because of their improved working conditions and higher wages. With their arrival the community had both increased considerably and become more scattered, so that the established Chinese being used to a more close-knit community regarded the new arrivals as antisocial. There was, moreover, a lack of common interest between the two groups, the former seamen and the latter restaurant workers. Yet some Hakka restaurateurs were apparently anxious to conceal their ethnic identity in the UK, conscious of their traditional inferior status (Garvey and Jackson, 1975). However, Watson (1977a) has claimed that despite the ethnic hostilities between Chinese dialect groups in the New Territories, the traditional dichotomy of Cantonese versus Hakka, though maintained in Britain, provokes little open hostility. Rather he suggests the two groups have much in common in their position in Britain and find it to their advantage to underplay ethnic differences in order to unite against their primary rivals in the restaurant trade, the Bengalis and the Cypriots.

In the late 1960s O'Neill (1972) examined the role of the family and community and the social adjustment of the Chinese in Liverpool by means of a participant observational study of 30 families and interviews with 150 other Chinese. She asserted that the Liverpool Chinese were an extremely heterogeneous group and questioned whether they in fact formed a community at all. If the community existed she suggested that it was based on rather superficial acquaintances, for the small intimate group of family and friends was much more significant to individual Chinese. Many differences were perceived as important by the Chinese: regional and cultural; first and second generations; rich and poor; Christians and communists; and the Liverpool-born Chinese and the Hong Kong-born immigrant. These divisions tended to be marked by different behaviour: the second generation being perceived to show less loyalty, the *nouveau riche* to take on a new lifestyle, the Liverpool-born to be more concerned with their relationship with the host community compared with the Hong Kong-born who were more aware of regional differences according to their place of origin. These distinctions cut across the Chinese 'community' and made interaction difficult. In practice, the Chinese did little to help one another, being concerned with their own families to the exclusion of others.

Another divisive factor was the secretive attitude of many Chinese, who were often concerned to hide information from other Chinese who might benefit. Lai (1975), for example, remarked that although the families whom she interviewed seemed friendly enough with the other families with whom they were sharing accommodation, they were perhaps less frank in their presence. Cheung (1975) noted in York that interaction among the Chinese in catering was severely limited to relationships by blood, marriage or place of origin and the proprietors could not visit another restaurant seen to be in direct competition. Moreover, researchers into the Chinese community of both Chinese ethnic and British origin all came under suspicion at the commencement of their investigations until a rapport was established. Several writers have also pointed to the social distance maintained between catering workers and Chinese professionals. According to Watson (1977a), the latter group are mainly highly educated urban Hong Kong migrants who attended Western-style universities, or those who have stayed on after completion of their courses in this country (Chann, in QCRC, 1981). The professionals interact almost exclusively with their British or Chinese counterparts. Even 20 years ago O'Neill's research in Liverpool largely confirmed this pattern for the locally-born second-generation Chinese, who were beginning to enter professional and technical occupations in banks, education, engineering and research. The Chinese professionals tended to become occupationally integrated into wider society and to move away from their Chinese roots. Being very mobile, they were thus a loss to the Chinese community to the extent, in some cases, of leaving England.

Given such intra-group differences, O'Neill concluded that the Chinese in Liverpool in the 1960s did not form a self-sufficient or independent community. But though the group was loosely knit and liable to friction, it did function to provide some occupational and social facilities. The 'community' was only felt to be important by those whose relationships depended upon it, namely, those who had failed in their aspirations to have an English way of life, old men, from the first phase of immigration, and those with no family life. Generally the family, region of origin or linguistic group were the important factors of allegiance rather than the 'community' as such. O'Neill claimed that the Chinese were not conscious of their racial unity, but rather of a way of life. Being Chinese was an explanation for thinking and behaving in a Chinese way – belonging to an ancient historical tradition individually interpreted, so that there were several models of what being Chinese meant. On the other hand, Watson (1977a) has maintained that some Chinese do think of themselves as members of a loosely organized 'community' incorporating all migrant and second-generation Chinese associated with the restaurant trade. Although this group lack an authority structure and are dispersed in their settlement, they maintain close ties and constitute 'a community of mutual interests'. Their 'encapsulation' in catering renders them insulated culturally from the wider society. These contrasting views exemplify the difficulty in determining whether or not a Chinese community exists, though differences in sample, place and time may largely account for the variation between these researchers' conclusions.

O'Neill identified three groups of Chinese who saw themselves as part of the Chinese rather than an English way of life. One group were successful second-generation Chinese of traditional family background who had maintained their loyalty largely by marrying Chinese spouses. A second group were those such as doctors or engineers who had aspired, but failed, to integrate with wider society since they were seen by the British as Chinese yet their professional status made them marginal members of the Chinese 'community'. A third group who identified with the Chinese way of life were the locally born Chinese or Anglo-Chinese women who married Chinese immigrant men. Interestingly, whether the second-generation Chinese in Liverpool moved towards a closer accommodation with a British way of life or adopted the Chinese way of life, they were accepted. It was difficult to maintain positive aspects of Chinese culture as these were not reflected in society at large and there was no community basis to preserve them. Family ties were of overwhelming importance both in terms of a sense of mutual responsibility between parent and child and of gaining independence through personal and family contacts. Any Chinese 'community' existed because of its relationship against outsiders rather than any sense of community between Chinese families. Cheung's (1975) research in York confirmed an absence of community feeling as the families were predominantly concerned about conflicting financial and business interests and doubted whether in the absence of any indentifiable leader the degree of cohesiveness was sufficient to organize any social activities on a community basis. On the other hand, at the same time in London Lai (1975) concluded that the similarities in background and a common occupational and housing experience since arrival in the UK had had a levelling effect on earlier differences and imposed similar habits and outlooks on the Chinese caterers and their families.

Evidence from these researches suggests that according to the time and place of research and the group under investigation different conclusions as to whether or not a Chinese community exists may justifiably be drawn. The studies reveal that the Chinese are socially and geographically divided and that the increasing influence of the wider society has served to diminish the significance of traditional allegiances to village or region of origin, lineage or clan. Moreover, economic rivalries together with the Confucian tradition of family self-help and the secular nature of Chinese culture and way of life lacking strong religious ties have made for difficulties in establishing community organizations. Despite these, recognition of the family as the focus of the Chinese way of life, the unifying bond of language and the perception of the Chinese as a group by the wider society combined to suggest a loose concept of a Chinese community. It is, nevertheless, one clearly different from that of many other ethnic minority groups, notably lacking in recognized leaders at local or national level.

ORGANIZATION OF CULTURAL ACTIVITIES

Social organization among the Chinese is comparatively informal and largely family-based. Generally social life centres on clans, informal Sunday meetings in restaurants, gambling-houses for the men and Mahjong teas for the women, a few trade associations and a variety of other Chinese associations, all continually changing, as well as some church activity, cinemas and informal meetings in commercial supporting services such as barbers' or grocers' shops (Simsova and Chin, 1982). Some 20 years ago O'Neill claimed that distinctively Chinese facilities were the result of a demand from the Chinese themselves, not a response to discrimination. Despite much dissatisfaction with available facilities there had been little enthusiasm to organize others, the relatively small size of the Chinese population, the long hours worked and the absence of necessary leadership being deterrents. Shops, restaurants and clubs bring together a scattered population. But generally the pattern of social life is family-based as the celebration of weddings and other festivals have not become family rather than community occasions. Indeed some families are relatively isolated and make new contacts only through existing friends.

Until relatively recently at least, only in London and Liverpool, the two longest-standing areas of Chinese settlement, have there been separate facilities on a large scale. In Liverpool, in the 1960s, Nelson Street and the surrounding area was the recreational heart of the Chinese 'community'. Chinese clubs and organizations existed, according to O'Neill (1972), but these were poorly supported and served little purpose for the majority of the Chinese in Liverpool. By contrast, Gerrard Street in Soho, London, which emerged as the focus of the Chinese community in Britain and to a large extent in Europe in the mid-1960s, although it similarly lacks space and is predominantly a business and recreational rather than residential area, continues to give every sign of a flourishing Chinese way of life. Gerrard Street, which has been described by Watson (1977a), Khan (976) and in ILEA (1975), offers authentic Chinese restaurants, a variety of recreational facilities, including gambling-halls and cinemas, and a number of specialized services such as printing shops, travel agencies, barbers, grocery stores, bookshops, solicitors' offices and taxi companies. These facilities are all run by Chinese, largely for Chinese. Clearly Gerrard Street is able to meet Chinese needs in terms of food, entertainment and information by providing 'a village network of alliances, personalities and interconnected concerns' (Khan, 1976, p.25). It serves as a focus for Britain's Chinese population: restaurateurs visit for supplies; families arrive there at weekends to meet friends, enjoy a meal, some entertainment and stock up on provisions; and it becomes an arena for social exchange between widely scattered people where for once Chinese are in the majority and the language of the street is Cantonese.

Gerrard Street and its immediate environs is the nucleus of a Chinese urban settlement in the UK and a fascinating urban development in its own right. Yet its isolated situation is all the more ironic since it is the focus of attention for so many visiting Chinese come to relieve their isolation in the provinces and to re-establish their Chinese identity. Gerrard Street is the meeting-place of the Chinese where something of the Chinese way of life can be re-experienced. Although the social isolation of Britain's provincial Chinese might not necessarily lead to the erosion of culture as suggested by Garvey and Jackson (1975), traditional social expansiveness as described by Tsow (in CAG & QCRC, 1979) may nowadays be limited to the family. A visit to London's Gerrard Street is probably for most provincial Chinese families a treat to be had at festival time. Since the early 1960s Gerrard Street has formed the centre for observing occasions of traditional cultural significance. Ng (1968) recorded that the Chinese New Year, Dragon Boat Festival and Ching Ming were celebrated there in the 1960s through club associations. By the mid-1970s the Chinese New Year Festival with its lion dance, was celebrated by 10,000 observers, predominantly Chinese (Khan, 1976). Even so the festival, which requires much practice and organization, lacked trained personnel and finance since no applications for a grant had been made. The Chinese New Year was also celebrated in Middlesbrough, Manchester, Liverpool and Huddersfield. Apparently the Chinese community in Liverpool did not, however, participate in various inter-ethnic and inter-cultural festivals (Khan, 1976). London, especially the Gerrard Street area, remains the cultural focus of the Chinese community as was demonstrated in 1980 by the Hong Kong in London mid-autumn Chinese festival with its traditional dragon dances, Kung Fu, Wu Shu and traditional Chinese junk on the Thames. Such events assist the Chinese, scattered as they are across the country, to renew their sense of community and culture.

Also Gerrard Street and the surrounding area has been the centre for a number of trade, cultural and recreational and welfare clubs and associations. Over the years these have all had 'stop–go' fortunes, so that Gerrard Street functions primarily as an area for entertainment rather than action. The purpose of the associations and clubs is to meet the personal and sociocultural needs of the Chinese whose inadequate command of English prohibits them from social interaction with the wider community (Ng, 1968). But it seems that in order to succeed a Chinese association must appeal to the specific interests of a certain group of migrants, such as those sharing a common surname, or it must be directed and organized by others from outside the group such as professionals, church members or political activists (Watson, 1977a). Associations for mutual benefit and general welfare have had particularly inauspicious histories. These have apparently often had little to offer migrants in return for participation and support, as membership has not been a prerequisite for employment. Although an immigrant might acquire status by being elected to a leadership position in various associations or clubs, and by mediating between the group and the host society, esteem and respect from fellow immigrants was more likely to be commanded through wealth and business success.

Considering Chinese trade associations in particular it is curious that although Chinese caterers have a community of mutual interest, even when they have been able to form trade associations these have not become the forum whereby leaders could act as intermediaries with the wider society for they could not claim to speak for the Chinese community as a whole (Watson, 1977a). Indeed catering trade associations seem to have had mixed success. The Association of Chinese Restaurateurs, formed in the early 1960s, attracted more interest from the provinces though it was primarily of benefit to restaurateurs in London. On the other hand, Cheung (1975) reported that few restaurant proprietors in York were members of the Chinese Association of Commerce, also established in the 1960s, thus indicating that this wider association did not seem to offer much to caterers. Apparently the Edinburgh Chinese Association, which attempted to signal the independence of the Chinese catering trade in Scotland, was short-lived, and the British Chamber of Chinese Traders had to confine its activities to the catering trade (Watson, 1977a). The existence of the Peking Restaurants Association again suggests a specific interest group. Indeed it seems that in some cities and towns economic competition and suspicion militate against the formation of associations for mutual benefit (Mackillop, 1980). Informal networks for news passed on during visits to restaurants, and gambling-halls which also serve as labour exchanges, seem to be as important as some of the larger associations and clubs (Watson, 1977a).

Over the years political clubs and associations have had mixed fates due to political changes in the Far East. Left- and right-wing political clubs have enjoyed greater or lesser prominence over time, but catering workers have been largely apathetic (Ng, 1968). Migrants have been primarily interested in their economic prosperity, have not been associated with any political movements in Hong Kong and could not risk deportation by open support for mainland China. Before the 1960s, the Kuomintang party had been active, in conjunction with the Chung Sam Workers' Club in London, Bristol, Cardiff and Liverpool. But with the recognition by the British government of the People's Republic of China in 1950, the Kuomintang party in the UK was disbanded. Although there were some right-wing attempts to continue propaganda activities, largely amongst Chinese students in the 1960s, the left-wing propaganda activities of Mao's China were much more successful, even in gaining recruits amongst the Chinese settlers (Ng, 1968). Propaganda films were shown regularly to large audiences of restaurant workers and students from Malaysia and Hong Kong. There was a left-wing club in Liverpool during the 1960s to stimulate interest in Mao's China (O'Neill, 1972) and pro-China organizations in Birmingham, Manchester, Leeds and Sheffield (Cheung, 1975). Both right- and left-wing political groups involved in the workers' clubs in Soho, London, in the mid-1970s were concerned about recently arrived adolescents with minimal British schooling (Khan, 1976). The left-wing clubs, orientated towards China, are ideologically and culturally opposed to the materialist values displayed in the Hong Kong films and in the Soho gambling-casinos, but they encourage the learning of revolutionary songs and dances of the new China, sometimes at the end of Chinese language classes. Although both left- and right-wing clubs exist in such towns as Liverpool, Manchester, Leeds, Birmingham and Glasgow, reflecting the gulf between mainland China and Hong Kong/Taiwan (Khan, 1976), and there are organizations like the Free China Centre and the Society for Anglo-Chinese Understanding to publish their achievements, in general most Chinese appear not to be politically committed, either in terms of their country of origin or Britain, and only luke-warm attempts have been made to recruit support for the People's Republic of China (Clough and Quarmby, 1978).

Turning to a consideration of recreational facilities, clubs and associations, the cinema is a popular form of entertainment with the Chinese. At first films were shown in the restaurants and then in local cinemas, gradually gaining in popularity from the weekly shows in Liverpool to screenings everyday in Leeds and other large cities (Cheung, O'Neill). Films became an important part of Chinese social life, providing a meeting-point for catering workers and their families, even though films are usually shown in the early hours of the morning and attendance may entail travelling over long distances. The films are usually of Hong Kong origin, often Kung Fu dramas. Simsova and Chin (1982) have pondered, however, about the impact of video on the Chinese (and indeed other groups) as home viewing will lessen the incentive to meet other Chinese at the cinema. In their survey Simsova and Chin found that Chinese themes on TV were not very attractive and that the Chinese preferred videos of Hong Kong TV. Many did not know of Chinese programmes or programmes with a Chinese theme and others had reservations about the way the Chinese were presented. The recent parliamentary report (GB. P. H of C. HAC, 1985) pointed to the need for more news and information programmes for the Chinese on radio and TV and that these could be in the small hours when many Chinese have their leisure-time. It noted that Radio Merseyside had weekly, and Radio Manchester monthly, broadcasts and thought these might have wider appeal. There are several Chinese newspapers available in Britain which usually include some British news relevant to the British Chinese community. The Hong Kong Government Office has a fortnightly *News Digest* with 19,000 subscribers.

By contrast, Chinese music would seem to be a minority specialized interest. Simsova and Chin (1982) found that ten per cent of their sample of 449 Chinese claimed music as one of their recreational interests. Music clubs, however, seem to have proved unstable, and although a Chinese music society with 600 members exists, it only results in about one performance a year. Khan's (1976) research into the arts of the Chinese revealed a centre for Chinese musical talent in Soho and an interest amongst students of other nationalities, suggesting a potentially wider audience. Simsova and Chin found that a third of their sample, particularly those who were older and the non-professionals, listened to Chinese music exclusively, and 54 per cent did so occasionally. Half of the sample, especially young people, liked folk music best. Indeed 46 per cent of the sample, especially the older members, had access to a record player, and 91 per cent, especially the younger, to cassette players. Fifty-nine per cent, of whom three-quarters were older, long-term residents, bought Chinese sound recordings, and younger Chinese wished to borrow these from libraries.

Although gambling has been reported widely as a traditional recreational activity for the Chinese in the UK, this is almost exclusively confined to the Chinese working in the catering trade. The gambling-halls are social meeting-places and restricted to Chinese only. Ng (1968) described in detail some of the gambling activities which usually take place during the restaurant workers' breaks. By the mid-1960s the increase in gambling-houses in London and Liverpool had caused concern to the kinsmen of Chinese immigrant workers at home, anxious to protect their interests. Gambling is also a popular pastime amongst restaurant workers in the provinces, for as Cheung (1976) reported, although there was no local casino, half his sample gambled constantly and nearly all had done so at some time, mostly on horses and greyhounds. Those whose families were in the UK were less likely to participate, and Simsova and Chin (1982) found that amongst students and professional Chinese gambling as a leisure activity was scarcely mentioned.

Amongst the younger generation of Chinese, in particular, sporting activities seem to be increasingly popular. O'Neill (1972) reported the existence in the 1960s of some Chinese sporting facilities in Liverpool. Cheung (1976) mentioned that some catering workers were interested in table tennis and that there was even a league of Chinese football teams, as there is also in Scotland (Barr, 1983). Simsova and Chin found that 37 per cent of their sample, especially men, claimed that sporting activities were their main form of recreation. In addition to the general popularity of Kung Fu, which requires proper training, both mental and physical discipline and hence proper provision, an interest in sports may well extend beyond the kind of facilities which can be provided by distinctively Chinese clubs and associations and thus encourage interaction with wider society.

Though clubs associated with trade, cultural and recreational interests have had mixed success, associations for welfare or mutual aid have usually received even less support. The Chinese way has been to provide welfare support within the family and the voluntary-run Chinese classes for children have been the only popular organization on a community basis – but one with growing success (see pp. 175*ff.*). Nevertheless, from time to time a few Chinese welfare organizations, usually reflecting the narrow concerns of a specific group, have succeeded. One such is based on a clan association of those with the surname Cheung, which sponsors welfare work in the Chinese community and provides Chinese language classes for caterers' children in Soho. The Chun Yee Society, one of the oldest welfare clubs founded in 1906 in London's East End, provides help with funeral expenses, temporary accommodation and, since 1971, Chinese classes. The oldest Chinese organization in Liverpool, also established in the early 1960s, is the Chinese Masonic Lodge. In the first half of the century, as well as making welfare provision, it was very active socially organizing family outings, and traditional celebrations. But it declined by the 1960s due to state welfare provisions and the fact that the second phase of immigrants considered its organization old-fashioned (O'Neill, 1972). Yet it still provides a meeting-place and some accommodation for the old single Chinese in Liverpool (Lynn, 1982). Another successful group is the Overseas Chinese Professional Association, composed mainly of doctors, solicitors and lecturers whose work is linked to Chinese language classes (QCRC, 1981; see p.198). Other successful groups, which have been in existence for relatively long periods, include the various Chinese evangelical Christian associations (see p.100).

Apart from such sources of welfare support from groups established by the Chinese themselves, the interests of the Chinese in the UK have been actively represented by the Hong Kong Government Office (HKGO) in London and its branches in Manchester and Edinburgh. The Office liaises between Hong Kong and the UK, especially with immigrant inquiries, visa and passport problems and represents Chinese community interests at governmental level. It has been particularly instrumental through its involvement in all the important educational conferences where the position of pupils of Chinese origin and their social and economic backgrounds have been discussed. As well as a library of works in English and Chinese and much information about Hong Kong, the HKGO offers great support in terms of textbook provision and other assistance to the voluntary language classes in the UK (see p.178). Nevertheless, Chinese often regard representation of their interests by this institution with ambivalence and many migrants prefer not to avail themselves of 'establishment' help (Lai, 1975; Baker and Honey, 1981).

Gradually, during the 1970s it became clear that there was a need for a Chinese Advisory Bureau and community centres which would be independent of any kind of governmental association (CRC, 1975). To go beyond the Chinese community is regarded as shameful and as one Chinese tag has it, 'in this world avoid entering the door of a government office as in death you would avoid entering hell' (GB. P. H of C. HAC, 1985). The Chinese Community Centre, in Gerrard Place, was set up in 1976 (QCRC, 1981) with an urban aid grant and began to deal with the problems of the Chinese community associated with housing, health, welfare and translation difficulties. Initially the Centre, which employed Chinese-speaking social workers, had to overcome much prejudice, since the local Chinese could not believe that the services were provided free of charge. However, over the years various barriers, such as clannishness within the Chinese community, have been broken down, so that the organization has received increasing requests for help, and co-operative relationships with the wider society have begun to be established. Although earlier attempts to form centres elsewhere, for example, in York and Sheffield (see Cheung, 1975; and Mackillop, 1980), received little support, more recently community centres have been successfully established in Liverpool and Manchester (Lynn, 1982; Powell, 1982, see p.118). In order to assess how these recent developments have come about it is necessary to consider Chinese perceptions of the majority white British society and other groups within it.

CHINESE PERCEPTIONS OF THE BRITISH AND BRITISH CULTURE

When Ng (1968) researched the Chinese community in London in the mid-1960s, he concluded that for most of the New Territories immigrants 'discrimination by the host society, although it undoubtedly exists is "passive"; the English people are thought to be neither "friendly" nor "hostile"' (p.48). This perception contrasted with that of the first-phase immigrants who as seamen, competing with English seamen for jobs, had suffered from discrimination and prejudice (May, 1978; Broady, 1955; Jones, D., 1979). Indeed one of the aims of the Chinese welfare associations had been to combat discrimination. In Ng's view the absence of perceived discrimination by the second phase of Chinese immigrants was largely because they were not competing directly for the same jobs. All researchers into Chinese in the UK have observed that the economic niche which they have adopted has permitted the Chinese to control their own lifestyles without adapting them to suit British social expectations. They have maintained the stereotype of an independent community, although their very economic survival depends on a symbiotic, socially defined role relationship between customer and caterer which has a considerable degree of interdependence but which has permitted them to remain by far the least assimilated of all Britain's immigrant minorities (Broady, Ng, Cheung and Watson).

As the observer–participant studies reported by Cheung and O'Neill show, the Chinese are aware of discrimination but do not feel themselves in the main to be objects of it. Indeed, it appears that they will go out of their way to avoid disrepute and discrimination. Only a few restaurateurs in Cheung's sample claimed discrimination, but more claimed to know of cases of it, for example, customers not paying for meals. Yet they saw their relationship with the wider society in terms of the supplier–customer relationship, and were prepared to be the losers financially to save incurring trouble and thought, without knowing of the Race Relations Act, that they might stand to lose more if they claimed discrimination. They did not resort to the law if cheated so as not to lose face for the Chinese community as a whole. O'Neill described this as a sense of 'collective accountability'. She considered that in the 1960s the Chinese in Liverpool were too greatly concerned about how they were perceived by the English. This seemed to spring from insecurity, but the genuine concern to maintain a spotless reputation appeared to be an extension of the traditional ethic of keeping 'face' for the family to include Chinese people in general. This seemed to be a reaction to outsiders rather than a feeling of togetherness within the Chinese community itself. The Chinese were aware of the possibility of discrimination and adjusted their lives and avoided contact with the wider society as far as possible. O'Neill (1972) claimed that apparent changes, possible because of lack of religious ties and dogma, were only functional and had no effect on Chinese attitudes. Living their lives without interference from wider society related to the traditional concept of an independent family life. The Chinese also saw themselves as outsiders who needed to earn respect and trust. Their relationship with British society was seen as a matter of respect not race. Hence they have been concerned to divorce themselves from other ethnic minority groups in the minds of British population. A further element in establishing good relationships between the Chinese and local people in Liverpool was their good reputation and their independence. Indeed the Chinese themselves, O'Neill claimed, believed in the stereotype, valued it and saw it as flattering.

These interpretations find echoes in more recent research and comment. For example, Chan (1983) has identified a presumption of 'inferiority' amongst many Chinese (though not necessarily cultural inferiority) who feel that since this country belongs to the British, racial and discriminatory practices against the Chinese are justified despite the birth of many of their descendants here. This belief reinforces their idea that there is no point in the Chinese striving for academic or political success and that the only alternative is to aim for economic and material success. In view of the desire to promote their economic position and to avoid trouble and disrepute, news coverage in the mid-1970s, connected with Triad societies and drug rackets, caused considerable consternation to the majority of law-abiding Chinese (Freeberne, 1978). Though according to Watson (1977a) only a minority of Chinese from rural Hong Kong were involved in illegal activities, because of the publicity given to the Triad groups a new stereotype of the Chinese restaurant worker as an infiltrator and drug purveyor was emerging and the Chinese were increasingly seen as threatening and secretive.

However, the police have usually been concerned to stress that the Chinese are probably the most law-abiding minority in the country. Voon (in CAG & QCRC, 1979) pointed to the often neglected aspect of police relations with the Chinese community and noted that traditional Chinese suspicion of government agencies was also transferred to the police. The tendency amongst the Chinese was to solve problems for themselves rather than seek external arbitration. Misunderstandings and misconceptions about the law had built up due to linguistic difficulties and there was a need for better understanding of the system and the function of the British police force. There was, however, growing concern about the number of young transgressors amongst the Chinese community and the difficulties of assisting them, since interpreters were only required to translate and not to explain. Nevertheless, in a CRE survey (1981) involving a nationally representative sample of 107 Chinese, 1,057 West Indians, Asians, Africans and Cypriots and 1,073 white respondents, unlike the other groups, nearly 20 per cent of the Chinese felt that relations with the police had improved. In fact 44 per cent of the Chinese (like the Cypriots) thought that the police tried to be fair. Moreover, of all the groups the Chinese were most likely to say that race relations had improved, though just as many thought they had deteriorated. The recent parliamentary report (GB. P. H of C. HAC, 1985) noted the well-merited reputation of the Chinese as a law-abiding community. Any crime was kept within the Chinese community but there was no evidence of Triad connections between the UK and Hong Kong, nor of a drug problem. However, there was mistrust of the police based partly on traditional suspicion of authority and also police corruption in Hong Kong. Although there was no hostility to the police here, very few Chinese were recruited into the police force. Few incidents of racial harassment were actually reported though there was evidence of abuse in restaurants and a demand for a greater police presence in respect of takeaways. It was suggested that the Chinese could benefit from more community policing.

It is interesting that the traditional Chinese attitudes of independence, wishing to avoid trouble and losing face, together with their low profile due to the economic niche into which the vast majority of Chinese have fitted, have almost undoubtedly led to the lack of notice which they have received from the general public and, in turn, less overt discrimination. On the other hand, these very attitudes and conditions make it particularly difficult to assess the degree of discrimination and, in turn, to more accurately gauge the true perceptions of the Chinese towards the British.

But does an apparently passive acceptance of the status quo necessarily mean the acceptance of racial or cultural inferiority? Watson (1977a), in particular, has maintained that the Chinese believe that their culture is infinitely superior to European cultures, and although they have few illusions about their role as workers in British society and prefer to maintain a low profile, they do not particularly wish to change their way of life. There did not seem to be evidence of cultural and ethnic redefinition such as that occurring within the West Indian and Asian communities. The acquisition of flashy cars or liking for British pop music and films, Watson argued, is only a superficial change reflecting Westernization in Hong Kong, not any fundamental embracing of Western culture. Nor at the time of Watson's research was there evidence of an Anglo-Chinese or a Sino-British culture emerging. This interpretation has been questioned, however, by Simsova and Chin (1982) as respondents in their study showed a higher-than-expected awareness of British culture, especially the mass media. Although the Chinese had pride in their own culture, which was the basis of all their interests, they were nevertheless willing to explore aspects of traditional British culture. But in view of the preponderance of students and professionals in their sample Simsova and Chin might only be justified in making this interpretation for a relatively small minority within the Chinese population.

Watson predicted that the second generation of Chinese would be less likely to remain so impervious to contemporary British culture. This clearly differs considerably from the traditional Chinese way of life, particularly in terms of family structure and outlook on life as exemplified in values and attitudes. Research has shown that the Chinese are against intermarriage with the white British (O'Neill, Cheung), though a pragmatic attitude has been adopted in the absence of Chinese women (Broady, Ng). Yet even from the limited research evidence available, it is clear that the Chinese at various stages of settlement in different localities have varied in their attitudes towards British culture. For example, whereas Cheung reported that the Chinese parents in York in the mid-1970s resisted aspects of British culture brought into their homes by their children attending school, in O'Neill's view the second-generation Chinese in Liverpool experienced little cultural conflict because they had often lacked contact with other Chinese families and there was no feeling of belonging to a Chinese community.

Cheung (1975) found that the Chinese saw the English as too enjoyment-oriented, failing to save or to live a life of deferred gratification. Contacts with the British were limited by language and the fact that Chinese work-hours were usually British leisure-hours. Even so, few Chinese took any opportunity to socialize although some went to parties given by English friends. Generally they appeared isolated and did not know what was going on in society at large. O'Neill (1972) and Watson (1977a) also noted that few of the Chinese caterers – even those able to converse in English – were interested in making English friends. Fong's (1981) study in Liverpool also confirms lack of social interaction as 18 out of 31 families had never visited an English or foreign family, and only 12 had sometimes done so. There has been some criticism of the apparent disinclination of the Chinese to interact socially with the larger community (Harris, 1980).

As a conclusion to her research O'Neill decided that the Chinese in Liverpool wanted to be integrated and independent – to be accepted but not necessarily to participate in the social activities of the wider society. Since the Chinese had deliberately encouraged the perception of a non-problematic community, O'Neill suggested that it was then difficult for Liverpudlians to see that the Chinese did in fact have problems. In turn, the

Chinese were beginning to assume that because of the lack of help from the police or social welfare organizations the local authority did not care. In many ways this ambivalence seems to have been deliberately fostered, though as O'Neill predicted, with the arrival of increasing numbers of Chinese in the 1970s and the obligation on them to interact more closely with wider society in the education of Chinese children, attitudes to society at large have shown some evidence of change. Chann (in SCSCRC, 1976) has suggested that there are two groups amongst the Chinese community: those who are conservative, wish to remain independent and self-sufficient; and those who feel that they should integrate into the community in which they live for the sake of their families, co-operate with various social agencies and authorities and make the best use of the resources available. Although in the last few years with the emergence of Chinese community groups and the growth of Chinese language classes the traditionally low profile of the Chinese may be changing, the extent to which greater social interaction is taking place is unclear.

CHINESE AND OTHER ETHNIC MINORITY GROUPS

But what of the perceptions of Chinese with respect to other ethnic minority groups in British society? It appears in Liverpool, for example, that from the earliest years of settlement the Chinese were anxious not to be associated with other ethnic minorities, notably West Africans, in the area (Broady, 1955; O'Neill, 1972). Indeed as Fong's (1981) evidence shows, although the majority of Chinese families in her sample had other ethnic minority families for neighbours only a few said that they liked them. Watson (1977a) noted that although the Chinese are conscious of divisions within their own community, based on kinship, dialect and village of origin, these are not so strong as the perceived differences between the Chinese and non-Chinese. However, the Chinese make few meaningful distinctions between various non-Chinese groups beyond that of 'European', 'Indian' and 'black'. The arrival of Vietnamese refugees in 1979–80, a high proportion of whom are ethnic Chinese, provoked an ambivalent reaction in the Chinese population in the UK (Bishop and Engelhard, 1979). Whilst many of the Chinese community, it was claimed, regarded the arrival of the Vietnamese as unwelcome publicity, and some resented the reception given to the refugees, others set up a committee to 'make a bridge between the Chinese community and the refugees'. Apparently offers of work for the refugees met with little response, although the Chinese were aware of the very different social background of many of the Vietnamese. Nevertheless, the committee alerted local Chinese associations to refugees coming to their areas, with the aim of providing assistance and reorientation to life in England, such as that given by the Chinese Christian group described by Mackillop (1980) in Sheffield. It will be of interest to monitor the long-term relationship between the Chinese and the newly arrived Vietnamese, although the recent parliamentary inquiry (GB. P. H of C. HAC, 1985) reported that links between the two communities did not appear to be strong.

It is possible that the arrival of Vietnamese refugees precipitated a greater involvement by the Chinese in their own community organizations and associations as well as *vis-à-vis* the wider community. For in the last few years there has been a rapid growth in the number, scope and orientation of Chinese community organizations. According to Ng (1968), Chinese immigrant associations differed from those of, for example, Indian immigrants in Britain, in that they promoted cultural activities and aimed to represent the Chinese to the wider society. However, if the latter was intended, there would appear from the foregoing evidence to have been a lack of success in representing the needs and interests of the Chinese to British society. Hence the recent expansion of community activity may indicate a renewed intention to make the voice of the Chinese heard. During the middle to late 1970s there were a number of conferences organized by Chinese professionals with the aim of developing greater understanding of the needs of the Chinese community in Britain and of their evolving culture in a British context. It was recognized (see, for example, CAG & QCRC, 1979) that language presented a major difficulty for communication and interaction and that it was necessary for Chinese professionals to pool their resources in order to promote understanding of differences in cultural attitudes, especially where social services, community help and education were concerned. Not only was there a need for representation of the Chinese in local government and other agencies concerned with ethnic minorities, but there was a complementary requirement for information to be translated in order that the Chinese could participate in British society. As a result of this conference, the Chinese Action Group was formed to co-ordinate and disseminate information and identify areas of need.

However, it is at the local level that the initiatives in developing Chinese organizations seem to have been taken. Whereas in the past Chinese associations have had their roots in clan, district or language groupings, the newer organizations are often locality or area related and are open to all Chinese. There are some 60 such associations (Chann, in NCC, 1984). In addition, there are certain interest groups such as the Chinese London Music Society or the London Association of Chinese Youth and Students. Many of the associations are affiliated to one of the two national federations of Chinese associations. The area-based associations, which organize social, recreational and educational activities, aim to foster better relations both within the Chinese community and between the Chinese community and British society. Indeed it appears that they actively seek further contact with the local people. Most of the groups are voluntary self-help groups, although some receive financial assistance through the Urban Aid Programme or the Inner City Partnership, and may be able to employ full-time social workers and advisers.

Although it is likely that the relatively recent growth of these groups has been a natural outcome in the gradual settlement of the second phase of Chinese immigrants, Chann (in NCC, 1984) has suggested that three factors in particular facilitated their emergence. First, there is a new second generation of Chinese who have grown up and experienced the education system in Britain and hence have a better command of English and knowledge of the British way of life than their parents, but are also aware of the problems and needs of the Chinese community. Some take an interest in community affairs, especially helping the elderly and more recent arrivals. Secondly, more Chinese professionals are taking a large part in community activities. Whereas Watson (1977a) had noted many had previously had little to do with other Chinese outside their immediate circle of friends, some involved in Chinese language-teaching classes became more aware of the needs of the Chinese community as a whole to the extent that they took action and initiated some associations. Thirdly, Chann has pointed to the increased awareness of Britain's multiracial society and the availability of some funding to assist in the formation of associations. Even so, as Chann hinted the very existence of these associations depends on the ability of the Chinese to come to a greater understanding and trust within their own local communities in order that the associations may truly provide mutual aid.

Two such recent large-scale developments are community associations in centres of Chinese population in Liverpool and Manchester, augmenting the association established earlier in London (see p.111). The Merseyside Chinese Community Service, inaugurated in 1977, was supported by the Manpower Services Commission with a grant for three community workers (Lynn, 1982). It provides interpretation services, assists with applications for welfare benefits, housing and immigration, offers cultural entertainment and broadcasts weekly on local radio. Indeed in 1982 a Chinese community centre with funding from central government and the local authority was opened. The Merseyside Chinese Centre and pro-Communist Wah-Sing Association also organizes social activities and Chinese language classes. A parallel development has occurred in Manchester where the Chinese Education, Culture and Community Centre was inaugurated in 1979. Since Manchester is the social and commercial centre for 10,000 Chinese, plus another 10,000 scattered over the north-west, the Centre – funded by Manchester City Council, the Commission for Racial Equality and the local Chinese – provides a social gathering-place, catering for 5,000 Chinese each week (Powell, 1982). It offers a wide range of activities: language classes for Chinese and English, Kung Fu, Chinese lion and dragon dancing, folk and classical music, painting and calligraphy. In addition, the Centre advises on social problems, and provides an interpretation and an escort service to hospital. The primary aim is to foster good relations between the Chinese and English communities locally. According to the recent report the *Chinese*

Community in Britain (GB. P. H of C. HAC, 1985), other community centres in Westminster, Camden and Tower Hamlets in London, and in Birmingham, Nottingham and Newcastle, have been assisted by grants under the Urban Programme. But concern was expressed that the interests of the Chinese 'community' were often not given priority by local authorities, nor was there much contact with the CRE, and it was suggested that the dispersal of the Chinese indicated a need for greater governmental and cross-authority support.

The need to facilitate interaction and understanding between the Chinese and wider British community is long overdue. The paucity of data on inter-community perceptions is in itself indicative. Stereotypes abound. The Chinese are perceived as self-contained, self-sufficient, independent, disliking interference; having their own culture; having an extended family network of care; having their own businesses in which they are hard-working and reliable; and being law-abiding. Some of the first Chinese settlers experienced overt discrimination as a result of their competition with the British for jobs. But even though the numbers of immigrant Chinese have increased – and particularly in the last decade – because they are scattered throughout England only forming communities in the larger urban areas, and having overwhelmingly remained in the catering trade, they have not been perceived as competitors in the job market, education, social services or housing, or as a burden on the wider community. Hence there has been less overt hostility between the Chinese and the indigenous population than with other ethnic groups. Indeed the Chinese seem to have gone largely unnoticed, rarely exciting even curiosity or friendliness. It is the very lack of interaction, the ethnic segregation of the Chinese in the UK, which seems to have kept an appreciation of each community by the other to a minimum. The stereotypes held by the British of the Chinese, compounded by barriers of language and culture, and the ambivalence of the Chinese in desiring to maintain a low profile, appear to have led to a lack of recognition of the needs and interests of the Chinese on the part of the British, amounting to some extent to institutionalized racism; and on the part of the Chinese, a lack of understanding of their rights as members of British society, and only a narrow conception of the British way of life. As important, however, is the loss of cultural enrichment which the Chinese as a group within British society are able to contribute since any serious appreciation of Chinese culture has been limited to a knowledgeable few or a superficial acquaintance at festival time. The emergence in the last few years of a growing number of Chinese community organizations is significant. It is indicative of a further orientation towards settlement in the UK but also the desire to maintain Chinese culture. It is important that the opportunities offered by the establishment of such organizations, with their twin aims of reviving Chinese language and culture and interacting to a greater extent with wider society, should be built upon. There is a very real sense in which greater first-hand understanding and appreciation on the part of both the Chinese and the British is urgently needed if mutual benefit is to be gained. This is the more necessary as more children of Chinese origin are born in this country and experience a full British education. But it is also vital that a proper assessment should be made of the contribution of the education of pupils of Chinese origin to this current crucial phase in the development of the Chinese community in Britain.

Part Three

The Education of Pupils of Chinese Origin

Introduction

Pupils of Chinese origin comprise the third largest ethnic minority group in British schools. Their numbers, however, are not always realized because, apart from one or two larger settlements, they are widely scattered across the country, with often only one or two such pupils in a school. It should not be assumed that pupils of Chinese origin necessarily have similar backgrounds or origins. Three groups may be distinguished. First, there are second- or third-generation Chinese pupils, children of mixed marriages usually with one Chinese and one white parent or grandparent. Such children will be likely to come from the older-established Chinese communities in parts of the East End of London, Cardiff and Liverpool.* A second group are second-generation Chinese pupils, born in the UK, with parents born in Hong Kong or China who have arrived via Hong Kong. These children will at present, and in future years, constitute the majority of pupils of Chinese ethnic origin in British schools. A third group are first-generation Chinese pupils who have arrived direct from Hong Kong, Singapore or Malaysia, or even via the West Indies, Guyana, Mauritius, Pakistan, India or Common Market countries (Garvey and Jackson, 1975). This latter group, who have not arrived directly from Hong Kong, may either have stayed in the above-mentioned countries for two or three years en route to Britain or have been born there, and hence in immigration figures are likely to be recorded as emigrants from such countries rather than of Chinese ethnic origin. Until recently first-generation Chinese pupils comprised the largest proportion of pupils of Chinese ethnic origin in schools.

Compared with pupils of West Indian or Asian origin, there is very little documented evidence on the post-war arrival of pupils of Chinese origin in British schools. Neither, apart from some research on second-generation pupils of Chinese origin from mixed marriages in schools in Liverpool

---

* In Merseyside, in 1981, 40 per cent of the non-white population was of mixed ethnic origin (OPCS, 1983b). In 1983 some 62 per cent of 26,000 persons of mixed Other Asian (non-Indian sub-continent Asian) and white origins were under 20 (OPCS, 1984). These figures obviously include persons other than of Chinese ethnic origin.

Table 20: DES figures including pupils of Chinese origin, 1967, 1970, 1972

		Total	*Boys*	*Girls*
Commonwealth Asian,	1967	3,601	1,939	1,662
excluding Indian and Pakistani,	1970	4,956	2,651	2,305
i.e. mainly Chinese origin	1972	8,008	4,314	3,694

Source: GB. DES, 1968, Table 27; 1971, Table 38; 1973, Table 38.

(Silberman and Spice, 1950), did this group of early second-generation Chinese attract much attention. The arrival of Chinese children in British schools in the early 1960s in Huddersfield is incidentally mentioned by Burgin and Edson (1967), and in the mid-1960s in Bedford by Brown (1970). When Jackson and Garvey (1974) conducted their research – the first study to focus on pupils of Chinese origin but which is largely anecdotal and impressionistic – they reported few second-generation Chinese pupils. However, it was suggested that there were more first-generation Chinese children entering the UK in the early 1970s than those from any other ethnic minority group (possibly excepting Indian children) and that the numbers of Chinese pupils would continue to rise by, it was estimated, 1,600–3,500 annually.

Table 20 indicates the growth in the number of Chinese pupils according to the DES Form 7 returns for the years 1967 and 1970 and, for the last year of the collection of such figures, 1972. Though the DES figures are imprecise, because of the method of categorization, since that time there has been no clear national record of the numbers of pupils of Chinese origin in schools. Even in the mid-1970s educational records at LEA level were deficient with respect to pupils of Chinese origin, though records might be kept of other ethnic minority pupils, and the numbers of pupils of Chinese origin may have been underestimated (Garvey and Jackson, 1975). Some indications of their numbers in a few localities may be derived incidentally. For example, in Derby records show a gradual increase during the 1970s from 41 Chinese pupils in 1973 to 59 in 1975, with some movement into the town both directly from Hong Kong and other towns in the UK (Fitchett, 1976). Records for Northamptonshire in 1977 show that there were 76 Chinese pupils among 4,575 ethnic minority pupils in primary and secondary schools (Northamptonshire LEA, 1980). Records kept by David Ladlow at the Language Centre in Liverpool, where half the pupils are of Chinese origin, are indicative, though they obviously do not show all such pupils in Liverpool schools (see Table 35, p.162; Lynn, 1982). One of the most accurate sources, the ILEA Language Census for 1983, shows that there are some 2,825 speakers of Chinese in education in London, an increase of 23 per cent since 1981, with 1,645 pupils in primary and 1,109 pupils in secondary education and a greater proportionate increase at the lower age range (see also p.141). However, as the recent parliamentary report (GB.P. H of C. HAC, 1985) confirms apropos of teaching E2L, there is evidence of little monitoring of pupils of Chinese origin by LEAs and variability of provision for their needs, and that even where there is centralized registration some may be slipping through the net.

Nationally the Nuffield Foundation project *Teaching Chinese Children* (1981) estimated that there were some 20,000 pupils of Chinese origin in British schools. Immigration statistics from 1971 to 1981 supplied by the Hong Kong Government Office (GB. Home Office, Control of Immigration Statistics for relevant years) suggest that Chinese children have continued to arrive over the last decade. Since they must be accompanied by an adult, and the number of 'others and dependants' related to those entering the UK on employment vouchers or work permits numbered approximately 19,761 during this time, the number of Chinese children is unlikely to have exceeded 10,000–12,000. A more accurate source of figures is the Labour Force Survey which indicates that in 1981 there were about 30,000 children of Chinese origin below 15 years of age, three-quarters of whom are UK-born (see Table 8, p.42). These figures are confirmed by Census data according to the membership of such children of a household whose head was born in the Far East (see Table 21).

There is still some movement of Chinese pupils between the UK and Hong Kong. In addition to some Chinese pupils arriving direct from Hong Kong, some UK-born children of Chinese origin have been sent back to Hong Kong to live with relatives and receive some education there before returning to the UK, often to join their parents at the age of ten or more

Table 21: Persons usually resident in private households whether born inside or outside the UK, by age, birthplace and birthplace of head of household in the Far East, 1981

	Birthplace	0–4	5–15	16–19
Far East = Hong Kong,	UK-born	10,320	15,214	2,898
Malaysia,	Outside UK	953	5,234	6,694
Singapore		31,721		

Note: Since only one per cent of heads of household of Chinese ethnic origin are UK-born (OPCS, 1983b, Table 9), and although children of heads of households born in China are omitted, these figures give the likely numbers of children of Chinese ethnic origin, though they may also include some persons not of Chinese ethnic origin. Source: Census 1981; OPCS, 1983a, Table 3.

(Chan, 1983). Such children often experience particular difficulties in their readjustment to the UK: within the family – many meet parents whom they do not remember, and often new siblings whom they have never seen; differences of language and culture and, in some cases, the change from a rural to an urban lifestyle; and some of these returnees suffer maladjustment to a considerable degree, often becoming withdrawn (Ladlow, 1980). However, the practice of sending children back to Hong Kong for an education in a Chinese milieu is declining as the Chinese become more settled in the UK, and with the wider availability of Chinese language classes. All children now coming from Hong Kong will have had some previous schooling, though this will vary from full-time education from the age of four onwards, or part-time education from seven or eight years of age, depending on whether the child comes from an urban or a rural area. It has been suggested that Chinese pupils from urban Hong Kong make the transition to the UK more easily than those coming direct from the New Territories (SCSCRC, 1976). But many experience bewildering changes in school atmosphere, teaching style and learning methods compared with schools in their country of origin (Chan, 1983). In addition to all these tensions, some pupils experience considerable frustrations with inadequate English, as their knowledge, it has been suggested, might otherwise match that of their classmates, especially in science and mathematics (CAG & QCRC, 1979).

Moreover, it is clear that the majority of UK-born pupils of Chinese origin also experience language difficulties on entering school, since although some may have learnt the alphabet from their relatives (Jackson, 1979) and some spoken English from their siblings, their home environment will have been largely Cantonese or Mandarin speaking (see p.143*ff.*). Another factor affecting social adjustment to school is that apart from one or two areas with larger Chinese populations the number of Chinese pupils in schools is likely to be very small. Indeed Jones (1980) has suggested that they rarely constitute more than five per cent of any school population. Thus Chinese children are likely to attend schools with few if any other pupils of Chinese origin. Although schools in urban areas are likely to have other ethnic minority pupils, in some rural parts of the country to which the Chinese have dispersed the schools which they attend may be all-white.

The distinctive dispersal of Chinese pupils throughout the UK has made for particular difficulties in assessing and evaluating their performance as a group. Even in individual cases communication difficulties have impeded finding out what a child actually knows and deciding how she or he can be effectively taught. Until recently, at least, the general indication from the literature on the education of Chinese pupils has been that they generally do quite well academically, apart from those arriving as adolescents with little English (CRC, 1975), and that Chinese children born and brought up in the UK are normally as well adjusted, bright and academically orientated as

British children (Lue and Tsow in CAG & QCRC, 1979). The slight stereotyping which exists suggests that pupils of Chinese origin are usually not lacking in intelligence and once they have mastered English they may make remarkable progress (Langton, 1979). However, such a generalized view may gloss over potential difficulties of language and social integration and contrasting home and school environments. It is, therefore, the function of this review of research to critically examine the evidence which does exist on these pupils and to point to particular areas of weakness and difficulty as well as strength and success. However, it must be observed at the outset that there is a dearth of quantitative data on the educational attainment of pupils of Chinese origin and that it has been necessary to draw overwhelmingly on qualitative descriptive evidence stemming from more subjective assessments.

The absence of 'hard' evidence' may be illustrated by the case of IQ testing. Although during the last decade it had been increasingly recognized that no standardized IQ test is appropriate to assess ethnic minority pupils, a certain amount of evidence from IQ testing has nevertheless been collected with respect to pupils of Asian and West Indian origin (see Taylor, 1981; Taylor with Hegarty, 1985). Yet a full search of the published literature has only produced one incidental record of IQ performance of pupils of Chinese origin in Britain. A study carried out in the London Borough of Redbridge in 1977, of top junior pupils in eight multiracial schools (representing 25 per cent of that year group), included five Far East Asian pupils – presumably Chinese – who attained a verbal reasoning score of 103.6. Their performance was second only to that of African pupils, higher than that of the white indigenous pupils (97.7) and the borough average (101.4) (BPPA & RCRC, 1978). Though not all the evidence on pupils of Chinese ethnic origin is of such dubious provenance nor quite so parlous, nevertheless it is difficult to avoid the conclusion that the relative lack of research data on this group's education indicates a lack of awareness, interest and concern about pupils of Chinese origin. Indeed attention to pupils of Chinese origin has overwhelmingly been in the context of language teaching.

Section 6
Language

As with other ethnic minority pupils, language can be seen as a central consideration in the educational performance of pupils of Chinese origin. Some of the difficulties experienced by newly arrived and UK-born pupils of Chinese origin in learning English have been documented (p.166*ff.*). But compared with larger groups of ethnic minority pupils the language background of Chinese pupils has, until relatively recently, not been investigated. So it is only now that the interactive effects of Chinese and English – the languages of home and school – on a child's cognitive development and educational achievement can begin to be explored.

This section examines research data on the language background of adults and children of Chinese origin in relation to home, school and society at large. The first sub-section focusses on the language knowledge of Chinese adults and children, their competence in Chinese dialects and English, use of these languages in the home in spoken and written form and attitudes towards these languages, and learning them and their significance for identity. A second sub-section reviews provision for teaching English as a second language, particular difficulties for Chinese pupils and available learning materials. Another sub-section examines the extent and organization of voluntary Chinese language teaching by the community, and attitudes towards classes. Finally, mainstream provision for Chinese is considered. The section draws chronologically on national and local studies to build up a picture of the language background to the education of pupils of Chinese origin.

Language knowledge
This sub-section examines the range of language knowledge of Chinese adults and children, both of Chinese dialects and English. It covers both oral–aural competence and literacy as assessed by self-reports, interviewers' judgements or teachers' assessments. Knowledge of Chinese dialects and English are considered separately and chronologically according to evidence from national and local surveys.

Knowledge of Chinese languages

The Chinese language, in its system of written characters, is the primary unifying bond between the diverse groups of Chinese in the UK. The main Chinese dialects spoken by the Chinese in the UK are Cantonese, the language of urban Hong Kong and Kwangtung province; Hakka, a dialect of the rural New Territories; 'Mandarin', spoken by those from mainland China; and Hokkien, the principal dialect of the Malay Chinese. Mutual intelligibility of different dialects may be variable. Language for the Chinese is not only significant as a means of communication, but is a most important vehicle of social learning. It conveys the values inherent in the culture, in the absence of an overriding religious basis, in the strong, natural bias towards the oral transmission of Chinese culture in daily communication (Tsow, 1980a). Indeed Timothy Mo, a novelist of Chinese origin writing in English about the Chinese in the UK, has gone so far as to suggest that there is a lack of interest in the written word amongst the Chinese, and that the Chinese character does not lend itself easily to writing (see Davies, 1983). Certainly the focus of research into language knowledge (though not necessarily use and attitude, see pp.142–59), both Chinese dialects and English, amongst the adult and young population of Chinese origin in the UK is more on the spoken than the written word. But it is not known to what extent this is influenced by current debate about the choice of a written standard form of Chinese for community language teaching.

It is, moreover, ironical when considering the relative significance of English and Chinese for the Chinese in the UK, that whereas English may have a unique claim to the title of world language in that although it is only spoken as a native language by ten per cent of the world's population it is the most generally known and used, both as a native and a second or subsidiary language, Chinese has more than twice as many native users world-wide (Crane, 1975). In the UK the status of Chinese as a minority language and the growing influence of English in Hong Kong (see pp.10–12) are likely to affect attitudes towards it. Moreover, as the second generation of Chinese ethnic origin grow into adulthood it cannot necessarily be assumed that they will have a Chinese dialect as their first language, as there is likely to be a shift towards English. These factors at least – the dialect of the country or region of origin, the complex interrelationship of spoken dialects and written form(s) (see p.190), literacy, language as a vehicle of culture language status, attitudes and vitality – have to be weighed in consideration of the Chinese language background in relation to the education of pupils of Chinese origin.

Given this complexity, it should not be surprising that there is no comprehensive national information about the number of Chinese languages spoken, read or written, or to what extent and by whom. Moreover, there has unfortunately not been a language question in the Census, and statistics on ethnic origin and country of birth only give an imprecise and inaccurate guide to linguistic affiliation (see pp.39–40).

Although Campbell-Platt (1978) found it impossible to construct a linguistic map from published sources about minority groups in Britain, she estimated on the limited basis of country of birth figures from the 1971 Census that Cantonese and Hakka speakers ranked as the eleventh and twelfth largest groups of overseas language speakers. Moreover, it is not known how many Chinese dialects are spoken in the UK, though it is generally thought that Cantonese speakers predominate, with smaller groups of speakers of Hakka, Mandarin, Hokkien, Malaysian Chinese dialects and Vietnamese. Tables 6 and 7 can only serve as a general indication of the likelihood of bilingualism in Chinese languages and the potential need for an educational response. A fragmentary but important picture of the range of Chinese language knowledge can only be built up from a few local surveys and in-depth studies reviewed here. But clearly different regions and cities contain different numbers and proportions of Chinese language speakers (see pp. 42–7, and below). Indeed the dispersal of the Chinese in the UK is a special characteristic, evident in nearly every small town and even larger villages.

It is likely that some adults of Chinese ethnic origin speak more than one Chinese dialect. Clough and Quarmby (1978) found that the Chinese students in their sample were multilingual and spoke at least one other Chinese dialect. A survey of the library needs of Chinese in London, although weighted in its population sample (students 66 per cent, professionals seven per cent, nurses 14 per cent, non-professionals, including housewives, catering trade and clerical workers, 11 per cent) revealed a great range of language knowledge (Simsova and Chin, 1982), as Table 22 shows. Although nearly all spoke at least two Chinese dialects, 58 per cent, especially Malaysians, chose to be interviewed in English. However, the small number of UK-born Chinese usually spoke one Chinese dialect.

Multilingualism is again indicated by an in-depth language study in London (Tsow, 1984) which included data collected on languages spoken by 138 parents, mainly living in London, aged over 35 and from the ABC

Table 22: Chinese languages spoken by respondents in a survey of library needs

Birthplace	N	Cantonese	Hokkien	Mandarin	Hakka
			Percentage speaking		
Hong Kong	209	99	4	35	24
China	31	64	10	77	15
Singapore	44	64	62	88	14
Malaysia	188	71		59	32
Taiwan	8	56		78	12

Source: Simsova and Chin, 1982.

socioeconomic groups, and whose children did not attend Chinese language classes. Of these parents, 43 per cent spoke English, 80 per cent spoke Cantonese, four per cent spoke Mandarin and 35 per cent spoke other Chinese dialects. They gave as their main language: English, 14 per cent; Cantonese, 67 per cent; Mandarin, three per cent; and other Chinese, 18 per cent. In the absence of further evidence, however, it is not clear to what extent multilingualism in Chinese languages is related to the social class of the respondents in these studies, though movement from the country of origin will have increased the need for linguistic versatility. Moreover, there is likely to be a shift towards English with the growth to adulthood of second and subsequent generations, especially perhaps in the older-established communities. For example, in 1979 one study in Liverpool (quoted by Lynn, 1982) found that out of 141 heads of household interviewed 91 gave Cantonese, 39 Hakka and five (three of whom had been born in England) gave English as their main language. Thirty-two said they could speak English reasonably well. Overall these figures also warn that it should not be assumed that the population of Chinese ethnic origin will necessarily have Cantonese as their first language.

Until relatively recently there had been no serious attempt to ascertain the range and extent of Chinese-language knowledge over several locations. The Linguistic Minorities Project (LMP) of 1979–83 (LMP, 1983a, and 1985, with more details) represents a major contribution to establishing a sociolinguistic baseline of linguistic diversity and patterns of language use. The LMP involved four surveys: the Schools Language Survey (SLS) documenting the linguistic diversity and extent of literacy in five LEAs; the Secondary Pupils' Survey (SPS), a sample survey in two LEAs of language use and perceptions; the Adult Language Use Survey (ALUS) of patterns of adult language skills and use in three cities; and the Mother-Tongue Teaching Directory Survey (MTTDS) which gathered information about mother-tongue teaching provision in the same three areas. Two of these surveys, ALUS and SLS, provide information on Chinese language knowledge of adults and children. In the context of establishing adult language knowledge it is relevant to describe the ALUS and findings in further detail here; reference is made elsewhere in this sub-section to other findings.

The ALUS involved minority language groups including Chinese language speakers in Bradford, Coventry and London. Interviews took place in Cantonese/Chinese, and only in English when the respondent asked to do so or initiated a language switch. A section of the questionnaire investigated respondents' self-assessments of language skills, including literacy. Although it was not possible to estimate the total population of Chinese speakers in London, a random sample was interviewed; whereas in Coventry and Bradford, with smaller Chinese populations, an attempt was made to conduct an interview in every household identified. Table 23 shows

Table 23: Main demographic features of the Chinese respondents in the Adult Language Use Survey

	Bradford	*Coventry*	*London*
Estimate of total populations	250	300	–
No. of households with member interviewed	50	43	137
No. of people in respondents' household	244	213	597
% of people in respondents' household aged below 17	51	43	33
% of people in respondents' household aged over 50	7	8	9
% of households in owner occupation	0	61	37
% of households in council housing	28	12	37
% of males aged 17–65 at work outside home or in family business	9	72	60
% of females aged 17–60 at work outside home or in family business	9	43	37
% of people in respondents' households brought up overseas	87	56	53

Source: Adapted from LMP, 1983a, Tables 5.1–5.3.

Table 24: Extent of multilingualism amongst Cantonese speakers

Cantonese speakers	N	*Additional Chinese languages known (percentages)* Mandarin	Hakka	Vietnamese
Bradford	50	15	13	97
Coventry	43	14	83	–
London	137	17	16	14

Source: Adapted from LMP, 1983a, Table 5.4.

the main demographic features of the Chinese respondents in Bradford, Coventry and London. An age and sex balance was largely achieved, but the findings should not be interpreted as necessarily representative of Chinese speakers in these cities nor of England as a whole. Indeed they are of great interest in indicating local variations.

Naturally the main languages spoken by the Chinese respondents in the ALUS were usually the language of the interview – Cantonese – and English, but in Coventry this was only the case for 70 per cent of Chinese speakers as many turned out to be speakers of Hakka. Table 24 shows the extent of multilingualism amongst Chinese speakers. High proportions in each location spoke three or more languages: Coventry 76 per cent, London 61 per cent. But the proportion of Chinese speakers in Bradford – all refugees from Vietnam – who reported knowledge of three or more languages was exceptional: 94 per cent.

In addition, respondents reported on the linguistic skills (spoken) or household members including children and non-family members said to know Cantonese very or fairly well:

Bradford	N = 233	66%
Coventry	N = 213	49%
London	N = 504	82%.

The ALUS also supplies information on the percentage of Cantonese speakers who reported that they understood and spoke, and read and wrote, Cantonese very or fairly well (Table 25). The relatively low percentages in Coventry and Bradford relate to the large numbers of respondents whose home language was another Chinese language. Further information on literacy in Cantonese and English is given in Tables 27 and 28. Evidence to the parliamentary committee investigating the Chinese in Britain suggested that most Chinese over 45 would have some knowledge of the written language but that a sizeable minority, estimated at 20 per cent, especially women, would be illiterate in Chinese (GB. P. H of C. HAC, 1985).

The knowledge of Chinese languages of pupils of Chinese origin should be set in this context of bi- or multi-lingualism. Clearly some pupils of Chinese origin, through their home and community environment, may have the chance to acquire or become used to operating with more than one Chinese dialect. Given the dispersal of such pupils across the country, it may be important in relation to decisions about E2L or mother-tongue teaching to know which Chinese dialect is the pupil's home language. A national survey in 1979 (Little and Willey, 1983) revealed the wide distribution of Chinese language speakers who were represented in 38 per cent of 118 schools. A further survey in 1983 also disclosed that 16 LEAs with primary schools with at least ten per cent of bilingual pupils named Chinese as one of the most

Table 25: Chinese adults' competence in Cantonese

Cantonese speakers	Respondents answering fairly or very well N	Understand and speak %	Read and write %
Bradford	50	88	28
Coventry	43	79	51
London	137	96	65

Source: Adapted from LMP, 1983a, Table 5.5.

frequently spoken languages (Tansley and Craft, 1984).

Three language censuses covering the whole of the ILEA in 1978, 1981 and 1983 (ILEA, 1979, 1982, 1983) provide evidence of considerable and increasing linguistic diversity among London schoolchildren and of the growing numbers of Chinese speakers analysed according to their distribution within the ILEA and by age, though unfortunately no distinction is drawn between different Chinese dialects, nor is any assessment available of their competence in these languages, as it is for English (pp.140–1). In 1978 teachers in all primary and secondary schools collected information on a class basis for every pupil for whom English was not a first language. Of the 128 languages recorded, 'Cantonese/Chinese' language speakers formed the ninth largest group, totalling 1,712. Most of the ten ILEA divisions had 100 or more Chinese language speakers, though the largest concentrations were in Camden (483) and Islington (240) with fewest in Greenwich (50) and Lewisham (84) (ILEA, 1979). In the second survey conducted within the ILEA in 1981 teachers in all primary and secondary schools collected information on pupils speaking a language other than or in addition to English at home. One hundred and thirty-one languages other than English were recorded and some 2,237 Chinese language speakers again formed the ninth largest group (five per cent) of overseas language speakers. As before, they were mainly concentrated in Camden (576) and Islington (316) with fewer in Greenwich (73) and Lewisham (126). The numbers of Chinese language speakers had increased between 1978 and 1981 by 30.7 per cent, one of the highest increases in foreign language speakers. This increase was fairly even according to age and consistent across the ILEA divisions although Chinese language speakers constituted 45 per cent of the roll of one school in Camden (ILEA, 1982). In 1983 the census used the same definition and extended its scope to include pupils in nursery and special schools. A total of 147 languages were recorded and Chinese language speakers totalled 2,825 rising to eighth position (5.6 per cent) in the groups of overseas language speakers. The largest numbers were still to be found in Camden (641) and Islington (374) and four divisions each had just less than 200 Chinese speakers. In fact Chinese speakers increased by 23.1 per cent over the 1981 figure, the second highest increase (after Bengali speakers, 65.2 per cent) of all the language groups. The increase was greater in the primary age range (26.7 per cent) than secondary (18.1 per cent) and since there are more Chinese speakers aged five than 15 it suggests that their numbers are likely to continue to grow in the next few years, especially since a particularly high proportion of Chinese speakers stay on at school to 16 and 17 (p.224). Indeed it would seem that this increase of Chinese language speakers within the ILEA has paralleled the increase of Chinese nationally during these years (see OPCS, 1982a, 1983a, 1983b) and may well continue.

In evidence to the recent parliamentary committee the DES estimated that some 70 per cent of Chinese pupils speak Cantonese, 25 per cent Hakka and five per cent Mandarin (GB. P. H of C. HAC, 1985). Fortunately in recent years more information has become available on Chinese pupils' Chinese language knowledge, mainly through three sources: a sample survey with techers' assessments in London schools (Rosen and Burgess, 1980); a CRE study of the views of Chinese parents and their children who were either attending or not attending voluntary language classes in London, Edinburgh, Manchester or Liverpool (Tsow, 1984); and the LMP survey of five LEAs country-wide (Couillaud and Tasker, 1983; LMP, 1983a).

In 1977–8 Rosen and Burgess (1980) collected teachers' assessments of the language knowledge of 4,600 pupils aged 11–12, in 28 schools in 11 London boroughs. In this accidental sample some 33 out of a total of 749 bilingual pupils spoke Cantonese (four per cent). Of these Cantonese speakers, 60 per cent were considered to be bilingual, regularly speaking both languages. Of the remainder, 27 per cent had Cantonese as their dominant language and only 13 per cent spoke it minimally. However, the fact that pupils of Chinese origin speak Chinese dialects does not necessarily mean that they can write or read Chinese. Rosen and Burgess found that 64 per cent of the 33 Cantonese speakers in their sample were considered to both read and write Chinese, and a further 12 per cent to read, but not write, Chinese.

In the CRE survey (Tsow, 1984) those parents whose children did not attend part-time Chinese language classes, who were mainly middle class, living in London and with children up to the age of 11, were more likely to claim that Cantonese was their children's second language. Some 48 per cent claimed that their children spoke Cantonese as their main language, one per cent Mandarin and seven per cent other Chinese dialects. Unfortunately, comparable evidence for the children of parents predominantly in the lower socioeconomic group whose children attended classes is not cited. However, of the 68 out of the 138 mothers who maintained that their child spoke

Cantonese or Mandarin as their main language, only nine mothers said that their child could write Chinese with any proficiency, 33 a little and 24 none at all. The significance of learning to speak, read and write in Chinese in relation to voluntary Chinese language classes is discussed elsewhere (see pp.155–6).

The LMP (1983a) Schools Language Survey (SLS), developed to assist LEAs to document linguistic diversity, also provides interesting information

Table 26: Pupils' knowledge of Chinese dialects in five LEAs, 1981

Place	Nos*	% of all language groups in schools	Literacy† % (of total)	Sex ratio boy/girl	6–8	9–11	12–15	15+
Bradford	142	1.0	56	49/51	39	34	30	–
Coventry	89	1.2	61	44/56	28	23	19	–
Haringey	147	1.9	69	55/45	54	41	33	–
Peterborough	84	3.5	69	50/50	22	21	21	15
Waltham Forest	109	2.0	57	55/45	34	36	23	–

Place	Language groups				
	Cantonese	Hakka	Hokkien	Mandarin	Chu-Chow
Bradford	70	26	1	–	1
Coventry	49	15	–	1	–
Haringey	102	10	1	5	–
Peterborough	49	13	–	–	–
Waltham Forest	67	4	1	3	–

Place	Language groups				
	From Hong Kong	Vietnamese	From Vietnam	Cantonese from Vietnam	Malysian Chinese	Unspec- ified
Bradford	4	23	2	15	–	22
Coventry	2	17	2	3	–	17
Haringey	4	–	–	–	1	24
Peterborough	3	11	4	1	–	14
Waltham Forest	8	2	1	2	3	20

*This figure appears to exclude Vietnamese speakers.
†Literacy means reading or writing in one of the spoken languages given.
Source: Adapted from Couillaud and Tasker, 1983; LMP, 1983a, Table 2.5.

on the bilingualism and biliteracy of pupils of Chinese origin. It was administered by teachers in Bradford, Coventry, Haringey, Peterborough and Waltham Forest in 1980–1 and records pupils' self-reports of the language(s) they spoke at home and their literacy in 'Chinese'. Table 26 provides information on the numbers of different Chinese dialect speakers, the age and sex of 'Chinese' speakers, their literacy and proportion of all language groups in schools in five LEAs. There was evidently some difficulty in identifying the Chinese dialects. Chinese dialects comprised a small proportion of the speakers of languages other than English in these five LEAs. Although Cantonese speakers are in the majority, the figures also reveal a significant minority of Hakka and Vietnamese speakers. The numbers of Chinese dialects varied within the five LEAs, ranging from six to nine, plus some unspecified Chinese dialects. Once again, the table also shows an increasing number of Chinese dialect speakers in the lower age groups. The overall literacy rate for Chinese speakers of 64 per cent was amongst the highest for all the language groups. Only amongst the pupils of Chinese origin in one of the five LEAs, Peterborough, was there a clear increase in self-reported literacy with age, and only in this LEA was the proportion of Chinese dialect speakers aged 12–15+ greater than in the lower age ranges.

Unfortunately, there is no clear indication of the extent to which pupils of Chinese origin may speak more than one Chinese dialect, though it seems that second-generation Chinese in the UK are less likely to be multilingual than their parents. Simsova and Chin (1982) found that for 53 young Chinese adults who had arrived in the UK before the age of 15, 91 per cent of whom spoke Cantonese and on average 1.7 Chinese dialects, this was slightly less than the overall average for Chinese adults.

In conclusion, on the evidence available it seems that a fair proportion of Chinese adults may speak more than one Chinese dialect. This may be related to social class. Cantonese predominates, although there are a range of Chinese dialects spoken, including significant minorities of Hakka and Vietnamese speakers, varying by location. Although it appears that pupils of Chinese origin have a certain competence in Chinese, unfortunately the degree of proficiency has not been assessed with any objectivity by these studies. Interestingly, one-half to two-thirds, a similar proportion to adults, claim literacy, possibly due to attendance at language classes. Clearly it is also important to consider knowledge of, and skills in, Chinese in relation to competence in English.

Knowledge of English
The remainder of this sub-section focusses on Chinese adults' knowledge of English and considers to what extent Chinese language skills interact with oracy and literacy in English. Bilingualism is likely to be a matter of the degree to which languages are spoken, ranging from a minimum

competence to complete mastery. Most bilinguals are likely to have a
dominant language, and those who speak English as a second language are
likely to have degrees of mastery. Fluency is sometimes deceptive and
literacy more difficult to assess. Chinese adults' and children's knowledge of
English is reviewed through local studies and surveys.

It seems likely that there will be considerable differences in the English
language knowledge of the two main groups of Chinese adults in the UK,
catering workers and students and professionals. Whereas the former will
generally have had little education or English tuition in their country of
origin, those in the second group with considerably more and often a higher
education, are likely to have had a considerable knowledge of English
before arrival in the UK and plenty of opportunities to extend their
proficiency during their residence here. In London Ng (1968) discovered
that the majority of Chinese restaurant workers were ignorant of English
and that there was hardly any social contact between them and society at
large apart from the waiter–customer relationship, so that it was possible for
Chinese kitchen staff never to exchange a word with British people. These
findings were confirmed by Watson (1977a, 1977b), who suggested that
most of the waiters only learn enough to handle the menus and that fewer
than 20 per cent are able to hold a simple conversation with their customers.
In order to overcome the language barrier each restaurant employs at least
one waiter or a manager who is competent in English and thus able to act as a
mediator for the others. Cheung (1975) also made similar observations in a
study of catering workers in York. Again competence in English was low as
although half could speak English only five out of a sample of 73 could speak
in English sentences. However, those with greater competence could
usually make themselves understood in English in writing, which he
attributed to the fact that they had completed their secondary schooling in
Hong Kong.

In a study in London Lai (1975) found that, according to their self-ratings,
only four adults (three men and one woman) amongst the 24 catering
families could speak a little English but their competence was not great.
Indeed most had no English in spite of being resident for 12 years or more.
Garvey and Jackson (1975) quote other similar instances. Women in
particular were handicapped, for men could understand more than they
could speak and were helped by their colleagues at work. The same few who
spoke English also had minimal competence in reading, but even they could
not write a letter in English. Lynn (1982) quotes a survey conducted in
Liverpool, in 1979, in which 109 out of 141 heads of household interviewed
said they had problems with the English language and only 32 could speak
English reasonably well. Lynn pointed to the difficulties for such people of
acquiring access to information as they did not read the local newspapers,
although 109 of the families regularly read the Chinese newsletter. Again
recently, Tan (1982) in a study of 50 Chinese families – predominantly

working in the catering trade in London – found that although there was a range of proficiency in English amongst the adults in the sample about 26 mothers and 21 fathers had difficulties in talking to shop assistants. Only 14 mothers and 24 fathers were rated as speaking some, or being fluent in, English. Tan suggested that most of the parents, except those working as waiters or at the counters of the takeaway shops, had very little contact with English people and hence no chance of practising English.

Yet Simsova and Chin (1982) have questioned whether the Chinese in the catering trade do still have little knowledge of and proficiency in English, as these studies have suggested. Moreover, data on a small proportion of non-professionals in their own sample tend to support other evidence. Although on average 58 per cent of their sample chose to be interviewed in English (Hong Kong-born 37 per cent, China-born 39 per cent, Taiwan-born 50 per cent, Singapore-born 64 per cent, Malaysian-born 80 per cent, UK-born 100 per cent and others 93 per cent), only 15 per cent of the non-professionals chose to be interviewed in English. More than 50 per cent of students and professionals, more women than men and those under 40, chose to be interviewed in English. Moreover, there were proportionately more in the Hong Kong-born group who displayed variations in their knowledge of English depending on their age on arrival in the UK, the elderly often having no English at all. Curiouly some 96 per cent of the sample in the literacy survey claimed to be able to read English, varying from 80 per cent of the non-professionals to 100 per cent of professionals. Simsova and Chin suggested that those who could not read probably did not agree to take part in the survey, hence the high rate of literacy. It is interesting, however, to compare the claimed literacy in Chinese: 82 per cent, 98 per cent of the non-professionals compared with 65 per cent of nurses. Moreover, amongst this sample Simsova and Chin found that there was a high educational level, with only three per cent who had finished their education before the age of 16, even those who were involved in catering. It has, however, to be remembered that the participants in this survey were library users and hence – even if catering workers – are likely to have been atypical. Indeed evidence to the recent parliamentary inquiry (GB. P. H of C. HAC, 1985) estimated that as many as 65–75 per cent of first-generation Chinese were unable to speak English and some who had been in the UK for 30 years had limited English.

The ALUS of the LMP (1983a) provides up-to-date information on the oracy and literacy of Chinese adults in English (see pp.130–3 for survey and sample details). High proportions of Chinese speakers claimed some knowledge of English (Bradford, 87 per cent; Coventry, 85 per cent; and London, 95 per cent). But self-rated ability to understand and speak, and read and write, English fairly or very well was considerably lower, and lower than skill in Chinese languages (see Table 25). Indeed the Chinese speakers' skills in English were amongst the lowest claimed by all language speakers

Table 27: Chinese adults' competence in English

| Chinese language speakers | N | Respondents answering fairly or very well | |
		Understand and speak %	Read and write %
Bradford	50	10	6
Coventry	43	44	30
London	137	47	42

Source: Adapted from LMP, 1983a, Table 5.5.

Table 28: Chinese adults' literacy skills in English and main minority language

Chinese language speakers	N	Literacy* in two languages %	No literacy in either language %
Bradford	50	58	6
Coventry	43	67	2
London	137	69	2

*Defined as ability to read and write at least 'not very well'.
Source: Adapted from LMP, 1983a, Table 5.6.

Table 29: Chinese household members' English and bilingual skills (percentages)

	N	English	Bilingual
Bradford	233	18	16
Coventry	213	55	26
London	504	61	51

Source: Adapted from LMP, 1983a, Table 5.7.

(Table 27). However, very few of the Chinese speakers were illiterate in both their Chinese dialect and English (Table 28). Finally, the spoken language skills of respondents' household members, including children and non-family members who were said to know English or English and a minority language very or fairly well, are shown in Table 29. These figures indicate that, with the exception of the newly arrived Vietnamese Chinese in Bradford, over half the household members had in principle the possibility of speaking in either English or in the minority language to the respondents. However, compared with other language speakers these figures suggest that Chinese children, like Bengali children, are less likely than other language speakers to have access to other household members speaking English, which may have implications for their opportunities to learn and use English (see ILEA data 1982, 1983).

Assessments of the knowledge and proficiency of Chinese pupils in spoken English are available from teachers' evaluations in three surveys in London. In Rosen and Burgess's study (1980) only 18 per cent of the 33 Cantonese speakers were rated as unambiguous speakers of English, whereas 82 per cent were considered to incorporate features deriving from Cantonese in their spoken English. This was the highest proportion for any of the overseas language speakers. Thus only 46 per cent of the Cantonese speakers, the lowest proportion of any overseas language-speaking group, were rated as fluent speakers of English, 36 per cent as intermediate and 18 per cent as initial speakers of English. These findings suggest that there might be particular difficulties in acquiring English for Chinese-language speakers. Yet it has been claimed (see Garvey and Jackson, 1975) that some pupils of Chinese origin, especially those who have received some form of secondary education in Hong Kong, may write English better than they speak it. Indeed some parents are reported to have paid for English-language tuition for their children in Hong Kong.

Competence in English was also assessed by teachers for four cohorts of pupils in ILEA language censuses in 1978, 1981, 1983 and 1985 (ILEA, 1979, 1982, 1983, 1986). In the 1978 census teachers rated the need of pupils for whom English was not a first language for additional English-language teaching. Although the Chinese-language speakers formed the ninth largest group of foreign language speakers, they comprised the fifth largest group of those judged by their teachers to be in need of additional English teaching. Some 57.4 per cent (982) of Chinese-language speakers were said to require additional language tuition. They were distributed proportionate to their numbers within the ILEA divisions, more in Camden and Islington in comparison with Greenwich and Lewisham. In the subsequent 1981, 1983 and 1985 surveys the fluency in English of pupils who used a language other than, or in addition to, English at home was assessed according to four categories: beginners with very restricted spoken English and only slight understanding, so that the diversity of linguistic demands in the classroom are significantly problematic; second-stage learners quite fluent in spoken English with a high proportion of non-native errors and an uneven vocabulary and syntax; third-stage learners with spoken and written English with few signs of non-native use, though lacking the full language range of English speakers of the same age and ability, thus a tendency to underachieve in language-based

Table 30: Stages of competence in English of Chinese-speaking pupils in ILEA, 1981, 1983 and 1985 (percentages)

	Beginners %	Second stage %	Third stage %	Fluent %	Total no
1981	17.2	21.6	24.9	36.4	2,237
1983	16.1	22.8	25.0	35.5	2,825
1985	14.7	26.4	27.3	31.2	3,546

Source: ILEA, 1981, 1983, 1986.

subjects; and those with full competence, having a command of written and spoken English comparable to that of native speakers of the same age and ability. Thus findings in 1981, 1983 and 1985 may be directly compared. In 1981, whereas just less than half the total number of foreign language-speaking pupils (46.7 per cent) were rated as fully competent in English, only 36.4 per cent of Chinese speakers were considered fluent. In 1983 a smaller proportion of foreign language speakers were rated fluent (43.4 per cent) as also Chinese speakers (35.5 per cent). Table 30 shows the stages of competence in English of Chinese speakers in 1981, 1983 and 1985. The only other foreign language speakers of whom a lower proportion were rated fluent in English were Bengali, Vietnamese, Japanese, Tagalog and Arabic speakers. In view of the relative recency of arrival of many of the Bengali and Vietnamese speakers these figures again tend to point to special difficulties for pupils of Chinese origin in acquiring fluency in English. The types of difficulty and the extent to which Chinese-language knowledge and cultural background are taken into account in E2L teaching are considered elsewhere (see pp.166–74). Census data are helpful in indicating trends but these need to be seen in the context of the possible influence of teachers' attitudes in assessing competence and differential language shifts within different areas. It would be particularly valuable educationally if assessment could be related to amount of E2L teaching received, frequency of use of English in the home, extent of knowledge of Chinese, and attitudes to English and Chinese within the home.

However, as yet such refinements seem a way off. Indeed, as with other areas of testing, there is a complete absence of published reports on the assessment of pupils of Chinese origin in the school context on conventional reading tests. Though evidence in relation to other ethnic minority pupils for whom English is not necessarily a first language, notably those of Asian origin, has suggested that conventional reading tests may not give an accurate assessment of the reading capability, not to mention potential of such pupils (see Taylor with Hegarty, 1985), nevertheless the omission of such data on pupils of Chinese origin must indicate that any testing of such pupils has not been recorded in a way in which it is possible to trace the particular scores of pupils of Chinese origin, or that such testing has never taken place – whether or not the inappropriateness of such tests for pupils of Chinese origin has been a factor. Only in the BPPA survey of top junior pupils in 1977 is there any record of testing, which may in itself be dubious and cannot be accorded weight. Some five Far East Asian pupils attained a score of 99.8, their performance being slightly inferior to that of African and 'other' pupils, but higher than that of indigenous pupils (98.7) and just lower than that of the borough average (100.1). But compared with their outstanding performance on verbal reasoning and maths (see pp.126, 211–12), their score for English suggests that in this area their potential may not have been fully realized (BPPA and RCRC, 1978). The only other mention of specific testing of English is a comment from a conference report (SCSCRC, 1976) which suggested that two areas of special weakness for pupils of Chinese origin showed up by NFER diagnostic tests were vocabulary and clause (see also p.168).

Generally it seems clear that Chinese adults' competence in English is likely to be greatly influenced by their previous and current opportunities to learn and practise English: Chinese professionals and most catering workers are likely to demonstrate widely differing English skills. There is unfortunately insufficient evidence on competence related to age, sex or length of stay, though there are indications that it may not necessarily increase with years in the UK. As might be expected, oracy is greater than literacy, but even so evidence suggests that the degree of proficiency is in question. This has implications for Chinese children learning English. Although, not surprisingly in view of school attendance, their English skills are greater than those of the adults, evidence of the relatively low proportion of Chinese pupils fluent in English must give rise to concern and indicate particular difficulties in learning English. In this context and generally, however, the linguistic ability of Chinese adults and children maintaining their Chinese language skills has yet to be recognized.

Language use
Research evidence on language use by Chinese adults and children focusses on language in use in the home between parents and children, siblings, with friends and other household members. Unfortunately, there is little evidence of language use in other social contexts, possibly because of the home- and business-centred life worlds of the Chinese and until recently, at least, their relative lack of participation in community enterprises. Neither is there any information on media influences. However, by contrast, there is a significant body of information on the reading habits and library usage of the Chinese which can usefully be considered. Data are not divided here according to use of English or a Chinese language because the studies, largely reflecting practice, make no clear division. Most of the studies

depend on self-reports by the respondents. Interestingly, most of the research has been undertaken within the last five years, possibly reflecting the burgeoning of interest in language development among the growing number of children from families speaking languages other than English, and the relationship between the use of the mother tongue and English. Although the language used at home has always been thought to be an important influence on a child's education, until relatively recently the potential of establishing proficiency in the mother tongue prior to learning English in school has not been seriously considered. The extent to which parents and children speak to each other in Chinese or English is, therefore, a matter of interest. Obviously language use is affected by proficiency in a language (pp.127–42) and also attitudes to language (pp.152–9).

Language use at home
Lynn (1982) has claimed that the mother tongue is constantly used by Chinese parents in the home. In a CRE survey (1981) involving 107 Chinese, nearly half of whom were aged 25–39, 53 per cent claimed to speak mainly Chinese dialects at home and 39 per cent mainly English. In a small-scale study Fong (1981) discovered that the parents in 28 out of 31 families in Liverpool claimed to speak Chinese with their adolescent children and only three parents spoke both Chinese and English, and none English alone. But this has to be compared with the frequency with which English is spoken by the children to their parents, with siblings and with friends. Of the 31 adolescents, 80 per cent of the 30 per cent who had recently arrived from Hong Kong could speak Cantonese fluently and conversed with their parents in Cantonese. However, the 30 per cent who were UK-born could not speak Cantonese very well so they conversed with their parents in both English and Cantonese. This, Fong noted, sometimes led to misunderstanding between parents and child, especially as the parents' English was limited to the vocabulary of their food business, and tended to result in a lack of fluent and accurate expression by children also. Overall some 77 per cent of the children spoke Chinese dialects with their parents and only 23 per cent mixed Chinese and English. None spoke English alone. There was a greater shift to speaking mixed Chinese and English with siblings (40 per cent), the same proportion speaking Chinese only and 20 per cent English alone. With friends the proportions using both English and Chinese were even higher: 55 per cent claiming to speak both, 30 per cent English alone and only 15 per cent Chinese exclusively. These data would seem to confirm the dominance of Chinese in parent–child interaction but an increasingly mixed pattern of spoken language use, especially amongst the peer group, and those pupils of Chinese origin who are UK-born.

A similar pattern was established by Ng (1982), who interviewed 251 adolescents (134 females, 117 males) aged 12–17 in ten Chinese language schools across the country. Some 93 per cent claimed that their parents spoke to them in a Chinese dialect (118 were speakers of Cantonese, 107 of Hakka and six of other Chinese dialects). Slightly fewer (86 per cent) claimed commonly to use Chinese dialects in speaking with their parents. About 14 per cent spoke to their parents in English, double the percentage who were spoken to in English by their parents. Although Chinese dialects were still predominant in communication with siblings and friends, Chinese was less commonly used. Nearly half claimed that they spoke English with their siblings and friends: 41 per cent of the children spoke to their brothers or sisters in English and 48 per cent were spoken to by their brothers or sisters in English; and 46 per cent claimed to speak to their Chinese friends in English and 37 per cent claimed that they were spoken to by their Chinese friends in English.

The CRE survey in 1979 (Tsow, 1984), which also took place in connection with Chinese language classes, provides further information on the extent of Chinese language use in the home and differences according to social class and birthplace of the children. Two groups of mothers were interviewed: 195 whose children aged eight plus were attending part-time Chinese language classes, and 138 mothers whose children aged up to 11 were not. The first group of mothers were predominantly born in Hong Kong, had lived in London for ten years or more, were aged 35 plus and belonged to the lower socioeconomic groups. The 138 mothers whose children did not attend the Chinese classes had similar backgrounds, except they were largely from the higher socioeconomic groups. The languages spoken at home by these two groups of parents and those spoken most frequently are shown in Table 31. The predominance of Cantonese and its frequency of use by parents is again demonstrated. There was a strong tendency for Chinese to be spoken by the parents regardless of length of residence in the UK. However, the longer parents whose children attended

Table 31: Languages spoken at home by parents of children attending and not attending Chinese language classes

| | Spoken by parents of non-attenders/attenders | | Spoken most frequently by parents of non-attenders/attenders | |
| | N = 138 | N = 195 | N = 138 | N = 195 |
	%		%	
English	43	35	14	9
Cantonese	80	80	67	69
Mandarin	4	2	3	
Other Chinese	35	37	18	

Source: Adapted from Tsow, 1984, p.15, and Table 6.

language classes had been in Britain, the more likely they were to speak English with their children: 40 per cent in the UK ten or more years, 26 per cent in the UK less than ten years. Even so, English was only used most often by nine per cent of these parents who were over 35 or with ten or more years' residence. A greater proportion (43 per cent) of the more middle-class parents of non-attenders claimed to speak English at home, but only most often by 14 per cent. Although these data demonstrate considerable linguistic maintenance on the part of the parents, there is also some indication of a gradual increase of Chinese and English usage by some parents and possibly those from higher socioeconomic backgrounds.

However, once again what the parents speak at home does not necessarily correlate with the languages spoken by the children. More of the children of interviewed parents who did not attend language classes were said to have English as their first language (51 per cent) and 48 per cent Cantonese (one per cent Mandarin and seven per cent other Chinese dialects). Further evidence is available from a sample of 312 children aged 8–14, predominantly from London but including 71 from Liverpool and Manchester, who were attending mother-tongue teaching classes, but not the children of parents who were interviewed whose children attended such classes. Pupils' claims of the languages they spoke at home and those spoken at home most often are given in Tables 32 and 33.

Again Cantonese was the language spoken at home by most of the pupils (72 per cent) and most frequently (48 per cent). This was especially the case for pupils born in Hong Kong or outside the UK and with less than two years in the UK, but also held true for those in the UK for up to nine years. Over a quarter of pupils claimed to speak other Chinese languages, and 14 per cent to speak them most frequently at home. Interestingly, they were more likely to have been born and to have lived in the UK for over ten years. However, some 62 per cent of Chinese pupils claimed to speak English and 38 per cent

Table 32: Languages spoken at home by pupils attending Chinese language classes

	Total	Birthplace Hong Kong and elsewhere	UK	Length of time in the UK (years) 1–2	3–9	10+
Base: all	312	148	164	49	188	75
	%	%	%	%	%	%
Cantonese	72	85	60	82	76	56
English	62	46	76	33	64	75
Mandarin	1	1	1	–	1	1
Other Chinese	26	19	32	22	24	32

Source: Tsow, 1984, Table 11.

Table 33: Languages spoken most often at home by pupils attending Chinese language classes

	Total	Birthplace Hong Kong and elsewhere	UK	Length of time in the UK (years) 1–2	3–9	10+
Base: all	312	148	164	49	188	75
	%	%	%	%	%	%
Cantonese	48	66	32	63	48	36
English	38	23	51	16	40	47
Other Chinese	14	10	18	16	13	18

Source: Tsow, 1984, Table 12.

most frequently. Three-quarters of the English speakers had been born and lived in the UK for more than ten years, and 43 per cent were from higher socioeconomic backgrounds, whereas 60 per cent of the Cantonese speakers came from lower socioeconomic backgrounds. Moreover, 51 per cent of the UK-born spoke English most frequently at home, the same proportion as the non-attending children who were said by their parents to speak mainly English at home.

Findings from the LMP tend to confirm trends in language use reported in other studies and reveal some differences according to location. Table 34 shows the patterns of language use between adult respondents in the ALUS (see p.132) and other household members, irrespective of language skills. Clearly use of Chinese languages predominates, though there is an

Table 34: Languages used between Chinese adults and all other household members

N = household members excluding respondents		% of interlocuters using only or mostly minority language* reciprocally with respondents	% of interlocuters using only or mostly English reciprocally with respondents	% of interlocuters using both English and the minority language reciprocally with respondents
Bradford	184	85	0	13
Coventry	157	57	10	19
London	446	73	6	14

*Minority language here includes Chinese dialects other than Cantonese.
Source: Adapted from LMP, 1983a, Table 5.8.

increasing pattern of use of both Chinese dialects and English even among the Vietnamese in Bradford, and especially among Chinese in Coventry, ten per cent of whom used mostly English. Whereas these figures obviously reflect language skills available to the speakers, further analysis of unconstrained choice of language use only served to confirm how few respondents and family members were said to have a fair knowledge of English and minority languages (see pp.138–40) and hence how few used English reciprocally all or most of the time. The ALUS also revealed the extent of use of English between children in the household. None of the 36 Vietnamese children in Bradford spoke only or mostly English, but interestingly some 60 per cent of the 30 children in Coventry were said to do so, compared with only 20 per cent of the 81 children in London (see pp. 133–6).

Overall the data demonstrate the dominance of Chinese languages in use in the home. This is particularly the case in parent–child communications, although there is a tendency for children to use Chinese less reciprocally with parents. Increasing use and frequency of English spoken by children in the home is related to birth in the UK, length of residence and socioeconomic background, which also appears to be related to adult usage. The studies also indicate a move away from use of Chinese alone by children as relationships become more peer directed. There is increasing use of both Chinese and English with siblings and friends, and of mostly English, especially with friends, even of Chinese origin. But again differences according to location suggest factors such as migration, birthplace and socioeconomic background, not to mention competence, are influential.

Reading habits and library use
Several studies have investigated the reading habits of Chinese adults and children and their library use. This information usefully complements the account of spoken language use at home. It is considered through studies of adults' reading of Chinese and English books and other materials, parents reading to children and Chinese children's reading habits.

Research conducted in 1975 by Clough and Quarmby (1978) in six London boroughs amongst adult non-library users in language classes, which included ten young Cantonese-speaking Chinese adults with an average education of seven years, found that six preferred reading Chinese, and read a Chinese-language newspaper. Although some did not know about the public library or that it was free, nearly all would have liked to be able to borrow Chinese-language books. In an investigation into the library needs of the Chinese in London (Simsova and Chin, 1982) more than half of the sample (499) read Chinese books. Though 82 per cent of the sample claimed to be able to read Chinese to a degree, half of those from the lower socioeconomic grouping did not read Chinese books at all. Those who claimed to read books in Chinese only for pleasure were mainly those in the lower socioeconomic groups, over 40 and born in China, Taiwan and Hong Kong. Only if respondents had lived in the UK for 20 or more years was their reading in Chinese adversely affected, though this sub-sample was very small. Some 52 per cent of the sample were active readers, having read one or more Chinese books during the previous month, and they comprised 62 per cent of the sample who were able to read in Chinese. Some 27 per cent of the active readers were avid readers, having read three or more books in the previous month, some 15 per cent of the total. A higher proportion of those from the lower socioeconomic classes were amongst the active readers in Chinese.

Simsova and Chin found that 40 per cent of those who read books in Chinese liked light fiction, 26 per cent classical and modern fiction and 34 per cent non-fiction,the latter tending to be read more by professionals in the sample. Within the range of light fiction, stories about fighting were particularly popular, followed by romances. Curiously some 58 per cent read about Chinese culture in English, with the lower socioeconomic group and longer-established residents and women buying fewer of such books and the professionals more.

Indeed some 53 per cent of the sample bought Chinese books. There are about seven Chinese bookshops in the Soho area of London, tending to fall into two types, those stocking romances and thrillers and others political works, manuscripts and paintings (Chin and Simsova, 1981). It appears that the Chinese, especially the non-student population, are culturally disposed to book-buying out of necessity, partly because the libraries in their own countries may not be well developed and also because those here do not generally stock Chinese-language material (see also Tsow, 1977). Approximately one-third of Simsova and Chin's sample did not own any Chinese books, although 15 per cent, often those of lower socioeconomic status, older and longer-term residents had 30 or more books. The professionals, especially those born in Hong Kong, tended to have larger collections of books. More than half had equal numbers of books in Chinese and English.

But only 28 per cent of the sample borrowed Chinese language books from the library, and these tended to be students. Thus only half of those who were members of the public library (overall 54 per cent) did not borrow from their libraries in Chinese, and as 82 per cent claimed to be able to read Chinese and 52 per cent were active readers, Simsova and Chin argued that this suggested that they would borrow books in Chinese from their libraries if available. Almost three-quarters of the respondents wanted access to more Chinese books in the libraries. Seventy per cent read only in Chinese, 78 per cent mainly and 79 per cent equally in English and Chinese. Some 40 per cent wanted access to materials to learn in Chinese. Simsova and Chin concluded that there was unquestionably a need for greater provision of Chinese books and language materials in libraries and that libraries should publicize their services in Chinese. There are Chinese collections in London: Bexley, Brent, Camden, Hackney, Hammersmith, Kensington, Lambeth, Southwark, Westminster (Simsova and Chin, 1982) and in at least six local authorities (Cooke, 1979). But although there is evidence of greater awareness of need, earlier reports indicated that provision was inadequate (Millward, 1977; CAG & QCRC, 1979). Appendix 5 in Simsova and Chin (1982) gives a detailed account of the technical difficulties for libraries initiating a Chinese collection.

Investigations have suggested that Chinese-language readers are interested in a wide variety of reading material, especially newspapers. O'Neill (1972), for example, discovered that the 30 Chinese families and others whom she studied took two newspapers in Chinese, one from China and the other distributed free in the UK by the Hong Kong Government Office. In York Cheung (1975) found that newspapers and magazines played an important part in providing the restaurant workers with links with their homeland and sometimes restaurateurs subscribed to particular periodicals for their workers. According to Harris (1980), Europe's only Chinese-language newspaper, *Sing Tao* printed in the UK, has a circulation of 10,000 six days a week. But according to Chin and Simsova (1981), some 33 Chinese language newspapers, mainly from China, Taiwan and Hong Kong are regularly available in London. In addition, some 362 Chinese-language periodicals can be obtained from seven Chinese bookshops in the Soho area, and periodicals and newspapers are also available from Chinese barbers, gambling-houses and provision shops (Sing Tao Newspapers, 1980). A language and culture guide from the Centre for Information on Language Teaching (CILT) in 1986 provides up-to-date information. Simsova and Chin (1982) also found that there was a tradition of reading newspapers amongst their Chinese sample, with 90 per cent of those able to read Chinese reading Chinese-language newspapers, especially men in the older age groups. Some 42 per cent of the sample bought Chinese-language newspapers and 23 per cent borrowed them from friends, but only eight per cent consulted them in libraries. Indeed three-quarters of the sample wanted access to Chinese newspapers in libraries, and Simsova and Chin drew attention to this gap in provision for Chinese readers.

Simsova and Chin's (1982) sample included 53 Chinese who had arrived in the UK before the age of 15, 57 per cent of whom were still under 25. Some 91 per cent spoke Cantonese and 53 per cent opted to fill in the Chinese questionnaire. Seventy-seven per cent read Chinese for pleasure, less than those who read English for pleasure (96 per cent). Some 52 per cent of the Chinese readers were active readers; and of these, 31 per cent had a large collection of Chinese books. Moreover, 60 per cent of active readers regularly read Chinese newspapers and periodicals. But with this bi-literate sample, there was a shift towards reading in English: 38 per cent read English and Chinese equally, 21 per cent mainly English and 23 per cent only

English. These young people were mainly employed in the public sector as almost three-quarters used only or mainly English and the remainder both English and Chinese. Forty-five per cent had large collections of books in English, half read in English about Chinese culture and affairs and nearly all read English-language newspapers. Two-thirds used the public library, a third as an information source. Such data provide information on a different group of young Chinese, who have not necessarily experienced much British schooling, but nevertheless comprise a significant minority amongst the population of Chinese in the UK, and may have an influence on the development of their own community.

Indeed some 96 per cent of Simsova and Chin's (1982) sample claimed to be able to read in English. Those of Chinese ethnic origin from Malaysia and Singapore and the UK-born tended to read only or mainly in English for pleasure. Indeed 46 per cent read only, and 30 per cent mainly, in English for work which demonstrates that they participated in the British mainstream economy and, therefore, cannot be seen as typical of Chinese parents in the UK. Some 17 per cent claimed to read equally in English and Chinese. Of the readers in English, 80 per cent were active readers of one or more books per month and, of these, some 38 per cent read avidly, three or more books per month. These readers tended to be under 40 and professionals, nurses or students, but some 67 per cent of long-term residents read actively in English and 22 per cent avidly. Indeed 41 per cent of the sample were active readers in both English and Chinese and 37 per cent were active in English, but not Chinese. The majority of the 11 per cent who did not read either English or Chinese claimed that it was because they were too busy. Overall some three-quarters of the sample of 499 Chinese adults claimed to read in English. All these read English newspapers and magazines. Some 55 per cent read the daily paper and 75 per cent read books. About half the sample claimed to borrow books in English from the library and 27 per cent read English newspapers in the library, and 72 per cent bought newspapers in English. Only 5 per cent had any books in English of their own. The book-owners were much more likely to be professionals, to have larger collections of books, to read either mainly in English or equally in English and Chinese, and to be active readers in English, including books about Chinese culture. Some 60 per cent of the sample interviewed in English (58 per cent) wanted more access to materials to enable them to learn English. A further postal survey conducted by Simsova and Chin, which included respondents from Glasgow and Liverpool as well as London, found a slight increase in the bias to reading in English with about one-third of the respondents reading in Chinese and English equally for pleasure and a slightly higher use of the public library service. However, against these findings for a sample weighted towards professionals and those from upper socioeconomic groupings has to be placed the lack of literacy in English reported in families from lower socioeconomic groupings (Lai, 1975; Lynn, 1982; and see pp.

138–9).

There is unfortunately little evidence about Chinese parents reading to their children, although Ladlow (1980) has claimed that many Chinese parents show interest in reading to their children and borrowing books in Chinese from the local library. Elliott (1981), who researched into the library needs of mother-tongue teaching schools in London in 1980 and interviewed ten Chinese pupils in ten schools, primarily first generation, aged 7–19, found that four claimed that their parents read to them in Chinese and seven had told them a story in Chinese – illustrating the oral tradition perhaps. By contrast, none had been read to by their parents in English.

Two studies provide some limited information on Chinese children's reading preferences and habits. Clough and Quarmby (1978) conducted a survey in six London boroughs of 397 ethnic minority children's use of public library services. Included in the sample were nine children of Chinese origin, of average age nine all, except one, UK-born. All, except one, claimed to speak and read in English, but five also claimed knowledge of Chinese dialects. In fact all, except one, preferred to read in English. Half had learned of the public library from their family, two-thirds visiting it weekly for a range of fiction and non-fiction books. Almost all of them had books of their own at home which were predominantly in English. Three-quarters of the children were satisfied with the library facilities, and although half of them consulted staff when they needed help, the other half were inclined to abandon their search. However, only one-fifth of their parents were library members. One-third of parents inspected the child's choice of books and one-fifth of the parents read to their children from them.

In Elliott's study (1981) which involved ten Chinese pupils, predominantly first generation, five claimed to be able to read Chinese and five a little, and nine claimed to read English, one a little. An equal number (eight each) of books in Chinese and English were claimed to have been read in the few months prior to the interview. The children's order of preference for reading in Chinese was for magazines, story-books, factual books and books on the parents' country, compared with comics, story-books, factual books, magazines and, to a lesser extent, books on the parents' country of origin, in English. Overall, however, the Chinese pupils seemed to have less voracious reading habits than children from other language speaking groups.

Once again, however, although these data from library and language class surveys are of interest, caution must be exercised in generalizing from them since such small numbers of pupils of Chinese origin are involved. This is partly due to the nature of the inquiries themselves, aiming to cover a wide range of language groups, but also partly a function of the dispersed nature of the Chinese population. The focus of these studies would suggest that reading has a special place in the life of Chinese adults and their growing children. But against this has to be set the relatively low rates of reported literacy in Chinese (see pp.132–3) and English (see pp.138–9) in more broadly based samples. There is a need for more evidence from local and sociolinguistic studies about language use for different purposes, at home, work and in community contexts, and for different Chinese language groups, before any distinct patterns can be established in determining language shift other than the to-be-expected increasing use of English amongst Chinese children. Indeed there would appear to be evidence of considerable maintenance of Chinese, even when the possibility exists of using English.

Language attitudes
Attitudes to a language are generally considered to be significant in affecting the acquisition of a proficiency in that language. It is therefore important to examine what is known from research of Chinese parents' and children's attitudes to English, Chinese dialects and the significance of the languages for their sense of identity. Unfortunately, there is a lack of sociolinguistic research on Chinese adults' and children's attitudes to the Chinese and English languages *per se*, unlike the situation with respect to South Asian adults and children. Hence attitudes to languages will be considered more indirectly here through evidence on Chinese adults' attitudes and motivation towards learning English and E2L provision; Chinese parents' attitudes to their children learning English and Chinese, especially through their own attempts at teaching and enthusiasm for their children to attend Chinese classes, and the children's attitudes to classes; and finally, the interrelation of language attitudes and identity.

As has been shown (see pp.137–40) many of the Chinese adults involved in the catering trade are unlikely to have a good command of English. This is also likely to be the case for many Chinese mothers at home. But what are their attitudes to learning English on their own account and that of their children, and how can this be facilitated? Cheung (1975), for example, found that most of the Chinese caterers in York had little knowledge of English when they arrived in this country, but restaurant proprietors and those who had established their takeaways felt the need to learn English because of increased contact with the wider society. The arrival of their families and improved working conditions motivated them to attempt to learn. On the other hand, Lai (1975) discovered a low motivation to learn English. Although some received a little help from their colleagues at work, it was obvious that their association predominantly with other Chinese at work did not provide them with the opportunities to learn English in the course of their daily lives. Neither, it seems, do many Chinese women feel motivated to attempt to learn English. It has been suggested that Chinese mothers need to acquire the attitude of mind to attend E2L classes (see Lue and Tsow in CAG and QCRC, 1979), for although they were said to be very keen on the education of their children, they were reluctant to find time for their own education in a very busy working life. Moreover, Fong (1981) found that parents refused to learn to speak English despite their residence in the UK for many years. As the Swann Report (GB. P. H of C, 1985) noted, some Chinese adults feel strongly that if they give up Chinese they will lose their cultural heritage and be unable to speak freely. But limited English also restricts interaction with the wider community.

Attempts to set up classes for Chinese adults to learn English have generally failed (Clough and Quarmby, 1978). Reviewing language tuition schemes for ethnic minority women, Mobbs (1977) found that few classes had substantial numbers of Chinese women learning English. It seems that as well as the pressures of home work and housework or working in the catering trade, which leaves many Chinese women little time for learning English, they are also naturally self-effacing and many may feel too shy to attempt to participate in language classes (CAG & QCRC, 1979; Lai, 1975). It has also been pointed out that classes are usually held during office hours or in the evening, but such hours are not convenient for those who ply the catering trade (see SCSCRC, 1976; Chan, 1983). Cheung (1975) found that fewer than one-third of his sample had registered for English-language classes held during the evening in local further education colleges, and suggested that they need persuasion to try the course and also to move from beginners' to intermediate grades. He pointed to the importance of the Chinese attending such classes as a group, as those who went alone and encountered difficulties tended to leave. They exhibited a reluctance to speak, both in and out of the classes, and had little opportunity to practice because they spent most of their time with other Chinese. If they moved to other jobs, they frequently dropped out of classes. Cheung reported that an E2L adult tutor had claimed that, although he had taught Chinese students for ten years, none had ever sat for an examination, although some had left after two or three years' attendance at classes speaking confidently. In Lai's (1975) sample only two men in the 24 families had attended English classes for a short time after their arrival in the UK. Two women had also attended classes and four had received some form of home tutoring. However, none of these Chinese, all in their twenties, had found the lessons particularly useful. In addition, the women had experienced child-care problems when trying to attend classes and many felt too shy to do so. Some claimed that they only felt confident amongst other Chinese. Lai noticed that even those who attended classes had a restricted vocabulary.

Many LEAs also operate home tuition schemes, such as that in Liverpool. But often even strenuous efforts over many years have only met with limited success (GB. P. H of C, 1985). There have been suggestions that bilingual Chinese–English teachers should be employed for adult classes (Lai, 1975; Chan, 1983). Although it has been considered controversial to employ bilinguals to teach English, a case quoted by Chan seems to show that the employment of a bilingual Chinese teacher has facilitated communication in the initial stages of teaching E2L to Chinese adults because of the greater understanding of the linguistic problems faced. This has also been acknowledged by the Swann Report which suggested that LEAs should give careful consideration to bilingual teachers for E2L to adults, possibly on a co-operative basis. Some E2L classes now take place within Chinese community centres, as, for example, at Manchester (Powell, 1982) and Liverpool which receive Urban Programme funds. Such locations may seem less forbidding to potential language learners. Evidence from the Department of Education and Science (DES) to the Home Affairs Committee on the Chinese Community in Britain (GB. P. H of C. HAC, 1985) made it clear that although there was an awareness of need for continuing E2L support for Chinese adults, responsibility for provision rests with LEAs. The Report itself noted an absence of overall governmental responsibility for this area, and, on the part of Chinese adults, a lack of time, social contact, poor educational background and lack of awareness of classes as well as the unsuitability of existing provision and the difficulty of learning English: 'Our evidence shows that the widespread failure to learn English has been a severe handicap to the Chinese community and we believe that greater knowledge of English would be of such profound benefit to both individuals and the community that efforts to increase the effectiveness of E2L teaching among the Chinese should be given a high priority.' The Report recommended that E2L classes for Chinese adults should be arranged for Sundays and early week-day afternoons, that bilingual assistants should be increased and that the potential of audio-visual aids should be explored since many families have video recorders to watch programmes from Hong Kong. Research from the DES-sponsored project on the training needs of E2L teachers by the National Association for Teaching English as a Second Language to Adults is expected to give further leads.

It has also been suggested (see, for example, CAG & QCRC, 1979) that classes should be provided in English for Chinese parents whilst their children are learning Chinese in the part-time language classes. Indeed in London 14 per cent of the parents of children attending Chinese classes in the Commission for Racial Equality (CRE) survey spent their time waiting for their children by learning English (Tsow, 1984). Such initiatives seem significant because they can give explicit recognition to the importance of sharing linguistic knowledge and skills and extending communication by developing a partnership in learning on the part of both parents and children: the parents with their knowledge of Chinese dialects but little English, and the children with some knowledge of Chinese and English and increasing skill in English. As with other linguistic minorities, Chinese children have been relied upon to act as interpreters for adult members of the family, especially mothers, and many become proficient in code-switching from English to Cantonese and back into English again with ease (Watson, 1977a). Moreover, in helping their parents to learn English, children may very well be extending their own learning by becoming more conscious of the differences between the two languages, as a case quoted by Garvey and Jackson (1975) shows.

There appears to be little evidence about Chinese parents' attitudes to their children learning English (see also p.231). Clearly their own lack of English may make it difficult for some Chinese parents to help their children directly in acquiring English. However, Cheung (1975) found that as Chinese parents had high hopes for their children in the UK they thought it was particularly important for their children to know English, since they saw their own lack of English as the reason for their restriction to the catering trade and they wanted their children to have the opportunity to choose a wider range of employment. Others thought that their lack of English also restricted them from contact with the wider society. A further reason for their positive attitudes towards their children learning English was that those who were in business on their own account needed someone with fluent English whom they could trust with their business dealings. Indeed Cheung observed that often learning English seemed for these parents the only essential matter in their child's education in the UK, as they felt very ambivalent about the cultural implications of a Western education (see p. 235). The ideal for them would be if their child would speak to them and their other children in Cantonese but also have fluent English.

Generally Chinese parents seem to have a very strong interest in and enthusiasm for their children to learn Chinese. However, for some parents their own lack of education and demands on their time may hinder attempts to teach Chinese to their child. Collins (1957) reported that in Anglo-Chinese families the father placed a great deal of importance on teaching Chinese to his children although, apart from a few phrases, he was generally unsuccessful in doing so. Tsow (1984) found that 62 per cent of the parents whose children attended Chinese language classes claimed that an adult family member taught the child to read and write in Chinese in the home. This was particularly likely to be the case amongst younger parents with only one or two children, and those who had been in the UK for ten years or more. But there was also a strong tendency for parents to consider themselves ill-equipped or unqualified to teach their children – in fact some 41 per cent were effectively not able to do so. Others lacked time and claimed that their children did not co-operate in learning. Ng (1982) also found that Chinese parents did not allow their children to forget Chinese traditions and thought that they needed to acquire Chinese culture and language. But she suggested that even those who took their children to Chinese language classes needed to show more interest in their learning.

One way of gauging Chinese parents' attitudes to Chinese and its perceived significance for their children is to consider their attitudes to their children attending part-time Chinese language classes. (Other aspects of parents' and children's attitudes to classes are reviewed later, see pp.186–8, 197.) It is clear that many parents wish to send their children to these classes to maintain their Chinese cultural identity and traditions. In the CRE study (Tsow, 1984) 78 per cent of 195 parents whose children attended Chinese language classes thought it was important for their children to learn Chinese because they had Chinese origins. A further 13 per cent considered it was important that they should know the Chinese tradition, and four per cent that they should not be Westernized. There was, moreover, almost as great a specific focus on language ability as such: 62 per cent claimed that they should know the mother tongue, 18 per cent that they should be able to write Chinese and 17 per cent that they should be able to read it. A quarter of the parents thought that it was important to learn Chinese to be able to communicate with other Chinese and that it would be particularly useful if their child were to return to Hong Kong. A knowledge of Chinese as useful for translation and knowing more than one language were also seen as significant reasons for learning Chinese by a minority of parents. It is of interest to note that a similar pattern of responses was given by 114 out of 138 parents, whose children did not attend mother-tongue teaching classes, but who would have liked them to do so.

Ng (1982) found that pupils of Chinese origin learning Chinese in language classes had a very positive attitude to Chinese and wanted to learn it. This was the case as much for the UK- as for the Hong Kong-born, but for girls more than boys. In fact Ng suggested that learning Chinese had to be seen as learning a second language for these children. But since the learning of English by Chinese pupils is often regarded as second-language learning in the state education system, this suggests that for some Chinese children there is no true first language. Whilst ideally exposure to both Chinese and English and opportunities for practising both languages could lead to considerable competence in both, even bilingualism, there is also a danger that lack of encouragement or opportunity might mean that some pupils never achieve full powers of expression in either language and may need to operate with a mixed code. The younger children in Ng's survey aged 12 or so had less positive attitudes to Chinese. Most had been born in the UK, considered themselves to be British and did not understand why they had to learn Chinese. Even those who were older realized that Chinese culture had no status in the UK. Ng suggested that attitudes to learning languages are vital to determining success or failure and that Chinese children's attitudes to second-language learning will be a function of their feelings about integration and its prospects in future British society. Some 69 per cent of the adolescents interviewed claimed that the Chinese language gave them a feeling of belonging and that they would feel out of place if they did not speak Chinese with other Chinese people. Seventy-five per cent felt that they would be ashamed if they could not speak the language of their parents' country of origin. Half said that receiving Chinese lessons improved their understanding of what happened at home and wished they could speak Chinese fluently. Moreover, 65 per cent claimed that their parents would not be happy if they always spoke English at home. Yet 61 per cent claimed that Chinese would be of no use to them in the jobs that they would like to do after they left school. Hence these pupils of Chinese origin regarded Chinese as relevant and important in the context of their domestic life but not in terms of their future career. This may go some way to explaining a difference in the degree of enthusiasm between parents and children for attending Chinese classes, as noted in the Swann Report (GB. P. H of C, 1985).

Attitudes to a language, to English or Chinese dialects, may also reveal attitudes towards identity. In comparison with evidence on this matter for pupils of West Indian or Asian origin there is minimal comment on the ways in which pupils of Chinese origin use language to establish an identity. But two interesting cases are cited by Lobo (1978) and Jackson (1979). Lobo mentions some children who, although able to talk Cantonese, refused to speak it every day at home, speaking English even to adult Chinese friends. Only with grandparents and occasional visitors who could not speak any English did they make the effort to talk in Cantonese. Lobo interpreted this as a desire to establish an identity as British, an attitude which may cause distress to some parents. Jackson also reports that within the Chinese family whom he studied in detail the eldest child, aged seven, refused to speak in Chinese at home after beginning school, answering his father in English even when addressed in Chinese.

Refusal to speak the mother tongue at home except when essential, as for example with a non-English-speaking parent, has been noted by many observers. Saifullah Khan (1980), for example, has pointed to the disturbing trend towards a situation whereby the actual dominance of English and loss of the mother tongue can cause considerable communication difficulties between parents and children. This obviously varies from one family to another, depending on the motivation of and opportunity for family members to learn English, the presence of older siblings at school and attitudes and orientation towards British and homeland societies. But the loss of communication is often obvious between the non-English-speaking mother and child in Chinese families. Ladlow (1980) has claimed that some Chinese children have refused to speak Chinese at home because their teachers have told them to speak as much English as possible. By contrast, he suggests that, though parents should be given support to develop English if they feel they wish to do so, Chinese children should be encouraged to speak constantly in Chinese at home, and with their Chinese friends, and to read Chinese books so that they can develop their vocabulary, preserve the mother tongue and communication with the family and be able to participate in the Chinese community in the UK. Ladlow considers that knowledge of two languages should be seen as an advantage, but that some Chinese parents do not speak sufficiently good English to offer linguistic assistance in developing their children's English and might reinforce errors. Though this is admittedly a difficulty, the encouragement which parents can give to their children attempting to learn English can boost their confidence and skill. As a recent study on collaboration between teachers and parents in assisting children's reading has shown (Tizard *et al.*, 1982), ethnic minority parents, including some Chinese with little proficiency in English, had a beneficial effect on their children's reading performance merely by hearing them read in English.

In conclusion, although many of the studies cited in this analysis of Chinese adults' and children's knowledge, use of and attitudes towards Chinese dialects and English are relatively small scale and often involve self-selected samples, nevertheless cumulatively their evidence does permit certain trends to be distinguished. From a research perspective, however, compared with some other ethnic minority pupils, notably those of Asian origin, the linguistic vitality of pupils of Chinese origin has not been a focus of investigation. It is clear that many Chinese adults and parents, especially those involved in the catering trade, have very little English and are solidly Chinese-dialect speaking, though in fact they may be able to communicate in more than one dialect. Nevertheless, there are considerable differences in language knowledge and use according to the educational background and socioeconomic status of adult Chinese, so that those who are students and professionals will demonstrate a much greater range of language knowledge, including considerable competence in English. Yet in terms of the present generation of pupils of Chinese origin such adults will be in a minority as parents. Thus Chinese dialects, especially Cantonese, are dominant in the home, particularly in communication between parents and children. All pupils of Chinese origin will have some facility in a Chinese dialect, though it is unlikely to be more than one, but even though they will speak such a language they are less likely to be able to read or write it. Indeed it seems probable that they will only acquire literacy skills to any degree if they attend Chinese language classes.

Although Chinese dialects predominate in the home at present, there is considerable evidence of use of both Chinese and English and a considerable increase in English usage, especially by pupils of Chinese origin with siblings and friends. Pupils of Chinese origin operate in both Chinese and English in their daily lives, though the point at which English may become the dominant language, and in exactly which context and when, the research evidence is inadequate to demonstrate. For it is clear from teachers' assessments of the English of pupils of Chinese origin that many are not rated as being fluent and that their English is likely to continue to need special attention for the length of their schooling. On the other hand, it is important to stress that pupils of Chinese origin do not form a homogeneous group in terms of language knowledge, use and attitudes. There are many differences in competence in speaking, reading and writing in Chinese and English, which will be affected especially by birthplace, education and socioeconomic background. Thus, tentatively, it appears that Hong Kong-born Chinese who have received substantial schooling there are likely to have their Chinese dialect dominant in all three forms, though in English their literacy may exceed their oracy. The UK-born pupils of Chinese origin tend to enter school being almost exclusively Chinese-speaking, though their knowledge of English may vary according to whether they have older siblings already in school, and the extent to which their parents can speak some English. As they progress through school and their proficiency in speaking, reading and writing English grows, English may become their dominant language and, unless they receive tuition in their mother tongue, it may not develop beyond the linguistic level of the home. Generally pupils of Chinese origin will display a range of facility in both languages, so that whereas by their secondary schooling some may appear fluent in both, others may have a greater proficiency in one, and some may still lack the competence to express themselves adequately in either. It is important, therefore, to pay specific attention to the available research evidence on the language needs of pupils of Chinese origin, both with respect to additional teaching of English and for mother-tongue maintenance.

Teaching English as a second language
In so far as pupils of Chinese origin have been singled out for particular attention within the educational system they, like many other linguistic minority pupils, have often been seen as requiring particular assistance with learning English as a precondition to their learning as such. As the previous sub-section has demonstrated, almost all pupils of Chinese origin come from a Chinese-language background which predominates in the home. Thus most pupils of Chinese origin, even the UK-born, will have very little, if any, English when they start school since they will have had few opportunities to learn English other than from older siblings or the media unless they have attended some form of nursery or perhaps child-minding provision. Moreover, during their school years it seems that they are often unlikely to have opportunities to extend their English out of the school environment, except with siblings and friends (see pp.143–6).

The lack of English of many pupils of Chinese origin has been evident to teachers from the time when they first began to arrive in schools, irrespective of whether this has been at the normal starting age or as they have entered this country at a later age. This has presented difficulties in two particular ways: first, in terms of the organization of arrangements for teaching English to such pupils since they are often widely dispersed in small numbers and in different schools over a large area; and secondly, because Chinese dialects and English are so obviously different types of languages this may have necessitated special and distinctive attention to be given to the teaching of English to Chinese pupils. Following an outline of research evidence on teachers' assessments of the need of pupils of Chinese origin for additional English teaching, this sub-section reviews the organizational arrangements made for E2L teaching to Chinese pupils, their particular difficulties in learning English and the kinds of learning strategies and materials which are available. Provision for and attitudes of Chinese adults to E2L teaching have been reviewed above (see pp.152–5).

Need for E2L teaching
It is clear that those for whom the mother tongue is a Chinese dialect may have more problems than are usual in learning a new language when they come to learn English. For example, Chinese is monosyllabic and does not use inflections; it lacks many consonants, especially clusters or final consonants; there is no declension or a rigid tense or time sequence; the printed form is in vertical lines from right to left; the written form is constructed of strokes comprising ideograms rather than an alphabet; the written form is different from the spoken form for Cantonese and Hakka speakers; and, perhaps most significantly, the linguistic form embodies a different system of thought (see Ladlow, n.d.l; Lynn, 1982). There is a need for teachers to have access to information not only about the cultural background of pupils of Chinese origin, but also the nature of the differences between Chinese dialects and English in order that they might be aware of the difficulties faced by Chinese speakers with the learning of English. For pupils of Chinese origin E2L teaching has not only had the function of language instruction as such, but often also has had a wider educational purpose of providing an introduction to British culture and serving to develop their social and life skills. The broader educational function of E2L teaching may be of particular relevance and importance for older Chinese pupils arriving at some time during their secondary education, as not only will their knowledge of English and experience of British ways of life be limited, but their subject knowledge may be behind that which would normally be expected for pupils of their age. Yet it is likely to have no less relevance for those who have been born in this country, starting their schooling, perhaps, with a knowledge of the alphabet, but otherwise living within a distinctively Chinese ethos at home.

Research evidence based on teachers' assessments of the English-language knowledge and proficiency of their pupils of Chinese origin has shown clearly that there is a need for continuous English-language tuition for many such pupils throughout their school lives. This is evident from the investigations which have taken place in recent years within the ILEA (see also pp.140–1). Rosen and Burgess (1980) found that within a small sample of Cantonese-speaking pupils aged 11–12 their Cantonese was dominant, fewer than half being rated as fluent speakers of English. Even then an overwhelming majority still incorporated some Cantonese features into their English. Similarly, the ILEA language census of 1978 (ILEA, 1979) provided clear evidence of the need of pupils of Chinese origin for additional English teaching. According to their teachers, more than half of Cantonese/ Chinese speakers in the ILEA required further help with English. Indeed by the time of the 1981 survey (ILEA, 1982), in which assessments were based on a finer categorization of proficiency in English, the proportion of Chinese-language speakers not yet fluent in English and therefore, by implication, requiring some additional help with their English had risen to nearly two-thirds. This proportion remained the same in the 1983 language survey. In comparison with other language speakers the figures suggested particular difficulties for pupils of Chinese origin.

Although records of Chinese pupils receiving E2L tuition are generally inadequate in publicly available documentation, indications of numbers can be gained from some research reports and the records of one LEA language centre. For example, almost all the 20 Chinese pupils in secondary education in York interviewed by Cheung (1975) were receiving additional English tuition in small groups. Clough and Quarmby (1978) recorded that during a visit to an ILEA language centre pupils of Chinese origin formed the largest group within the centre, numbering some 35 out of 110 11–16 year-olds in 1975. Fitchett (1976) cited figures to show that in Derby from 1971 to 1975 some 44 pupils of Chinese origin, mostly directly from Hong Kong, entered a language centre. By far the best available records are those compiled and kindly supplied by David Ladlow at the English Language Centre, Liverpool, from summer 1969 to autumn 1984, especially as (according to Fong, 1981) over 90 per cent of Chinese children arriving from Hong Kong receive special English tuition at the language centre. Figures in Table 35 show that the number of pupils of Chinese origin receiving E2L lessons in any one term has always been high, and that there is usually a higher proportion of pupils of Chinese origin than pupils from other ethnic minority groups. In the autumn of 1983, for example, there were 18 Chinese pupils at infant level receiving special English tuition in withdrawal groups taught by peripatetic teachers in their own schools, nine at junior level were attending the language centre in the mornings and 27 at secondary level were taught either by peripatetic teachers in their own schools or attended the language centre full time. The figures overall may also give some indication of the numbers of pupils of Chinese origin who pass through schools in Liverpool. These Chinese pupils can be dispersed in several schools. Other figures quoted by Lynn (1982) show that in the summer term, 1981, for example, 15 junior pupils were in eight schools as were 15 secondary-age Chinese pupils. It is of interest to note, moreover, that the number of Chinese pupils receiving E2L lessons is declining from 118–137 in summer 1973 to 70–136 in spring 1984 and the corresponding proportion of Chinese pupils has fallen from 75–80 to 45–50 per cent in the last decade.

Table 35: Pupils receiving lessons in English as a second language: Liverpool, 1969–84

Term	Schools			Pupils			Chinese (and latterly Vietnamese)	Nationalities	Teachers
	Primary	*Secondary*	*Total*	*Primary*	*Secondary*	*Total*			
Summer 1969	4	4	8	15	29	44	19	8	1
Autumn 1969	4	6	10	25	72	97	69	7	2
Spring 1970	4	5	9	28	69	97	73	7	2
Summer 1970	4	5	9	27	58	85	65	6	2
Autumn 1970	4	3	7	22	41	63	52	4	2
Spring 1971	6	2	8	23	45	68	59	4	2
Summer 1971	8	2	10	42	45	87	73	6	2
Autumn 1971	5	7	12	47	73	120	102	7	2
Spring 1972	4	7	11	47	71	118	102	5	3
Summer 1972	8	6	14	61	63	124	106	9	3
Autumn 1972	8	6	14	66	56	122	104	8	3
Spring 1973	10	6	16	76	62	138	119	9	3
Summer 1973	10	7	17	77	60	137	118	10	3
Autumn 1973	8	9	17	81	91	172	146	12	6
Spring 1974	9	8	17	62	79	141	128	8	6
Summer 1974	9	10	19	61	70	131	118	8	6
Autumn 1974	15	11	26	65	65	130	107	8	7
Spring 1975	16	6	22	89	53	142	108	12	7
Summer 1975	18	9	27	108	58	166	121	14	7
Autumn 1975	18	11	29	100	73	173	131	11	7
Spring 1976	20	11	31	87	77	164	139	10	6
Summer 1976	20	10	30	71	78	149	128	7	7
Autumn 1976	18	8	26	87	49	136	100	14	7
Spring 1977	16	7	23	81	47	128	93	11	7
Summer 1977	13	9	22	75	50	125	96	10	7
Autumn 1977	15	10	25	86	76	162	115	15	7
Spring 1978	17	10	27	80	64	144	103	14	7
Summer 1978	16	9	25	78	65	143	97	15	7
Autumn 1978	24	11	35	76	65	141	94	19	7
Spring 1979	25	11	36	87	63	150	99	20	7
Summer 1979	25	10	35	75	65	140	91	15	7
Autumn 1979	33	10	43	81	49	130	86	16	7
Spring 1980	29	7	36	79	51	130	80	15	7
Summer 1980	29	6	35	91	49	144	88	17	
Autumn 1980	24	5	29	83	53	136	78	23	
Spring 1981	23	9	32	82	54	136	85	20	
Summer 1981	23	11	34	88	49	137	86	15	
Autumn 1981	31	8	39	109	50	159	89	15	
Spring 1982	28	9	37	100	46	146	88	14	
Summer 1982	31	9	40	105	52	157	93	13	
Autumn 1982	30	8	38	111	51	162	89	14	
Spring 1983	26	7	33	112	48	160	83	18	
Summer 1983	30	7	37	115	52	167	86	20	
Autumn 1983	27	8	35	87	54	141	68	19	
Spring 1984	27	12	39	80	56	136	70	16	
Summer 1984	20	10	30	77	55	132	61	16	
Autumn 1984	30	7	37	99	52	151	61	19	

Source: Adapted from Lynn, 1982, p.24; and information from Mr D. Ladlow, English Language Centre, Liverpool.

Organizational arrangements for E2L teaching
The arrangements made for E2L teaching for pupils of Chinese origin have not been well documented compared with the provision made for other ethnic minority pupils, especially those of Asian origin. But it is clear that in addition to normal class teaching there has been a diversity of approach ranging from *ad hoc* arrangements, withdrawal groups, remedial placement and peripatetic teaching to tuition in language centres. Arrangements have often been affected by the dispersal of the Chinese. Some Chinese children may be found in a school which otherwise has no ethnic minority pupils or special arrangements for E2L support. Some indication of the effect of various types of E2L organization on pupils of Chinese origin may be gauged from the literature.

Arrangements may be on a very *ad hoc* basis. For example, because of his contacts with the Chinese families in York, Cheung (1975) became involved in teaching English to a few young children who had just started school. There were otherwise no special arrangements for giving them E2L tuition as they were so few in number. The case study of Tommy, described in detail in Chapter 7 of Garvey and Jackson's (1975) report, confirms the existence of *ad hoc* arrangements and demonstrates the progress which can be made and the benefits to be derived from individual tuition. Little and Willey's (1983) national survey of 70 LEAs in 1979 revealed a continuing diversity of approach to providing E2L teaching for pupils of Chinese origin where they were in small numbers in schools. They quote the example of one LEA which would only fund the travelling expenses of two voluntary Chinese-speaking tutors to teach a non-English-speaking Chinese pupil.

Townsend (1971), who some ten years earlier had described the arrangements made by LEAs for special English teaching, noted that pupils of Chinese origin sometimes constituted very small groups where part-time withdrawal arrangements within the school were in operation. In the mid-1970s in some schools pupils of Chinese origin continued to be withdrawn from certain lessons for extra tuition in English (SCSCRC, 1976). Some of these withdrawal groups may depend on the visits of peripatetic teachers. But since these and other teachers are so hard-pressed, it is necessary to keep the amount of tuition received under review to ensure that it is sufficient to develop the child's proficiency and understanding most efficiently. In Liverpool provision has developed, so that full-time teaching takes place in a language centre, with peripatetic teaching as an important alternative or supplementary arrangement. In 1969 two peripatetic teachers were appointed to take withdrawal classes in a number of junior and secondary schools which included pupils of Chinese origin, and they also gave advice to teachers in schools where classes could not be arranged. The work was extended to include infant schools when a third teacher was appointed in 1972 and short, regular withdrawal classes for infants in their own schools are still taken by a peripatetic teacher who tests the children and also gives advice to class teachers. Peripatetic teachers also undertake follow-up work in secondary schools with pupils who have already received some tuition at the language centre up to the second stage of E2L. Where possible, these pupils are prepared for the CSE examination in English as a second language.

Sometimes when pupils of Chinese origin receive all their schooling in ordinary schools, they are placed in remedial streams in order to give them additional help with English. Although there is no evidence on the extent to which this takes place, it has widely and for a long time been regarded as unsuitable (Townsend and Brittan, 1972; CAG and QCRC, 1979) as the example of Tommy, quoted by Garvey and Jackson (1975), shows. Pupils of Chinese origin may lack proficiency in English, though they may not necessarily be slow learners, and placement in remedial streams may have a particularly depressing psychological effect and reduce their motivation and retard their progress in learning (SCSCRC, 1976).

Yet it has also frequently been argued that it is important for pupils learning E2L to take their place within an ordinary school in order that they may mix not just with other overseas language speakers, but the full range of children, so that there are opportunities to socialize and to practise English with their peers. This may be particularly important for pupils of Chinese origin in view of their lack of opportunity to practise English outside school (Fong, 1981). Indeed Jones (1980), who visited some schools with larger concentrations of Chinese children in Soho and Liverpool which made specialist teaching possible, reported that the Chinese pupils themselves claimed that they learned English more quickly when they were more integrated in the ordinary school, as when in groups of Chinese they conversed in their Chinese dialect whenever possible. It has also been argued (SCSCRC, 1976; Lynn, 1982) that it is important that Chinese pupils should be in the mainstream in order to maximize the development of their understanding of British culture and society through the medium of the school.

Many LEAs maintain language centres which tend to focus on the development of linguistic skills and will always have a large proportion of overseas language speakers. In Liverpool the provision of a language centre in 1973 with six teachers enabled some 60 children or so who attended different schools, but who were at similar stages of learning English, to be taught together and in suitable classes. Such arrangements are now made for some 30–40 junior pupils from some 20–30 schools who attend morning sessions, returning to their own schools for the afternoon, and full-time attendance for about 30 secondary pupils, usually recent arrivals, who are then subsequently placed in secondary schools or further education colleges. Attendance may vary from a few weeks to over a year and usually depends on age, so that whereas younger children may stay there two years before they are sufficiently able to take their place within the ordinary school, senior-age pupils may remain there for about four terms (Lynn, 1982). But even in such a favourable environment there may not be sufficient individual attention because of the lack of teaching staff, as there are usually some 15–20 pupils learning E2L in a class (Fong, 1981). The language centre in Liverpool in action is described incidentally by Hopkins (1977). There are difficulties in assessing the proficiency of pupils and when the time is appropriate for them to be transferred from the language centre and integrated into ordinary schools.

Lynn (1982) argued that it would be preferable for the language centre to be placed within a school, so that there might be some continuity in the pupil's experience of schooling through familiarity with the school's location, ethos and social environment, thus obviating the need for further readjustment. In fact the Language Centre in Liverpool was re-sited in January 1982 within a comprehensive school. But according to Lynn, when pupils transfer from the language centre, they are then placed in remedial classes within schools and still have to adjust again later to the ordinary classroom situation. This must serve to emphasize differences between pupils whose first language is or is not English and to make their adjustment doubly difficult. On the other hand, others involved in E2L teaching have suggested that there is a need for all requiring E2L teaching to attend a language centre as a matter of course, and that there should be an ongoing programme of basic studies for those who have experienced an interrupted school career and a more advanced class for those who might be more academically able. Again others have argued that 8–10 year-olds requiring E2L teaching might spend all their time in separate language classes, apart from being attached to their own schools for various social activities, and only returning to their classes in the term prior to transfer to secondary education. In this way it has been suggested that children learning English should benefit from a much more structured approach than is available within the ordinary class situation and have a greater exposure to written material. It appears that there is a case for re-examining E2L arrangements for Chinese pupils. The recent Home Affairs Committee Report (GB. P. H of C. HAC, 1985) recommended that:

LEAs should examine their language provision, including methods of identifying children needing it and monitoring its effectiveness, so as to ensure that pupils become proficient in English as soon as possible and none leave school without proficiency; that the DES provide authorities with advice and assistance to that end; and that the Inspectorate make it a priority to investigate the effectiveness of language provision at all stages of schooling.

The report pronounced itself against 'remedial' approaches, advocated the appointment of peripatetic teachers for continuing support, greater resources for nursery teaching and using the mother tongue, and Chinese teachers funded under Section 11 (see pp.173–4).

Finally, it is interesting to note some supplementary English classes described by Jones (1980) for some Chinese adolescents aged 14–16-plus who had been in the UK about four years. Although they spoke English, they needed additional help with their English in order to be able to attempt examinations. The same organization also ran Chinese classes. English classes included discussion, some formal teaching and written work. Indeed their Chinese teachers were of the opinion that more individual tuition was required within the state education system in order for such pupils to augment their proficiency in English. The Home Affairs Committee (GB. P. H of C. HAC, 1985) also reports that for the last 13 years or so the Burnage Chinese Group in Manchester has run a supplementary school for some 20 pupils of varying ages needing individual attention and exam-coaching in English. A 97 per cent success rate has been claimed at O-level and CSE. Birmingham Community Centre is also reported to have plans for a similar venture.

Difficulties in learning English
Although it had been realized that Chinese dialect speakers had particular difficulties in acquiring proficiency in English, until recently the nature and extent of Chinese language 'interference' had not been described in a way which would be accessible and helpful to E2L teachers. The need for reliable and substantial information on the differences between Chinese and English as well as appropriate language learning materials was regularly asserted through the 1970s (see CAG & QCRC, 1979). Tsow (1980b), in particular, argued that attention should be focussed on the differences between Chinese and English – differences which often go beyond the linguistic to the conceptual. Pupils of Chinese origin have thus to learn a new system of thought as well as a new language when learning English. Difficulties may be particularly great for Chinese adolescents for, as Cheung (1975) reported, such pupils may operate at a conceptual level in Chinese, needing first to absorb material in their native dialect then translating their responses into English. However, this makes for problems with both understanding and expression. He found there were particular difficulties with understanding such concepts as 'how', 'what', 'when' and 'why', and that explanation in the pupil's own language was of assistance. Similarly, Jones (I., 1979) noted that a natural tendency of Chinese adolescents to think in Chinese before writing in English caused characteristic grammatical errors. But Tsow (1980a) has suggested that a Chinese child's syntactical mistakes in English may be explored to illuminate the cultural context of language: 'The process of transposition from one mode of cultural thinking into the linguistic pattern of another merits a positive approach in education because it illustrates the extent to which different cultures, and their languages, represent different

ways of "seeing things"' (p.6). The need to take account of the cultural context of language with respect to Chinese–English interference may well not have been fully realized to date.

Instead the focus of attention has been upon particular linguistic difficulties in second-language learning for pupils of Chinese origin. During the 1970s it was gradually recognized that a greater awareness of the structure of the Chinese dialects of pupils of Chinese origin would assist E2L teachers and a number of small-scale guides to the differences between Chinese and English were produced (Hill, 1976; Jones, I., 1979; Ladlow, n.d.1, n.d.2, 1980). The Nuffield Foundation's project, established in 1977, was the first research attempt to explore such differences systematically. The resulting guide for teachers which provides information about the culture and history of Chinese-speaking pupils, published materials of use in English teaching, and detailed analyses of differences between written English and spoken Cantonese became available in 1981. The book includes in its appendices the Hong Kong Education Department's recommended syllabus for English-language teaching in secondary schools and the structured syllabus for primary school teachers. These are helpful in indicating the kind of language teaching which Chinese pupils who have arrived in Britain during their adolescence would have been likely to have experienced in Hong Kong. It is emphasized, however, that since most teachers in Hong Kong are not native English speakers, Chinese pupils may be more proficient in reading and writing than listening or speaking and may need greater practice in oral work. This is borne out by Gibbons (1982) and by Lee (in ILEA: English Centre, 1979).

Some common difficulties which appear consistently in the literature on linguistic aspects of the education of pupils of Chinese origin are worth briefly mentioning in general here. Ladlow (1980) noted that the lack of conversational ability demonstrated by many Chinese pupils from rural areas of Hong Kong is an additional difficulty during their learning of English. In this situation knowledge of the child's background is essential in order to offer the right kind of help. Undue pressure to speak should not be brought to bear on children during their early months in school in England, whether they are young children starting school or recent arrivals from Hong Kong, as a period of reorientation and listening is necessary. Both Ladlow and participants in conferences about the education of Chinese children (see CAG & QCRC, 1979) have stressed the danger of referring such children for speech therapy, as has sometimes been the case.

On pronunciation Ladlow's (n.d.1) contrastive analysis is particularly instructive showing that there are especial difficulties for Chinese dialect speakers learning English as Chinese has fewer consonants, especially final consonants (e.g. 'can't') and no clusters of consonants, which tends to lead to the splitting of English words into separate syllables. Not so much difficulty is experienced with vowels, except for the difference between long and short vowels (Hill, 1976). But some English sounds (e.g. the difference between 'l' and 'r' and between 'f' and 'v', and with no Cantonese equivalent) require considerable effort to master. So there is a tendency to compromise with approximations (Jones, 1980). As Cantonese is monosyllabic a small range of possible words are distinguished by tones which differentiate meaning rather than the grammatical structure of statements or questions in English (Hill, 1976; Ladlow, n.d.1). This frequently results initially in a lack of intonation in spoken English (Jones, I., 1979).

But grammar, too, can be difficult for pupils of Chinese origin to master. In contrast to English, Chinese has no inflexions or declensions in terms of plurals, nouns, adjectives and personal pronouns (Ladlow, n.d.1) or to denote comparatives, subject, object and gender, and frequently lacks indefinite and definite articles (Hill, 1976). Moreover, several writers have pointed to the lack of conjugation of verbs ·which entails particular difficulties in forming tenses in English. A typical mistake would be the use of the infinitive instead of the gerund (Nuffield Foundation, 1981; Jones, 1980). Word order also presents problems as it differs from that used in English. Observation of set word ordering is the only way to make communication meaningful in Cantonese. This is illustrated in a particularly helpful comparison of written English word order and spoken Cantonese in Chapter 3 of the Nuffield Foundation guide, so that teachers can see the points of mother-tongue interference experienced by Cantonese-speaking pupils. However, written Chinese in the Mandarin form differs further. Whilst pointing out that Chinese dialects cannot be categorized into parts of speech so neatly as English, Jones (I., 1979) supplies a useful analysis of particular grammatical difficulties with illustrations of the English of pupils of Chinese origin. The SCSCRC report (1976) mentioned a lively debate between E2L teachers as to whether Chinese pupils would benefit from the use of grammar exercises and structural drills contained in grammar books such as they may well have been used to in Hong Kong, or whether a more situational approach and active use of English would be more effective in E2L learning.

Another potential area of weakness is that of vocabulary (SCSCRC, 1976) which may be limited, though sufficient for everyday use (Jones, 1980). In contrast to the adoption of words in English from many different roots (Latin, Greek and international words), more words in Chinese are derived from Chinese roots only (Ladlow, n.d.1). Chinese also lacks abstract terms, so that the Chinese child may have difficulty in expressing the abstract concepts of English (Jones, I., 1979). A lack of vocabulary shows up particularly in reading, as although an attempt may be made to analyse long words, lack of knowledge of the meaning of key words in any passage will reduce comprehension (Garvey and Jackson, 1975). This also is an area where extra help is needed (Fitchett, 1976). It may be improved by rote word learning, thus capitalizing upon traditional Chinese skills, or by increased reading (Jones, 1980). But it may sometimes also be difficult to assess comprehension as pupils of Chinese origin may be reluctant to 'lose face' by admitting that they do not understand (Lynn, 1982). Mixing in the context of the ordinary school may increase vocabulary considerably, so that understanding may be much greater than ability to speak (Garvey and Jackson, 1975).

Learning to read English may necessitate eye training for the older Chinese pupil due to the difference in the direction in which the two scripts run (Jones, I., 1979; Lynn, 1982). A child who has learned to read and write Chinese, thereby having a developed visual memory, may find the 'look and say' method of learning English particularly helpful, especially in the initial stages of reading (Ladlow, n.d.1; Jones, I., 1979). Phonic work may be introduced at a later stage, and although it may take a long time to grasp, it may have beneficial effects on accent (Fitchett, 1976). Memorization skills used in learning Chinese may also be transferred by literate Chinese to the acquisition of English spelling, though this may result in a failure to see links between sound and spelling (Hill, 1976). Ladlow (n.d.2) considers it important for teachers to try to learn some Cantonese for Chinese cultural and historical terms, as pupils may not recognize these when transliterated into English. He provides an appendix on the spelling and pronunciation of Cantonese words to assist teachers introducing aspects of Chinese culture into their teaching.

The written form of Chinese, composed of separate horizontal, vertical and slanting strokes and with bending hooks, has a slight pictorial or phonetic element (Lynn, 1982; Ladlow, n.d.1). It is obviously very different in appearance and in its written construction from the alphabet. Jones (I., 1979) has suggested that Chinese pupils who can write Mandarin may well need practice in drawing patterns before learning to write English. But some pupils may find writing English relatively easy because of their practice in this skill in Hong Kong schools (Lee in ILEA: English Centre, 1979). Chinese education has traditionally emphasized the skills of calligraphy and Chinese pupils may transfer such skills to writing English, learning to copy neatly, though possibly without real understanding (Hill, 1976). Pupils may prefer to copy from the board in class rather than to engage in verbal exchange with the teacher (Lynn, 1982) and may copy their work over and over again at home in order to assist learning (Garvey and Jackson, 1975). Finally, developing listening skills may be particularly important during the early stages of language learning as it may have a significant influence on speaking ability (Ladlow, 1980).

Learning English as a second language is likely to be significantly affected by the attitudes of pupils of Chinese origin to English, the learning opportunities which they have, the strategies used to teach them, available teaching materials and the awareness and skills of teachers. The attitudes of

Chinese pupils to learning English are likely to be particularly crucial in determining the level of proficiency which they acquire. Ng (1982) has suggested that Chinese pupils' attitudes towards English may well be a function of their feelings about their social integration and the prospects which exist for social and economic integration. But Tsow (1980b) has also importantly pointed out that the language-learning environment must be encouraging, otherwise the child may be caught in a conflict situation between the attitude of the school towards his mother tongue and his parents' attitudes towards the learning of English. In other words, each must be sympathetic towards the other in order for learning to occur. Chinese students in secondary schools in York, some recent arrivals, others resident up to four years, with completed primary schooling in Hong Kong said that they found English particularly difficult. They also wished they had arrived in the UK earlier in order to have a better subject knowledge (Cheung, 1975). Both Lai (1975) and Fong (1981) also reported that students had particular difficulties with English and disliked it. Also Cheung (1975) quoted a teacher in further education who, over the course of ten years, had taught English to 70 Chinese. He claimed that they were particularly work-oriented and that English was learnt solely for the practical needs of work and finding their way in the country, not with the aim of achieving any intrinsic competence or gaining a qualification. On the other hand, those adolescents reported by Jones (1980) to be attending supplementary English language classes even though they were helping their parents to run catering establishments, recognized their need for additional English tuition in order to succeed in examinations which might allow them to compete in the labour market for jobs outside catering.

Pupils of Chinese origin observed in the Liverpool Language Centre have been judged to be less assertive and inquisitive than other ethnic minority children, so that their reserve and timidity often makes them inconspicuous in class (Fong, 1981). They tended to be unwilling to contribute in class and to speak only when explicitly asked a question by a teacher. It has been suggested that Chinese children may not like to assert themselves as it may mean 'losing face' and that the Chinese concept of education is much more passive (see pp.272–4). This style of learning makes it difficult to assess language competence (Ladlow quoted by Lynn, 1982; Fong, 1981). Indeed, in Ladlow's view, based on over 15 years' experience of teaching English to pupils of Chinese origin, they tend to be slower in speaking and understanding English than children from other ethnic backgrounds (Lynn, 1982). Teachers in one ILEA school with more than 50 per cent Chinese pupils also claimed that they were slower in learning English compared with other ethnic minority pupils (Lai, 1975). Fitchett (1976) noted similar opinions but claimed that, in his experience at the English Language Centre in Derby, Chinese children responded as well as other ethnic minority pupils, though perhaps less obviously so. The kind of attitude towards learning displayed by pupils of Chinese origin may affect the assessments which teachers make of their competence in comparison with other E2L learners.

But it has also been suggested that the particularly strong family and cultural influence of Chinese pupils' homes, in which parents often speak little English and offer limited opportunities and support for speaking English, is likely to be a factor in influencing the development of proficiency in English (Lai, 1975; SCSCRC, 1976; Fong, 1981). Such factors suggest that pupils of Chinese origin may well be subject to certain tensions engendered by a differential attitude between home and school towards the learning of English and the maintenance of their Chinese mother tongue. If Ng (1982) is correct, the perception of this mismatch in attitude may lead to emotional distress which may serve to hinder effective language development, in both Chinese and English.

It is important for particular teaching materials and strategies to be developed for E2L teaching to pupils of Chinese origin, especially perhaps, as the Swann Report has observed, for materials which can be used by teachers with only one or two Chinese pupils and no specialist E2L support. The Nuffield Foundation guide (1981) makes specific suggestions for language-learning programmes for Chinese children, depending on whether they are to be taught in a multiracial class, language centre or withdrawal group, and according to their age and level of attainment. Moreover, the literature suggests that pupils of Chinese origin are likely to need continuing support with English language throughout their school lives and across all subjects of the curriculum (see SCSCRC, 1976). Although the Nuffield guide stressed that teachers should use as many written and visual materials as possible which relate to the cultural and geographical background of pupils of Chinese origin, from the list which it cites it appears that there is a shortage of such teaching materials, especially in so far as pupils of Chinese origin are shown in a British context (see pp.289–94). Evans (1981) recommended the Bradford Keystone Infant Language Scheme which includes some illustrative material of Chinese children but noted that the Schools Council's 'Scope' series does not deal with specific language difficulties of Chinese-speaking pupils. However, Evans also mentioned that teachers of newly arrived Vietnamese pupils were constructing a 'survival' manual of trilingual information sheets (English, Vietnamese, Chinese) relating to daily needs in social situations in Britain which could form a basis for class discussion. One of the earlier curriculum development projects, the Bilingual Education Project set up in 1977 at the Centre for Urban Educational Studies (CUES), has produced the *World in a City* materials (CUES, 1982), described by Wright (1980). These aim to build on the mother tongue of recently arrived secondary-age pupils receiving E2L help for a large part of the school week, so that they may learn through the simultaneous presentation of material in their first language and English.

Amongst the seven languages covered is Chinese. The materials are suitable for use in various learning situations – individual, in pairs, in the mainstream class, in withdrawal groups – and provide survival information in the area of humanities, and social and integrated studies on, for example, aspects of family life, religion and employment, practice work in particular skills and comprehension questions. The ILEA has produced the 'First Few Weeks' series of booklets for use by teachers, parents and children providing vocabulary for coping with day to day communication in, amongst other languages, Chinese and English, available from the Learning Materials Service (LMS). The BBC has also included some material in Cantonese in the schools TV series *You and Me*, stories in seven languages and English for four- and five-year-olds (audio cassettes available) in the *Mother Tongue Song and Story* radio series for four- to seven-year-olds (booklets available), and in the *Minority Languages: Magazine 1985* radio programmes for adolescents (teachers' notes available). However, generally relatively little attention has been given specifically to including Chinese in E2L materials.

Greater emphasis has been given to E2L approaches for linguistic minority pupils as a whole and more recently to supporting children's bilingualism in the mainstream at the primary level. Again the ILEA and the erstwhile Schools Council have been primarily involved in these curricular developments. The early Second Language in the Primary School Project from 1975 in the ILEA was concerned to develop materials to support learning English through collaborative learning in phased learning activities (video cassette, teachers' book and story-book available from LMS). The Bilingual Under Fives Project from 1978 aimed to provide the bilingual schoolchild with opportunities to communicate in his mother tongue in school and to involve parents and siblings in a task and activity-oriented programme (materials and teachers' book available from LMS). The Schools Council Language in the Multicultural Primary Classroom Project (1981–3) devised strategies linking language growth with conceptual development across the curriculum, based on the enriching contribution of bilingual pupils to the education of all the class (teachers' guide available). Part of the work of the Schools Council/EC Mother Tongue Project (1981–5) has focussed on developing a handbook for monolingual teachers, *All our Languages* (Houlton, 1985), outlining strategies for supporting classroom language diversity across the curriculum by working with parents and local communities and developing resources, especially taped stories in pupils' mother tongues. Other useful sources are: *Supporting Children's Bilingualism* (Houlton and Willey, 1983) which includes a list of recent projects; an annotated bibliography of materials supporting E2L learning (Hester *et al.*, 1977); Brown's (1979) book on the young bilingual child; Twitchin and Demuth's (1981) chapters on mother tongue (Chapter 12) and E2L (Chapter 13); and publications from the National Council for Mother-Tongue Teaching and Centre for Information on Language Teaching.

The awareness of teachers of English language needs of pupils of Chinese origin is obviously a crucial factor in successful development of proficiency. The attitudes of teachers may vary considerably, from those reported by Cheung (1975) who did not understand why such pupils were not taught English at home by their parents, to those in language centres whom Lai (1975) found to know much more about the pupils of Chinese origin and to have a better relationship with them. But in general it seems that there is a need to raise the consciousness of teachers about pupils of Chinese origin, their cultural traditions and their contemporary situation as a minority group in Britain, both in initial and in-service training courses. There is still a need to develop the sensitivity of teachers to the use of language in classrooms and its influence on learning (SCSCRC, 1976) as well as the specific training of more teachers of E2L directed towards the needs of pupils of Chinese origin (Lynn, 1982). A survey in 1982 (Craft and Atkins, 1983) on provision by teacher training institutions for courses in teaching minority languages revealed that the response had instead been to offer a range of E2L courses. Whilst student teachers were likely to emerge from ITT with some awareness of linguistic diversity in schools, they were much less likely to be trained to offer language support across the curriculum or strategies for working in multilingual classrooms. Initial teacher training courses which involve a multicultural element in which pupils of Chinese origin feature specifically may be few and far between. However, Little and Willey (1983) reported that one LEA with a low concentration of ethnic minority pupils had started to consider how to provide an in-service course for teachers on the problems of teaching English to Chinese children. The DES evidence to the Home Affairs Committee (HAC) (GB. P. H of C. HAC, 1985) also reveals that HMI have run two training courses on the Chinese, the second of which, in 1982, focussed on the Cantonese language.

Another traditionally controversial area, deserving of further exploration, is the employment of bilingual Chinese teachers to teach English to pupils of Chinese origin. They may be able to facilitate explanations of different linguistic structures and to assist those pupils whose subject knowledge and skills may be well developed but who cannot communicate with their teachers (Cheung, 1975; CAG & QCRC, 1979; Rathbone and Graham, 1983) (see also pp.297–8). A Commission for Racial Equality (CRE) survey of mother-tongue teaching in LEAs revealed that only one or two developed Cantonese as a medium for teaching E2L (Tsow, 1983b). The DES evidence to the HAC acknowledges that research suggests that in the nursery and early primary years children whose mother tongue is used in the classroom learn English more quickly and make more rapid progress with schoolwork. Using Chinese at this level depends on the number of Chinese pupils and the availability of fluent teachers. If teachers are available, applications for grants can be made under Section 11 as ILEA has done to support two full- and one part-time teacher of Chinese to work in the mainstream (GB. P. H of C. HAC, 1985). In conclusion, this review of the research evidence and literature concerning provision for E2L teaching for pupils of Chinese origin has revealed a considerable need for attention to be given to specific ways in which such pupils may be encouraged to develop greater proficiency in English throughout their school lives. Even where specific arrangements exist to focus on the initial stages of English-language learning the teacher–pupil ratio may be inadequate, suitable teaching materials may be lacking and E2L teachers may need to have more specialized knowledge of the particular difficulties which Chinese pupils face in learning English because of the considerable differences between the two languages. These difficulties would appear to be greater than those normally experienced by other ethnic minority pupils learning English as a second language. They may be additionally compounded by the learning styles of Chinese pupils and the restricted opportunities which they have for practising English in an out-of-school context.

Only now is more attention being given to the particular needs of pupils of Chinese origin in learning English. The focus previously had been on the kind of linguistic mistakes made because of mother-tongue 'interference' in English-language learning rather than consideration of cultural influences in learning language. To date there does not appear to have been any research on young pupils using knowledge of Chinese as a basis for developing language as such, prior to teaching English at a later stage, as for example experiments have been undertaken with pupils speaking South Asian languages. This lack of attention and rather negative approach is perhaps indicative of the general educational attitude towards pupils of Chinese origin. Their dispersal is obviously a factor influencing language-teaching arrangements. But this should not be allowed to be an excuse, and might be remedied by school consortia or cross-LEA arrangements. Sensitive provision is vital, especially since there is evidence to suggest that once such pupils have acquired fluency in English, they are often able to realize their academic potential within the examination system. But for others who do not reach this point there are inherent dangers of semi-lingualism, an inadequate language knowledge and lack of fluency of expression in either Chinese or English. Though there is evidence of increasing English language use amongst pupils of Chinese origin, even in the home context, it is clear that their homes exercise a strong cultural and linguistic influence towards a pattern of socialization in the Chinese tradition. This need not be in conflict with the aims of the school in teaching English if there is a proper recognition of the value of both languages and the enrichment of bilingualism. It is, therefore, of interest and significance in terms of the influence which it may have on the attitudes of pupils of Chinese origin to learning English and their schooling in Britain, to compare the attempts which the Chinese 'community' has made to maintain Chinese culture and language in its voluntary provision.

Mother-tongue teaching

Amongst the Chinese in the UK language is the main vehicle for the transmission of culture to the second generation. Chinese parents are evidently concerned both that their children should not grow up ignorant of Chinese cultural traditions, and that they should also have pride in their cultural roots, which in many ways are considered to be superior. Although Chinese families live in a predominantly Chinese milieu, the language of the home being largely that of a Chinese dialect, parents are not often in a position to be able actively to further their child's linguistic skills, especially literacy, as they often have little time, or due to their own lack of education, many may be scarcely literate themselves or feel ill-equipped or unqualified to teach their child (Tsow, 1984). Some parents, however, do make considerable attempts to ensure that their children acquire some reading and writing skills in Chinese (Garvey and Jackson, 1975; Jackson, 1979). The concern of many Chinese parents that their children should not be divorced from their Chinese heritage by experiencing their education in British schools has resulted in the voluntary provision of Chinese language classes by the community itself. In recent years these have grown on an increasing scale. Indeed the parliamentary inquiry on *The Chinese Community in Britain* (GB. P. H of C. HAC, 1985) noted that the subject of mother-tongue teaching was the most commonly mentioned in all areas and by people in all walks of life.

This section examines the extent of mother-tongue teaching provision by the Chinese community, its organization and administration and, most importantly, the attitudes of parents and pupils towards such classes and the kind of instruction and level of proficiency achieved within them. It is fortunate that a fairly clear account, at least in terms of the organization of classes, can be given by drawing in detail upon two recent research surveys (Tsow, 1984; Ng, 1982) and information compiled by the Hong Kong Government Office (1982, 1984; and Chann, 1982, 1984). It is instructive to compare this account with information which it is possible to piece together on mainstream provision for Chinese teaching and examination entry (see pp.201–10).

AIMS It is the central aim of the voluntary part-time Chinese language classes to promote a knowledge of Chinese culture amongst the pupils of Chinese origin who attend, with an emphasis on the written and spoken language as central to that culture. Indeed the specific focus on language may be most apparent, the aim being to develop a sufficient knowledge of the language, so that children may be able to converse, read newspapers and novels and write simple letters, which entail learning about 4,000 characters, the minimum number for everyday use (Chann, 1982; Jones, 1980). In addition, the classes may also have a distinctive ethical orientation and, in some cases, linguistic maintenance may facilitate religious instruction

(CRE, 1982a). Cheung (1975) claimed that socialization into Chinese values was a prime purpose of the Chinese language classes. He quoted a teacher in what was then one of the largest Chinese language schools in the UK:

> Besides helping the Chinese children with the learning of the Chinese language so that they do not forget Chinese culture, they emphasise even more a moral training guided by the virtues of 'Lei' (courtesy), 'Yee' (righteousness), 'Steng' (honesty) and 'Han' (filial piety) so the child will not be filled with the atmosphere of deterioration which dominates the western culture of today.

The need felt by the Chinese community to preserve such values and cultural orientation through Chinese language classes has been demonstrated by the provision which has been made over a number of years and the support which the establishment of voluntary part-time Chinese language classes has obtained. The classes, initiated by concerned parents or associations, have become an important part of community education and indicate the desire of Chinese parents for their children to receive an education in Chinese culture, and the willingness to make such provision if it is lacking from the state education system. The CRE research (Tsow, 1984) demonstrated that parents' main reason for sending their children to these classes is the desire to maintain their cultural identity. They consider it significant that their children should know Chinese, especially to be able to communicate through the spoken word, but also to be able to read and write in the language. According to teachers in the Chinese language classes, speaking Chinese was a particularly significant reason for setting up classes – as were, to a lesser extent, learning about Chinese religion and culture, writing the language, promoting communication within the family and encouraging preservation of the local Chinese community (see also Barr, 1983).

HISTORY AND DEVELOPMENT   The foundations for the significant expansion of Chinese language classes during the last few years were laid in the 1960s. But there is an even longer history of provision for Chinese language teaching by the community, as there was apparently a Chinese class in the Limehouse area in the East End of London in pre-war days (Chann, 1982, 1984). The Chung Hwa School, founded originally over a restaurant in 1928, acquired its own premises in 1933 (Jones, 1980) and, according to Ng (1968), was officially opened by the Chinese Ambassador in Pennyfields in 1935. The school was financed by money donated by a prominent Hong Kong citizen who had already founded an English-language school in Kowloon. The school aimed to provide facilities for Chinese and Anglo-Chinese children to learn 'their own language, customs, culture and folklore' and, in addition, various activities, such as sport and drama, were offered and the school ran an employment agency. The school was independent of the state education system and was attended in out-of-school hours by some 20 British-born Chinese children who were taught by a specially recruited teacher from China, assisted by Chinese university students studying in the UK. However, neither the London school nor its Liverpool counterpart survived the war, although several attempts were made to re-establish the school in the late 1940s. They were unsuccessful, Ng suggested, because by that time the Chinese community in the East End was already in the final stages of disintegration (see p.34). However, during the 1940s when the Chinese community in Liverpool was augmented (see p.34) a mutual aid association, the Progress Club, provided classes for Chinese language, history and culture (Jones, 1980). According to O'Neill (1972), these classes flourished briefly, but declining interest later caused them to close. Collins (1957) also refers to a language school in the Chinatown area of Liverpool which only operated for a short time as Mandarin was taught, and not being the spoken language of the immigrants, it received little support.

It was not until the early 1960s when Chinese women and children began to join their husbands in England that Chinese language classes came into operation again. For example, Ng (1968) recorded that in 1963 the Overseas Chinese Service in London organized classes for Chinese children aged 4–12 'to learn the Chinese language, customs and ethics', so that they would cultivate 'a good character and never forget Chinese culture'. Lessons given in Cantonese, however, only attracted a very poor enrolment. Classes sponsored by the Chinese Chamber of Commerce in Soho commenced in 1968 (Chann, 1982, 1984). At that time there was one teacher and some 20 pupils, whereas according to Cheung (1975), by 1974 the numbers had grown to more than 150 pupils. Indeed, according to Campbell-Platt (1978), in 1975 Fong claimed that the Chinese Association of Commerce was discussing with the ILEA the possibility of operating a full-time bilingual school for Chinese pupils. Over the years the school associated with the Chinese Chamber of Commerce has developed to such an extent that it is now the largest organization for Chinese language teaching numbering some 926 pupils in 1984 (HKGO, 1984) and provides systematic instruction from the beginners' stage through to O-level. Another school associated with a kinship group – the Cheungs – was established in the 1960s to teach the Chinese language to children of workers in the catering trade. This still flourishes with some 189 pupils in 1984 (Jones, 1980; HKGO, 1984). Despite these examples of successful growth, the classes set up during the 1960s often had mixed fortunes and some in the North of England soon had to close down due to lack of interest on the part of pupils or a lack of teaching staff (Chann, 1982, 1984).

The early 1970s saw a revival in Chinese language classes in the voluntary sector. O'Neill (1972) noted that the classes in Liverpool which had fallen into desuetude in the 1940s were once again flourishing. By the mid-1970s the Chinese school in Leeds was said to be the largest Chinese language school outside London. But compared with provision made by other linguistic minorities Saifullah Khan (1976) concluded that the dispersal of the Chinese in the UK was a serious hindrance to the formation of mother-tongue classes. Nevertheless, Cheung (1975) reported that in more populated Chinese areas such as Glasgow, Edinburgh, Newcastle, Middlesbrough, Leeds and Sheffield classes had again begun to be organized. By the late 1970s the school in Sheffield had ceased to function, either through difficulties with accommodation or teaching staff (Mackillop, 1980), although other classes began under the auspices of the Chinese Christian Fellowship, and there are now two schools there. Hence provision has fluctuated, many classes having mixed fortunes. But generally the pattern of expansion set the trend which has continued to the present day. The development of some classes is well documented, as in the case of the setting up of a school for the teaching of Cantonese in Edinburgh, a direct result of a conference initiated by the Standing Committee of Scottish Community Relations Councils (1976). One year later some 65 children aged 4–16 were enrolled and it was also hoped to introduce classes in Mandarin. Barr (1983) outlines existing provision in Scotland where some classes are also attended by Vietnamese and Scottish children. She claims that classes are particularly necessary for Chinese children who are fostered privately, full-time, with Scottish families.

Generally with the arrival of increasing numbers of Chinese children and the birth of Chinese children in the UK a need for Chinese language classes was beginning to be made known. Elliott's (1981) survey of mother-tongue schools in London showed a steady increase in the number of Chinese language schools from three in 1970 to 14 a decade later. But the most dramatic increase in the number of classes has been very recent. In 1982 Chann (in NCC, 1984) reported that of about 60 known part-time voluntary Chinese language classes, 56 of which are associated with the Hong Kong Government Office, some 40 have been established in the last five years. Indeed the HKGO list of classes for 1984 in the UK totalled 84, demonstrating continuing expansion. Chann has attributed this to four main factors: parents' realization that a language and cultural gap exists in addition to a generation gap, and that mother-tongue teaching and learning something of the Chinese cultural heritage may help to bridge these gaps; that classes have become better organized due to the involvement of Chinese professionals; the increased willingness of many LEAs to permit the use of local school premises at weekends either free of charge or for a nominal fee; and the assistance provided by the Hong Kong Government Office in terms of textbooks, workbooks and grants towards running costs.

Evidence, however, suggests that existing provision is largely a response to its own need on the part of the Chinese community, as although there has been a change in awareness and support on the part of some LEAs, in the light of the mother-tongue teaching debate and increased consciousness generally of the need to make greater provision for minority languages, this has mostly yet to be applied to Chinese (see also pp.199–210). In a national survey in 1971 (Townsend and Brittan, 1972) only two out of 132 primary and 98 secondary schools reported that local Chinese communities made arrangements for Chinese to be taught to children outside school hours, a much lower figure than for other linguistic minorities. But in 1979, in another national survey, three LEAs with ten per cent or more ethnic minority pupils reported that Chinese language classes were organized by the Chinese community, as did nine LEAs with 2.5–10 per cent ethnic minority pupils (Little and Willey, 1983). Yet again, LEA awareness of Chinese community provision was a lot less than for South Asian language teaching and there was no evidence in the case of Chinese of any support given by LEAs to the voluntary sector. However, in another national survey by the CRE in 1980–2 (Tsow, 1983b) 47 per cent of the LEAs responding (87) made some contribution to voluntary mother-tongue teaching provision, in 90 per cent of cases in the form of accommodation. Chinese, generally Cantonese, was reported to be taught and 26 per cent of the LEAs responding (76 per cent) assisted voluntary Chinese classes. In a further survey by the Schools Council in 1983 (Tansley and Craft, 1984) 16 out of 63 LEAs with primary schools with at least ten per cent bilingual pupils mentioned Chinese as a language occurring most frequently. Fifteen out of 49 LEAs able to give details about community schools knew of a total of 36 Chinese schools in their areas. However, comparison with figures cited by the Linguistic Minorities Project (LMP) (see pp.181–2), even allowing for difficulties in classification of schools and classes, suggests LEAs do not have a clear picture of voluntary provision and that these figures are an estimate nation-wide (see also pp.203–4). Fortunately, in the case of Chinese community schools other national and local sources help to piece together a picture of expanding provision.

TYPES OF ORGANIZATION   There are four main types of organization of voluntary Chinese language classes. First, those organized by Chinese associations and groups linked by commercial interests, trade orientations or clansmen, and based on self-help welfare and mutual interest. A second group of classes are organized by church groups, mainly Christian denominations, in which Anglicans and nonconformists predominate. Other classes are organized by students from Hong Kong. And a fourth group are those formed most recently and attached to community centres, which may be directly aided by government grants, as in Liverpool, Manchester and London, or have the encouragement and assistance of local CRCs (Chann, 1982; Tsow, 1984). The CRE research undertaken in 1979 (Tsow, 1984) which included interviews in Chinese language schools with 69 teachers, predominantly male, half aged 16–24 and the remainder almost all 25–34, and two-thirds of whom were in the C1 socioeconomic grouping, confirmed these generalizations. Although about a third of the teachers did not know the origins of their language classes, more than a third were teaching in schools which had been in existence for five or more years. Some 21 teachers claimed that parents had been particularly instrumental in founding the language classes, sometimes with the assistance of local Chinese organizations or community centres. Local Christian groups had set up eight of the schools represented by the teachers. A distinctive feature of Chinese language class provision is that some classes have been established by overseas students' associations, the students seeing their contribution to language teaching as voluntary community service during the period of their UK study.

NUMBER OF SCHOOLS, CLASSES AND PUPILS   It is difficult to be precise about the number of Chinese language schools, classes and their enrolments since these fluctuate, their locations change and the distinction between schools and classes is difficult to draw with any rigour. Tsow (1983a) has suggested the size of classes within a Chinese language school may vary from five to 60 students in one room, and, moreover, that demand exceeds supply. Fortunately, however, information available from the Hong Kong Government Office (HKGO) and the 1981 Commission for Racial Equality (CRE) survey of mother-tongue teaching in LEAs (quoted by Tsow, 1983a) enable a reasonably accurate statement to be made concerning Chinese language classes. Tsow suggested that there were about 50 classes in existence with some 480 teachers and approximately 6,700 Chinese pupils across the country. However, according to the HKGO list for September 1984, 83 Chinese language schools in the UK are associated with the Office and have a total of 8,924 students studying Chinese language and culture. The classes are divided into three areas coming under the jurisdiction of the three Hong Kong Government Regional Offices in Edinburgh, Manchester and London. In Scotland and the north-east of England there were 17 schools with 1,304 students; in the north, north-west, Midlands, east and Northern Ireland there were 28 schools with 2,891 pupils; and in the London areas, south-east, south-west and Wales some 4,729 pupils studying in 38 Chinese language schools. These figures confirm a huge increase in the numbers of pupils and schools in the last few years and suggest that almost a third of children of Chinese origin under 16 are now attending classes. It is also interesting to note that the London HKGO also oversees three schools in Holland with 591 Chinese pupils, one in Denmark with 125 pupils and one in Dublin with 17 pupils. Not surprisingly, the greatest concentration of Chinese language classes in the UK was in Greater London, which reflects not only the size of the population, but also the availability of teaching staff. The 1984 HKGO list shows the following national distribution of Chinese mother-tongue schools: Greater London (16); Edinburgh, Leeds, Liverpool and Manchester (3 each); Birmingham, Bristol, Cardiff, Glasgow, Luton, Newcastle, Sheffield, Swansea (2 each) and one in each of the following towns or areas: Aberdeen, Banbury, Banffshire, Belfast, Bolton, Bradford,

Brighton, Canterbury, Chatham, Coventry, Derbyshire, Doncaster, Dundee, Dunfermline, Elgin, Fife, Gloucester, Grantham, Gravesend, Guildford, Hatfield, Huddersfield, Hull, Irvine, Leicester, Middlesbrough, Nottingham, Oxford, Perth, Peterborough, Plymouth, Portsmouth, Preston, Southend, Southampton, Stirling, Stoke-on-Trent, Surrey, Worcester and Worthing.

The greatest number of pupils in the Chinese language classes are to be found in the London area – some 3,200 or so. The size of schools in various locations varies considerably from the 12 pupils at the Worthing Chinese Sunday school to the 926 pupils who attend the Chinese Chamber of Commerce Chinese School (HKGO, 1984). There are several particularly large schools, e.g. the Newcastle upon Tyne Chinese school (267 pupils), the Wah Sing Chinese Community Centre in Liverpool (308), The Kung Ho Association of Sunday Schools in London (363 pupils in three locations), the Manchester Chinese Education Culture and Community Centre (403), The North West Chinese Association's Language Centre (501) and the Overseas Chinese Education Centre (652 pupils in four locations). But many of the schools have 20–50 pupils. Numbers may fluctuate quite considerably from year to year in different locations as, for example, in the case of the Midlands Chinese Association Sunday School attached to Sidney Stringer School in Coventry. When visited by Jones (1980), it had a maximum possible attendance of 80 children, whereas in the Hong Kong Government Office record it had an enrolment in 1982 of 20 students and 17 in 1984.

It is perhaps more instructive, therefore, to consider the extent to which

Table 36: Number of Chinese language classes, pupils and ages in three LEAs, 1981–2

	Bradford 1981	Coventry 1981	Haringey 1982
1 Year in which first surviving class began	1979	1979	1972
2 Number of classes in 1981–2	5	3	11
3 Number of pupils on roll	75	20	194
4 % of pupils attending regularly	93	85	88
5 Pupils on roll as % of pupils in LEA using Chinese at home (SLS)	51	22	*
6 Age group of pupils:			
8	35	1	74
8–10	28	11	74
11–13	6	3	25
13+	6	5	17

*The Chinese classes were actually held in Finsbury Park, outside Haringey, but 43 of the total of 194 pupils were from Haringey; in the Schools Language Survey (SLS) some 147 pupils reported speaking Chinese at home.
Sources: Adapted from LMP, 1983a, Table 4.1, 4.2, 4.3; 1982a, 1982b; and 1983b, Table 6.

provision in a certain locality is taken up according to the potential number of students. Fortunately, it is possible to make such an assessment in the case of Chinese pupils in Coventry, Bradford and Haringey in the light of information collected in the Mother-Tongue Teaching Directory (MTTD) Survey in 1981 and 1982 and the Schools Language Survey conducted by the Linguistic Minorities Project (LMP, 1983a, 1982a, 1982b, 1983b). The MTTD covered classes provided by community organizations as well as those initiated by the LEA or its schools, inside or outside LEA premises and during and after school hours. All the Chinese classes dated from the 1970s. Table 36 gives details of the number of Chinese classes, pupils and their ages in the three LEAs. In Coventry the information from the MTTD incidentally validates the figures given by the Hong Kong Government Office report, showing that in 1981 there were some 20 Chinese pupils attending three language classes in Cantonese, and Mandarin, 85 per cent attending regularly. It is of interest to note, however, that these classes commanded a relatively low level of support by only 22 per cent of the 89 Chinese-speaking pupils in Coventry according to the Schools Language Survey. By contrast, in Bradford there was a relatively high take-up, some 51 per cent of the 148 Cantonese-speaking pupils in Bradford being enrolled in the five Cantonese-Mandarin classes. The majority of pupils in classes across the three locations were aged less than ten. The classes were all held at weekends for two to three hours. No LEA gave any support in terms of teachers' salaries or accommodation. The classes lacked funds and no examinations were taken. Sometimes the classes received textbooks from the HKGO and drew on parents' fees for exercise books and paper. It is important that these findings should be set in the context of the socioeconomic position of the Chinese, and their attitudes and relationship to the education system, as well as the development of LEA language policies. Generally the LMP showed that teachers' qualifications, payment and training opportunities, and materials and examinations, were in urgent need of consideration. In the case of Chinese classes, given the predominance of provision in the voluntary sector (see also pp.202–4), the LMP argument for greater communication between LEAs and voluntary class organizers regarding all aspects of provision to meet and support needs and demands must have especial force.

FINANCE   All Chinese language classes are run on a voluntary non-profit-making basis depending much, in the tradition of self-help, on the special effort of individuals and groups. Chann (1982) and Tsow (1983a) differ somewhat in their descriptions of the sources of finance for Chinese language classes. Chann claims that the HKGO makes an annual cash grant towards running costs of most established and reputable classes, but that a few obtain similar grants from the Urban Aid Programme through LEAs and others engage in fund-raising activities or donation campaigns. Tsow (1983a), on the other hand, claims that parental donations and subsistence from associations, groups or church congregation funds form the main sources of finance and that donation drives are rare because of the continuous support and mutual understanding between the client and servicing groups. Few establishments, she claims, receive grants. In a survey of 45 Chinese language schools across the country with between 25 and 500 pupils in each totalling 3,170 pupils, Ng (1982) found 21 schools were supported financially from the HKGO, 12 from the Chinese community and ten by their churches. Some classes do not charge a fee, others a nominal fee, payable monthly or annually, and used, for example, to offset travelling expenses for volunteer teachers (Chann, 1982; Tsow, 1983a). Approximately half of the schools in Ng's survey charged no fee, but she suggested that the classes might be improved if teachers were paid and more money were available for materials and equipment, and that a parental contribution would increase appreciation by both parents and children. In the CRE survey (Tsow, 1984) 61 per cent of 195 parents of children who attended Chinese language classes paid fees. This was much more common outside London (92 per cent compared with 50 per cent of London parents). Almost all of those who did not pay fees said they would still send their children to classes if fees were due. The benefit of paying fees was largely seen by parents as helping teachers and improving the quality of teaching and teaching materials. Information from teachers in the survey confirms these findings: 50 out of 69 reporting that tuition was free, although in just under half of these cases parents were said to make voluntary contributions. However, some of the teachers thought that lack of finance hindered the provision of other activities such as outings (Tsow, 1984). Running costs are variable from school to school. The majority involved payments of rent and travelling expenses. The Chinese Chamber of Commerce Chinese School, however, with its own freehold property, has to maintain the building and also pay for teachers who are engaged permanently on a salaried basis (Chann, 1982).

ACCOMMODATION Accommodation for the Chinese language classes is again variable, many meeting in local schools, church halls, community centres, on university premises or at the sponsoring Chinese organization's rented or freehold properties (Chann, 1982). In Ng's (1982) survey one Chinese language class rented premises from the LEA, five used them free of charge, nine had Chinese Community Association accommodation, eight had free use of church premises and there were also other forms of accommodation arrangements. Many of the clubs, centres or church premises may be unsuitable for teaching purposes. Some meeting-places are too large and require temporary partitions, as in the case of the Manchester Community Centre (Powell, 1982). In others the smallness of rooms require a shift system in order to fit in a number of classes. The Chinese Chamber of Commerce Chinese School with its own premises has ten teaching-rooms and two toilets, but such facilities are beyond most smaller schools, which generally lack library facilities. Tsow (1983a) claims that not more than one-tenth of the total Chinese language classes in the UK use state school premises. Some LEAs, such as ILEA and Newcastle (GB. P. H of C. HAC, 1985), provide premises free of charge, others make a small charge. There are often difficulties in making arrangements for use of premises. Moreover, rooms in schools and church halls have to be rearranged for the Chinese language classes and then dismantled and re-established again at the end of the session, which can be particularly frustrating as no Chinese cultural environment can be established. Ng suggests that Chinese language classes should utilize the premises of schools closing due to falling rolls. In fact the premises of Chinese Community Association schools are often furnished with furniture bought from state schools which are closing down. Dissatisfaction with accommodation was one of the major complaints of the teachers in Tsow's survey (1984), nearly half reporting a need for new or improved premises. A third of the teachers complained about lack of physical space and that the rooms were cold, miserable and poorly decorated. Accommodation was clearly a matter of priority in the concerns of the teachers in the Chinese language classes. Other voluntary mother-tongue classes experience similar problems with accommodation (CRE, 1982a).

CLASS TIMING AND DURATION AND LENGTH OF ATTENDANCE   The voluntary class year coincides with the state school year, commencing in late September or early October and ending in June or July with breaks, which might be as long as a month and a half for Christmas and Easter. Most of the terms average 12 weeks with as much as three and a half months in the summer vacation. A small minority of classes run for 18-week periods and continue through the summer vacation, though there is sometimes difficulty in obtaining students for teaching during this time (Chann, 1982; Tsow, 1983a, 1984). Classes are held at various times throughout the week in after-school hours and at weekends, these, especially on Sundays, being particularly popular. Only the Chinese Chamber of Commerce Chinese School runs classes on both Saturday and Sunday to accommodate the large number of children, though elsewhere classes are often held simultaneously (Chann, 1982; Tsow, 1983a). A majority of the classes in Ng's sample were held on Sunday. Most of the 195 parents in the CRE survey (Tsow, 1984) said that their child attended on Saturday or Sunday, although outside London 26 per cent of parents said Wednesday. Of the 312 pupils aged 8–14 in the CRE survey, 60 per cent attended classes on Sundays, the proportion rising to 73 per cent outside London and 70 per cent in the lower social class grouping. Ng has argued that attendance on Sundays may be seen as an additional burden on children, preventing social integration with the wider community. On the other hand, attendance at Chinese language classes serves to affirm identity and continuity with the Chinese social community. In the CRE survey most children (62 per cent) attended on Saturday, though there was generally a wider choice of days. Of the weekdays the most popular day for classes was Wednesday, especially outside London (17 per cent) and with children from the higher socioeconomic group.

The weekday lessons are normally held from 5.00 pm to 7.30 pm, and classes normally last for one to two hours (Tsow, 1983a, 1984; Ng, 1982). At weekends the LMP (1983a) found that they lasted two to three hours, though they may last for up to four hours with breaks between sessions (Chann, 1982). In the CRE survey it was most common for parents to say that their child attended classes for two hours each week (49 per cent). But whereas 96 per cent of the parents outside London made this claim, it was the case for only 32 per cent of those in London where the length of attendance varied from one hour to four or five hours, though this might have included some travelling time. Most of the children (84 per cent) attended Chinese language classes once a week (Tsow, 1984; also Ng, 1982). Some 34 per cent of the children stayed for the duration of the language class, 26 per cent for 2½–3½ hours and fewer than ten per cent for less than an hour. It is not necessarily the older children who stay for the longest period and distance evidently has a significant influence on the length of time spent in the classes, for although 77 per cent out of London stayed for two hours compared with 21 per cent of London children, some 30 per cent of London children stayed for 2½–3½ hours.

In Ng's survey the 251 children had, on average, been attending Chinese language classes for 5.4 years. In the CRE survey half of the parents had children who had been attending classes between six months and two years, a quarter had only been attending for up to six months in 1979. There was little difference in the length of attendance according to the length of residence of the parents, though there was a slight tendency for the children of parents who had been living in the UK for longer than ten years to have attended classes for longer. Some 73 per cent of the parents whose children attended mother-tongue teaching classes would have liked their children to spend more time in the classes, two-thirds believing that they would learn more, and nearly half that they would have more contact with the Chinese language, culture and people. However, parents who did not want their children to spend more time in these classes (27 per cent) were concerned that their children should not be overstretched, and a minority implied that they did not wish learning the mother tongue to take place at the expense of learning English. But most of the parents did not think that their child's attendance at language classes prevented them from joining in other activities. Indeed, in the children's survey, some 42 per cent, especially the 12–14 year-olds, attended classes in the summer holiday, and three-fifths of those who did not expressed an interest in doing so (Tsow, 1984).

PARENTS' ATTITUDES TO ATTENDANCE   It is generally agreed that Chinese parents are very enthusiastic about their children attending Chinese language classes and make great efforts to ensure that they attend regularly

(Jones, 1980; Chann, 1982). For example, most of the parents in Lai's sample (1975) felt that it was very important for their child to learn the Chinese language and 14 of the children, aged 6–16, attended classes twice a week in London.

The CRE survey (Tsow, 1984) is a particularly useful source of information concerning parents' and children's attitudes towards Chinese language classes as shown through their knowledge of the classes, decisions about attendance, reasons for attendance and non-attendance, and reasons for choice of classes. Some 312 children aged 8–14, mostly living in London but 71 in Manchester and Liverpool, were interviewed. There were two samples of parents: 195 mothers whose children attended part-time Chinese classes (but were not those interviewed), who predominantly lived in London, were born in Hong Kong, aged 35 plus, had lived in the UK for ten or more years and belonged to the lower socioeconomic group; and a second group of 138 parents, again usually mothers, predominantly living in London, aged 35 plus and from the upper socioeconomic group, with children mainly less than 11 years of age who did not attend Chinese classes. In fact there was some difficulty in obtaining a sample for this latter group, formed partly from subscribers to the Hong Kong *Reader's Digest*, and contacts made by the specially trained bilingual interviewers who had on average to consult seven Chinese householders before isolating an appropriate respondent. Those parents whose children attended classes mostly heard about the classes by word of mouth from friends and neighbours (52 per cent) or from friends and relatives whose children attended the classes (nine per cent); ten per cent mentioned newspapers and nine per cent advertising of some sort. Similarly, 88 per cent of those parents who did not send their children to language classes had heard of their existence, mainly by word of mouth, 66 per cent from friends and 21 per cent from newspapers or other forms of advertising. The survey found that 67 per cent of the parents, especially those from the lower socioeconomic group whose child attended mother-tongue teaching classes, took a joint decision regarding attendance. Middle-class fathers were more likely to make the decision alone. In the children's sample 41 per cent said that both parents decided that they should attend classes, though where one parent made the decision this was more likely to be the mother in the lower socioeconomic group (28 per cent) and father (22 per cent) in the higher socioeconomic group. Six per cent of the children claimed that they themselves were responsible for the decision to attend, most likely those who were older and who had been born in Hong Kong. Family support and interest apparently play a significant part in influencing attendance, as just over one-third of parents whose children attended language classes in fact had three or more children attending, and many had two in classes. Moreover, in the children's survey, some 72 per cent claimed that other family members were also learning Chinese.

The Linguistic Minorities Project (LMP, 1983a) also provides information on parents' awareness of and child's attendance at Chinese classes in three LEAs from the ALUS. Differences in response from households with children under 21 may have reflected local levels of provision and the Bradford respondents were Vietnamese. Whereas only four per cent of 47 Bradford respondents were aware of provision, 70 per cent of 103 respondents in London and 82 per cent of 33 respondents in Coventry knew of mother-tongue schools. However, knowledge of classes did not necessarily correlate with child's attendance. In only 17 per cent of households with children aged five to 18 in Coventry and 29 per cent in London had at least one child attended a class in the previous four weeks. This was below average for all the households surveyed. Reasons for non-attendance were distance to travel in London and that parents or children were too busy or thought the classes not very valuable given their other priorities in both Coventry and London.

Parents' reasons for their child's attendance at Chinese classes are usually to maintain cultural identity and tradition (see pp.155–6). It is interesting to note, however, that in the CRE survey (Tsow, 1984) the reasons of those 83 per cent of parents whose children did not attend Chinese language classes but who would have liked them to do so were very similar: 70 per cent claimed that Chinese was the mother tongue, 49 per cent that children should know their own language and 29 per cent wished them to be able to read and write Chinese, with a substantial minority being concerned to ensure communication with their child. Two-thirds of those parents who had a child in language classes, but also had children who were not attending, said it was because they were too young. Some 14 per cent of the children were said to have an adequate or superior knowledge of Chinese already, six per cent said that they were too busy with school work, but only two per cent that they did not like the classes or were unable to find a vacancy. The reasons given by those parents whose children did not attend language classes but who would have liked them to have done so (121) were mainly those of inconvenience, 34 per cent of the parents claiming that they were too busy to accompany the children and 30 per cent that there were transport problems. However, 26 per cent claimed that the children were not interested, six per cent that they had been before, six per cent that they found Chinese difficult and 15 per cent that they were too busy. Some 17 per cent said that they were too young, but only seven per cent claimed that they were teaching the children at home and six per cent that they already spoke Chinese. Seventeen per cent of parents who did not wish their children to attend a class gave as their reasons predominantly that the child was concentrating on school work, did not want to learn Chinese and did not have time to do so.

Thus, although these reasons do suggest that there may be a different orientation towards Chinese amongst those parents who do not send their children to classes, and especially those who do not wish to do so anyway, it is clear that inconvenience, including difficulties with transport, is a major factor in the decision not to send the child to a class. This tallies with the reasons given by those parents who chose to send their children to language classes, 38 per cent of whom gave the convenience of location as their main reason for their choice of the particular school which their children were attending. However, convenience was only a major factor in London (50 per cent compared with six per cent elsewhere), as outside London parents were more concerned by lack of choice (22 per cent compared with four per cent in London) and the fact that the school which their child was attending was the only one they had heard of (32 per cent compared with ten per cent). In London parents were also influenced by the fact that friends and relatives sent their children to the same school (21 per cent) and the reputation of the school and its teachers (18 per cent).

TRAVEL TO CLASSES   It is often claimed that the attitude of Chinese parents towards the transmission of their culture to their children can be gauged both by the extent to which they are prepared to travel long distances to take their children to Chinese language classes, and also by the waiting-list for enrolment. Fong (1975, quoted by Campbell Platt, 1978) claimed that some Chinese pupils travelled up to 100 miles to classes. Simsova and Chin (1982), who visited some Chinese language schools in London, noted that parents were highly motivated and often travelled long distances to bring their children to classes. Some mothers travelled for two hours each way to the Overseas Chinese Education Centre (QCRC, 1981). In the CRE survey (Tsow, 1984) 38 of the 69 teachers thought that their pupils had to travel five or more miles to classes and ten suggested that pupils travelled 15 miles or more, indicating that classes are not particularly conveniently located for most children. Parents were less likely to consider journeys over ten miles convenient in terms of distance. Eighty-five per cent of the parents of children who attended these classes said that the distance was not inconvenient. Although 58 per cent had less than four miles to travel, 28 per cent travelled five miles or more, and this was particularly likely to be in London (39 per cent). Only in two per cent of cases were parents sufficiently inconvenienced by the distance of the class to consider moving their child. In the children's survey 12 per cent travelled five to ten miles and seven per cent 20–40 miles. Outside London a quarter of the children travelled 10–12 miles. Those who travelled the greatest distance, and who tended to be travelling for longer, were Hong Kong-born. Thus the classes apparently attract attendance from a wide catchment area, which fits with expectations according to the known dispersed settlement of the Chinese population.

Seventy-five per cent of the parents claimed that their child, especially if under 12, was accompanied by one or both parents when travelling to classes, ten per cent by a brother or sister and only five per cent alone. In the children's sample 84 per cent claimed to be accompanied by siblings, parents, friends or others when travelling to classes, 27 per cent of those who travelled alone being aged 12–14. The relatively high use of car transport to classes, especially outside London, may indicate a certain level of prosperity achieved by the Chinese community. For example, 50 per cent of the parents outside London said that their child travelled by car, in which case they were almost always accompanied by parents, whereas only 29 per cent of children in London travelled by car. Two-thirds of children said by their parents to travel by bus were accompanied by one or both parents, though a quarter travelled alone. Forty per cent of the children in London travelled by bus, compared with 21 per cent outside London, and 37 per cent travelled by underground. There was more than twice as great use of a car outside London to travel to classes (70 per cent compared with 31 per cent). Of the 52 per cent of parents who had access to a car to convey their child to language classes, some 73 per cent had children who were UK-born and 59 per cent belonged to the higher socioeconomic group, including 40 per cent from the semi-skilled group. Ng (1982), however, noted that there was often very poor attendance at Chinese language classes in the winter because of transport difficulties and the long distances which many of the pupils had to travel to attend. She suggested that parents should help each other in transporting their children to classes and also that the larger schools should diversify, so that classes could be located more conveniently in smaller towns.

WAITING-LISTS   Another way of assessing the enthusiasm and commitment of Chinese parents to the language classes may be the long waiting-lists for enrolment, especially in larger cities (Chann, 1982). Tsow (1980b, 1983a, 1984) has often claimed that demand for tuition exceeds supply and that the schools are over-subscribed with long waiting-lists. She cited the case of Manchester where in 1980 a newly set up Chinese language school with 350 students had some 300 on the waiting-list, and by 1982 this had risen to 400 (Powell, 1982). The Overseas Chinese Education Centre in London also claimed a long list (QCRC, 1981). Yet in the CRE survey (Tsow, 1984) only ten per cent of the parents whose children did not attend Chinese language classes were said not to do so because they were awaiting a vacancy. For various reasons there is probably a certain turnover in the number of pupils who attend classes, though there is no explicit evidence on those who drop out. Chann (1982) noted that some young children who begin Chinese drop out, but counselled that parents should persevere as the children would eventually settle and enjoy the lessons. Ng (1982) claimed a certain discrepancy in parents' attitudes. She observed that whilst they make strenuous efforts to get their children to a Chinese language class, they need to show more interest in the actual process of learning, which might be developed by their own involvement in literacy programmes (see pp.152–7).

AGE RANGE OF PUPILS   The age range of pupils attending Chinese language classes can be from 3 to 18, though mainly from the ages 5–14. In the

Linguistic Minorities Project (LMP) the majority of pupils were aged less than ten (see Table 36). Overall there appears to be an equal sex ratio, though the Commission for Racial Equality (CRE) survey (Tsow, 1984) found slightly more boys attending classes. The age distribution was broadly similar for boys and girls, but there were slighly more boys aged 10–13 and slightly more girls aged 14 or over. In Chinese classes pupils are graded according to ability, not age. This may mean, for example, that pupils aged five to nine may all be in one class (Tsow, 1984). The class is grouped according to the standard achieved in Chinese and may be at kindergarten, beginning, intermediate or advanced level (Cheung, 1975) and corresponds to Primary Grade 1–6 of the Hong Kong system of primary education. Some schools provide higher-level classes up to the fifth-year grade of secondary school, and a few teach to GCE O- and A-level standard.

LANGUAGE TAUGHT   Most of the Chinese language classes use Cantonese as the teaching medium, since most of the Chinese in the UK are from southern China where the most popular spoken Chinese is Cantonese, though there are also other variants such as Hakka and Hokklo (see pp.10–12). In classes provincial Cantonese is both the medium of instruction and the spoken language taught. This differs from Mandarin in terms of pronunciation, colloquism and idioms. Mandarin, a European term, is still used loosely to refer to the written form of Chinese either in the traditional overseas norm of Guoyu/Baihuawen and other forms in use in Hong Kong, Singapore and Malaysia, or the simplified script of 2,000 characters, Putonghua, adapted by the People's Republic of China in 1956 (Chann, 1982; Tsow, 1984; Martin-Jones, 1984). There are only a few classes which teach in Mandarin or which offer Mandarin as a taught language, for example, at Ealing (Chann, 1982). Some parents would, however, be interested to encourage their children to learn Mandarin. In the CRE survey 23 of the 70 parents whose children did not attend Chinese language classes and did not speak Chinese would have liked their child to speak Mandarin. On the other hand, 50 chose Cantonese. In Ng's survey (1982), whereas 30 schools used Cantonese as the medium of instruction, only three used Mandarin. Both Hakka and English were also frequently employed to explain linguistic points or to communicate with the children, half of whom spoke Hakka. Ng suggested these children experienced a certain frustration because the medium of instruction was Cantonese, the language of the more urban educated teachers, and questioned the extent to which English was used to supplement Cantonese as the medium of instruction. The extent to which English should be used as a medium of instruction and the degree to which teaching materials and approaches should be adapted to the linguistic and cultural experience of Chinese children in Britain are complex and controversial issues.

It is not clear from the literature whether there is any bias towards written or spoken language in the Chinese classes. Jones (1980), for example, claimed that since the children speak some Chinese dialect, but if they are UK-born or have emigrated young they will not read or write Chinese, the classes concentrate on acquiring literacy. Ng (1982) considered that the pupils whom she had observed spent too much time reading and writing, although a good deal of the time was necessary to acquire the skills, as she noted that the children wrote the Roman letters next to the Chinese characters to remind them of pronunciation. Yet evidence from the CRE survey suggests that there is a significant bias towards oracy rather than literacy in the learning of Chinese. According to the 69 teachers interviewed, speaking Chinese was a much more significant reason for setting up the classes. Thirty-nine teachers opined that the main objective of the classes should in fact be for the children to learn to speak Chinese and, in particular, that they might be able to communicate with their parents or friends in their native tongue (14). Other main objectives were that the children should learn about Chinese culture, their background and inheritance in order to carry on the tradition (15) or to learn about religion (12). Learning to write in Chinese and to understand Chinese characters was given as a main objective by only four teachers. Tsow (1984) suggests that the emphasis on the spoken form is conditioned by two factors: expediency in communication, and the difficulty of mastering written Chinese characters. Learning the language is in itself, however, inseparable from learning the cultural background, inheritance and religion.

CULTURAL CONTENT   Indeed Jones (1980) argued that if the attempt, as he saw it, to equate Chinese culture with calligraphy failed, then there would have to be a rapid change to disseminating Chinese culture through other disciplines such as history or literature, in order to preserve a Chinese cultural orientation amongst the second and third generations. He claimed that Chinese classics of poetry and folk literature, available in translation, would serve the purpose of introducing Chinese children to the best in Chinese literature whilst also improving their English. Ng (1982), too, has recommended that the greatest attention should be paid to developing an appreciation of Chinese literature, history and art. Tsow (1984) has argued that, although classes concentrate on language learning as such, the texts used have a content which is particularly concerned with the transmission of an ethical code, for example, respect for the old or the importance of family harmony being emphasized in the stories presented. In some schools subjects such as Chinese painting and music lessons are also taught in Cantonese and in classes run under the auspices of the churches, religious lessons and Bible lessons form the main content. Ng found that Chinese literature was the most popular subject in 31 schools, and 12 taught social studies, nine focussing their Chinese language teaching on the Bible. Learning Chinese songs was a popular curricular activity and 25 per cent of those parents whose children attended language classes in the CRE survey also identified singing as the most common additional activity (Tsow, 1984).

TEACHING METHODS   There is relatively little available information on the method of instruction in Chinese language classes. However, although many of the teachers are highly educated, they are likely only to have experienced the kind of teacher-directed learning in their own education in Hong Kong, where teaching methods are more formal, and may not understand the techniques of teaching children. In the CRE survey 70 per cent of children attending Chinese language classes spent most of their time in formal studies such as sitting down to read and write. This emphasis (despite the teachers' emphasis on spoken Chinese) seemed to prevail throughout most of the classes, both in London and elsewhere (Tsow, 1984). In an observational study of ten Chinese language schools Ng (1982) discerned that the teaching methodology was largely determined by following a textbook and there was little evidence that the teaching methods, content and activities were planned. She felt that the teaching was dull and unlikely to generate motivation, and she suggested that curricular innovations, both in the range of content and the methodology employed, were long overdue, and recommended that mainstream educationists should be consulted. The CRE survey showed some awareness on the part of teachers in the Chinese language classes of the need for contact with mainstream teachers and for participating in sessions on teaching methodology (see p.193). The Home Affairs Committee report (GB. P. H of C. HAC, 1985) recommended that further education colleges should offer short-courses in language-teaching skills for voluntary teachers.

THE TEACHING FORCE   Almost all teachers in the Chinese language classes are said to be very enthusiastic and devoted (Ng, 1982; Chann, 1984). A unique feature of the Chinese mother-tongue classes is their reliance on overseas Chinese students as a large proportion of their teaching force. They may be GCE O- or A-level students, undergraduates or postgraduate students. Parents, clergy and professionals, including university lecturers, also teach in the Chinese language classes. Although the academic qualifications of these teachers is varied, and may be very high, they are not necessarily qualified as teachers or specifically as language teachers. Some, however, may have qualified and taught Chinese in Hong Kong, Malaysia or Taiwan (Chann, 1982; Tsow, 1984). The predominance of youthful students in the teaching force of Chinese language classes is confirmed incidentally by the sample of teachers interviewed by Ng and in the CRE survey. In the latter about half of the 69 teachers interviewed were aged 16–24, and almost all of the remainder were aged 29–34, only five being 35 plus. Males tended to predominate and almost two-thirds came from the C1 socioeconomic group, 14 from AB, five from C2 and none from DE. Only three of the teachers were qualified. In Ng's (1982) small-scale survey of 31 teachers, 14 female and 17 male, their ages ranged from 20 to 50, the majority being 21–35. More than half had taught Chinese in the UK for one to five years, and although half of the sample were university graduates or students, 26 were not trained to teach. Tsow (1983a) has estimated that there are some 480 teachers in Chinese language schools, and in a survey of mother-tongue schools in London Elliott (1981) found that almost all of the eight Chinese schools in the sample had a teacher–pupil ratio of one to ten which compared very favourably with many of the other mother-tongue teaching schools.

REASONS FOR TEACHING   The great majority of the teachers in the Chinese language schools teach out of interest, because of a perceived need on the part of the children, see themselves as members of the Chinese community offering a much demanded service, and may also gain socially through the contacts which they make in teaching (Ng, 1982; Tsow, 1984; QCRC, 1981). Students may sometimes be the motivating force behind the formation of the school, as in the case of the school in Coventry described by Jones (1980). Tsow estimated that 98 per cent of the teaching staff are part-time volunteers (1983a). Only a few are paid (see p.182–3), although some groups attempt to reimburse travelling expenses. One of the main difficulties experienced by the Chinese language classes is the turnover of teachers because most of the teachers are transient students (Chann, 1982; Ng, 1982). Within a school the teaching force may fluctuate considerably as new students join or others withdraw when, for example, they come under pressure at examination time (Jones, 1980; Tsow, 1983a). The recent decline in the number of Chinese students from abroad due to the increase in overseas students' fees has affected the staffing of some classes and is causing some concern (Tsow, 1983a).

CONTACT WITH OTHER VOLUNTARY AND MAINSTREAM TEACHERS   Another difficulty revealed by the Commission for Racial Equality (CRE) survey is that the teachers in Chinese language classes have little contact with teachers from other part-time classes (43 out of 69 had none), nor do they have contact with teachers in mainstream schools (57 out of 69 had none). There was, however, a considerable awareness on the part of the teachers in the Chinese language classes that they needed to be better informed about teaching methodology and 26 expressed strong support for the idea of participating in sessions to increase their teaching skills. Ng (1982) also found that although 26 out of 45 schools held staff meetings there was little communication between teachers about teaching methodology. She recommended the introduction of an annual residential in-service teaching course for Chinese-language teachers, and Tsow (1983a) has also recommended that short part-time courses should be organized by consultation between teacher training institutions and voluntary teachers. According to Chann (1982), since 1981 an annual seminar has been organized by the Hong Kong Government Office (HKGO) to provide a forum for the exchange of experiences between Chinese language class organizers and teachers, though it is not clear to what extent this conference is meeting an in-service training need. Moreover, as Tsow (1984) has pointed out, there is at present a lack of structure to facilitate communication between part-time language teachers and full-time teachers in the mainstream. This could be particularly beneficial in terms of greater mutual awareness not only of the aims, methods and content of the two parallel types of education, but also of different perceptions of the needs of pupils of Chinese origin experiencing both types of educational provision.

Administration is another difficulty sometimes encountered by the Chinese language schools. Many of the teachers lack experience of community organization but have to be responsible for administration, policy decisions and contact with outside organizations and agencies, negotiating with LEAs for accommodation and also with the HKGO and other UK governmental bodies for grants. This is a task which requires considerable skill and expertise if maximum benefit is to be derived from financial assistance which may be available.

TEACHING MATERIALS   It is estimated that the Hong Kong Government Office (HKGO) supplies some 70 per cent of Chinese language classes with textbooks (CRE, 1982a) and in the research studies reviewed this source is invariably mentioned. According to Chann (1982), the textbooks supplied to Chinese language classes are those in use in Hong Kong. There are four Chinese readers for the kindergarten level and two for each year with a workbook for Primary Grade 1–6. The texts are colourfully illustrated. Tsow (1983a) has described one of the most popular texts which includes general knowledge, stories, historical episodes, letter writing, festivals, translations of nursery stories in Chinese as well as a grammatical text. There is a strong value content to the text and about half of the Chinese language classes are also supplied by the HKGO with civics textbooks and related workbooks to widen the scope of language learning. Books are sometimes used with an older age group than that intended. Textbooks at the secondary level are not supplied and have to be purchased by the schools running classes at this level. In one year the four schools run by the Overseas Chinese Education Centre cover the language syllabus for half a school-year in Hong Kong (Lue, 1982). Yet nearly half the teachers from the CRE survey (Tsow, 1984) said that these books were inadequate for their teaching requirements. Teachers thought that the subject-matter needed to be more varied and relevant to Chinese living in England; that books suitable for varying levels of competence and for different age groups were required; that books were insufficient, out of date, suitable for full-time rather than part-time teaching and orientated much more to the written than the spoken word. In particular, teachers wanted more story-books and those with information about the cultural and traditional backgrounds of China. Some teachers had attempted to develop their own books to meet the needs of their pupils, and according to Chann, if considered suitable, these are passed on to other classes.

It appears that there are very few other teaching aids available for use in Chinese language classes. Chann (1982) mentioned a pilot scheme being tested in two London classes using video cassette tapes produced in Hong Kong which, if successful, could be made available to those classes able to take advantage of them. Tsow reported that audio-visual aids are generally minimal, with the exception of pictures and workcards. And Ng (1982) found that only half the teachers in her survey used teaching aids because it was difficult to get appropriate materials. In the CRE survey two-thirds of the teachers felt that teaching aids and materials were inadequate. Many required a blackboard, projectors and other audio-visual aids, cassettes, posters and maps. In some schools stationery seems to have been in short supply, and strictly allocated, whereas in others it was more freely available (Tsow, 1983a). Whilst, as Tsow has pointed out, there is evidently a need to train voluntary teachers in the production of teaching materials suitable to their needs, it would appear that in some cases the facilities already available within libraries have not been fully exploited by some mother-tongue teaching schools (Simsova and Chin, 1982). Since, according to Elliott's (1981) survey, there was a very mixed response from eight Chinese language schools in London as to their own book collection, three having none, it would seem important for Chinese mother-tongue teaching schools to organize access to public library provision, such as that in Brent, which in 1980 had more than 300 books in Chinese or about Chinese culture and was regularly servicing requests from other libraries (see also p.149). Since recent years have seen a considerable amount of research on the library needs of ethnic minorities, it is possible that public library provision in Chinese may now be more extensive.

ATTAINMENT There is very little evidence about the level of attainment of the pupils who study in the Chinese classes. Chann (1982) claimed that in most classes tests of achievement are given regularly. However, according to Tsow (1983a), the tests, which are imported from Hong Kong, use the traditional script, though some of the books used in the classes imported from the People's Republic of China are printed in the new simplified script. Ng (1982) recorded that in 30 out of 45 schools surveyed the children's academic performance was assessed regularly every two to three months, in 13 of the schools. Yet two-thirds of the 31 teachers interviewed claimed that the children's proficiency in Chinese was not up to the expected level, even though the children participated actively in class. Achievement may ultimately be tested by examinations at O- or A-level, though very few pupils reach this stage of proficiency as there are few classes which organize teaching to this level. In classes which aim at promoting fluency and encouraging a love of literature there may not be anything to be gained by following an examination syllabus (GB. DES, 1984). Examination performance in Chinese must therefore be seen as a measure of the attainment of mainstream pupils, both of white British and Chinese origin, though largely from overseas (see pp.204–5).

LIAISON WITH PARENTS Ng (1982) claimed that half of the children studied for the sake of their parents, yet only some of the parents were interested in their progress and their expectations were not particularly high. The CRE survey revealed that parents would continue to send their children to classes, even if they had to pay, or pay more. The existence of waiting-lists for classes can also be interpreted as a further indication of demand and perceived need. Although most teachers in language schools have some contact with the parents of their pupils, apparently fewer than half claimed that parents participated in school activities, and only 11 teachers stated that formal yearly or half-yearly meetings were convened specifically to discuss the child's progress. Meetings to discuss difficulties with the child's learning were mentioned by only five teachers. This parlous evidence may suggest that parents are satisfied with the informal evidence which they have of their child's linguistic development and cultural understanding, and given what in many cases may be lack of ability or time to teach their children themselves, they do not necessarily wish to participate more actively in the education of their children and are pleased to leave this to the Chinese language classes. Indeed there was some indication that teachers did not see the need to establish further contact with the parents (Tsow, 1984).

PUPILS' ATTITUDES   Pupils' attitudes to their attendance at Chinese language classes may significantly influence the level of proficiency which they manage to attain and their enjoyment of the meetings. Chann (1982) claimed that many children look forward to going to classes, even though some beginners may find it difficult and lose interest. On the other hand, Langton (1979) claimed that primary-age children seem to enjoy their experience at Chinese language schools very much, but some secondary-age children are reluctant to attend, possibly because of the increasing influence of the peer group at an age when identity is paramount. Yet Fong (1981) found that 21 out of 31 secondary pupils claimed that they were always interested in learning Chinese and nine 'sometimes'. Once again, the most illuminating data comes from the two investigations conducted by Ng (1982) and Tsow (1984).

Ng discovered that about half of the 251 Chinese children interviewed in ten language schools claimed that they liked to attend the Chinese lessons and did not think it was a waste of time. Even if they were allowed to stop going, 136 said that they would not stop. Those who enjoyed the lessons and found them useful claimed that they would like to spend money buying Chinese books. But half of the children wished that they did not have to attend extra lessons in Chinese at the weekend. Even so, two-thirds to three-quarters of the sample had a positive attitude towards the Chinese language (see pp.156–7), though they saw it as being largely of domestic significance. Although 59 per cent said that they learned much about the Chinese language in the lessons they were critical of teaching methods. Seventy per cent wished that the lessons could be improved, for example, through more discussion (63 per cent) or that more individual attention could be offered by the teacher in the class (52 per cent). Some 79 per cent wanted to know more about the history and culture of China and 82 per cent wanted more conversation practice. Fifty-seven per cent thought there was not enough teaching material and equipment. It is of interest to note that although half claimed that they had been offered an opportunity to perform in class, only half of this group said that they liked to answer the teacher's questions in the class, and fewer (46 per cent) liked to ask about what they wanted to know or did not understand (27 per cent). Yet 53 per cent said they would like to help the teachers if they were to put on an exhibition about the Chinese language. Ng (1982) concluded that there was not enough active participation in the lessons.

In the CRE survey (Tsow, 1984) of 312 children aged 8–14 in language classes the most frequently cited reason for liking classes, especially by the 12–14 year olds, the girls and those born in Hong Kong and elsewhere outside the UK was the opportunity for meeting friends (32 per cent). Twenty-eight per cent overall claimed they enjoyed learning and improving their Chinese, though there was a considerable difference in this response according to birthplace: 37 per cent of those born in Hong Kong and elsewhere indicated their enjoyment of Chinese compared with 20 per cent of the UK-born. By contrast, some 28 per cent of the UK-born claimed that they liked writing in the classes compared with 19 per cent of the Hong Kong born, though there was a more equal distribution according to birthplace in their attitudes towards reading (20 and 18 per cent). Interestingly, twice as many of the UK-born, compared with the Hong Kong-born, claimed that they liked attending the language classes for 'playing' and almost as many for 'studying'. Yet seven per cent of the children spontaneously described their classes as 'boring'. Although this might indicate a certain dissatisfaction with the classes, when asked to describe their dislike about the language classes, one-third of the children said 'nothing particularly'. Their greatest complaint was that their classmates were 'naughty' (14 per cent). However, the largest number of complaints in total were directed against the facilities offered at the Chinese language classes, the smallness of the desks and classrooms (23 per cent) and an unfavourable comparison was drawn between these facilities and those in the mainstream schools attended by the pupils. Overall, some three-quarters of the children considered both their voluntary and mainstream teachers to be 'nice, kind and friendly'. However, there was some indication that the teachers in the language classes were considered to be more patient, even though they were seen as slightly more strict and as giving too much homework. It would seem therefore from these findings that pupils of Chinese origin have, on the whole, positive attitudes towards their attendance at Chinese language schools. However, as the Swann Report (GB. P. H of C, 1985) noted, Chinese children may be less enthusiastic than their parents about attending Chinese classes.

EXTRA-CURRICULAR ACTIVITIES Some of the Chinese language schools organize extra-curricular outings and visits as well as social activities such as Chinese evenings (Tsow, 1983a). The majority of teachers in the CRE survey (Tsow, 1984) involved their pupils in extra-curricular activities, such as visiting museums, galleries and theatres, as well as sports. Expeditions specifically connected with Chinese culture were also undertaken, but lack of finance and the young age of some children involved in the classes may hinder further activities. However, although a third of the children in the survey said that they liked their language class because they met friends, and 60 per cent who did not attend classes in the summer would have liked to have done so, it seems that they were not particularly interested in out-of-school activities with their Chinese peers. In fact 76 per cent of the pupils in these language classes went straight home after the end of their lesson, and 57 per cent did not wish to find further companionship out of lesson-time, although their responses may have been constrained by the knowledge that the lack of physical space at the classes may have prohibited any social activities.

SUPPLEMENTARY SCHOOLS   A few of the part-time Chinese language classes also serve a tutorial function offering supplementary subject-oriented education. Jones (1980) described such provision for a group of Hong Kong-born adolescents who arrived in the UK during their secondary education and needed more help with their English (p.170). One such establishment where classes in English and in Chinese are offered is the Overseas Chinese Education Centre, Shepherd's Bush, London. Classes also take place in maths, chemistry and physics (CAG and QCRC, 1979; QCRC, 1981). In the CRE survey two per cent of parents whose children attended Chinese language classes said that their children also learnt English or social sciences and one per cent said geography or mathematics. Two teachers interviewed confirmed that the primary objective of their classes was that the children should receive help to cope with their ordinary schooling (Tsow, 1984). In a national survey in 1979 Little and Willey (1983) discovered that three LEAs claimed to support supplementary schools organized by the Chinese community.

COMMUNITY FUNCTION OF CHINESE SCHOOLS   It is important to note the significant role which Chinese language classes are playing in the development of the Chinese community. Whereas other organizations over the years often seem to have failed to have brought about any great degree of social cohesion amongst the Chinese population in the UK (see pp.105–12), the strength of the Chinese culture and the desire for continuity of the Chinese language and traditions to be passed on to the second generation have proved to be a rallying-point for many adult Chinese, so that the Chinese language classes are not only serving the particular function of transmitting culture to the younger generation, but are also becoming focal points of social life for the Chinese communities (QCRC, 1981; Simsova and Chin, 1982; Barr, 1983). According to Chann (1982), where the Chinese community is relatively small and scattered, language classes have become the unifying force of the community providing a regular meeting-place for parents, children and overseas students. In this way some of the classes have become community centres in which friendships may develop, personal or communal problems may be discussed and assistance given. Social and communal activities are also organized. The CRE survey revealed something of this increased social interaction. In many cases the weekly class attendance of Chinese pupils is the occasion for a social outing for the whole family in which shopping, socializing and attendance at Chinese language classes become combined activities. Although shopping was said to be the most frequent activity whilst the children are attending classes in London, some ten per cent of the parents said that they waited for the child at the school and 16 per cent claimed to 'chat with friends/parents and visit friends', this figure rising to 28 per cent of parents outside London. This suggests that the Chinese language classes are seen as an opportunity for socializing by adults.

ENGLISH CLASSES   Another function of some of the Chinese language schools is to provide English classes for the mothers of the children whilst they learn Chinese. Apparently, however, this is not a new development, as Ng (1968) recorded that the Overseas Chinese Service and one of the Chinese workers' clubs had tried to organize English classes conducted by English-speaking Chinese for catering workers. These apparently met with little success despite the workers' desire to learn English, largely because the hours spent working did not leave sufficient energy or time to attend classes, and since the medium of instruction was generally English, few could follow the lessons. In the CRE survey 14 per cent of the parents who accompanied their children to Chinese language classes claimed to spend their time learning English. Indeed, some of the parents indicated that this was a factor in the choice of school (Tsow, 1984). The provision of simultaneous programmes for parents, including British culture, could increase the active involvement of parents in the Chinese schools (Ng, 1982). The meeting-points which the Chinese language classes provide have not been fully exploited in terms of extending inter-community knowledge and appreciation.

LEA SUPPORT   The organization of English lessons at the Chinese language schools and the very existence of classes themselves sometimes brings these establishments into contact with LEAs from whom hire of school premises and financial help are sometimes also requested. There is evidence of variable success, depending upon the relationship between the language classes and the local LEA, which may be constrained both by difficulties of linguistic communication and knowledge about the channels of communication (Chann, 1982; Tsow, 1983a). Probably no more than ten per cent of Chinese schools throughout the UK use state school premises, sometimes free, sometimes rented. The LMP MTTD survey (1983a) showed that, unlike some other minority language classes, no Chinese classes in Bradford, Coventry or Haringey received LEA support in terms of accommodation or teachers' salaries. But in implementing its policy on mother-tongue teaching recently Wolverhampton, for example, supports Saturday Chinese classes by paying teachers (*Mother Tongue Project Newsletter* 5 September 1984). It has frequently been recommended that more local authority support should be available to parents and self-help community groups for language classes. Tsow, in particular (1984), has pointed to the need for LEAs to promote dialogue about professional matters between voluntary and mainstream teachers and that they should make facilities and financial support available. The Home Affairs Committee report (GB. P. H of C. HAC, 1985) records that Strathclyde gives £20,000 to support Chinese teaching, the ILEA £2,760 to the Overseas Chinese Education Centre and that West Glamorgan supports a Sunday school where parents learn English and their children Chinese.

The existence and growth of Chinese language classes across the country demonstrates not only the typical self-reliance of the Chinese community, but also the strength of their commitment to Chinese culture and language, and the desire for it to be transmitted to the second generation. There is every reason to suppose that the demand for Chinese-language tuition will continue. Many of the classes were already established prior to the recent debate in mainstream education circles about the importance of mother-tongue teaching and arrangements for it. Though there has been expansion in recent years, as with other linguistic groups, it is likely to slow down as provision already exists in most large cities. The self-help, part-time classes run by the Chinese community appear to be one of the better-organized networks of voluntary provision for mother-tongue teaching. But despite their considerable success, especially socially in terms of community focus, their organization is less effective than it might be and this is likely, in turn, to reduce their efficacy in Chinese-language teaching. It is clear that the Chinese language classes suffer from poor accommodation, lack facilities and teaching resources, and experience considerable problems of teacher turnover and lack of trained teachers. Whilst the dispersed nature of settlement of the Chinese population means that the location of many Chinese language classes is inconvenient for parents or children who may have to travel long distances to satisfy their desire for a Chinese education, it would appear that parents could offer more mutual help with transportation and that a wider network of classes in smaller towns would also be of considerable benefit. It would seem a relatively straightforward matter for LEAs – aware of the support of the Chinese and other linguistic minorities for language tuition – to take a more positive attitude towards assistance, particularly in the matter of accommodation and some technical resources. Similarly, an expansion of the role of teacher training institutions to take account of the short-term, in-service needs of voluntary language teachers would be likely to have considerable benefit.

The positive attitude which not only Chinese parents, but also children of Chinese origin whether Hong Kong- or UK-born display towards Chinese dialects (despite the suggestion that with the focus of language classes on Cantonese speakers of Mandarin, Hakka and Hokklo are ill-served), has significant implications for the education of pupils of Chinese origin in the UK. Chinese language classes are often a focus for the hopes and fears of Chinese parents attempting to maintain a Chinese orientation in the upbringing of their children. Moreover, the Chinese cultural and linguistic orientation of second-generation Chinese may be seen not only as a resource and enrichment to them as individuals, but as extending the cultural diversity and vitality of British society. Experience elsewhere suggests that even where bilingual education is advanced in the state system, Chinese community groups have continued to provide voluntary part-time language and culture classes (Tsow, 1983a). In the light of the continuing debate about the provision by linguistic minority groups for teaching in their own language and culture and the extent to which provision should be made in the mainstream system (see Taylor with Hegarty, 1985) it is obviously also relevant to examine the ways in which the state education system can materially assist linguistic minority groups to make their own provision more effective and efficient. This should be a two-way process and draw on the successful provision for Chinese-language teaching by the self-help system of the Chinese community. It is necessary, therefore, to examine the extent to which the state education system has been aware of the needs of the Chinese community for Chinese-language teaching and mainstream provision made to date.

Mainstream Chinese

In recent years, as the debate initiated by the EEC directive in 1977 about the provision of mother-tongue teaching in mainstream schools has developed, it has become commonplace to read of recommendations that, despite the complex theoretical and practical issues involved in provision, there should in fact be a greater awareness of need and that action should be taken to satisfy demand (see also Taylor with Hegarty, 1985; Thomson, 1983). This has been no less the case with respect to offering Chinese language classes in the mainstream. Arguments have also been advanced for the inclusion of aspects of Chinese culture in the curriculum (e.g. Jones, I., 1979; see pp.289–98). The growth in the number of voluntary part-time Chinese language classes organized by the Chinese community has run alongside the developing awareness in educational circles at large of the need to consider mainstream provision for mother-tongue teaching. In consequence there is now a growing body of evidence of various LEA initiatives, though still often on a piecemeal basis, which will take account of some minority language needs (see, for example, CRE, 1982a; LMP, 1983a;

Tsow, 1983b). This sub-section will therefore assess the level of demand there has been and may be for teaching Chinese in the mainstream, the extent of provision, the level of achievement and some of the special difficulties associated with provision. The focus here is on teaching Chinese as part of the modern language curriculum in secondary schools. Recent approaches to support Chinese pupils' bilingualism and use of the mother tongue in E2L learning have been reviewed earlier (see pp.171–4).

Though voluntary part-time language classes have been available to Chinese children in the main urban centres since the late 1960s, there is no research evidence in any of the national surveys until the very end of the 1970s of any demand by Chinese parents for the inclusion of Chinese in the mainstream curriculum. Conversely, it would not appear from the dearth of evidence that there has been any particular realization by schools of the intensity of Chinese parents' desire that their children should grow up knowing something of the Chinese language and culture. But in any case, as various contributors to the Centre for Information on Language Teaching (CILT) conference on less commonly taught languages in 1975 pointed out, the educational system has been unaware of the significance of Chinese as a world language, and the likelihood of an increasing demand for interpretation and translation in Chinese to facilitate future trade.

Until recently there has been very little evidence of any provision being made for teaching Chinese to pupils of Chinese origin in the state system. Provision is largely on an *ad hoc* basis and may be associated with the work of language centres. The CAG and QCRC Conference, in 1978, reported that in the London borough of Islington Chinese classes were available in the language centre, with the aim of giving this subject the same status as that of other school subjects, although the classes were held immediately after school. Other schools had been invited to participate, but timetabling difficulties had frustrated co-operation. Both reading and writing in Chinese were taught up to O-level standard. This arrangement still existed in 1982 (Simsova and Chin). The Language Centre in Liverpool makes arrangements for pupils of Chinese origin of secondary age to receive lessons in their mother tongue for a few hours each week, either in school-time or immediately after school, and a number of pupils have been prepared for O-level Chinese (see Tables 39 and 40, pp.219, 220).

In recent years there is slight evidence of increased provision, sometimes in response to demand. One interesting account of provision made by the North Westminster Community School as a result of a petition from Chinese-speaking children is given by Groocock (1983). This led to the hiring of a Chinese teacher with the help of an Urban Aid grant. In addition to the confidence gained by the Chinese-speaking pupils, other children in the school developed an interest in the language, and it was claimed that the teaching helped to improve social relationships and an appreciation of bilingualism. Moreover, in 1982 at a national conference on Chinese children in Britain (NCC, 1984) Lue mentioned that he and other organizers of the Chinese language schools had been approached by state schools with a view to arranging Chinese language classes in the mainstream where there were few resources to undertake such teaching. More liaison between the two types of schooling was proposed, and that teachers in Chinese language schools should keep a record of pupils' mainstream schools and notify headteachers in order to demonstrate the need for provision.

In a recent interesting article Wright (1985) has outlined a course in Chinese, available at the instigation of the headteacher, since 1978 from Year 3 as an option in the modern language curriculum in a school in Bracknell, Berkshire. Usually 20 out of 300 pupils in a year-group elect to take Chinese and, in 1985, there were 40 14–16-year-old students including three ethnic Chinese (two from Vietnam and one from Hong Kong). The third-year introductory course, which also includes cultural aspects, leads to the Oxfordshire Modern Language Achievement Certificate in Chinese at Level 1. The two-year course starting in the fourth year emphasizes language and leads to the Southern Region Examinations Board CSE or the Cambridge O-Level, which include an oral test, listening comprehension and translation into and out of Chinese; native speakers may take the London University O-Level. Cambridge also offers an A-level examination for non-native speakers. Wright reports a dearth of suitable published teaching materials at an elementary level, and he and a colleague have developed their own. He lists other useful and helpful sources including the Chinese Language Project at the Faculty of Oriental Studies, Cambridge. Berkshire LEA provides a Chinese language assistant for conversation classes. Wright argues that there are sound educational reasons for offering these language classes, and a ten-week, sixth-form general studies course on China to develop an awareness of China, its culture and civilization, to break down stereotypes and to open up vocational prospects. Parents are reported to be supportive.

Unfortunately, three recent national surveys confirm the generally parlous state of provision of Chinese teaching in the mainstream. In 1979 Little and Willey (1983) discovered that 13 LEAs claimed that minority languages were taught in the curriculum, but Chinese was not mentioned apart from a very few arrangements for examination entrance (see p.205). In a second survey, in 1980–2 (Tsow, 1983b), it was discovered that of the 60 LEAs responding, 26 per cent had mainstream mother-tongue teaching, and in 83 per cent of these cases there was some curricular provision. Chinese was one of the 12 languages taught but only in two LEAs, and only one provided instruction up to O-level (see also p.179). At the other end of the age range, another national survey in 1983 (Tansley and Craft, 1984) found that although 23 LEAs provided mother-tongue teaching in 252 schools as part of the primary school curriculum, none offered Chinese despite an awareness in 16 LEAs of Chinese being one of the most frequently spoken languages for which community provision was made. Generally LEAs are showing greater willingness to consider the introduction of minority languages in the mainstream curriculum for a variety of objectives and reasons and the growth of provision is mainly linked to the existence of formal LEA policies. However, Chinese is obviously seriously under-represented in the state system. The HMI inquiry in four LEAs, namely, Ealing, ILEA, Manchester and Walsall (GB. DES, 1984), demonstrated varied provision in the mainstream and in supporting community schools, but, as so often, references to teaching Chinese were incidental and exceptional. The parliamentary inquiry (GB. P. H of C. HAC, 1985) recommended that the DES should examine possibilities for provision such as peripatetic teachers, centralizing arrangements in colleges or language centres, distance teaching methods or the concentration of Chinese pupils in a few schools. The dispersal of the Chinese-speaking population, the number of dialects concealed by the term 'Chinese', the large-scale existence of voluntary provision, lack of parental demand to mainstream schools and possibly ambivalence of attitude towards mainstream provision, lack of trained and qualified teachers, teaching materials and timetabling pressures are all serious constraints on provision. But there is little evidence of serious appraisal by LEAs of possibilities for provision for Chinese, which is remarkable given the numbers of Chinese speakers and its status as a world language – and with China's rapidly increasing importance in the world, politically, economically and culturally.

One way of assessing the level of interest in Chinese-language learning is to consider examination entrants. However, a caution must be sounded at this point. Interpretation of figures, for examination entrance rather than passes, must take account of the fact that a large but unknown number who take examinations are not pupils of Chinese origin permanently resident in the UK, but overseas students of Chinese ethnic origin or in the UK to complete their education. The figures also include a small number of white British students. The relatively small proportion of permanently resident pupils of Chinese origin amongst course entrants is borne out by three further factors. First, few of the Chinese language schools teach Chinese to this standard (Chann, 1982) and, as has been indicated, there are relatively few mainstream classes; secondly, there may often be only a low level of intention on the part of pupils of Chinese origin in mother-tongue teaching classes to reach examination standard (Elliott, 1981); and thirdly, O-level Chinese has been designed for British students and consequently requires a higher level of English than Chinese, so that examination performance may be more related to foreign language than mother-tongue learning (CAG & QCRC, 1979; Tsow, 1980b). An example of relatively low examination entrance for Chinese is shown from the national survey conducted in 1979 by Little and Willey (1983) in which, although 43 per cent of 150 heads of modern language departments said that their schools made arrangements for pupils to take examinations in the languages of ethnic minority groups, even if they were not taught in school, only three per cent made such arrangements for O-level and one per cent for A-level Chinese.

It seems, however, that overall there are proportionately more entrants for examinations in Chinese than for other Asian languages. The Centre for Information on Language Teaching (CILT) report (1975) noted that in 1973 there were 568 entrants for GCE O-level in Mandarin and 175 for A-level. By 1979 the number of entrants for O- and A-level examinations in Chinese (see Table 37) accounted for 60 per cent of the entrants for examinations in Asian languages (GB. P. H of C, 1981). A comparison of the figures in Table 37 with the 1973 figures for Chinese examination entrants shows the steady increase in numbers during the last decade. Again it is necessary to reiterate that these figures will include probably a majority of entrants who are not pupils of Chinese ethnic origin permanently resident in the UK.

Table 37: GCE O- and A-level entrants in Chinese: University of London Board, 1978–81 (summer)

	1978	1979	1980	1981*
O-level	821	1,117	1,344	1,346†
A-level	137	138	201	222‡

*This figure includes entrants in January.
†In addition there were 94 O-level entrants through the Oxford Delegacy of Local Examinations, one through Associated Examinations Board, 41 Cambridge Board and 15 Oxford and Cambridge = 151, making a total of 1,497 in 1981.
‡There were eight A-level entrants through the Oxford Board.
Sources: Reid, 1984; and University of London figures.

Just as the provision for the teaching of Chinese in the school system is minimal, so very few institutions of higher education, polytechnics or universities offer Chinese. Figures quoted in the CILT report (1975) show that, in 1973, there were 26 students of Chinese on advanced courses in further education, including polytechnics and colleges, and eight universities offered 14 courses in Chinese language and studies to 123 undergraduates and 13 postgraduates. Chinese requires special resources at the elementary stages, and some courses had additional support from linguistics departments (Perren, 1975), as did Modern Standard Chinese taught at the University of York in the last two years of the BA course, which aimed to give students a basic competence and introduction to the writing system. In 1974–5 there were 26 students and in 1975–6 22 (Verma, 1975). Chinnery (1975) also described a degree course in Chinese at Edinburgh University which, because of its organization, was available to a wide range of students in their first and second years, and attracted many who had previously not touched upon China in the school curriculum, nor learnt Chinese at school. In addition to two parallel courses in spoken and written Chinese in the first year, and two parallel courses at second-year level in modern and classical Chinese, there was a year's course in Chinese civilization, usually attended by a majority of students who were not Chinese language students, thus further spreading a knowledge of Chinese culture (see also CILT, 1986).

At this level also difficulties are experienced with teaching material, especially recorded or audio-visual material. Sloss (1975) described the Chinese Language Project, established at Cambridge in 1969 to investigate the initial acquisition of viable skill in basic modern Chinese and to develop techniques and materials for instruction. Interestingly, the project assessed that 1,000 hours of study would be necessary to obtain a 'minimal but minimum viable level of skill' in Chinese. Three categories of students who wanted to acquire basic instruction in Chinese were identified: those who would go on to regular undergraduate courses; existing scholars from other fields who wished to specialize in Chinese; and students from government, services, the media, industry or commerce who require the language for practical non-academic purposes (see also SCSCRC, 1976). The needs of this latter group may be only now being addressed. Powell (1982) reported that the Manchester Chinese Education, Culture and Community Centre was offering classes in Cantonese and Mandarin and had many applications from bankers, insurance workers, police and immigration officers. Thus there would seem to be evidence of a certain general need for opportunities to study Chinese – not only for pupils of Chinese origin, but other white British pupils and indeed adults, including those in education and social services (see also CILT, 1986).

One obvious requirement for extending provision for Chinese teaching in the mainstream is the availability of trained teachers of Chinese. Some university departments specialize in Chinese, but there were only six in 1982–3 (GB. P. H of C. HAC, 1985) and less than three other institutions of higher education offering undergraduate courses (Craft and Atkins, 1983). Clearly not all graduates in Chinese intend to teach it. On the other hand, there may be native speakers whose qualifications abroad are not recognized in the UK or who are trained to teach but not as language teachers. More information on teachers who speak a minority language, such as on the register being built up by ILEA, would be helpful. A national survey of teacher training institutions in 1982 (Craft and Atkins, 1983) revealed a total absence of initial or in-service provision for training teachers of Chinese and no suitably qualified teacher training personnel. There was only one report of an LEA language centre running a short course for teachers wishing to teach Chinese. A working party of the National Congress on Languages in Education in 1982 (Reid, 1984) recommended that both initial and in-service teacher training courses should be systematically developed for 12 of the most widely used languages of minority communities, including Chinese, and welcomed the Royal Society of Arts (RSA) initiative in 1982 in setting up a working party on the training of teachers of minority languages, for which Broadbent (1984) made specific recommendations. In 1983 the RSA successfully piloted a part-time, one-year course, leading to a certificate in the Teaching of Community Languages, at centres in ILEA, Birmingham, Haringey, Edinburgh and Manchester. The parliamentary inquiry (GB. P. H of C. HAC, 1985) suggested that the DES should give a greater lead on training and that the expertise of teacher training workers in the China Overseas Christian Mission and the Education, Culture and Community Centre in Manchester should be drawn upon. But although there has been much discussion of priorities for the development of training for minority language teaching in an attempt to break the vicious circle of recruitment and provision between schools, universities and training institutions (see further, for example, Atkins, 1985), it is obvious that to date there is no supply of teachers able to teach in Chinese, or child psychologists or social workers able to function adequately in Chinese. This is a major impediment to the introduction of Chinese in the mainstream on a wider scale.

However, Chann (1982) claims that most Chinese parents would like Chinese to be made available as an optional second language in mainstream schools. This is borne out by the CRE survey in which 87 per cent of parents whose children attended Chinese classes, and 83 per cent of those who did not, said that they would like their children to be taught Chinese as a mainstream subject (Tsow, 1984). Of the latter, 43 per cent thought that it would be convenient and 22 per cent that it would save time if they could be taught at school. A quarter of the respondents stressed the importance of learning the Chinese mother tongue. Some thought that the children would concentrate more and have no excuse not to learn. On the other hand, among those who did not want their children to be taught Chinese at school, there was a feeling that it would not be practical, that it was no use in England and that it would detract from other lessons. Apparently these parents had not thought about the possibility of making Chinese available to non-Chinese pupils. Moreover, some 58 per cent of teachers in the Chinese language schools were unaware of recent policies or discussion relating to mother-tongue teaching. Indeed there was more ambivalence in their response to the possibility of Chinese being incorporated into the mainstream curriculum. Of the 64 interviewed, 35 were in favour, 22 against and 12 uncertain. Those in favour of Chinese being available as an optional second language stressed the importance of Chinese as a widely spoken language, felt that it should be taught in the mainstream, that such teaching would assist Chinese children to progress in the language and culture and that it might interest others. Those who were against mainstream Chinese thought that it was not useful or necessary for British students, that the Chinese language classes were adequate, fitted the needs of Chinese pupils and gave better tuition in a difficult language, and that there would be little demand in the mainstream as a whole.

The Swann Report (GB. P. H of C, 1985), however, presents a different picture on this point. Unlike the views of other linguistic minority communities, the committee claimed that the Chinese representatives consulted had stated that the majority of the community preferred to retain the responsibility for mother-tongue provision, but would welcome LEA support in terms of accommodation, materials and INSET, and recognition which might affect pupils' attitudes. However, the views cited by the Report suggest that a variety of perspectives and interests exist. The parliamentary inquiry on the Chinese in Britain also recommended that LEAs should limit their support to assisting with accommodation, grants and playing a part in management and liaison (GB. P. H of C. HAC, 1985).

Unfortunately, there is a lack of evidence on the opinion of pupils of Chinese origin about incorporating Chinese into the mainstream curriculum. Lue (in NCC, 1984) has claimed that Chinese children would prefer to study Chinese as an extra-curricular activity at the end of the school-day rather than as a timetabled subject. In the Secondary Pupils Survey of the Linguistic Minorities Project (LMP) in Peterborough and Bradford, although many monolingual pupils were aware that Cantonese or Chinese was spoken by classmates or in the locality, few suggested that they would like to learn Chinese at school (Table 38). However, Wright (1985) has noted the attraction of learning Chinese, and particularly its unique script, for monolingual pupils.

Despite the positive attitude of Chinese parents in the Commission for Racial Equality (CRE) survey to the possible provision of Chinese language teaching in ordinary schools, it would appear that to date there has been

Table 38: Number of monolingual pupils aware of 'Chinese' spoken locally and wanting to learn it at school in two LEAs

	Peterborough			Bradford		
	Classmates' language	*Local language*	*Wanting to learn at school*	*Classmates' language*	*Local language*	*Wanting to learn at school*
Language						
Cantonese	47	2	19	29	3	19
'Chinese'	53	120		14	107	

Source: Adapted from LMP, 1983a, Tables 3.4 and 3.5.

little recognition of this interest and few attempts to build upon the dual language proficiency of many pupils of Chinese origin, even as a bridge for learning English (see pp.171–4). Advantages for incorporating Chinese in the mainstream curriculum have been claimed by teachers, educationists and the Chinese community. Among the former Prager (1977) has argued that to include minority languages such as Chinese in the curriculum would increase the number of foreign language examination passes, improve the standard of English because of the required translation into English which would carry over into all subjects, thereby possibly leading to a re-assessment of the learning ability of ethnic minority pupils; maintain cultural links for such pupils; lessen the cultural distance between home and school; and increase self-respect among ethnic minority pupils and, if there was a take-up by other pupils wishing to learn these languages, then the multicultural curriculum would be broadened and there would be a greater appreciation of bilingualism and improved pupil relationships. On behalf of the Chinese community Chann (1982) has claimed that to include Chinese in the mainstream would mean that it would be better organized and more professionally taught by trained teachers, using textbooks and materials more suited to the UK context, and that the language would be given a more appropriate status. Other Chinese professionals who have argued in favour of some mainstream provision have also indicated the likely coexistence of voluntary Chinese classes.

Indeed it is obvious that there are a number of especial difficulties in implementing the teaching of Chinese in the mainstream, both at a theoretical and a practical level. For example, Tsow (1980b) has consistently argued that there should be opportunities for choice as to which Chinese dialect is taught. This may require consultation with parents in different localities as to what is appropriate. Others (e.g., Lue in NCC, 1984) have indicated the difference in aims and objectives of the Chinese schools and the mainstream schools, particularly in so far as traditional Chinese values are incorporated in the materials used in the Chinese language classes. It is possible, too, that the contrast between the more formal teaching methods of the Chinese language classes and the individual learning environment of many mainstream classes might become more apparent to pupils if Chinese were to be taught within the ordinary school. Perhaps the greatest practical difficulty for mainstream provision – or one that is generally seen to be so because of the stress on quantitative rather than qualitative criteria in assessing needs – is the dispersal of the Chinese community itself. However, dispersal is not unique to pupils of Chinese origin, and it may be questioned to what extent it is justifiable to make provision for other more numerous ethnic minority groups to have their languages taught within schools and not to do so for pupils, like the Chinese, who may be less numerous but have no less a degree of need or interest (see Derrick, 1977).

In the past it has been suggested that initiatives for mother-tongue teaching should come from individual schools (CAG & QCRC, 1979). A government statement indicated qualified support for mother-tongue teaching 'if children come from homes in which no English is spoken they can be taught at an early age – *provided there are enough of them to make it economic* – English grammar in parallel with their own language . . . there is no reason why children should not learn their original language as the second modern language' (Boyson, 1983, p. 20). Numbers are apparently dominant in the decision concerning provision. The Chinese community is well aware of this difficulty having attempted to provide classes which would be sufficiently accessible to be viable. This confirms the need for greater liaison between the two types of schooling, so that provision might be mutually compatible and complementary. Indeed the other main factor in the difficulty of establishing provision for teaching Chinese in the mainstream, namely, the lack of competent teachers, might be slightly ameliorated by drawing on trained teachers amongst the teaching force of the Chinese language schools. There is a need both to increase the teaching skills of voluntary teachers through recognized courses of training and to encourage bilingual Chinese, including second-generation pupils, into teaching (see pp.296–8) as well as other Chinese speakers.

Tsow, in particular (1984), has argued that LEAs should seek both educational and administrative means to teach Chinese within the school curriculum from pre-school to secondary level as part of their commitment to the promotion of equality of opportunity and good race relations. Since the Chinese population is so scattered, it may be necessary for one or two schools within an LEA to establish a teaching programme, and for this to be made widely known, or for arrangements to be made between neighbouring LEAs. Whilst mother-tongue provision during recent years has served to bring about some interesting initiatives with respect to more numerous linguistic minority groups, especially in the case of South Asian languages (see Taylor with Hegarty, 1985), it would appear that wider discussion has as yet had little impact on increasing the opportunities for pupils of Chinese origin to study their mother tongue in the ordinary school. Their dispersal in small numbers in schools throughout the country and the lack of competent trained teachers are factors to be weighed in considering the establishment of mainstream provision. But in the long term administrative obstacles should not be allowed to become attitudinal impediments to matching the enthusiasm and commitment of Chinese parents to ensure their children have some knowledge and appreciation of Chinese culture and language. The need of each Chinese pupil to examine his identity through an exploration of his cultural heritage may be just as great, if not greater, whether he is one pupil alone in a class or school or one amongst many Chinese pupils. That the opportunities for learning Chinese should also be available to other pupils in school can only serve to broaden the nation's cultural and linguistic vitality.

Section 7
Mathematics

In contrast to the considerable amount of information on the linguistic proficiency of pupils of Chinese origin there is a dearth of data, either qualitative or quantitative, on the mathematical ability of pupils of Chinese origin. Existing comment suggests that pupils either have a natural aptitude for mathematical and scientific subjects, or that this is an area where there is less linguistic interference and greater opportunity for their talents to be demonstrated.

Teachers in two primary and three secondary schools in London with large numbers of Chinese pupils reported them to be diligent and competitive academically, and particularly good at mathematics and handwork (Lai, 1975). This finding is confirmed by Fong (1981) in an observational study of 31 Chinese adolescents, two-thirds of whom were in three secondary schools and the remainder in the Language Centre, Liverpool. Teachers assessed their abilities in mathematics positively and noted their generally better achievement in non-verbal subjects. The Chinese pupils themselves claimed that mathematics, chemistry, physics and art were their best and favourite subjects. Whilst it would be understandable if achievement were better in non-verbal subjects, it should be remembered that these subjects also have a linguistic content and require a certain linguistic proficiency. An example quoted by Cheung (1975) of a Chinese pupil who could do a mathematical problem if he knew a certain calculation was needed demonstrates the linguistic and conceptual interference that can occur even in apparently non-verbal curricular subjects. Other instances, for example, that of Tommy in the E2L teaching case study (Garvey and Jackson, 1975), indicate that Chinese pupils often have a natural flair for mathematics. The fact that Arabic rather than Chinese numerals are normally used in schools in Hong Kong, may facilitate mathematical adaptation for newly arrived Chinese pupils.

Data from tests of mathematical ability and examination performance are extremely parlous but serve to confirm general impressions. For example, in the 1977 BPPA and RCRC survey the five Far East Asian pupils in the top junior forms of eight multiracial schools in the London Borough of Redbridge attained an average score of 109.8, higher than any of the other groups, and greatly exceeding the schools' (97.3) and the borough average (101.6) (BPPA & RCRC, 1978). Figures for CSE and GCE O- and A-levels and 16+, compiled by Ladlow at the Language Centre in Liverpool, confirm the relatively high proportion of examination passes in mathematics, and at higher grades, for previous pupils of Chinese origin in 1981–3 from seven Liverpool secondary schools (see Tables 39–41, pp.219–21). Relatively high proportions of passes, and at higher grades, were also obtained in science subjects and art.

These limited data suggest that the ability of pupils of Chinese origin in mathematics is relatively high compared with other subjects, though the extent to which there is some linguistic interference is unclear. Indeed complacency about performance is unwarranted since the absence of information demonstrates that there has been no attempt at a proper assessment of performance.

Section 8
School Placement

A consideration of the school placement of pupils of Chinese origin involves three main aspects: provision for pupils arriving in the UK with some educational experience in their country of origin; streaming; and special needs.

The particular difficulties experienced by some Chinese pupils arriving in the UK after commencing their schooling elsewhere, and especially older students, have been commented upon frequently (Lai, 1975; Cheung, 1975; Fong, 1981; Lynn, 1982; see also pp.124–5). Difficulties in adjusting to British education are generally related to age and previous education, language, especially knowledge of English, and differences in the learning environment. Having visited three London secondary schools with Chinese pupils, Lai (1975) noted that particular difficulties had been experienced by Chinese students who had started their primary education relatively late in Hong Kong (compared with the usual six years from the age of six to 12, see pp.18–22), which they had not completed before their arrival in the UK when they were placed in secondary education because of their age. In York Cheung (1975) also discovered that those children who arrived between 10 and 14 suffered more problems of adjustment due to inadequate language and differences between the educational systems, compared with children arriving between the ages of five and nine. Children from the rural areas of the New Territories who had often started their primary education two or three years later, and may have taken nine years to complete a six-year course because of the system of promotion to a higher class only on successful examination performance, sometimes arrived in the UK at the age of 14, having just completed their primary education, only to be placed in the third or fourth year of the secondary school according to their chronological age. Sixty per cent of the adolescents in Fong's sample who came from the rural New Territories reported such problems in school placement in Liverpool on arrival. Many such pupils will have only just begun to learn English and may also be subjected to great pressure in attempting to catch up in subject learning. Moreover, the learning environment itself often contrasts greatly with that in Hong Kong schools (see p.21) which is teacher-centred with pupils being encouraged to be quietly obedient. The more challenging individualized learning methods in UK classrooms, together with changes of teachers and classrooms, may be bewildering, and the inability to communicate with teachers and peers worsens the situation and results in frustrating tensions (Fong, 1981; Lynn, 1982). The initial UK school experience of Chinese pupils placed in large comprehensive schools, with little English, lacking an understanding of the educational system and trying, in addition, to adjust to a new home environment in a different social context must be traumatic indeed, and should be a matter of some concern. LEA policies for the reception and monitoring of newly arrived pupils requires better documentation, given the well known problems of adjustment.

As with other ethnic minority pupils, there is some evidence that pupils of Chinese origin tend to be found in the lower and remedial streams of schools. An early investigation by Feeley (1965), for example, revealed that Chinese pupils were placed in the lower streams at a boys' secondary modern school in the East Midlands, whose catchment included the town's older housing which was beginning to be inhabited by new immigrants. Although it is difficult to be certain, owing to the ways in which figures for ethnic minority pupils are reported, it appears that Chinese children (included in the categories 'rest of Commonwealth' and 'non-Commonwealth') were not especially represented in special schools, schools for the blind, deaf, physically handicapped or maladjusted according to the last statistics of education collected by the DES, in 1972 (GB. DES, 1973). There may, however, have been a slight tendency for their over-representation in ESN schools. The CAQ & QCRC Conference Report (1979) suggested that referrals of Chinese children for assessment of ESN should be investigated as their only problem was lack of English. More recently Fong (1981) has also reported that Chinese pupils tend to be placed in the lower streams of secondary schools, again because of their lack of English. However, lower stream placement may seriously demotivate pupils who are otherwise keen to learn, and for Chinese pupils who may previously have experienced a more passive learning environment disruptive pupils found in some of the lower streams may be an unwelcome peer group. There may be an argument for placing Chinese pupils who show application and ability but lack English with more diligent and capable workmates, so that they may mix with pupils with whom they may have more in common, and from whom they may have a greater opportunity to benefit linguistically by working in a co-operative learning situation. Various peer-tutoring methods can have considerable academic and social pay-offs, both across the curriculum and in home–school relationships (Taylor-Fitzgibbon, 1983).

There is some evidence that pupils of Chinese origin are naturally quiet, well-behaved and shy in the classroom. Various cultural factors in their upbringing may predispose them to be inhibited in their interactions with teachers and peers. Some 70 per cent of the Chinese pupils studied by Fong were considered to show degrees of under-reaction in the classroom situation as measured by teachers' opinions on the Bristol Social Adjustment Guide. This may result in them receiving less attention by classroom teachers who may be preoccupied with more behaviourally demanding pupils. Indeed the lack of demonstrated emotional or disruptive behavioural tendencies on the part of pupils of Chinese origin, unlike some other ethnic minority pupils, is confirmed by their complete absence from school support centres and educational guidance centres according to an ILEA survey (1981). It would appear therefore that, apart from concerns about the social, linguistic and educational adjustment of newly arrived Chinese pupils, particular difficulties in the placement of Chinese pupils are likely to result from a certain social isolation due to their dispersed settlement and hence the fact that there are often only one or two Chinese pupils in a school. In a national survey conducted in 1979 by Little and Willey (1983) only Chinese pupils were specifically mentioned by more than one or two LEAs as differing, in middle and secondary schools, from other ethnic minority pupils who were not new arrivals in the UK, seven LEAs stating that Chinese children had special educational needs, usually related to their isolation within the school and community. This brief review of evidence on aspects of the school placement of pupils of Chinese origin indicates a number of hidden problems often largely masked because of the non-assertive nature of Chinese pupils themselves.

Section 9
Examinations

There is a paucity of evidence on the examination performance of pupils of Chinese origin at CSE and GCE O- and A-level due to the absence of ethnically based educational statistics and research. Although judgements cannot therefore be made on this customary criterion of educational attainment, three factors – of language knowledge, length of schooling and parental attitudes – are cited as relevant to examination performance. It may be assumed that teaching style and methods are also influential, but as usual there is an absence of information on this point.

Lack of proficiency in English is a crucial factor in examination performance, especially for Chinese pupils who arrive in the UK during the latter years of schooling. Jones (1980), for example, records the difficulties of some 14–16 year-olds in the UK on average for four years, who arrived with some elementary English but requiring further help and attended a supplementary English class. Though they spoke English confidently, they lacked the range of vocabulary and grammatical accuracy needed to succeed in the examinations which they were attempting. Even O-level Chinese requires some translation into English, and since it was designed for English speakers learning Chinese, requires a higher level of English than Chinese. There was a report of the examination being redrafted in Chinese (CAG & QCRC, 1979). But the Swann Report (GB. P. H of C, 1985) again noted that some Chinese pupils had difficulty in passing it not because of their ability in Chinese, but because of their command of English. A conference in Scotland in the mid-1970s suggested that an O-grade in the Scottish Certificate of Education in English for overseas students should be introduced which would be acceptable as an alternative to further education colleges and universities (SCSCRC, 1976). But when full attention is given to developing the English language proficiency of pupils of Chinese origin, they may well be able to attempt examinations in a remarkable space of time, as a case study quoted by Garvey and Jackson (1975) showed. Though Tommy arrived in England with no English, some three years later he was attempting CSEs in four subjects – English, History, Biology and Mathematics. Cheung (1975) drew a distinction between the performance of those Chinese pupils who arrived in the UK during their secondary schooling and those born in the UK. Only one of the late arrivals was reported to have gained a Certificate in Secondary Education, whereas the UK-born were said to be sufficiently successful in their examination performance to enter professional occupations. Yet at a conference in 1982 (NCC, 1984) participating educationists reported that pupils of Chinese origin were leaving school without any examination qualifications, particularly in areas where they were not able to receive intensive English-language tuition in language centres. Though the Swann Report (GB. P. H of C, 1985, p.666) rejected this approach to E2L teaching, it acknowledged that even though evidence generally suggested Chinese pupils were doing well they might 'be underachieving in relation to their true potential primarily because of a lack of necessary language support' and an inappropriate curriculum.

Throughout the literature there are comments (see e.g. Garvey and Jackson, 1975; Lynn, 1982) suggesting that despite the desire of Chinese parents for their children to receive a good education, some mismatch between the family's traditional expectations and the school's expectations may develop when a pupil has the ability to further his education by taking O- and A-levels. Although teachers may try to encourage able Chinese pupils to succeed in examinations, some Chinese parents may not allow their children to study sufficiently or provide suitable study conditions, but may continue to require help from the student in the family business. Lynn quotes just one example out of several over a number of years, in which a Chinese pastor attempted to explain to parents that a student must study and not work in the family business, but despite the parents' apparent agreement, he was still expected to work each evening for two-and-a-half-hours. Yet there are also continual reports that Chinese parents expect their children to have homework and that, on the whole, Chinese children are very home-based. It seems that it is at this very time when Chinese pupils need to devote themselves to their studies in order to achieve examination success, which may open up wider choices in the job market, that the conflicting demands of school and home, with the traditional expectations of parents to provide for the child's entry into the family business or the catering trade, most obviously coincide.

Hard evidence on examination performance of pupils of Chinese origin is almost non-existent. Data recorded by Verma and Ashworth (1981) show that in one school pupils of Chinese origin constituted the largest ethnic minority group (18 per cent) in one class in the top form of a mainly CSE 'non-academic with GCE crafts' stream and five per cent of another class, whereas they comprised only three per cent of a 'GCE with some CSE' stream. The most interesting data on examination performance available have been kindly supplied by Ladlow, on the RSA, CSE, GCE O- and A-level and 16+ performance of pupils of Chinese origin in 1981–4, who were previously students at the English Language Centre in Liverpool. Tables 39–

41 show that these Chinese pupils have a range of subject and grade achievement in CSE and GCE O-level and particular attainments in maths, sciences and art, with generally higher grades. However, it should also be noted that they do achieve passes in English language, mainly at CSE level, which is a tribute to the ability and application of such pupils and testifies to the skills of teachers in the English Language Centre and those offering continuing support during schooling.

Unfortunately, there is no way of knowing whether such results are typical, either of pupils of Chinese origin in Liverpool or such pupils nationally. Still less is there any record of such pupils who fail to achieve any examination success at all. On the other hand, in evidence to the Home Affairs Committee (GB. P. H of C. HAC, 1985) the ILEA's Education Officer observed that Chinese pupils 'perform considerably better than other minority groups in public exams' (p.xxxiv). There are, however, indications that attention to English language is necessary throughout the school life of pupils of Chinese origin and that this will have a considerable effect on examination performance and hence qualifications essential to employment success. The Home Affairs Committee report also noted the evidence collected during visits that two-thirds of Chinese pupils in Manchester fail CSE English (p.lxxix) and concluded that 'We regard the extent of the language difficulties afflicting even some British-born Chinese as one of the most serious findings' (p.xxxv). The general lack of evidence on examination performance demonstrates that, as in other areas of the education of pupils of Chinese origin, the fact that they are often in relatively small numbers in a school means that their performance often fails to be monitored and recorded. A comparison of evidence from different localities on the examination performance of pupils of Chinese origin is urgently required for diagnostic purposes, to identify need and increase awareness for provision.

Table 39: Achievements of former pupils of the English Language Centre, 1981; results of 19 candidates in seven Liverpool secondary schools

	RSA			CSE						O-level						A-level			
	1	2	3	1	2	3	4	5	U	A	B	C	D	E	U	C	D	E	O
English literature						1			1		1								
English language		1	1			3	7	2	2*		1	1	1						
Mathematics		2	3			1	2	3		2	2	1	1				1		
History			1				2	3	1			1							
Geography	1					1	2	1				1							
Physics		1	1			1		1			2		2						
Chemistry											2	1			1	1	1	1	1
Biology	1	1*	2							2	4	1			2			1	1
Art	3									2		3			1				
Woodwork	1		1			1													
GED		2	1																
Typing	2	2	1			1	1												
Needlework	1	1	1																
Computer studies	1	1	1																
Commerce		1	1					1											
General studies								1											
Sociology														1					
Greek										1	1*							1	
Chinese										1		1							
French											1								

*One of these is non-Chinese.

Table 40: Achievements of former pupils of the English Language Centre, 1982; results of 16 candidates in seven Liverpool secondary schools

	CSE						O-level						A-level					
	1	2	3	4	5	U	A	B	C	D	E	U	A	B	C	D	E	O
English language	2		1	2	3*													
Mathematics		1	1	2	2	3	1	1	2									
History			2	1														
Geography	2		2	2														
Physics		2	1	2	1*	2			2	1								
Chemistry	1			1*							1	1						
Biology		1	1					1	1									
Art	2	2						1	1									
Woodwork									1									
GED	1		1	2*		1			1		2							
Computer studies	2	1		1					1	1								
Commerce				1					1	1								
Chinese					1		1	1	1									
Arabic												1						
ESL			2															
Home economics			1	1														
Motor maintenance	1		1			1			1									
Navigation									1			1						

*One of these is non-Chinese.

Table 41: Achievements of former pupils of the English Language Centre, September 1983 to July 1984; results of 16 candidates in six Liverpool secondary schools

	RSA		CSE						O-level						16+					A-level						
	P	F	1	2	3	4	5	U	A	B	C	D	E	U	1	2	3	4	5	A	B	C	D	E	O	U
ESL			1	1																						
English language		1	2	2	2	1	1*				1		4*			2	3*									
English literature				2	2		1				2						1*					1				
Mathematics	2*	1		1	2	2				1	2	1	1*				1*					1				1
Additional further mathematics											1												1			
Physics				1	1			1		1	2*	1	1	2			1	1					1			
Chemistry				1	1			1		1		1	1													
Biology				1							1*	1	1													
Art								1			2*	1														
GED/Technical drawing	1	1*				1					2*	1	1													
Commerce							1	1					1													
Computer science						1					2			2												1
Navigation														2												
General studies													1*													1
Sociology													1													
World studies		1																								
History						1*				1																
Geography	1																									
Shorthand	1																									
Typing	1																									

*One of these is non-Chinese.

Section 10
Further and
Higher Education

Just as there is a lack of data on the examination performance of pupils of Chinese origin so their participation in further and higher education is also not well documented. In addition to ability, language is again a factor which seriously affects their representation in forms of further and higher education, but it appears that parental attitudes, the need for information about further education opportunities and guidance by teachers are also important influences on the take-up of further education by Chinese pupils.

It is important not to confuse the large number of Far East Asian students in further and higher education with pupils of Chinese origin who have experienced some, if not most, of their education in the UK. There is a tradition in the Far East Asian countries for the most able students, who are already literate in English, to complete their education in the UK either on A-level courses in further education colleges, with the hope of entering university later, or as direct entrants into higher education. It is generally agreed that by far the majority of students of Chinese ethnic origin in establishments of further and higher education are from overseas. Garvey and Jackson (1975), for example, claimed that there were thousands of overseas Chinese students in British universities, especially in post-graduate science. Wang (1981) noted that there were many Chinese university students in Liverpool, the overwhelming majority from overseas. According to Chann (1976), the 1971 Census figures included some 5,000 students from China, Hong Kong, Malaysia, Singapore and other Far East Asian countries. Clough and Quarmby (1978) claimed that in 1974 there were 1,776 students of Chinese ethnic origin from Hong Kong, 974 students from Singapore and 6,982 from Malaysia in institutions of higher and further education in the UK. Not all will have been of Chinese ethnic origin, but there are also some Chinese students from the People's Republic of China such as those sent by their government for study at the University of Sheffield for up to three years (Mackillop, 1980). Research conducted by Simsova and Chin (1982) into the library needs of the Chinese in London provides a good example of the representation of Chinese students in the UK and shows their use of educational facilities: some 66 per cent of the sample of 499 were students, mostly from Hong Kong (42 per cent) and

Malaysia (35 per cent), three-quarters men under 25. They were in the UK to complete their education, often in scientific and technical subjects, and many helped with the Chinese language schools. This was seen by the students as a contribution to community service and voluntary work during their studies and appears to be a unique feature of mother-tongue teaching classes (Tsow, 1983a, 1984; Chann, 1984). But it is clear that by far the majority of Chinese students in further and higher education and professionals in the UK have been predominantly educated in Hong Kong and, in the case of the students, are here to complete their education.

Parental attitudes may be a vital factor in the decision of able pupils of Chinese origin to stay on at school or enter further or higher education. It was reported at the SCSCRC Conference, in 1976, that in some cases considerable persuasion had been necessary to get Chinese parents to allow their children, especially girls, to stay on at school beyond the statutory leaving age. Lynn (1982) has observed that at this time there may be a conflict of expectation between home and school, for although Chinese parents want the best for their children, they tend to think that if they or a friend can provide employment, then it is best for the child to leave. Even though teachers may try to persuade parents to permit an able child to stay on, when parents do not agree it is likely that the child will obey the parents' wishes and leave school to enter the family business. However, other teachers have suggested that many pupils of Chinese origin are ambitious, fully alive to the possibility of further education and are both willing and expect to 'go it alone', if necessary. The reluctance of Chinese parents to allow their children to continue in education beyond 16 has, however, also been reported by some of the LEAs in the survey conducted by Little and Willey (1983). On the other hand, Jones (1980) mentioned that some Chinese parents have encouraged their children to take full advantage of the state education system in the hope that they will be sufficiently successful to obtain university places. Doubtless, Chinese parents, like any other group, will display a range of attitudes towards the continuation of their children in education beyond the statutory school-leaving age, and their attitudes will be particularly affected by socioeconomic circumstances, especially if they need additional help to run the family business.

It is difficult, however, to glean information on the numbers of pupils of Chinese origin with UK schooling who have continued into further and higher education. Lai (1975) in a survey in London found that none of the young Chinese aged 16+, most of whom had been educated in Hong Kong, were undergoing any form of further education. Yet Fitchett (1976) claimed that some pupils of Chinese origin had entered further education in Derby, though their numbers were unknown; Mackillop (1980) stated that many Chinese school-leavers in Sheffield were taking advantage of opportunities for further education; and Garvey and Jackson (1975) cited some examples of young Chinese in further education hoping to prepare for university entrance. It seems likely that the number of pupils of Chinese origin staying on at school and entering further education will have increased during recent years and may be proportionately greater amongst those who have received more education in the UK. Tan's recent study (1982) in London, for example, disclosed that some 15 17–18 year-olds out of 36 13–18 year-olds were still in school, suggesting a high rate of staying on. Moreover, the 1981 ILEA Language Survey (ILEA, 1982) revealed that there were more 16–19-year-old Chinese-speaking pupils in London schools than Chinese speakers aged 15, which suggests that Chinese pupils have a high rate of staying on. Their staying on compared with that of Urdu-speaking pupils, though, was not quite so high as that of Gujerati-speaking pupils. Indeed in the 1983 Language Census (ILEA, 1983) some 55 per cent of Chinese speakers aged 15 in 1981 were still in secondary schools when aged 17. This was a much higher proportion than for any other group of language speakers and compared with 19.9 per cent in ILEA as a whole. Unfortunately, there is no information about the reasons for staying on and the types of courses pursued by these pupils.

As a result of an observational study, Ng (1982) suggested that the performance of pupils of Chinese origin might be similar to that of pupils of Asian origin, but that they were poorly represented in higher education. This is confirmed by Wang (1981) and the few exceptional examples cited by Garvey and Jackson (1975) and Jones (1980). Pupils of Chinese origin pursuing their studies and entering institutions of higher education appear to be still comparatively rare. According to Fong (1981), lack of English, especially skills in the written language, is the main barrier to achieving good examination performance and hence restricts opportunities for higher education despite ability. Ladlow (1980) claims that Chinese parents make many sacrifices to ensure that those children with ability do go on to higher education.

It would seem that with respect to ethnic minority pupils, including pupils of Chinese origin, teachers have a particular responsibility to give realistic and appropriate guidance as to opportunities for further and higher education and careers, and that information to parents is likely to significantly widen and influence the perceived choices available (see pp. 254–5, 277–81 for consideration of Chinese parents' and pupils' attitudes towards employment). The CAG and QCRC Conference (1979) recommended that improved links should be made between schools and further education colleges with respect to the needs of pupils of Chinese origin, so that, for example, there might be a greater acceptance of students with lower proficiency in English on training courses. It was suggested that further education programmes in local colleges should be publicized more widely and disseminated through channels in the local Chinese community. In particular, there needed to be a greater awareness of and access to job training programmes for young Chinese. Chan (1983) has pointed to the continued lack of special provision for pupils of Chinese origin to undergo skill training in Scotland, so that many with a low level of English drop out of education at 16 and enter the catering trade. The recent report on the Chinese in Britain (GB. P. H of C. HAC, 1985) acknowledged that the extent of involvement of Chinese pupils in further education, TOPS or YTS courses was unknown, and it queried the English language qualifications for further education course entry. Although in recent years attention has importantly begun to be paid to approaches to further education in a multiracial society (see, for example, CRE, 1982b; FEU, 1983; Murray, 1984), it remains the case that the specific needs of Chinese pupils have been largely overlooked.

The particular difficulty associated with the education of pupils of Chinese origin, in addition to developing their skills in English, is to open up opportunities for opting out of the cycle of employment in the catering trade, especially since the desire of many pupils of Chinese origin and their parents is for them to experience a wider range of employment. Lynn (1982) considers that a step towards enlarging job choices is to provide Chinese parents with information concerning further education opportunities which may, in turn, stimulate parents to encourage their children to acquire academic qualifications. Fong (1981), too, has argued that teachers have a special responsibility to guide pupils of Chinese origin to have realistic aspirations and expectations and to advise them about attainable goals in further and higher education and with respect to likely future jobs. It would appear that there is much more work to be done in this field, especially in times of economic recession when there may be more pressure on pupils of Chinese origin to be absorbed into the catering trade despite restrictions on its opportunities for expansion. Proper guidance for pupils and parents of Chinese origin is vital if aspirations, expectations and attitudes are to be commensurate with ability and opportunity, so that educational achievement can be appropriately matched with available employment. But perhaps the most fundamental responsibility of the education system to pupils of Chinese origin is, as a Bristol teacher has expressed it, 'how to make sure that Chinese pupils have as good a basic education as possible, so that they *can* break away from the family business if and when they wish'. It is clear from this review of aspects of the education and performance of pupils of Chinese origin that insufficient is known, at the level of research, about the abilities, skills and achievements of these pupils or of the kind of education which they are receiving. It is to be hoped that there is a greater awareness of their needs, interests and aptitudes at the local level by teachers, advisers and specialists. But until there is more publicly available evidence on a national scale, it is difficult to assess strengths and weaknesses on little more than a broadly descriptive basis. This being so it is all the more important to examine the complementary and in many ways more adequately documented evidence about the attitudes of Chinese parents and children, their school peers and teachers in order to gain a better understanding of the context in which the education of pupils of Chinese origin takes place.

Part Four
Home and School

Section 11
Chinese Parents

In any consideration of the education of pupils of Chinese origin the attitudes and influence of their parents and the relationship between home and school must be considered central. It is important to examine research evidence on the attitudes of Chinese parents to their children's education to determine the degree of their congruence with the objectives of the education system as practised in the particular schools which their children attend. The educational experience of Chinese parents and their knowledge of the British education system are likely to influence their attitudes towards the philosophy of schooling inherent in the British system. Home–school contact may be particularly significant in promoting the mutual understanding of teachers and parents. These factors and cultural differences relevant to aspects of the curriculum and school organization, as well as parents' attitudes to extra-curricular activities, will be explored. Finally, the interrelation of parents and children – two generations with life experiences in two different cultural milieux – will be examined, especially with regard to parents' aspirations for their child's future employment. This review of research on parents' attitudes permits an assessment of the likely influence of Chinese parents on their children's education.

Parents' education
The education of Chinese parents is often considered to be relevant to their attitudes to their children's education and to their ability to assist their children to grow up in the two cultural orientations of home and school. All the evidence indicates that, apart from the professionals, many of the Chinese parents in the UK, especially those who are older, and women, have had very little or no schooling. According to Ladlow (1980), many had their education interrupted or curtailed by the Japanese war and occupation.

Parents in the 30 families and others studied in the late 1960s by O'Neill (1972) in Liverpool had not normally enjoyed much education. In O'Neill's opinion they were thus largely unable to convey to their children central ideas of Chinese culture. This was a peculiar difficulty in mixed Chinese-British marriages where the mother was invariably British, though conversely, the mother's familiarity with the British educational system was advantageous. Amongst the Chinese families studied by Lai (1975) in London the illiterate were more likely to be women or in the 45–51 age range. As a group their educational experience varied, but was generally modest:

	Illiterate	Private tutoring	Some primary education	Complete primary education	Some secondary education	Complete secondary education
Males	2	7	6	4	1	4
Females	6	2	4	6	3	2

Their educational opportunities had been limited and their experience reflected the traditional preference within Chinese culture for males to be educated if a choice were necessary. Lai questioned whether the educational background of these parents equipped them for preparing their children to cope with their educational experience in Britain. Similarly, in York Cheung (1975) discovered that the majority of his sample had completed six years of primary education in Hong Kong. Those who had completed secondary schooling were much more likely to be literate in Chinese, and to some extent in English. There was a greater range of educational experience amongst the Chinese parents in Tan's sample (1982) in London. All but one of the 50 mothers had two to 14 years of schooling. The majority (70 per cent) had only completed primary school education in Hong Kong, although one-quarter had some secondary school education, and two of the mothers had continued their studies to A-level after settling in the UK. Interestingly, the fathers' educational experience overall was less extensive, ranging from three to 12 years. Although 78 per cent had primary school education, fewer (20 per cent) had some secondary school education.

Thus while the claim in the QCRC Conference report (1981) that the majority of Chinese in the UK are illiterate seems slightly exaggerated, the CAG & QCRC Conference report's (1979) view that most Chinese parents are not formally educated to any high degree would seem accurate. Mothers are likely to have less educational experience than fathers and older parents are less likely to have had many years of schooling. The majority of parents will only have completed primary education. They are unlikely to have any knowledge of English before arrival in the UK, and their lack of English and lack of educational experience has led some commentators (Ng, 1982; Tsow, 1977) to suggest that when combined with the pressures and time spent in making a living, parents are very often unable to understand their children's educational experience in the UK or to give them support and guidance to reach their educational goals.

Parents' knowledge of and attitudes to the British educational system and their children's schooling

It is likely that Chinese parents' attitudes to their children's schooling will be influenced by their educational expectations, in turn conditioned by their own experience and knowledge of the education system in Hong Kong. Any group of parents will display a range of attitudes to education which will depend both on their own learning experiences and also the extent to which they have been informed about or become aware of the educational system. The first encounter with British education, for most Chinese parents, will be mediated through their children. As yet there are very few Chinese parents who will have experienced full or partial schooling in the UK, though Chinese professionals and students who have stayed on and reared a family are likely to have a more accurate appreciation of the system because of their own experience and their greater fluency in English. Chinese parents' attitudes to education have occasioned considerable comment, though little actual research. Nevertheless, there is a fair amount of agreement relating to their use of the state education system, attitudes to education *per se*, understanding of the system, especially relating to teaching methods, awareness of the significance of parental choice, support and guidance, and attitudes to the value and cultural system inherent in British education.

Most Chinese parents in the UK utilize the state education system for their child's schooling. For example, in the CRE survey 69 per cent of the 138 Chinese parents whose children did not attend part-time Chinese language classes had children in state primary schools, and 38 per cent in state comprehensives. Only four per cent of parents had children in public junior schools and one per cent in public secondary schools (Tsow, 1984). Those who can afford to pay may opt to place their children in private education (Jones, 1980). Fitchett's monograph (1976) includes an interesting account of a visit to a private junior Catholic school in Derby with a roll of 20 per cent Chinese children, predominantly born in the UK of non-Catholic families. The Chinese parents were attracted to the school because of its quiet and gentle but firm discipline and an ethos in which graciousness, good manners and behaviour were considered important. The parents whose children attended this school were said to be 'well-to-do', either working in or owning restaurants or takeaway shops. They were evidently prepared to pay fees and to transport their children to the school by car and taxi. The description given by Fitchett contrasts markedly with the report of many Chinese children given in Garvey and Jackson's account (1975). The children in Derby appeared contented, confident and well adjusted, enjoying their school and secure in their home background. The standard of their work impressed their teachers, especially by its artistic, neat quality.

Some Chinese parents, for mixed social, economic and cultural reasons may leave their children to be educated in Hong Kong, at least until secondary age. Others also, apparently for mixed reasons, have sent their children back to Hong Kong for some, if not all, of their education (Cheung, 1975; Jones, 1980). Increasingly in recent years parents who neither wished nor could afford to send their children to Hong Kong for their education, but who wished them to grow up with an appreciation of Chinese language and culture, have sent them to part-time Chinese language classes in out-of-school hours (see pp.185–8). However, it has been claimed that a British education is generally preferred to a continental education (in Germany or Holland), so that if the child's father has moved to work in Europe, Chinese children will usually be left in this country for their schooling (QCRC, 1981). In the main, therefore, Chinese children are educated in the state system. To what extent do parents encourage their children to take full advantage of it?

Traditionally the Chinese have valued education as a means to advancement and teachers and scholars have been held in high regard. In the UK the traditional attitude may perforce have been tempered by situational realities necessitating an increased focus on economic survival, especially since most parents' lack of formal education has limited their involvement in the academic aspects of the education of their children (CAG & QCRC, 1979). In Liverpool, in the 1960s, O'Neill (1972) discovered that Chinese parents placed great value on formal education in Britain as a means of improving socioeconomic status, and had a great desire for their children to enter professional occupations. Although Chinese parents were beginning to realize that an English education undermined an adherence to Chinese ways, primarily through the changes it effected in the bonds between family members, O'Neill observed that there was no overt conflict between Chinese parents and the schools which their children attended because their respect for education as such outweighed any dislike of the particular system of schooling. The underlying philosophy of education was different from their expectations, but this was not always apparent whilst the children were in the early years of schooling, so that their independence, for example, was only asserted later. In York, Cheung (1975) also discerned an ambivalence in the feelings of Chinese parents about the UK education system. They displayed an instrumental attitude to schooling, focussing on the learning of English as the main benefit, as it was thought that a better command of English would lead to wider career, and hence economic, opportunities. But again, parents were less happy about the cultural orientation of British education (see pp.234–6). More recently Chan (1983), too, has claimed that Chinese parents tend to weigh education in monetary terms; whilst they want their children to do well at school, the prime emphasis is always on material wealth, and education is a means to such a goal. In Chan's view many Chinese feel inferior in the UK and that it is pointless to strive for academic success, so they aim for economic success as an alternative. Yet in Fong's (1981) study, in Liverpool, all the parents claimed without qualification that they would like their child to be well educated. They wished their children to gain educational qualifications or practical skills, so that they might attain high-status jobs or become professionals. Thus Chinese parents are generally ambitious for their children and keen that they should succeed at school in order that they might have a better life than they themselves have had (Chann, 1976).

Chinese parents have a positive instrumental attitude to education for its potential economic benefits, though they may regard the British education system with some ambivalence because of its value orientation. Yet the consensus in the literature indicates that Chinese parents have a considerable lack of understanding of the British education system as such. Lack of ability to communicate in English with schools, lack of time due to work pressures and, for both of these reasons, lack of parental involvement in schools (see pp.236–9) have conspired to limit their knowledge of British education often to the information mediated to them through their children. Not surprisingly, as the CAG & QCRC Conference (1979) pointed out, parents' ignorance of the British educational system and teaching methods have often led to misunderstanding and dissatisfaction. Cheung (1975) found that British schooling was little understood by Chinese parents in York, to the extent that some entrusted another young Chinese, partly educated in the UK, to make arrangements for their children to be enrolled at a school some distance from their home. Lai (1975), in London, also recorded that Chinese parents were ignorant of their children's schooling: from their impressions they were relieved that their children appeared to enjoy their time in the primary school, but concerned that they did not seem to be learning enough at the secondary level. Garvey and Jackson (1975) reported that many of the Chinese parents with whom they came in contact were 'mystified' about their children's experience of schooling. More recently in Liverpool Fong (1981) discerned that Chinese parents did not understand the schooling system or know how their children were progressing in their schoolwork. Moreover, Chinese parents' lack of understanding of educational philosophy has not gone unnoticed by teachers and LEAs (Little and Willey, 1983).

Chinese parents generally have a different concept of education based on their own experience of a more formal education in Hong Kong, so that they often fail to appreciate teaching styles and methods or the ethos of the school in a UK context (Ladlow, 1980; NCC, 1984). The clearest evidence of the lack of knowledge – or at least the willingness to pass an opinion – about British schooling is provided by the CRE survey (Tsow, 1984.) Of the 195 parents whose children attended part-time Chinese language classes, nearly one-third failed to comment on their children's ordinary school. Twenty-one per cent said that they had no opinion (six per cent more than those who would not comment on Chinese classes), and nine per cent maintained that they could not comment because they could not speak English which was a barrier to communication with the school. On the other hand, 36 per cent of the parents expressed satisfaction with their children's school and 19 per cent thought the quality of teaching was good. There is evidently a need for effective communication to be established between schools and Chinese parents not just to make complaints or give information, but to facilitate mutual awareness on the one hand of parents' expectations and perceptions, and on the other of the kind of education which their children's schools are providing.

One way in which cultural expectations of Chinese parents leads to misunderstanding and dissatisfaction with the schooling of their children in Britain is through the different concept they have of teaching methods. Their suspicion of teaching styles is exemplified in a lack of understanding of the educational significance of 'play', especially in the early stages of learning. Lai (1975), for example, reported that Chinese parents in London thought of their children's primary schools as 'institutions for play'. Similarly, Garvey and Jackson noted that Chinese mothers were dismayed by their young children's reports of play activities at school, for they felt they must learn English through hard work. As Ladlow and Lynn have pointed out, the Chinese concept of education is to 'study books', so that many of the play and learning activities in British schools seem irrelevant and incomprehensible to Chinese parents. Young children are expected to learn by studying books and writing, rather than through free expression. In Hong Kong (see pp.18–22) even nursery school children receive homework and children rise to the next grade through examination assessment, not according to their age. The strength of some Chinese parents' concern is illustrated by an example cited by Lynn of a child who asked to be removed from the Language Centre, in Liverpool, because his parents felt that as his language learning focussed on verbal exchanges and play activities but homework and written assignments were not given every day, he was not being taught the English language. Ladlow has counselled that teachers should try to appreciate differential perceptions and expectations and not feel that parents do not show an interest in their child or school if they do not see the educational relevance of play. Although some parents have some appreciation of teaching methods in British schools (see, for example, Tsow, 1984), it would appear, especially perhaps in the matter of the education of younger children or E2L beginners, that parents expect formal teaching methods to a greater extent than they may generally be employed (NCC, 1984).

Another aspect of the education of their children in the UK which often fails to be appreciated by Chinese parents, namely, the importance of parental choice and involvement, may also in part be attributed to cultural expectations – of non-interference. Chinese parents expect schools to get on with the business of teaching and they are prepared to leave matters concerning education to the school (Lynn, 1982; NCC, 1984). Parents assume it is the professional responsibility of teachers to guide the child as to his best interests in all aspects of education, especially in subject, school and career choice (Ladlow, 1980). Lai (1975) discovered that secondary school age children in London had largely been assigned to their secondary schools without the active involvement of their parents. Parents relied upon learning about secondary schools from other Chinese parents and only a few had taken the advice of the head of the primary school or had exercised any choice. Those who did sometimes avoided schools in Soho, with a large concentration of Chinese pupils, in order that their children might improve their chances of learning English, though they were more concerned about their protection when in smaller numbers (see p.264). Yet although the expectations that the school will fully guide and advise Chinese pupils may have been reflected in a certain lack of opinion about schooling expressed by parents in the CRE survey (Tsow, 1984), it must not be assumed that this indicates lack of interest or support. For example, two-thirds of the parents in Fong's sample in Liverpool (1981) claimed that they always cared about their child's schoolwork, and this was largely corroborated in separate evidence given by their children. Thus parents with little educational experience, little knowledge of English and little time to spend with their children may, nevertheless, stress the importance of education and take considerable interest in their child's learning, especially at home. But as Mackillop (1980) for example reports, Chinese parents who are professionals, and who also take an interest and pride in their children's education and competence in English, are able to take a much more active part in their child's education at home and in school.

For those less Westernized or urbanized parents who form the majority of Chinese parents in the UK, however, the education of their children in Britain has caused considerable anxiety (Watson, 1977a). For though British educationists may have perceived Chinese parents as having an instrumental attitude to education, lacking understanding of teaching methods and of the need for parental involvement, Chinese parents have themselves been less than enthusiastic about the British school system because of the different values which are embodied in the content and process of teaching. Like other ethnic minority parents, they fear that their children, especially those in urban environments, will be attracted to British lifestyles and abandon Chinese cultural values, particularly that of loyalty to the family. Thus as well as anxieties about lack of formal teaching, Chinese parents are often concerned about what they perceive as a lack of discipline, in particular, the absence of manners and courtesy and obedience (see pp. 250–3). This they judge not only from their children's behaviour, but also – in the absence of their own ability to comprehend what is taking place in the school – through their children's reports of school-life (see Garvey and Jackson, 1975). There is a sense in which to Chinese parents behavioural traits are symptomatic of something much more profound in terms of a want of appreciation of, and adherence to, Chinese cultural traditions, especially in terms of family support.

This was apparent among the Chinese families studied by O'Neill (1972), who noted that although the children had often been successful in education, which she attributed to parental encouragement and the children's application, there was a paradox, in that achieving the very success so much desired by the Chinese parents for their children served to alienate them further from a Chinese way of life. Any form of education involves the transmission of cultural attitudes and values in the content, process and context of teaching. A significant aspect of Chinese education at home and school was to teach attitudes in support of the social structure (see pp.14–17). This, in turn, revolved around the concepts of filial piety, obedience and loyalty. Yet these values largely fail to find a place in British education, where the underlying philosophy is that of encouraging critical thinking and individualism. This focus, together with the situation of Chinese families in a Western cultural environment, and often their own lack of ability to explain the values of Chinese cultural traditions to their children, has occasioned considerable anxiety on the part of Chinese parents in research studies in the past 25 years. According to Cheung (1975), Chinese parents in York had ambivalent feelings about UK education because, as they saw it, in the process of succeeding in the education system their children were transformed into 'Gwei Shing' (Gwei = devil/ghost = Westerners; Shing = character; i.e. a Western non-Chinese character). Becoming Gwei Shing in Chinese parents' eyes meant losing the child as a family member because he would no longer be able to continue to support the social structure and family system.

Chinese parents sometimes deliberately took special action to attempt to ensure that their children would not lose their cultural inheritance. Sometimes the child would be wholly educated abroad, as it was generally thought that by adolescence the child would have developed a Chinese character and could safely be exposed to a British education without changing. Sometimes children were sent back to Hong Kong to finish their education with a first-hand experience of Chinese culture and family relationships within a traditional social structure and environment. Both these practices were continued into the mid-1970s, and though they may have been ostensibly undertaken to provide a Chinese education there were often other underlying socioeconomic motives (see pp.36–8). In recent years these practices have been largely discontinued as the orientation of Chinese parents has changed and, for the majority, their settlement in the UK confirmed. But this has not lessened the desire of Chinese parents for their children to grow up with a knowledge and appreciation of Chinese traditions and practices, to which they should largely adhere in their daily lives, hence the motivation for the establishment and recent rapid growth of voluntary part-time classes for Chinese language and culture. These classes have come to be the focus for the hopes of many Chinese parents to ensure that continued allegiance of their children to traditional concepts such as respect, loyalty, self-reliance and obedience. In this way Chinese parents hope to provide an antidote to the values which they perceive to be inherent in the British education system and contrary to those of their own culture.

Other ways in which the school's organization and aspects of the curriculum are perceived by Chinese parents to conflict with their own attitudes and interests are examined elsewhere (see pp.239–43). It is important that Chinese parents' poor understanding of the philosophy of British schooling and its methodology, which may be due to lack of information or misinformation, and their reluctance to voice their reservations, should not merely be interpreted as passive acceptance. It is ironical that the very attitudes and distinctively Chinese characteristics, which they are concerned to transmit to their children, serve to condition their own approach to schools and teachers about what they regard as their children's distinctive needs and interests as Chinese. Nowhere is the influence of these attitudes more apparent than in the context of parental participation in schooling through home–school contacts.

Home–school contact

A number of culturally conditioning factors can be discerned as typically influencing the attitude of Chinese parents to their child's schooling in respect of home–school contact. These may be described as: a characteristic reluctance to approach any form of authority, especially associated with government; the precedence which teachers have in Chinese social hierarchy, and hence the respect accorded to their professionalism, to the extent that Chinese parents prefer to withdraw rather than criticize teachers or the arrangements for the schooling of their children; and Chinese parents' lack of appreciation of the importance accorded to parental participation. The combination of these attitudes makes Chinese parents very reticent about entering school, especially if they are an isolated family (Ladlow, 1980). There are, in addition, significant conditions due to their position in Britain. First, the long hours worked in the catering trade makes school involvement difficult, as events often take place at the busiest times of their working lives. Secondly, and more fundamentally, the limited proficiency which many Chinese parents, especially mothers, have in English seriously restricts meaningful communication between parents and schools. For a majority this will be the single most overriding problem, and may affect home and school interaction to a greater degree than with any other ethnic minority group. Hence it is not surprising, though a matter of considerable concern, that all sources agree that home–school contact with Chinese parents is minimal. The degree of interaction may be examined through evidence on Chinese parents' visits to schools for various purposes and events, and the extent to which teachers attempt to communicate with parents, either indirectly or by home visiting.

All evidence suggests that visits made by Chinese parents to schools are extremely rare, both at primary and secondary level (for example, Lai, 1975). Indeed a teacher with experience of teaching Chinese children for 16 years (quoted by Lynn, 1982) claimed only to have met the parents of one of his Chinese pupils. Yet, as this teacher himself realized, parents' absence from school did not necessarily mean disinterest. Indeed Fong (1981) discovered that over 90 per cent of the parents in a small sample in Liverpool had visited the school once or twice when their children first started. They usually depended on the assistance of an interpreter or social worker acting as a go-between for their contact with the school. Fong argued that parents should make a greater effort to attend schools more often, utilizing such assistance where necessary, in order that through better contact teachers might have a greater appreciation of their home background, daily life and culture.

It is interesting to compare Chinese parents' contact with mainstream and voluntary language schools. In the CRE survey (Tsow, 1984) most teachers claimed to have contact with the parents of their pupils, although this was not often to discuss the child's progress or problems in learning. Even so, fewer than half of the teachers said that parents actively participated in the school's organization or outings. Yet such a degree of contact is greatly in excess of that experienced in the mainstream. The CAG & QCRC Conference (1979) urged that positive attempts should be made to contact Chinese parents about school events, and reported that whilst some schools had successes in attracting parents to international evenings, others had markedly failed to involve parents. Chinese parents are apparently reluctant to attend even social functions, such as open-days, because of long working hours, embarrassment and fears that lack of English would make the visit meaningless (Lai, 1975; Fong, 1981). Moreover, what is perceived as an unwelcoming aspect of some schools may inhibit further contact, as in the case of a Chinese parent with fluent English who attended a parents' meeting (Chan, 1983). Given the present staffing resources in schools with only the occasional Chinese speaker, even in areas with relatively large numbers of Chinese pupils, it is unlikely that direct communication with Chinese parents in their own dialect and school involvement can be facilitated.

Interaction might be developed through the skills of Chinese pupils themselves who play a vital role in establishing links, however tenuous, between the schools and Chinese parents. There is little likelihood of written communications being sent home in Mandarin and the relatively poor literacy of many Chinese parents would not ensure that any communication could be read or understood. It is, therefore, generally agreed amongst those with experience of attempting to communicate with Chinese parents that their children should convey messages orally. Ladlow (1980), for example, recommends that when parents are expected to visit school, the message should be given orally to the child and a verbal answer requested the next day since it may be weeks before a letter can be interpreted to parents (see also Garvey and Jackson, 1975). This places a further onus on pupils of Chinese origin and implies trust, apparently accorded by Chinese parents, that replies will be forthcoming (Fong, 1981; Lynn, 1982).

But Cheung (1975) provides an interesting insight. Since parents were rarely in a position to read notices sent home from school, in many cases the Chinese pupils themselves decided whether to bring the notice to the attention of their parents, as they knew that language difficulties and the timing of events would often prohibit parents' attendance at school functions. In effect, therefore, the Chinese children themselves often took the decision about parents' attendance. Since many children did not see the point of their parents going to the school, they implicitly reinforced a situation in which parental absence prevailed. Moreover, given the lack of facilities to communicate in Chinese, pupils of Chinese origin are often also required to interpret to parents their own school performance, for example, the grading on reports (Ladlow, 1980). But how satisfactory can this be? Chinese parents' lack of understanding of the British school system and their lack of school contact argues strongly for the urgency and importance of finding ways to communicate information if there is to be any real appreciation by Chinese parents of the orientation of British schooling. Cassette tapes in Cantonese explaining the objectives and teaching approaches of the school and inviting participation by parents might be a useful start (Tsow, personal communication).

Parent–teacher interaction is often confined to meetings occasioned by problems with the social or academic position of the child. But it is important that teachers' requests to parents for interviews should not be confined to problem-centred situations (CAG & QCRC, 1979). Ladlow (1980) suggests a Chinese pupil's good points should be emphasized, especially if parents have little command of English, in order to establish a better relationship. It would seem that home–school visiting could be particularly beneficial in facilitating greater mutual understanding as a more positive and active approach is demanded. By visiting the homes of Chinese pupils, especially if accompanied by a bilingual Chinese, a teacher may obtain more knowledge and information about the child's family background and establish a trusting and positive relationship between home and school. But even if communication is restricted through the child, as Fong points out, at least the teacher will be able to see the child's living environment and make direct personal contact with parents. It is important to make arrangements in advance, emphasizing that it is a social call to meet the family, and to be careful to fulfil the appointment as agreed. The teacher's visit is likely to give the family honour and respect (Ladlow, 1980). Others have suggested that meetings with parents would be more acceptable at community centres of Chinese schools (GB. P. H of C, 1985).

Such teacher–parent encounters are an essential preliminary to establishing a link which may encourage parental participation in their child's schooling to a greater degree (Ladlow, 1980). It is important for Chinese parents to realize the significance of the involvement. Although, for example, a parent support programme in Liverpool had attempted to involve Chinese parents, their response was always negative, yet other ethnic minority parents had welcomed the establishment of such a group (Lynn, 1982). The renamed Parent School Partnership, established in 17 schools, including the Language Centre, employed two bilingual teachers whose task was to visit parents, inform them of the Centre's work and encourage them to further their own education through various activities, including English language tuition, so that they can, in turn, help their children. According to Chann (1976), who cited instances of English classes for Chinese mothers in London and pre-school children in Huddersfield, experiments have shown that Chinese parents can be encouraged to play a greater part in helping their children to gain the most from their educational experience. But the task is not to be underestimated, since any initial communication requies the involvement of Chinese speakers. The usefulness of bilingual skills in establishing links between home and school has not been fully recognized. Chinese professionals and students might also be involved in providing information to Chinese parents and in exploring perceptions about schooling. For, as Chan (1983) has pointed out, though the attitude of Chinese parents may need to be changed, so school policies and practices relating to home–school contact must also be carefully re-evaluated.

Parents' attitudes to school organization and aspects of the curriculum
As with other ethnic minority groups, the Chinese may have a particular cultural orientation which predisposes them to hold certain attitudes towards aspects of the curriculum and the organization of their children's schools. Though the eclectic religious background of the Chinese may not prescribe such a dogmatic attitude as some of the religions of South Asian parents to those aspects of the life of the school which are generally agreed to impinge more directly on religious beliefs and social customs, nevertheless there may be matters in which the cultural orientation of Chinese families in the UK does not accord with school practices. An assessment is made of research evidence and of Chinese parents' views on discipline, diet, physical education, dress, religious education, single-sex schools and the possibility of separate Chinese schools. Thus the extent to which Chinese parents' wishes for the education of their children have been accommodated can be evaluated. Attention has already been drawn to the vital unifying role of the Chinese language in transmitting Chinese traditions and culture and the significance which Chinese parents accord to the socialization of their children through learning Chinese (pp.155–6). Moreover, attitudes to values which Chinese parents perceive to be mediated in schools, judging by

their observations of the effect of school experiences on the behaviour and attitudes of their children, may be more important than their attitudes to the aspects of education discussed in this sub-section. But again, given the paucity of research evidence on voiced requests to school authorities on the part of Chinese parents, it is difficult to be certain how to interpret strength of feeling on some of these matters.

There is a consensus that many Chinese parents think that schools are too liberal and lax in discipline. In the course of their own education Chinese parents will have perceived teachers as authoritarian figures, for in Hong Kong school is viewed as an important disciplinary agent. They may, therefore, use the threat of 'telling the teacher' to a child when he is disobedient (Ladlow, 1980; Lynn, 1982). Lai (1975), for example, reported that Chinese parents with children in secondary schools in London were concerned about discipline because of their children's reports of bullying. They were generally disappointed in the extent to which the school failed to protect their children. Examples quoted by Garvey and Jackson (1975) confirm Chinese parents' emphasis on discipline and the frequently expressed view that children should not be confused by too much choice. In the unfavourable comments on their children's mainstream schools made by parents in the CRE survey (Tsow, 1984) lack of discipline and insufficient hard work were mentioned by one in ten of parents. For Chinese parents the concept of 'discipline' may involve not just obedience, diligence and respect, but, in addition, the cultivation of good manners and courtesy. Interestingly, Tan (1982) found that Chinese parents often considered language and social customs, especially those relating to the development of good manners, as far more important than observing traditional dietary practices. They were less concerned if their children wished to follow a Western pattern of eating than if they showed signs of disrespect and indiscipline. Garvey and Jackson reported that Chinese parents may attempt to counteract what they perceived to be the liberal atmosphere of the school by stricter controls at home. They would prefer a greater stress on discipline, courtesy and the virtue of hard work (see Jones, 1980; and p.234) because they fear that the more liberal environment of the school and informal teacher–pupil relationships will lead to a loss of respect for parents and traditional Chinese values enshrined in their social system, and also contempt for learning.

It is somewhat ironical in view of the concentration of Chinese parents in the catering trade and the well-known differences in ingredients and cooking methods between Chinese food and traditional British food, that only one study has investigated Chinese parents' perceptions of school meals. Amongst the 50 families whose food ideology and habits were studied by Tan (1982) 40 had school-age children and 32 families allowed their children to eat school meals. Those who did not gave as their reasons fathers' dislike of the idea, their wish to have control over what the children ate, that the school meal was small, 'cold' (thermally) and expensive, and that home cooking was more nourishing. The mothers overall were well informed about the content of school meals but divided as to whether the school or home meal was more nourishing. They allowed their children to eat school meals despite this doubt because it was convenient and cheap; they thought children should learn to appreciate British food habits since they were living in this country; that they should get used to school meals at junior school since they would have to eat them at secondary school; and that teachers did not permit children to travel home to eat at lunchtime. The parents' attitudes to provision for Chinese diet in the school meals service may be seen as symptomatic of the attitude of Chinese parents to the educational system as a whole given the important cultural significance of food for the Chinese:

> The mothers always regard themselves as inferior to the institution. They are reserved in commenting on the policies of school meals, suggesting changes or making comments on the price of school meals. They do not like to criticize for fear of offending the authority and, moreover, they feel powerless to make improvements in official matters. The way that the mothers choose to react is to make up any dissatisfaction; for instance to make up the inadequacy of school meals they have created a food event, 'tea-time'. Some believe that the authority should know what is better for the children, and, if they are not doing their best, then there must be reasons for that; and others feel that for a payment of 35 pence per meal, one should not be expecting much in food quality. (Tan, 1982, p.139)

School meals were perceived by the Chinese mothers as 'unbalanced' although some of the items are enjoyed by children, have been categorized under the Chinese system of food and may be purchased by mothers for home consumption. However, mothers prepare cooling drinks and steamed foods (see p.85) to restore the dietary balance and equilibrium of the body base. The mothers also adopted a new food event – tea – at 4 pm when the children returned from school, to supplement school lunches. At this drinks are served, together with bread, biscuits or cake, although sometimes some cooked foods are supplied. Indeed, teatime has become incorporated into the daily food schedule and is still taken during the vacation and at weekends. This may be seen as an interesting cultural adaptation, but also one that the mothers feel incumbent upon them in view of the perceived inadequacy of school meals. But, as Tan argues, if it is a generally accepted principle that the food preferences of ethnic groups should be respected, as in the provision of vegetarian meals, halal meat or kosher food, should not the dietary preferences of the Chinese also be respected? The Chinese do not enunciate a preference on moral or religious grounds, but believe health to be enhanced by certain patterns of food preparation and choice. This attitude deserves consideration by school meals services, for it should at least be possible to include some Chinese food options in meals in schools with a sizeable Chinese catchment.

Physical education lessons may be a novelty to Chinese pupils, especially those who have received some education in Hong Kong where gym may be optional or non-existent. Moreover, in view of the traditional focus of Chinese upbringing on modesty this may lead some Chinese children, especially girls, to be unwilling to undress in a common changing-room or to take part in PE (Jones, I., 1979). Langton (1979) also suggests that greater provision should be made for table-tennis and basketball within the school's PE curriculum since these are often more popular with Chinese pupils. There are, however, no cultural or religious taboos associated with clothing for pupils of Chinese origin, as there are for some pupils of Asian origin.

Similarly, there is no evidence of any objection by Chinese parents to their children receiving religious education in schools, which is predominantly in the Christian tradition. Indeed, when Chinese in the UK hold religious beliefs they are almost invariably associated with a Christian denomination, often of an evangelical tendency. In fact, as the Hong Kong Government Office (HKGO) list (1984) of Chinese language schools and classes shows, at least 19, a significant proportion, of the schools are associated with religious organizations. In the classes the Chinese Bible or catechism are used, but it is not clear whether the linguistic or the religious purpose is dominant (Tsow, 1983a). Thus religious education would not seem to be particularly problematic with respect to pupils of Chinese origin, although Jones (1979) has suggested that the Christian tradition alone may seem somewhat narrow to the traditional broad-minded Chinese approach to religion (see p. 12). Comparative religious education should, therefore, be particularly welcome to Chinese parents. For them the Confucian emphasis on social ethics in practical daily living, as exemplified in the family and social structure, is of paramount importance, comparable in significance to religious faith (see p.13). There is a real sense, therefore, in which to recognize Chinese parents' values and beliefs would be to broaden the social studies curriculum to give it a multicultural dimension which would include taking account of Chinese social ethics. This already forms part of the syllabus of some of the Chinese language schools (see Tsow, 1983a, 1984).

Although, traditionally, Chinese social life has entailed a certain sexual segregation, the desire for single-sex schooling in the UK does not seem particularly strong amongst Chinese parents, if the absence of reports of parents' preferences is indicative. However, Jackson (1979) reported a dislike of mixed schools on the part of the Chinese family described in his case study and Jones (I., 1979) mentions an instance in which a Chinese boy refused to co-operate in a language-learning activity with a girl, illustrating that the transmission of traditional attitudes may surface in desire for segregation in the classroom.

It is clear that Chinese parents have strong and positive attitudes towards education and that they desire that their children should have a knowledge and appreciation of Chinese culture and language. The strength of their feeling is evident in the support which they have given to the establishment and growth of part-time Chinese language classes. Yet, unlike some of the South Asian minority groups, there has not been a particular drive on the part of the Chinese towards setting up separate full-time Chinese schools. A Chinese school was established in London before the war specifically to enable Chinese children in the UK to receive a Chinese education. But it is not clear whether the children attended this school on a full-time basis (as Ng, 1968, implies; see also Clough and Quarmby, 1978) or in their spare time (Jones, 1980). O'Neill (1972) claimed that towards the end of the 1960s some Chinese parents in Liverpool, who wanted their children to be Chinese in the fullest sense and to identify themselves completely with the Chinese way of life, would have liked to see a Chinese school established there like the Chinese schools in American Chinese communities. Fong (1975, reported by Campbell-Platt, 1978) states that in the mid-1970s the Chinese Association of Commerce was discussing with the ILEA the possibility of operating a full-time bilingual Chinese school, but this does not seem to have materialized. There is no evidence of a renewal of such interest in recent years, despite the rapid growth in part-time Chinese language schools, and moves by other minority groups to establish separate schools.

The general lack of research on parents' attitudes to aspects of the curriculum and school organization seems to be due to traditional Chinese attitudes of deference to authority, non-interference, self-sufficiency and withdrawal rather than criticism, as well as the lack of research undertaken. But it is unclear whether the cultural differences reported, for example, with respect to discipline and diet, are relatively slight because of the superficial similarity of the social lifestyles of the Chinese in the UK and, unlike some other Asian minority groups, the lack of clear religious and cultural prohibitions, or whether Chinese cultural preferences and interests in these matters are as strong and profound, but because publicly unexpressed and uninvestigated they are covertly unacknowledged.

Extra-curricular activities
Extra-curricular activities may be considered according to the degree of association with the school, such as school outings and summer holiday school activities and homework, set by the school but carried out in the home context, or the degree of the association with the home such as spare-time activities, hobbies and attendance at youth clubs. The extent to which pupils of Chinese origin participate in these activities may vary considerably – according to whether the family is isolated from other Chinese families; whether the family runs its own business and requires help from the

children; and whether parents are willing to let children participate in activities out of the home, for generally the home is the focus of social activity for pupils of Chinese origin.

Ladlow (1980) has claimed that Chinese pupils, especially adolescents, often have little opportunity to take part in out-of-school activities since their lifestyle usually involves working for some hours in the family business or minding younger children. However, he argues that this should not be seen as wholly detrimental as it fosters family unity and responsibility. Even so, this is likely to restrict the social mixing of pupils of Chinese origin with their peers and may make it impossible to join in school-based, extra-curricular activities such as school trips and clubs (Lynn, 1982). It has been suggested that the older girls in Chinese families are particularly likely to spend more time at home, thus missing the social mixing which occurs in after-school clubs. Fong (1981) also found that, in Liverpool, Chinese pupils in school seldom joined in any school-based clubs or activities in out-of-school hours as they went home immediately at the end of the school-day. These research findings and observations contrast to some extent with the claims made by parents in the CRE survey (Tsow, 1984) whose children did not attend part-time Chinese language classes. Although 29 per cent of the parents claimed that their children did not take part in any activities after school hours, among those who did the most popular school-based activities were associated with sport (57 per cent). Moreover, 39 per cent of the parents claimed that their children went on school outings. The majority of the teachers in Chinese language schools also claimed that their pupils were involved in activities run in association with but outside the hours of these schools, most commonly visits to museums, galleries and theatres, but also sporting activities, and in the main non-Chinese-oriented. But it may also be noted that 76 per cent of the children attending Chinese language classes interviewed in the survey went straight home afterwards, and 57 per cent did not wish to spend any additional time at the school participating in social activities.

However, it is also interesting to note that of the 58 per cent of children who did not attend Chinese-language classes during the summer, nearly 60 per cent, especially 12–14 year-olds, were interested in doing so. Some LEAs organize school-based summer holiday schemes. One such is the South Liverpool Holiday School, a language-enrichment scheme for ethnic minority children, associated with the English Language Centre and held regularly since 1971. The scheme covers pre-school to secondary age groups, utilizing the assistance of university and sixth-form students. Unfortunately, the extent to which pupils of Chinese origin participate in such school-based summer holiday activities is unknown. Garvey and Jackson (1975) recommended that LEAs should make special provision of this kind which would enable the considerably different needs, outlook and behaviour of Chinese children to be accommodated. They described a summer holiday project in Hammersmith, in 1973, staffed by volunteer Chinese students and part-time English teachers and evidently enjoyed by the Chinese pupils attending. The aim was to assist educational adjustment, both through developing proficiency in English and by paying attention to literacy in Chinese, dramatic and other social activities with a distinctively Chinese orientation. Such summer activities enable continuity of attention to developing proficiency in English as well as allowing opportunities for social interaction with other Chinese and non-Chinese pupils.

The extent to which pupils of Chinese origin have spare-time activities will largely depend on how much they are expected to help in the family business, as Cheung (1975) discovered in York. Children whose parents ran takeaways were often involved in helping, whereas other children had more time to themselves, for example, to play with their Chinese friends. According to Ladlow (1980) and Lynn (1982), it is not customary for Chinese parents to permit their children to play outside the home as they like to give their children constant supervision, although where a number of Chinese families live nearby children may sometimes be seen playing together outside. However, many Chinese parents are pleased for their children to visit their friends' homes, be they Chinese or English, to develop friendships. According to case studies and pupils' own accounts (Fitchett, 1976), most out-of-school activities are home-based: helping with housework (both boys and girls), child care, doing homework, watching TV and, especially for the girls, sewing and other domestic pursuits, rarely going outside the home for social activities. Fong (1981) also found that seven of the 31 children whose families ran fish and chip shops assisted in the shop until late at night, and the children whose parents worked in restaurants took care of themselves, preparing meals and cleaning the house. Usually they stayed at home doing homework, reading books, watching TV and playing with their brothers and sisters. Rarely did the younger children go out to play since they were generally not permitted to do so. Those who had arrived recently in the UK were often afraid of going out because of the different environment and the language barriers. Parents were often concerned that they might be involved in some form of trouble and only boys and older children had more freedom in their social activities. Fong's evidence also suggested that the children in the Chinese families were unlikely to be involved in social activities with other Chinese families to any great extent.

It is interesting to find that the more middle-class parents whose children did not attend Chinese language classes were less likely to claim in the Commission for Racial Equality (CRE) survey that their children were involved in working in the family business or with housework or child care, though it is possible that parents may not have thought to mention those activities specifically as undertaken by Chinese children in their spare time. Although a third of the parents claimed that their children did 'nothing specific', sports were the most popular activities cited. Nearly one-fifth of parents claimed their children watched TV, and almost as many that they played with friends or went on outings, spent time reading, writing or painting, and some ten per cent that their children listened to music. By comparison, only four per cent said that their children helped in the shop or supermarket. This was corroborated exactly by children attending Chinese language classes. This is not without interest since, following Garvey and Jackson's (1975) observational study of Chinese children in which they alleged that the Chinese children worked on average three-and-a-half hours each evening, it has often been assumed that this was the norm. In fact, almost one-third of the children in the CRE survey claimed that they spent their spare time watching TV, although ten per cent mentioned some kind of sporting activity, such as ping-pong or playing in the park. A further seven per cent claimed that they regularly helped their mothers, but over one-fifth claimed to spend their time doing homework after they left the Chinese language classes.

In fact what Chinese parents have perceived as a lack of homework has generally been a source of discontent with their children's schooling (see CAG & QCRC, 1979). The expectation that their children would receive homework from the age of five onwards has been conditioned by their own experience of schooling in Hong Kong (see p.21). Researchers are agreed that Chinese parents are often puzzled at the lack of homework (Lai, 1975; Garvey and Jackson, 1975; Ladlow, 1980; Lynn, 1982). For example, Fong claimed that the Chinese parents in Liverpool feared inadequate learning at school because their children did not bring any work or textbooks home to study. Moreover, in the CRE survey eight per cent of parents whose children attended Chinese language schools claimed that the reason they did not like the mainstream school was because there was insufficient homework, and three per cent of those same parents gave as their specific reason for liking the Chinese language school the fact that homework was given. Complementary evidence is interesting, as in the same survey six per cent of the 8–14-year-old Chinese children claimed to dislike the Chinese language classes because they gave too much homework, whereas none claimed this as a reason for disliking their mainstream schools. Pupils of Chinese origin apparently usually do complete their homework tasks (Lynn, 1982), though homework may be done after closure of the family business (Garvey and Jackson, 1975; see also p.286) or undertaken in crowded living conditions, amidst multifarious activities, including the preparation and serving of food, caring for siblings and the ubiquitous presence of the TV. But, as Ladlow (1980) has pointed out, Chinese parents' expectations of homework as soon as their child starts school can be put to good use, as a means of assisting the improvement of English. At the initial stages sentence copying and learning or matching and copying pictures and phrases are suitable. More advanced pupils might undertake free writing composition and keep diaries as a means of practising and extending their English. Chinese pupils who are keen to advance themselves through education may even welcome homework (Fitchett, 1976).

There is relatively little evidence about Chinese pupils attending social activities which are not organized either by the mainstream school or Chinese language schools. In Liverpool in the late 1960s O'Neill (1972) noted that Chinese children rarely attended scout or youth clubs and there was no specific Chinese community provision for children or adolescents. Garvey and Jackson (1975) observed that it was fashionable for some young Chinese to attend lessons in Kung Fu which had become a virility cult. Occasionally Chinese pupils might also visit the cinema and even discothèques on a weekly basis (Fitchett, 1976). There are other reports of Chinese boys attending youth clubs specifically for sporting activities such as table-tennis and billiards. The fact that sporting activities were frequently mentioned by parents and children alike in the CRE survey suggests that, since it is unlikely that specifically Chinese facilities will be available, sporting activities may encourage both social and inter-racial mixing. The CAG & QCRC Conference (1979) noted that with the exception of a youth club in Soho, and the provision of some extra-curricular activities associated with Chinese language classes, there was a lack of facilities and organizational arrangements specifically geared to the leisure needs of Chinese youth. Both that report and Garvey and Jackson recommended that the Chinese community should make greater efforts to establish contact with Chinese youth and make provision for leisure activities. With the growth of Chinese community centres, at least in the inner city areas of London, Liverpool and Manchester, it is possible that in recent years such facilities have become more available. But for young Chinese living in relative isolation from other children in provincial towns and in cramped housing conditions, and with the pressures of home and schoolwork, life may remain much as described by Garvey and Jackson and offer few opportunities for peer-group socialization.

In general, as in other areas of the education of pupils of Chinese origin, there are inadequate data from which to generalize about their extra-curricular activities. The lack of take-up of school-based activities by Chinese pupils might be a matter of some concern if the implications for social interaction and greater understanding between ethnic groups is considered. In some ways this mirrors Chinese parents' lack of interaction with their children's schools and may in some measure reflect obedience to parents' wishes to restrict social interaction and the need to undertake home-based activities, though the evidence is ambiguous on this point. Apart from sporting activities, the spare-time hobbies of Chinese pupils would appear to be predominantly passive and domestic. Activity patterns will obviously vary considerably according to personal taste, the circumstances of particular families and parental attitudes, depending greatly on the extent of adjustment to a Western lifestyle. Since the evidence suggests that contact between Chinese families may be on a weekly or less frequent basis and associated with other activities such as attendance at Chinese language classes, many pupils of Chinese origin will have little opportunity for regular extended socialization with other young people outside the school context. As more UK-born Chinese pupils reach adolescence it seems likely that increasing pressure will be put upon Chinese parents to relax their restrictions on socialization outside the home, which may entail considerable changes in the traditional parent–child relationship.

Chinese parents and their children
Not surprisingly, there has been even less research into the relationships between first- and second-generation, and even second- and third-generation, Chinese in this country. There are undoubtedly particular difficulties in undertaking home-based research since rapport and trust must be established over a period of time, and it is also an arena in which interpretations are particularly subject to cultural bias. Traditional family loyalty and close counsel, depending on the hierarchy of relationships, may permit only impressions and insights. In examining research evidence on relationships between Chinese parents and their children the length of residence of the families in the UK, and other factors such as their location, occupation and the time of the research itself, will be influential. For example, although O'Neill's (1972) research was conducted in the late 1960s, in Liverpool, the second generation were already adolescents or even adult. Relationships analysed here, however, mainly concern those between parents who have emigrated to the UK since the Second World War and their children, either born in the UK or who have arrived from Hong Kong at a later age to rejoin their parents. These two factors will affect the nature of the relationship: that between parents and children experiencing reunion after separation for many years with different lifestyles; and between children born in the UK, having grown up with the experience of British schooling and come increasingly under the influence of British values and way of life, and who may be growing apart from their parents and the emphasis on Chinese culture and values within their homes. Both generational and cultural differences in perception and outlook interact in these relationships. This sub-section examines evidence on the extent to which communication between parents and children in Chinese families is related to changes in values and attitudes, linguistic proficiency and use and, in particular, whether social problems are evident. Another factor, significant in assessing the relationship of Chinese parents and their children, is the attitude of parents to their child's future employment.

The Chinese language itself and the particular dialect of the home is crucial to the parent–child relationship in Chinese families since relatively few parents, apart from professionals, are likely to be able to converse with any fluency and subtlety of expression in English. In contrast, whereas Chinese children will invariably grow up in the home speaking Chinese, at some stage during their school career they are likely to have similar proficiency in Chinese and English, and because of the length of time they spend in an English-speaking environment and the communications with their siblings and friends which are more likely in English, at some point their proficiency in English is likely to overtake that in Chinese. Thus one of the main reasons why parents have been anxious to send their children to Chinese language classes is a practical concern that they should still be able to communicate directly through the Chinese language with their children. Indeed, as Ng (1982) discovered, children who attended the Chinese language classes appreciated the significance of their learning Chinese for improving communication in the home. Three-quarters said they would be ashamed if they could not speak their parents' Chinese dialect, two-thirds claimed that their parents would not be happy if they always spoke English at home and that they themselves would feel out of place if they did not speak Chinese with other Chinese people, and half claimed that the Chinese lessons improved their understanding of what happened at home, and they wished that they could speak Chinese more fluently. Yet several researchers and commentators have pointed to a breakdown in communication between Chinese parents and children simply because they did not speak the same language. For example, O'Neill (1972) observed that amongst the 30 Chinese families whom she studied in Liverpool the father typically lived in a Chinese cultural environment, with Chinese friends, and spoke very little English, whereas his children were typically English in their orientation and spoke little Chinese. Eventually communication became inadequate and almost non-existent. The gap between Chinese parents and children could be very wide, especially if the parents had only modest education. More recently Fong (1981), in a study of a similar number of Chinese families in Liverpool, has noted a trend to miscommunication between Chinese parents and children specifically because of communication difficulties. Whilst the recently arrived children from Hong Kong were able to speak Cantonese fluently and converse easily with their parents, most children who were locally born spoke English fluently and Cantonese poorly, hence conversed with their parents in English and Cantonese. However, since the parents' English was mostly limited to the vocabulary of the food business, sometimes the children and parents misunderstood each other and could not express their own views and ideas fluently and accurately.

Language can also be the focus for family communication difficulties especially when recently arrived children from Hong Kong are adjusting to cultural differences. Adaptation to the British way of life may be particularly problematic for adolescent arrivals, for they have to cope with both a new cultural environment and an adjustment to parents whom they do not really know, having perhaps only seen them occasionally during infrequent visits back to Hong Kong, and even perhaps new brothers and sisters. Some newly arrived children may suffer extreme problems of adaptation which may result in linguistic withdrawal (Ladlow, 1980; Lynn, 1982). In one case a child refused to speak at all in school and was referred to a speech therapist as it was suspected that he was dumb. The child was rejecting English, refusing to comply with what he was expected to do at school and only speaking Chinese at home. This discovery was only made when a Chinese-speaking home–school liaison worker visited the child's home, since his parents were unaware of his behaviour, as they had not received any of the letters sent home from the school explaining the difficulty. In this case, which may occur more widely, the child had been recently reunited with his parents after a gap of some years and had also made several trips back and forth to Hong Kong, so that he appeared to have become confused about his family and cultural orientations. Five per cent of the children in Fong's (1981) sample claimed that they did not get on well with their parents specifically because they had been separated from them when young and brought up by their grandparents and relatives, and having rejoined their families in England, their parents were often too busy at work to devote any time to them.

Some communication difficulties between Chinese parents and children arise when the children attempt to assert a British identity by deliberately refusing to speak Chinese at home. This situation may occur for a number of reasons. For example, in another case quoted by Lynn (1982), a teacher had told a child that he must speak English all the time, as by doing so he would be able to converse in English much better. This instruction the child followed to the letter, practising continuously at home and refusing to speak to his parents in Chinese, though they could not speak English. Hence Ladlow (1980) has suggested that teachers require a greater understanding of the significance of Chinese spoken in the home, and that they should indicate the equal value of Chinese and English by stressing that the child should speak Chinese at home as much as possible, in order to develop vocabulary by conversation and to ensure that the family continues to have a means of communication. Other examples in which Chinese children have refused to speak Chinese to their parents in an attempt to establish a different cultural identity, thereby provoking both linguistic and generational difficulties in communication, have been cited by Garvey and Jackson (1975), Lobo (1978) and Jackson (1979) (see pp.157–8).

Intergenerational relationships may also be confounded on account of the values and cultural orientation which Chinese parents maintain in the home and which may be very different to those experienced by Chinese pupils in their schooling. The traditional values of loyalty and obedience, respect and deference, permission and restriction, and trust and self-reliance, which Chinese parents try to preserve within the family, come under particularly critical scrutiny from young Chinese growing up in this country and are often put to the test in daily family life. O'Neill (1972) found that Chinese parents generally bemoaned the loss of loyalty both to the family and to the wider Chinese community by their children. They considered 'being a good son or daughter' most important. Yet most of the young Chinese whom O'Neill observed obeyed their parents to a greater extent than their English peers. They believed their parents sincerely wanted the best for them and appreciated their concern, but not unquestioningly, and made their protest through verbal retorts, though they were prepared, finally, to obey their parents because they wanted to make them happy. Conversely, Chinese parents did not want to force their children to do anything which would make them unhappy, and a kind of compromise was a traditional Chinese way of face saving. Such adjustment was possible in England because parents accepted that their children had been brought up in very different conditions and that they were often in a better position to make decisions for themselves. Indeed parents preferred respect to obedience and this was the way in which they had reinterpreted the meaning of 'being a good son or daughter'. Mutual intergenerational obligations and responsibilities remained, but these were secured by love and respect rather than obligation and authority. In the late 1960s in Liverpool, when the Chinese community had yet to be revived, the second generation had not been able to identify with a Chinese way of life, and had become more integrated into a British way of life, achieving their independence through personal and family contacts distinct from those of the community. Family ties in the form of a sense of mutual responsibility between parents and children were perceived as much more important than a community allegiance.

Chinese families in different locations, provincial and urban, may be at different stages of social adjustment to life in the UK. This is likely to be reflected in parent–child relationships. As a result of their three-month study of Chinese families across England, Garvey and Jackson (1975) painted a picture of Chinese family life which was autocratic and firmly disciplined, with little democracy in family decisions, orders being given by parents, usually the father, and unquestioningly obeyed, since loyalty was always expected. Garvey and Jackson suggested that, due to anxiety about the social life world outside the family, girls colluded in the restriction of their liberties. Children accepted parental expectations and adopted submissive attitudes and, in deference to their parents, problems were rarely discussed (see also Fong, 1981). In this situation children relied on each other for support and younger siblings would turn to older brothers and sisters for love and comfort. Naturally it is at adolescence, when Chinese youth contrast their social life with that of British teenagers, that restrictions are most keenly felt, but Garvey and Jackson noted that any rebellion against parental strictness led to deceit rather than open confrontation, with brothers and sisters closing ranks in the face of parental authority in order to protect each other. However, Garvey and Jackson recognized that there were differences from family to family and that parents' attitudes may vary considerably according to their rural or urban background, life experiences, economic situation and the opportunities for daily interaction with their children. When the business commitments of Chinese parents make such demands that their children may be overlooked and may not experience close interaction with their parents, children may grow away from them (see Wilson, 1977) and even latent hostility may develop towards parents. In such cases Chinese parents might not have the time, experience or understanding to help, advise or support their children (Garvey and Jackson, 1975; Fong, 1981).

Since research evidence on intergenerational relationships is likely to be subject to a particularly high degree of cultural and subjective bias, it is important to consider evidence collected by a Chinese interviewer, Fong (1981), who questioned children and parents separately in their homes. Some 30 per cent of the children were UK-born, 40 per cent had lived in the UK for less than five years and 30 per cent had recently arrived. All were of secondary school age. Interestingly, there was a considerable congruence between the Chinese parents' and children's perceptions of their relationships. Seventy-five per cent of the children said they liked to live with their families and got on well with parents and siblings. Some two-thirds of the children claimed always to get on well with their parents, although it was more likely for the same proportion to claim that they only got on well with the siblings 'sometimes'. Whereas 75 per cent of children were happy and satisfied with their lives, under apparently stable conditions, and many had no interest in being integrated in the wider community, 25 per cent were unhappy because they could not get on well with their parents and had little freedom in their social activities. Half the parents in the sample never allowed their adolescent children to go out and join others alone. The other half were equally divided between those who always or sometimes permitted their children to go out. Those who wished to engage in sporting activities and whose participation was restricted by their parents perceived life as dull and monotonous. Nevertheless, two-thirds of parents claimed that their child always obeyed and respected them, and the remainder that they sometimes did. By comparison, it was more likely that the child would claim to sometimes obey and respect his parents, with just under half of the sample stating that they always did so. Again some two-thirds of parents said that they always trusted their child, although the remainder were equally divided between those who sometimes and those who never did. Half the children said that they thought their parents always trusted them, and the majority of the remainder that they sometimes did. Traditionally children are expected to ask permission of their parents whenever they do anything, the remainder that they sometimes asked permission. Moreover, when in trouble children are traditionally expected to ask for help from their parents, but fewer than half the parents claimed that their child would always ask for assistance, the majority stating that they would only sometimes do so.

These Chinese parents' and children's perceptions, though of limited generalizability, may be tentatively seen to indicate the degree of movement away from traditional Chinese cultural practices. But many parents who come from a rural background, with only a modest education, also experienced difficulties in their adjustment to life in the UK, and were often unable to prepare their children to adapt to a new lifestyle. Both some of the recently arrived adolescents and some of the locally born Chinese children were eager to return to Hong Kong as they had been unable to reconcile differences between the two cultural backgrounds (see pp.268–9). In other cases there were intercultural and intergenerational problems because parents were unwilling to allow their children to become Anglicized. These interpretative comments suggest that there were more psychological tensions underlying the superficial and generalized responses of both parents and children. As Wang (1981) has commented, 'the problem is that the more the parent is chauvinistic about being Chinese, the more the children become uncertain about their position in Britain, where they feel their futures are destined'.

Any tensions between the generations on account of cultural differences are largely confined within the home. O'Neill (1972) found that parent–child conflict rarely resulted in juvenile delinquency, drug taking or membership of youth gangs. If there is any bad behaviour, the Chinese parent is said to feel so responsible for the correct upbringing of his child that he will see a misdemeanour as his own. Lai (1975) confirmed that the parents in the 24 families in London all thought that their children's upbringing was solely their responsibility. They displayed a striking reluctance to discuss any intergenerational problems and were unaware that there were social work agencies to advise with family difficulties. Despite one or two instances of truancy, the parents in general thought they were coping well. They might turn to their relatives sometimes for help, but none asked for help outside the family. Any misbehaviour was accepted fatalistically. Yet Chann (in SCSCRC, 1976) noted that cultural and generational gaps and 'a youth problem' were emerging. At about the same time Cheung (1975) reported that some of the Chinese children in the families whom he studied in York had become known to some social workers. He implied that there were tensions in the Chinese homes since children often spoke more freely in school. At a conference in 1982 (NCC, 1984) a Chinese social worker in Camden reported increasing social problems amongst Chinese teenagers, especially truanting from school, and Chan (1983) has suggested that recently arrived Chinese adolescents were grouping together in youth gangs and displaying violent and aggressive behaviour. Such reports are, however, relatively rare. Generally any difficulties between parents and children are kept within the family, and young Chinese are more likely to be 'quietly rebellious'.

Many Chinese children find the contrast between the culture of society at large and that of a traditional Chinese background very confusing. The major difference focusses upon the significance given to the family unit. It is considered important for the Chinese family to work together for the good of the family, so that individual expectations are in many ways unknown. This contrasts markedly with the individualism prevalent in British society yet, in the main, according to Lynn (1982), traditional family ties remain the strongest for pupils of Chinese origin. This, she claims, is especially true when parental expectations and aspirations for their children's employment are considered. O'Neill (1972) found, in Liverpool, that most Chinese parents did not want their children to follow them into the family business, but sought a good education for them as a preparation, hopefully, for entry into one of the professions. In fact, according to O'Neill, many children had been successful in this way. The parents' desire for their children to work in the wider community did not imply loss of parental control, for family enterprise did not have the same meaning as it had in the country of origin and was mainly a practical means of supporting the family. The parents were usually glad for their child to work in other employment because they appreciated that their own working life was so hard. Prestige was particularly attached to professional occupations, but all parents were anxious for their children to do well. Similarly, Cheung (1975) reported that the Chinese parents in York had high hopes for their children's employment and thought it crucial for their children to be proficient in English, so that they might opt out of the catering trade and choose their own employment. Again Fong also found that the Chinese parents in Liverpool had high expectations of their children, wanting them to gain educational qualifications or practical skills so they might obtain high-status jobs. But how realistic are these expentations in view of the facility with English required and an economic climate of high youth unemployment? Whilst some Chinese parents react with angry disbelief that a British education has apparently been of little avail, and their children can only obtain similar employment to their non-English-speaking parents in catering (Langton, 1979), others may expect their children to follow in their family business when leaving school (Lynn, 1982). According to Lynn, many Chinese parents tend to think that if they or friends or relatives can provide employment, then it is best for the child to leave school, and often at school-leaving age there will be a job waiting. However, it is important for schools to provide Chinese parents with information about further education opportunities, so that they might encourage their children to continue to study and obtain qualifications which will provide them with wider choices within the job market.

Indeed, if Chinese are seen in positions within the wider employment market, then, Lynn argues, this may encourage Chinese parents to allow their children to compete openly with others. Yet it is also important that parents' expectations should be realistic, and it would be wrong to raise false hopes, particularly in view of current lack of opportunity in young people's employment prospects. Chinese parents may be only too well aware of this, whilst at the same time earnestly wishing that their children might be able to escape from the catering employment cycle. Being able to offer their child some employment in the catering trade when they leave school at least means that the child is not unemployed and that he will have something practical to build upon later in life (Ladlow, 1980). On the other hand, it is important that Chinese parents who have children who are able to benefit from further or higher education should be persuaded of the necessity of allowing their children every opportunity to continue in education and not necessarily assuming help in the family business. Indeed increasing frustration may be felt by both Chinese parents and their children if, because of the economic recession, those who have educational achievements and wish to enter the wider employment market are unable to do so and have to be absorbed into the family business, against both their own and their parents' aspirations.

This tension about employment prospects for children of Chinese origin may contribute significantly to the parent–child relationship, which may already be complicated by linguistic and cultural difficulties in communication. It is always particularly difficult to evaluate largely qualitative research data on parent–child interaction, especially amongst ethnic minority groups where there is an additional danger of cultural bias in interpretation of stated claims and observed behaviour. In no case is this greater than that of Chinese parents and their children, particularly in view of the paucity of evidence. Whilst it would appear that Chinese parents do have high expectations for their children's education and employment in the wider economic sphere, traditional virtues of self-reliance, self-sufficiency, responsibility and loyalty to the family lead Chinese parents to make contingency arrangements for their children's employment in catering if other educational and economic opportunities are unavailable. This appears a wholly pragmatic adjustment. Moreover, although there may be tensions within the family unit about the degree of adherence to traditional values, lifestyles and cultural practices, it is extremely difficult to judge, from the evidence available, the severity of miscommunication between Chinese parents and children. It seems, for instance, entirely understandable that Chinese parents should want to ensure a means of communication with their children through the Chinese language. It is perhaps more on the orientation and degree of differences in perception based on differential rates of adjustment to Western living that parents and children are likely to experience disagreement. The greatest intergenerational disagreements may occur in respect of social interaction. But to date there is little evidence of serious juvenile problems, and disputes seem, in traditional style, to have been kept firmly within the family. Whilst the extent of communication difficulties in the relationships of Chinese parents and children should not be exaggerated, there are nevertheless indications that psychological tensions over and above those normally to be expected between generations may exist. A range of personal, social and economic factors will affect Chinese families' adjustment to living in the UK, which will also both influence and be influenced by the perception which the second-generation pupils of Chinese origin have of their position in British society, especially as they participate in that society in their schooling. The following section looks at these perceptions.

Section 12
Chinese Pupils

Attitudes to and interaction with peers

The pupil of Chinese origin may differ from his peers, including those from other ethnic minorities, in the degree to which he experiences social isolation. Due to the dispersal of the Chinese population in the UK, pupils of Chinese origin may not share their schooling with many or indeed any other Chinese pupils. Moreover, their socialization is likely to be very home-based and dependent upon their immediate family, because there may not be many other Chinese families or organizations in the immediate locality. In addition, Chinese children recently arrived from rural or urban Hong Kong need to readjust to new living conditions and another social life. These factors are likely to affect the socialization and sociability of pupils of Chinese origin not only with other Chinese pupils, but with their peers in general. Language, lifestyle, culture, temperament, character and the inter-personal perceptions of Chinese pupils and others are also influential in determining the extent of social interaction with their peers and the quality of the relationship which they may enjoy. In comparison with the evidence on inter-ethnic attitudes and friendship of pupils of West Indian and Asian origin research on pupils of Chinese origin is again limited. Much of the evidence drawn upon here is of a descriptive, anecdotal and impressionistic nature.

A number of barriers inhibit friendship between pupils of Chinese origin and other children and adolescents. Above all, there is their possible lack of proficiency in English, so that, for example, although some Chinese pupils may initially tend to join in playground games their lack of English may hamper their understanding of the rules, which prevents participation and socialization (Garvey and Jackson, 1975). Lack of English may also be a barrier for adolescents, inhibiting social interaction (SCSCRC, 1976). The lifestyle of the Chinese in the UK and, in particular, the degree of control which partners have over their children's social lives may be another constraint. For example, Fong (1981) reported that pupils of Chinese origin were rarely allowed out to play or socialize with other children or adolescents. Moreover, there was little social interaction with other Chinese families, so that the child's social life world was confined to the immediate family. Research suggests that few pupils of Chinese origin participate in school-based extra-curricular activities or belong to clubs or organizations other than Chinese language classes (see pp.243–8). Chinese adolescents often find that their lifestyle is so different from that of their British peers that they are reluctant to make friends (Ladlow, 1980). They may also conceal their work in their parents' business from their social peers (Garvey and Jackson, 1975).

Newly arrived Chinese children may require additional patience on the part of teachers and pupils alike if they are to adjust to the social environment of the school in which they find themselves. Such a pupil will be unlikely to benefit from the secure and established social networks and religious organizations which his South Asian counterpart would enjoy. Rather he is likely to be the only Chinese child in the school, unable to communicate well with his peers or adults there and, in addition, having to rediscover relationships after years of separation. In such circumstances it is understandable that some Chinese children might appear withdrawn and unresponsive, especially since the cultural background stresses reserve and modesty. Such a child may need constant attention and gentle involvement in co-operative learning tasks if he is to gain confidence for social interaction (Fitchett, 1976). But such children may not appear particularly attractive to their peers as possible friends. Two quotations illustrate Chinese pupils' perceptions of their first experiences of schooling on arrival in the UK:

When I first arrived in England I didn't know a single word and due to lots of misunderstanding there was a little bit of discrimination, but when they knew me better this stopped and I found very little trouble with other people. (15-year-old Chinese pupil, quoted by Fitchett, 1976, p. 25)

When I first came to this school there were no Chinese people here, except in higher classes. I was the only Chinese girl in my year, and I was a bit nervous. I thought it was funny seeing coloured people – Greeks. I thought in this country there were English people. I didn't know there were many different races. The first day the people in my class were quite friendly to me and they kept asking my name. All I could say was my name. The next day I learnt to say yes or no. (11-year-old Chinese pupil who arrived in the East End of London in 1975, quoted by Twitchin and Demuth, 1981, pp.18–19)

Even where Chinese pupils are in schools with other pupils of Chinese origin, it must not be assumed that there will be social interaction between them because they are Chinese. As Jackson and Garvey (1974) found, Mandarin-speaking Chinese may be particularly isolated since this language is not necessarily comprehended by the majority of pupils of Chinese origin who speak Cantonese or Hakka. Moreover, where there are Vietnamese and Chinese pupils in the same schools, although they share a common Chinese ethnicity, they may not mix socially. It has sometimes been suggested that pupils of Chinese origin may find it easier to make friends with other ethnic minority pupils rather than with their white British peers because they can explore aspects of the British way of life together and they may not necessarily be attracted to the same social and cultural pursuits enjoyed by the majority population (Lee in ILEA:English Centre, 1979). On the other hand, the Swann Report (GB. P. H of C, 1985) claimed that 'the Chinese language tends to encourage a sense of "superiority" over other cultures and this seems to have led to some Chinese children being prejudiced against other ethnic minority pupils, especially Asians and West Indians, and against indigenous white pupils' (pp. 667–8).

In addition to ethnic and cultural differences, the personalities of Chinese pupils as individuals and their characteristics as a group may also influence inter-ethnic attitudes and social interaction. Several commentators and researchers have noted the quiet, unassertive and incurious demeanour of Chinese pupils (Garvey and Jackson, 1975; Lynn, 1982; Fong, 1981). Others (Fitchett, 1976; SCSCRC, 1976) have claimed that many take a long time to overcome their natural shyness and are unlikely to take the first step in making friends. In Britain a natural oriental shyness may be compounded by self-consciousness of being Chinese, hence a member of a minority ethnic group and culture. The SCSCRC report (1976) suggested that if Chinese could be found to lead and encourage social activities amongst Chinese youth, this would help both with problems of linguistic communication and establishing parents' trust. When young Chinese were in the habit of socializing, they in turn would encourage their friends. Other sources (e.g. ILEA, 1975) have suggested that the gentler, quieter temperaments of Chinese girls may be incompatible with the more outgoing, ebullient temperaments of some West Indian and English girls, and make friendship unlikely. Rather it appears that some Chinese girls are more inclined to have Spanish, Italian and Asian friends. Some Chinese pupils may be popular amongst their classmates. However, Fong (1981) found that Chinese pupils were unassertive even amongst friends: of 31 pupils, none had always been the leader, 19 sometimes and 12 never.

Another factor which may be associated with the ability of Chinese pupils to make friends with their peers is age. It appears that it may prove more difficult to make friendships with increasing age. It has been claimed (CAG & QCRC, 1979) that Chinese toddlers have no difficulties in mixing with non-Chinese children and that there should be more opportunities to mix in playgroups. In London Lai (1975) discovered that whereas in primary schools with pupils of Chinese origin social mixing was good, in three secondary schools visited the older Chinese boys were not socially integrated. But it is likely that a whole constellation of factors will influence the social interaction of Chinese pupils and their peers on a daily and a long-term basis. The pupils whom Cheung (1975) interviewed in York had few close English friends. The extent to which they had to assist their parents in the family business seriously intruded on their opportunities for social interaction. To Chinese pupils an English friend may be a prize (Garvey and Jackson, 1975). There is a tendency amongst pupils of Chinese origin to keep to themselves (e.g. Wang, 1981). Garvey and Jackson (1975; Jackson and Garvey, 1974) give many examples, from their observational study, of the social isolation of some Chinese pupils. Arrival, departure and breaktimes apparently make pupils of Chinese origin, especially those lacking fluency in English, particularly vulnerable, and they may opt out, preferring to keep their own company and trying to go unnoticed. Fong (1981) also recorded observing that the Chinese children in Liverpool schools often preferred to group together during the recess and lunchtime breaks and not mix with other children. If the school were too big for them to meet one another, they just wandered off alone or to the library. It is difficult to interpret indications of the social isolation of some Chinese pupils found throughout the literature as this may be due to any number of factors, including a response to hostile behaviour on the part of peers (see p.264), a lack of fluency in English and therefore inability to participate in games and conversation, or merely a desire for some respite from being close-confined with others both at school and at home. It is, therefore, important to consider the evidence from the few sociometric and inter-ethnic studies which have involved pupils of Chinese origin.

It is interesting that the earliest research on pupils of Chinese origin in 1946–7 investigated their social integration and that of other mixed-race children in Liverpool (Silberman and Spice, 1950). At that time there were already considerable numbers of second-generation, mixed-race children with white mothers and fathers of Chinese, West African, West Indian or Asian origin who had been drawn to the city as seamen. The Chinese in Liverpool then had a loose social organization with recognized local leaders and could be regarded as a community group (see also Broady, 1955; cf. O'Neill, 1972). Data on the occupations of fathers in the city at the time show that about half the Chinese fathers were seamen and the others predominantly laundrymen, shopkeepers and semi-skilled workers. At the time of the research race relations in the city were said to be good on the whole, and the researchers claimed that the coloured population should be seen as part of a localized group of the very poor, rather than as a separate group defined by colour.

The friendship study was conducted in six schools, three local authority, three Church of England, an infant, junior and senior school of each type with a total of 1,048 children. Some 861 white pupils, 52 Chinese, with one or both parents of Chinese origin, and 135 'other coloured' children with one or both parents of African, West Indian, Arab, Burmese or Indian origin were involved. An assessment was made of the standard of clothing of the pupils.

The Chinese children were the best-dressed group, 94 per cent having clothing of a superior quality which was well kept, or clothing which was mended and well kept, compared with 75 per cent of the white pupils and 68 per cent of the other coloured pupils. The friendship test was in two parts. First, pupils were asked to send a letter to their best friend in the classroom and, in the second week, to send a second letter to the second-best friend, followed a week later by a further letter again directed to the claimed best friend. In practice, sometimes a Christmas card was sent to a friend and sometimes a vote was made for a friend. The second part of the test assessed antipathies. The children were asked to imagine a trip in a charabanc to the sea but to nominate 'the three children you would leave behind: three spoil-sports, the nastiest children in the class'.

A detailed statistical analysis revealed that on the first friendship test white children did not discriminate against coloured children, including Chinese pupils, when choosing friends, and similarly coloured children did not discriminate against white children. However, children with superior clothing did discriminate against those with inferior clothing in their friendship choices, but not vice versa. The findings of the rejection test were more ambiguous. Boys, coloured children and children with inferior clothing were more often rejected ($p < .05$). There was a significantly greater rejection of coloured children in the local authority schools. Children with inferior clothing were rejected more frequently than those with superior clothing, and occasionally by members of their own group. Differentiation in friendship and rejection choice took place more frequently between children of different clothing standards and between white and coloured children when the coloured group included pupils of Chinese origin. A further analysis showed that although there was no difference between the distribution of white and coloured children in different clothing groups, within the coloured group the Chinese, who constituted 25 per cent, were the better dressed and the other coloured group worse dressed than the white pupils. Although it was not possible to analyse the results of the friendship and rejection test to take account of this difference in clothing standard, the researchers acknowledged that in future studies Chinese pupils should be treated as a separate group, and that 'in those few cases where differentiation on the basis of colour occur it may be an artifact of social status' (p.56). Moreover, since discrimination existed on the basis of clothing standards, had an analysis been made in which the Chinese and other coloured groups had been treated separately, prejudice against the other coloured children and preference for the Chinese might have been found.

This is an interesting early study for two reasons. It demonstrates the possibility – which seems to have been since ignored – of undertaking research in which a fair proportion of pupils of Chinese origin are involved. And it also indicates that at that time in Liverpool pupils of Chinese origin from Chinese –white backgrounds were not being discriminated against, and because of their more prosperous appearance, may have enjoyed some social advantages over other mixed-race pupils. However, in view of the findings of some subsequent research that both white and coloured pupils show less ethnic preference for children of mixed race, and as this study may be very situation-specific relating to Anglo-Chinese pupils in an established multiracial city, before the advent of the majority of Chinese pupils with ancestry in the New Territories, too much weight should not be placed upon these findings in an analysis of race relations and schooling today. Moreover, other research conducted at the same time suggested that stereotypes of the Chinese may not have been favourable. James and Tenen (1950, quoted by Bagley and Verma, 1975) found that British girls of secondary-school age, whilst perceiving blacks in largely favourable terms, saw the Chinese (and Japanese) as cruel, fierce, bad, sly and war-like. They may have been influenced by contemporary events in the Far East. Attitudes to Chinese on the basis of colour remain ambiguous or unclear (Jeffcoate, 1984).

The 1946 friendship study conducted in Liverpool may be compared with another involving pupils of Chinese origin some 35 years later in Liverpool (Fong, 1981). A simple friendship test was administered fo 11 pupils of Chinese origin in the Language Centre and 20 other Chinese pupils in three secondary schools. Each pupil in the same class as the Chinese pupils was asked to choose five friends from the class to be invited to a birthday party in their house on the following Saturday. A wide range – but low rate – of friendship was indicated. Two-thirds of the Chinese pupils were invited by 10–20 per cent of their classmates to their birthday parties. The most popular Chinese pupils were those who had been at their schools for several years. Newcomers and isolates were not invited. According to Fong, during the test the Chinese pupils' peers were anxious and eager to know whether they had been nominated by the Chinese children and some were keen to make friends with Chinese pupils. Chinese pupils were seen as behaving well in class, being bright in certain subjects such as mathematics and art, and as kind and helpful, but too quiet and shy. Interviews with the Chinese pupils at home showed that they almost unanimously liked their classmates, but were almost equally divided between those who said they liked a few and those who said they liked a lot. Two-thirds of the Chinese pupils claimed that they were liked by a few of their classmates and, of the others, all except one claimed that a lot of their classmates liked them. Twenty-three out of 31 Chinese pupils said that they sometimes liked to make friends with English children, and of the remainder all, except the two newcomers, claimed they always liked to make friends with English pupils. However, they were more likely to say that they liked to make friends with Chinese pupils, 18 claiming that they always did so and 12 sometimes. Importantly, all except two of the Chinese pup ls wanted to have more friends and 26 out of 31 wanted these to be both Chinese and English.

The Commission for Racial Equality (CRE) investigation in which Chinese children attending part-time Chinese language classes were interviewed (Tsow, 1984) also incidentally gives information on the socialization of pupils of Chinese origin with other Chinese pupils. Travelling to the language classes was a social activity for only a few Chinese pupils accompanied by their friends (six per cent). But a third of the sample claimed to enjoy their language classes because they met with their friends, and 38 per cent of the 312 8–14-year-olds said that they would like to spend some time at the end of classes playing or talking with other Chinese children. By comparison, only one in five said they enjoyed their ordinary schools because they met their friends there. The Hong-Kong-born were more likely to make this claim: 24 per cent compared with 15 per cent of the UK-born claimed to 'meet many friends', and 11 per cent compared with seven per cent claimed that their classmates were 'nice'. Overall six per cent associated their everyday school, compared with the language school, with more friends.

Interestingly, no children in the CRE survey (Tsow, 1984) spontaneously claimed that they disliked their everyday school because of racism, although only two per cent claimed to like school because their teachers 'treat foreigners and English the same'. Only two per cent of Chinese parents whose children attended part-time Chinese language classes claimed that they disliked their child's mainstream schooling because of racial discrimination, whereas six per cent commented favourably because they claimed there was no racial prejudice. Yet the literature on pupils of Chinese origin is replete with claims of name-calling, bullying and other forms of racial harassment. It appears that the physical appearance of pupils of Chinese origin, especially the configuration of the Chinese face, gives rise to name-calling such as 'chinkie' and 'yellow-bug' on account of skin colour (Garvey and Jackson, 1975). Chinese names also seem to present an opportunity for joking 'you wong or right' or 'here's ching chong give us a song' (Lynn, 1982). Cheung (1975) recorded that most of the Chinese pupils he interviewed in York experienced social difficulties with their classmates and were bullied constantly. Garvey and Jackson give many examples of systematic racial harassment, name-calling and bullying experienced by pupils of Chinese origin, especially in the playground, irrespective of their numbers in school. Contrary to Silberman and Spice's (1950) evidence, Garvey and Jackson suggested that because of their physical appearance and their quiet demeanour, Chinese pupils may be perceived by white and black pupils as belonging to neither group, and suffer, in consequence, intimidation from both: 'Chinks are funny. Well they can't be in one gang or another, can they? They're not black, and they're not white now are they?' Fong (1981) also reported that some of the Chinese children in her sample complained that they had been teased, made fun of and bullied by their

264 Chinese Pupils in Britain

peers. Lynn (1982) has claimed that in some Liverpool schools Chinese children are said to suffer more from name-calling than children from any other ethnic group. Although Chinese children do not assert themselves within the classroom or playground and tend to isolate themselves because of lack of English which prevents them from joining in certain games, the more they try to opt out, the more they are noticed and picked on. Some children may prefer attending the language centres as the presence of a greater proportion of pupils of Chinese origin diminishes the likelihood of name-calling. The school should, therefore, actively disavow name-calling as a matter of course.

More seriously, pupils of Chinese origin may be subject to severe taunting and bullying during journeys between home and school (Lee in ILEA:English Centre, 1979; Garvey and Jackson, 1975). In the late 1960s O'Neill (1972) reported a growing lack of acceptance of Chinese pupils in Liverpool schools and that they were often picked on by groups of white and coloured children. Younger Chinese may be especially vulnerable and their only protection may be to stay together in groups in the playground and on their way to and from school (Lobo, 1978; Lee in ILEA:English Centre, 1979). Fighting may develop as a result of harassment and become commonplace (Cheung; Jackson and Garvey). Chinese pupils are perceived by their peers as both quiet and tough and may be violent if extremely provoked (Garvey and Jackson, 1975). Kung Fu techniques may be adopted as a defence, ironically, since these are often admired by other pupils who have a desire to emulate them without appreciating the necessary mental and physical discipline involved. Indeed fear of Kung Fu used in retaliation by pupils of Chinese origin may ultimately restrain racial harassment. Whilst the instances of racial aggression and violence between pupils of Chinese origin and their peers should not be exaggerated, Chan (1983) has warned that this is spreading.

Chinese parents are clearly concerned about intimidation of their children and any possible resort to aggression and violence. Cheung (1975) claimed that the parents of pupils in York, whilst supporting their children, advised them to be deaf to bullying. London parents (Lai, 1975) were disappointed that inadequate protection against bullying was given by their children's school. When bullying and violence persist, Chinese parents may temporarily withdraw their children from school or place them elsewhere (Jackson and Garvey, 1974; Lynn, 1982). Subsequently Chinese parents may be unwilling to allow their children to attend schools in what they regard as 'no-go' areas.

In conclusion, research suggests that many Chinese pupils suffer from a lack of friends amongst other race peers and may be subject to racial harassment of various degrees, much as their South Asian peers. Similarly, it is likely that they experience such treatment because of poor English, physical appearance and their upbringing which encourages them to be self-contained, non-assertive and modest. In some cases, especially when pupils are new in a school or where there may be only one Chinese pupil, such behavioural dispositions may be sufficient for some of their less other-regarding peers, safe in a majority, to take advantage. Instances of racial harassment cannot be ignored by schools. But the eruption of racially discriminatory activities should not be the only occasion for an examination of, and injunction against, racism. It should be an integral part of the school's business to promote a proper understanding by pupils of other pupils, regardless of race, as persons in their own right and deserving of equal respect and fair treatment. There is a need for such teaching in specific subject areas such as social studies and moral education and across the curriculum. Such principles should also be exemplified in the daily life of the school, both in its organization and atmosphere, particularly in teacher–pupil relations. Only where such an environment exists will the proper conditions for learning obtain and positive relationships, desired by many Chinese pupils and their white and other peers, be promoted. Whilst there are some such multiracial schools, research suggests that many need to adopt and pursue more positive policies in order that, in so far as pupils of Chinese origin and indeed other ethnic minority pupils are concerned, the Chinese saw 'within the four seas all men are brothers' may be realized.

Pupils' self-perceptions and identity

An important factor in the ability of Chinese pupils to benefit from educational opportunities in Britain is likely to be their orientation towards their future life and whether they see this in the UK or Hong Kong. Self-perceptions will both influence attitudes to British education and be influenced by it. A pupil's sense of identity will develop by living with his family in the UK and through an experience of schooling, in which little recognition is accorded to the Chinese culture or language (see pp.282–98). Since it is therefore unlikely that Chinese pupils will remain unaffected by an awareness of British culture and social life, it is important to examine research evidence on the extent to which pupils of Chinese origin suffer confusion or are able to adjust as they daily negotiate between the two cultural and social life worlds of home and school. It is, moreover, of interest to scrutinize the research, again largely inadequate, anecdotal and impressionistic, for evidence of any redefinition of identity on the part of pupils of Chinese origin.

The self-perceptions of pupils of Chinese origin will be most affected by the orientation of their family lifestyles, whether primarily towards their Chinese cultural roots and traditions in Hong Kong, a Chinese lifestyle adapted to living in the UK or a predominantly British way of life. Orientations will not only vary from family to family, but will also depend to some extent on the family's social interactions with other Chinese families and to what extent it has the sense of belonging to a Chinese community. This is likely to vary considerably according to whether the family lives in an established Chinese settlement or a provincial town. In addition, the time when the research was conducted may have an influence on pupils' self-perceptions.

For example, Collins (1957) claimed that the second-generation Chinese in Liverpool appeared to be content in their own community and did not want to be Anglicized. Yet a decade or so later O'Neill (1972) found that most of the second-generation Chinese she interviewed in Liverpool felt more closely involved with the local society as a whole than with the Chinese community. Although their parents continued to be the main source of Chinese influence, relatives were less important than English friends. The socialization of the second generation in Chinese culture and the Chinese way of life had been weak, and they did not see themselves as part of it. O'Neill thought that they were able to become occupationally and socially integrated in the wider society because of their relatively small numbers. In consequence, they had tended to choose marriage partners amongst the British though this had also been necessitated by a lack of choice amongst Chinese in the UK. The second generation, who were Anglo-Chinese, were not greatly distinguished from the local population and those who were only a quarter Chinese barely identifiable as such. Nevertheless, a small minority continued to see themselves as part of the Chinese rather than the English way of life. They were more likely to be those who were successful and from traditional Chinese families, those who had aspired and failed to become integrated in the wider society and locally-born Chinese and Anglo-Chinese women married to Chinese immigrants (see p.105). Interestingly, O'Neill noted that, regardless of whether the second generation of Chinese adopted a Chinese or British identity, they were accepted by their families. There were particular difficulties in trying to integrate positive aspects of Chinese culture because these were not reflected in society at large, and there was no community basis on which they could be preserved.

But by the time O'Neill was completing her research she had already observed changes amongst the Chinese in Liverpool with the arrival of greater numbers of post-war Chinese immigrants whom she suggested might have a greater desire to maintain a Chinese way of life. This has been amply demonstrated by the increased voluntary provision of Chinese language classes by the Chinese community which have, as a primary aim, the maintenance of Chinese identity through Chinese language and culture (pp. 175–6). Language and identity are closely intertwined, though sociolinguists are only now beginning to explore interconnections with respect to the emerging identities of linguistic minority pupils. Regrettably, there appears not to have been an explicit study in this connection with respect to pupils of Chinese origin, though a number of researchers have usefully pointed to dimensions of the question. For example, Rosen and Burgess (1980) have suggested that whilst the proficiency of pupils of Chinese origin in one of their two languages, Chinese or English, may be much lower than that of a British second language learner, their biculturalism may be much more profound, as many will be to a greater or lesser degree living in two cultures:

A Chinese girl may live for part of her time in a Chinese culture and part of her time in a British one and part in a mixture of the two if her home has undergone a degree of anglicization. The Chinese culture will in any case be that form of it which has developed in this country. She will not only be absorbing cultural meanings for the same activities, eating for instance, but possibly taking up values and attitudes which have no analogies in the two cultures. It does not follow that the two cultures match perfectly the two languages. Jewish culture has persisted outside the speaking of Yiddish. Nevertheless language is a highly salient dimension of ethnic identity. It is a highly explicit carrier of cultural meaning. (pp. 51–2)

Barr (1983) claims that Chinese classes are particularly necessary for children who are fostered privately, full-time, with Scottish families. Yet although these children's main language is English, and they have communication difficulties with their parents when they visit, their Chinese identity remains strong. Evidence from the Merseyside Chinese Youth Association to the Home Affairs Committee suggested that teenagers' inability to speak Chinese exacerbated the alienation between parents and children and argued that a knowledge of Chinese bolstered pupils' self-worth (GB. P. H of C. HAC, 1985).

Chinese parents see the Chinese language as vital for the transmission of the Chinese culture and the values enshrined in it and hence as a significant element in the identity of their children (see pp.155–6). Since it seems relatively few pupils of Chinese origin are literate in Chinese, culture must be transmitted orally. Hence the activities of daily life form the drama through which Chinese cultural values are enacted. But since this takes place within British society, those values will be modified according to the degree of cultural adjustment to the British way of life. For pupils of Chinese origin their greatest contact with this is likely to be in school. In this context, moreover, the culture of their homes may not be explicitly recognized. As Chan (1983) has pointed out, for example, the school curriculum reflects a European, if not British, cultural bias which creates an unfavourable learning environment for pupils of Chinese and other ethnic minority origin. It should not be surprising if Chinese children are confused about choosing their identity.

As a result of her researches, Ng (1982) concluded that pupils of Chinese origin did have identity problems. Most of the younger pupils of Chinese origin who were born in the UK considered themselves to be British for this very reason. They were too young to understand why their parents wished them to attend Chinese language classes to learn Chinese. Older pupils, who were mostly born in Hong Kong, knew that they were Chinese but were not reconciled to it because Chinese culture has no status in the UK. Some status should be given to the Chinese language, at least by making it available as an optional school subject (see also pp.207–10):

> Chinese pupils can dress like English, they can behave like English, they can adopt an English way of life, but deep in their hearts they know they are not English however little they know about their own culture. Furthermore, their parents may not allow them to forget they are Chinese. In a rather different way, the British will never allow them to forget they are Chinese. The Chinese immigrant does not suffer difficulties that are experienced by those immigrants who are markedly of a different skin colour, but they do have facial features that will always render them distinctively Chinese. (Ng, 1982, p.79)

Moreover, Ng has suggested that the attitude of pupils of Chinese origin to learning English will be a function of their feeling about the prospects for social and economic integration which exist for them in the UK. Chinese parents, she suggests, are unlikely to be able to give the kind of support and guidance which may be needed by the second generation growing up in the two cultures (see also Fong, 1981).

Lynn (1982) has also claimed that the Chinese pupil may be confused by the culturally diverse milieux and expectations of school and home and that adaptation must be an integration of both cultures, so that they are compatible in the child's personality and perceived identity. But how is the integration to take place and how do pupils of Chinese origin reconcile their identities in the face of two lived cultures? Some researchers have predicted growing acculturation of the second generation of pupils of Chinese origin (e.g. Clough and Quarmby, 1978). As a result of his socioanthropological investigations, Watson (1977a) doubted that the relative imperviousness of the Chinese and their culture in Britain would last beyond the first generation. But he argued that in the 1970s young first-generation Chinese, whilst displaying superficial signs of assimilation or acculturation in the appearance and lifestyles, had not necessarily experienced a change in personal identity. Neither had there been the kind of ethnic redefinition which some young West Indians and Asians have undergone by constructing a new identity which accords particular significance to certain aspects of their cultural backgrounds in the British context.

Watson (1977a) was impressed by the adaptability of those pupils of Chinese origin whom he observed in school. It is the extent to which adaptations and adjustments are made in the integration of the experience of living two cultures which affects the pupil's perceived identity. Research literature suggests that a range of attitudes and life stances are held by pupils of Chinese origin. For example, Fong (1981) concluded that Chinese children, whether locally born (30 per cent), immigrants in early childhood (40 per cent) or recently (30 per cent), experience considerable difficulties and problems in adjusting to life in the UK. These were so severe that half of the children, especially – but not exclusively – those who emigrated recently, were eager to return to Hong Kong because they missed the lifestyle, their relatives, friends and classmates. They had failed to adjust and integrate and had a feeling of not being accepted by the community. Others, who wished to become more Anglicized and who felt settled, looked forward to a visit to Hong Kong. Several vignettes by Fitchett (1976) provide illuminating insights into the social life worlds of pupils of Chinese origin in and around Derby. These also display a range in the degree of identity with a British way of life. Some pupils said that whilst they had no desire to live permanently in Hong Kong they would like to make visits back; others saw their future identity closely linked with their families in the UK and the family business; others, born in the UK, for this reason at least saw themselves as British; yet others with families and business connections in other European countries identified themselves with both Britain and Europe and saw their future in a wider perspective. Other reports (for example, QCRC, 1981) have claimed that pupils of Chinese origin are likely to regard themselves as British. But what exactly does this mean? Ng (1982), whilst suggesting that pupils of Chinese origin would not return to the land of their ancestors, has doubted whether even third- or fourth-generation Chinese will be culturally or linguistically assimilated. Langton (1979) argued that most second-generation Chinese, whilst still retaining close links with Hong Kong, identify Britain as their home and have begun to volunteer their services to the Chinese community with the aim of improving standards of living in Britain. The Swann Report noted the strength of Chinese ethnic identity in Britain (GB. P. H of C, 1985).

On the basis of interviews with young Chinese children in Derby, who seemed to be quite excited that an interest was being taken in them, Fitchett (1976) concluded that:

> In spite of the apparent alienation from host peers, lack of social contact, a routine 'family-bound' existence, work in the restaurant and take-away shop, all the children displayed a high degree of contentment and philosophic adjustment to their new life in England.

> The most agreeable impression gained was that these young people were not only adapting themselves to new conditions and would therefore survive, but would also with hard work and a practical view of things, make a success of their lives. (Fitchett, 1976, p.18)

Yet Fitchett was concerned that these might be superficial impressions and the children might have concealed deeper psychological tensions. He observed that pupils of Chinese origin often took longer to adjust to school than, for example, their Asian peers. Curiously, whilst a not inconsiderable amount of research has been undertaken on the self-concept of pupils of Asian and West Indian origin, no inquiry has apparently been mounted to consider the psychological aspects of the self-perceptions of pupils of Chinese origin and particular tensions which they experience in attempting to integrate the cultures of their home and school lives in the formation of their personalities and identities. In the absence of this evidence any comments on the self-perceptions of pupils of Chinese origin must be inconclusive.

Yet there are pointers to suggest that pupils of Chinese origin may experience even more stress than other ethnic minority pupils in attempting to reconcile the contrast in their home and school lives and to form a stable identity in both existences. Chinese pupils are particularly socially isolated, depending very much on their home environment for any social activity. Yet at the same time the social structure and the linguistic differences within those homes are unlikely to provide opportunities for discussion of the problems in growing up which Chinese children may be experiencing. Moreover, Chinese parents may be ill-equipped to guide and support their children as it seems they have little knowledge at first hand of the kind of contrast which school environments may present. Furthermore, in his upbringing, the Chinese child will be encouraged to be self-reliant and self-contained, which in itself would suggest a tendency to internalize any difficulties in adjustment or in establishing an identity. The Chinese pupil may feel that few can appreciate this position and may only be able to share feelings with siblings. Yet it should be a proper part of the educational role of the school to be fully alive to the needs of all pupils for personal and social development. Pupils of Chinese origin and others whose home backgrounds differ from the culture of the school have to learn to integrate aspects of their lives, to form stable yet flexible identities whether they choose the personal individuality typical of the British way of life, or that which may be possible in the adaptation of Chinese and other cultural norms in British society. In examining the attitudes of pupils of Chinese origin to school some light may be shed on the extent to which Chinese pupils perceive schools to be serving such a function.

Attitudes to school
The attitudes of pupils of Chinese origin to school are obviously a crucial factor in their response to their educational experiences. Once again, there is a relative dearth (Fong, 1981; Tsow, 1984) of information in this area with only two researches having incidentally collected information about pupils' attitudes to school as such. However, there are examples throughout the literature of the attitudes of pupils of Chinese origin to their schooling in terms of: their overall orientation; perceived contrasts between schooling in

Hong Kong and in the UK; their opinions of their teachers and teacher–pupil interaction; their attitudes to learning; their social behaviour; views about school meals; the curriculum; and their opinion of attending school. Though research has been slow to inquire into the attitudes of pupils of Chinese origin, another reason for the lack of evidence in this important area may be the reserve of many pupils of Chinese origin and apparent reluctance to talk or write about themselves, as other ethnic minority pupils have done. However, once persuaded, as in the case of Lee (in ILEA:English Centre, 1979) that their views will help other Chinese pupils to discuss their difficulties, then they may gain in confidence and enthusiasm as they attempt to express their perceptions. In view of the relative isolation of many Chinese pupils it may be especially important to develop opportunities which allow them to express their observations and attitudes, either in taped or written work, and to communicate their views to their peers, including other Chinese pupils, to know that they are sharing similar experiences.

Many pupils of Chinese origin have a positive attitude towards schooling, reflecting the traditional value placed on education in Chinese culture. Many Chinese parents value education particularly as it may lead to wider career opportunities and a different way of life, though they may have reservations about aspects of British schooling (see pp.232–43). They usually wish their children to succeed in education, though economic necessity may oblige them to call upon the assistance of their children in the family business rather than allowing them to devote themselves full-time to their studies. As the family becomes more settled and established financially in Britain the traditional love of learning predominates and academic excellence in the child is encouraged (Jones, I., 1979). Pupils of Chinese origin are generally said to have an academic orientation to schooling and some have claimed that 'the large majority . . . get on well, academically and socially in their British schools' (Langton, 1979). Two-thirds of the Chinese pupils interviewed by Fong (1981) claimed that they were moderately successful in school, and one-fifth saw themselves as achieving well. However, their social integration in schools was less successful (see p.262) and Fong suggested that Chinese pupils should be encouraged to join in school clubs and extra-curricular activities and, if possible, be given positions of responsibility commensurate with particular skills, so that they might develop confidence and security socially in the daily life of the school.

For those Chinese pupils who arrive in the UK in their secondary years having already experienced some schooling in Hong Kong, the contrast between the two educational systems and school practices, particularly with respect to teaching methods, school organization and discipline may be bewildering. It may shock such pupils to find an emphasis on the development of critical reasoning and teaching methods which invite them to challenge the teacher's presentation of material and to examine the evidence itself. Such approaches in many respects directly contradict their learning experiences in Hong Kong (see pp.18–22) in which the teacher's authority is paramount, deference and obedience expected without question, and learning is teacher dominated. Newly arrived Chinese pupils interviewed by Cheung (1975) in York found teaching methods and more individually based tuition in smaller classes and the need to move around within the school for lessons confusing in contrast to their previous experience (see also Garvey and Jackson, 1975). Frustration in their ability to communicate with teachers and peers may also hinder their adaptation to the new learning environment (Fong, 1981). Yet when they have settled down, Chinese pupils may consider that they are not worked hard enough in their school in Britain and may welcome more homework (Fitchett, 1976). The CRE survey (Tsow, 1984) found that a small minority of pupils attending Chinese language classes were more likely to complain that they were taught too little and did not work hard enough in their mainstream school (six per cent) compared with their language classes (two per cent). On the other hand, Fong found that half the children in her sample gave as one of their reasons for liking the UK the fact that they liked studying here for there was not so much schoolwork to do.

Discipline and the relative freedom of teacher–pupil interaction are also aspects of school life in the UK which cause Hong Kong educated pupils some discomposure. Two-thirds of the Chinese pupils in Fong's study claimed that they never made trouble in class and the remainder that they only sometimes did. Three per cent of the pupils in the CRE survey, predominantly the Hong Kong-born, complained about other 'naughty' pupils in their mainstream schools. Other reports suggest that Chinese pupils dislike lax discipline and, if academically orientated and hard working, they are particularly irritated by disruptive influences when placed in lower streams because of language difficulties. A further and illuminating insight into the attitudes of some pupils of Chinese origin to their teachers and schooling is provided by Cheung who described how Chinese pupils in a school failed to receive notices of a forthcoming medical examination and were not given song-books for use in school assembly, yet did not assert themselves to ask for these because they considered that they would receive them if someone thought they should. The attitude that the school will automatically do the best for them has probably been transmitted by parents (see pp.233–4). In general newly arrived Chinese pupils perceived the comparative freedom of the school environment in the UK with surprise, and critically. Indeed in the CRE survey Chinese pupils attending language classes often contrasted their strictness with the implied freedom of their everyday school.

The opinions of pupils of Chinese origin of their teachers and the kind of relationship which they have with them are particularly likely to influence their school performance. The Confucian ethic of respect for the teacher has meant that traditionally teachers have been perceived both as authorities and in authority. They are to be respected for their learning and knowledge, deferred to as elders, and may even be perceived as having a wider disciplinary agency (Jones, I., 1979; Ladlow, 1980). The contrast between teacher–pupil relationships in Hong Kong and the UK is described by Lee:

> In primary school in England, you and your teachers can talk to each other about everything, but in Hong Kong you have to respect your teacher. You respect them here, but it's different. There, if you see your teacher you have to bow, even when you're five, and when the teacher comes in the monitor calls out 'Stand Up!' and you all stand up to say good morning. You can't talk to your teacher like a friend, or ask him any questions. (ILEA:English Centre, 1979, p. 135)

Fong (1981) found that half the pupils in her sample claimed to like a few of their teachers, with the majority of the remainder liking a lot. In the CRE survey (Tsow, 1984) 14 per cent of the Chinese children, particularly girls rather than boys (18 compared with 11 per cent), cited liking their teacher as their main reason for liking their mainstream school. Overall some three-quarters of the children thought that their mainstream and Chinese teachers were 'nice, kind and friendly'. A small minority of pupils claimed only mainstream teachers 'let us do what we want', 'play with us', 'treat foreigners and English the same' and 'understand us more'. Compared with the language class teachers, mainstream teachers were marginally more likely to be said to 'explain well', 'treat us well' and to be helpful. Although some ten per cent of pupils claimed as positive attributes of their mainstream teachers that they did not shout at children and taught well, these positive attributes seem to have been offset by other more negative perceptions that teachers were bad-tempered and 'different', which might be an evasive answer and implying that not all teachers were perceived as teaching well or treating their pupils well. Indeed some 24 per cent of pupils claimed their mainstream teachers shouted at them, this being their most negative attribute.

Half the children in Fong's sample claimed that they always obeyed and respected their teachers and the remainder sometimes did so. Nearly two-thirds of the pupils thought that they were liked by a few of their teachers and the majority of the remainder claimed to be liked by a lot. The teachers themselves generally liked the Chinese pupils for their obedience and respect as well as their quiet manner (see p.282–4). Yet Fong suggested that sometimes Chinese pupils are neglected by their teachers for these very reasons (see also Chan, 1983). Indeed the few pupils who claimed that they did not like their teachers said it was because of the lack of individual attention and the feeling of neglect. The Chinese pupils wanted to be more friendly with their teachers, but their characteristic shyness, customary deference and lack of English inhibited them from being more outward going and they tended only to interact and talk with their teachers individually.

Fong's study also provides some interesting insights into the attitudes of Chinese pupils to their learning. Pupils sampled claimed that although they had learning difficulties they tried hard to achieve a creditable performance. But they did not participate to a great extent in answering or asking questions in the classroom. Two-thirds claimed to answer questions only sometimes and the majority were seen as unresponsive by their teachers (see pp.283–4). Cheung (1975) has suggested that this behaviour is associated with the important Chinese concept of 'saving face'. As he explains it, 'at school the student might try to ask little questions, for fear of losing face if the question was silly, or for fear of causing the teacher to lose face if he couldn't answer' (p.65). But, on the whole, the pupils in Fong's sample claimed to pay attention in class and to be hard-working – a third of the sample said they did this consistently. From her observations Fong judged that they were, on the whole, steady, meticulous and disciplined workers and, although most were initially cautious when facing new learning tasks, after the first attempt they seemed to like the challenge of something difficult. Yet two-thirds claimed that they sometimes had problems with their classwork and nearly a quarter that they always experienced difficulties. Whereas 90 per cent of those with problems concerning classwork sought help from their teachers, some of the shy pupils asked for help from classmates. They very much appreciated approval or encouragement by their teachers. Other accounts have suggested pupils of Chinese origin may spend much time during the evening meticulously copying work completed during the day at school in an effort to improve their writing and memorize the material (e.g. Garvey and Jackson, 1975). These observations suggest that some pupils of Chinese origin would benefit from additional tuition in study skills and various co-operative learning enterprises on projects and in study groups which might assist in the adoption of new learning strategies and in encouraging socialization with other pupils.

Some earlier research reported that some pupils of Chinese origin may regard certain curricular subjects such as physical education as a waste of time (CRC, 1975; Jones, I., 1979). Yet the CRE survey (Tsow, 1984) discovered that sporting activities were cited by 40 per cent of the Chinese children interviewed as the most popular aspects of the curriculum. Since there are other indications that pupils of Chinese origin may find sporting activities attractive in their spare time (see p.244–7), the significance of an apparently increasing involvement in sports may be pondered. Whilst academic and sporting activities are not mutually exclusive, the question may be posed as to whether some pupils of Chinese origin, like some pupils of West Indian origin, may be using sporting activities as a means to achievement when academic success may not be attainable. Alternatively, sporting activities may be welcomed as a way of meeting friends or of temporarily getting away from the cramped conditions of their homes. Other popular subjects cited by the Chinese pupils in the CRE survey were mathematics (29 per cent), liked mostly by those from lower socioeconomic backgrounds (55 per cent), English (24 per cent) and art (21 per cent). By contrast, drama, German and spelling were most unpopular. In Fong's (1981) sample mathematics, chemistry, physics and art were claimed as the favourite and best subjects of the Chinese pupils, whilst French and English were the subjects they liked least.

Regrettably, neither of these studies give any information on whether Chinese pupils would like to be able to study Chinese in the mainstream school or whether they consider aspects of Chinese culture are adequately represented in the school curriculum. Several researchers have observed that on the whole the curriculum in schools does not facilitate learning about Chinese paintings, calligraphy, theatre, music or the Chinese language. Wang (1981), who has been working to promote traditional Chinese artistic and cultural activities with young people, argues that provision should be made within the school timetable for both Chinese and English pupils. On the other hand, both Fong (1981) and Lynn (1982) have argued that it is important for newly arrived Chinese pupils and those who have just started school to develop an understanding of their environment and cultural life in Britain by visiting museums, libraries and exhibitions. Pupils who participated in the SCSCRC Conference in 1976 claimed that even when they were learning English at a language centre, they preferred to attend their ordinary school for at least part of the day in order not to miss part of a subject. They did not wish to be singled out and treated as 'special'. Both Fong and Lynn have also argued that Chinese pupils should be prepared to return to ordinary schooling as soon as possible, in order to participate in lessons with their peers and to improve their colloquial English through hearing and practising with native language speakers.

Pupils' opinions of school meals are available from a study by Tan (1982). A group of 36 Chinese teenagers, 23 male and 13 female, aged 13–18, half of whom had lived in the UK for fewer than five years and who attended four secondary schools in central London, were interviewed. The fathers of 26 of these Chinese teenagers were cooks and a third of their mothers did kitchen work. Thirty-one of the teenagers ate school meals, but they were equally divided in their like or dislike, irrespective of their length of residence in the UK. Overall 71 per cent of these teenagers preferred to eat Chinese meals, although there was an increasing likelihood that those who stayed in the UK longer would develop a liking for English food. Fifty-six per cent of the sample said that Chinese food was better for health, but most of those who said that they would choose to give Chinese food to their children claimed that they would do so for cultural reasons. The adolescents were aware of their mother's classification of food on the hot–cold axis and at school they experienced teaching about Western nutrition. How could children use this additional knowledge? How do they reconcile the dual system of nutritional concepts? Does use of Chinese at home and English at school emphasize or conceal the differences between conceptualizations of food? Tan speculated as to whether through their exposure to Western ideas, in school and through the media, a change in the attitudes of these young Chinese towards diet would occur in their adulthood, although adults' attitudes were unchanging (see pp.84–6).

In view of the various difficulties which pupils of Chinese origin appear to experience within school it is pertinent to inquire whether they like attending school or whether some feel alienated from it. Two-thirds of the children in Fong's sample claimed that they always liked going to school and the remainder that they sometimes did. Moreover, 90 per cent had never pretended to be ill or to get out of things at school. Tsow (1984) found that 20 per cent of the Chinese pupils interviewed at Chinese language classes claimed that they liked 'everything' about their mainstream school. Yet in Fong's sample two-thirds of the children were only sometimes happy in their class. A minority seemed on balance to like most things about their mainstream schooling. But the majority obviously have mixed feelings and do experience some difficulties.

It is when these difficulties become disproportionately problematic that a minority of pupils of Chinese origin become alienated from school. For example, in London Lai (1975) found that some Chinese pupils were playing truant and the attendance records of girls was causing concern (see also Garvey and Jackson, 1975). Sometimes there were difficulties in enforcing the children's attendance at school, particularly if both parents were in full-time work. More recently it has been claimed that truancy amongst pupils of Chinese origin in London is increasing (NCC, 1984). Garvey and Jackson suggested that unhappiness and dissatisfaction amongst pupils of Chinese origin in school may lead them to anger and despair because they feel their problems are overlooked. Others (e.g. Voon in CAG and QCRC, 1979) have reported increasing concern about the growing, though limited, number of young Chinese breaking the law who had been discovered to be backward at school, mainly because of disinterest resulting from language disability. This report suggested that particular attention should be paid to the social and educational needs of Chinese teenagers who could not keep pace with schoolwork.

Moreover, Chan (1983) has claimed that, although Chinese pupils used to give the impression that they were bright, quiet, obedient and good at science subjects, there are increasing indications that many Chinese children fail to adapt adequately to the education system. Although he cites as influential factors parental attitudes towards education, which may stress material gains rather than educational achievements, the omission of any aspects of Chinese culture in the curriculum, difficulties of socialization with classmates and poor employment prospects outside the catering trade, Chan also claims that the needs of some Chinese children may be overlooked and neglected by their teachers simply because they are reserved and quiet. The very fact that Chinese pupils are undemanding does not mean they have necessarily adjusted to the values and norms implicit in British schooling, for in some cases such inexpressiveness may be an indication of feelings of alienation from school and British society. Cultural factors in upbringing make it difficult to evaluate the extent to which such traits are broadly characteristic of Chinese pupils in general or an individual and explicit response to the school environment. But some Chinese pupils exhibit extreme symptoms of withdrawal in response to their perceptions of schooling. For some this may be a temporary phase only, and with time they may learn to adjust, at least superficially, to the ethos, curriculum and social interaction in school. Indeed DES evidence to the Home Affairs Committee (GB. P. H of C. HAC, 1985) suggested that the reticence and passivity of some Chinese children might be a defence against hostile attention preceding harassment. Thus it clearly behoves teachers of Chinese pupils to be aware of some of the difficulties which they experience in their schooling 'to cultivate links with the home and adopt an active and sensitive pastoral role' (p.241) in order to facilitate their natural well-being in school, so that they may realize their proper ácademic and social potential. To this end it is important to examine teachers' views about their pupils of Chinese origin and the extent to which they consider themselves trained to assist in the adjustment and integration of Chinese children in their classes.

Job expectations and the transition from school to work
Chinese parents have high aspirations for their children's employment (see pp.254–5) but they may be aware that expectations may not be realized and, therefore, make provision for the employment of their children in their own, relatives' or friends' business. To what extent do parents' views influence the employment aspirations and expectations of pupils of Chinese origin? What research evidence is available about the extent to which pupils' job aspirations are realized in the transition from school to work in an economic climate of high youth unemployment?

The trend for pupils of Chinese origin to aspire to jobs outside catering had already begun in the late 1960s. O'Neill (1972) found that most of the second-generation Chinese were anxious to move into work outside the Chinese sector, regardless of their education and proficiency in English. However, career choice might have been influenced by a latent awareness of their position as members of a minority group, vulnerable to prejudice and discrimination. Similarly, in York in the mid-1970s Cheung (1975) found that most young Chinese interviewed did not wish to work in catering because of the long hours and hard work involved, but only a few said that their parents suggested that they find another trade. Garvey and Jackson (1975) claimed that of all the young Chinese whom they encountered during their three-month study not one expressed a wish to enter the catering trade. They had seen enough of the hard work and long hours which their parents put in, and although it was a convenient net to fall back into if their aspirations were not satisfied, they were aiming to escape from the food business.

Claims that second-generation Chinese would not necessarily wish to work in the family business, despite the guarantee of financial reward, persisted throughout the 1970s (see e.g. Freeberne, 1978). Harris (1980) also reported that the second generation were setting their sights higher, beyond the catering trade, and that the better educated were more aware of other opportunities. But limited evidence available from pupils' statements suggests that although they might be ambitious and aspire to professional jobs, they might have a limited knowledge of the range of occupations available (see Lee in ILEA:English Centre, 1979). In Fong's sample secondary-age Chinese pupils, like their parents, had high employment expectations. Nearly all of them aspired to higher education and did not care for the catering trade because of the long working-hours and monotonous routine. Ng's (1982) nation-wide survey of 251 Chinese teenagers attending ten Chinese language schools found that they did not intend to work in their parents' takeaway or restaurant businesses, which seemed to be largely substantiated by the fact that 61 per cent claimed that Chinese would be no use in their future employment.

These rather generalized findings consistently indicate that pupils of Chinese origin will not be content to work long hours in a routine service industry, in poor conditions such as those which their parents have experienced in the catering trade. Though adolescents' aspirations seem ill-defined, evidence from these studies may be taken as indicating a desire to diversify and to aim at a wider range of jobs. But how realistic are such aspirations? In some cases parental pressure to enter the family business may be considerable (pp.254–5). But does the education system assist Chinese youth in realizing, if not a professional position, at least the opportunity to escape from the food business?

By the early 1970s O'Neill (1972) noted that in Liverpool many of the locally born Chinese were to be found in a wide range of occupations: manual work, shop assistants, bank cashiers, working in bars, working in education, engineering, research and medicine. But the sample, who often had one English parent, with some experience of further or higher education, and were not randomly selected but informal contacts, might well not have been representative. Even so, O'Neill could not discover any Chinese headteachers, counsellors or top managers. Those who had been upwardly mobile tended to be lost to their community, having become occupationally and socially integrated. By contrast, she also reported the disillusionment of recently arrived young Chinese with only one or two years of UK education who had no other choice but to work in the Chinese sector. Cheung made similar observations whereas, by contrast, some of the UK-born had become professional, such as teachers, computer specialists and engineers. Some restaurant workers believed that the UK-born Chinese fared no worse than the English when it came to jobs.

But there was growing concern in the mid-1970s amongst the Chinese community about the employment of the second generation. The SCSCRC report (1976) suggested that some Chinese youth felt a moral responsibility to work in the family restaurant, in line with traditional expectations, even though their parents had given them complete freedom of choice. Others, who lacked awareness of available career opportunities had opted to work in catering. Late arrivals with less proficiency in English found that they were too old for craft apprenticeships by the time they had achieved the necessary linguistic standard. The CAG & QCRC report (1979) emphasized that catering should not be taken for granted as an employment outlet and that young Chinese should be encouraged to develop the skills to take up opportunities to participate in the mainstream economy. More training schemes were required in which students with lower language proficiency could be enrolled. In particular, schemes in which young school-leavers, who might otherwise be unemployed, had been trained to work amongst their own communities should be extended to Chinese pupils.

Twitchin and Demuth (1981) reported a job-training scheme set up by Camden CRC in 1979 – Operation Springboard – to help ethnic minority youth with poor English. This provided language tuition and experience in local firms. Interestingly, a young Chinese boy was offered a job in a hardware store when the manager realized that it was a business asset to have a fluent Chinese speaker on the staff where a significant proportion of the customers were Chinese. Many schools are now involved in work experience programmes, but there is a need for more information on how these affect the employment aspirations and prospects of minority youth, especially Chinese.

It has been claimed (Mackillop, 1980) that unemployment amongst second-generation Chinese is relatively unknown because they have been absorbed into their own ethnic employment channels. But it should not be assumed that this is either desired by pupils of Chinese origin or their parents, or that it is necessarily a reliable form of employment. As Fong (1981) has pointed out, high aspirations may be difficult to realize because the opportunities for further and higher education and jobs are very much linked to proficiency in English. In view of current high levels of unemployment which affect ethnic minorities disproportionately severely, pupils of Chinese origin may have little choice but to enter the catering trade. However, Chan (1983) has suggested that the catering trade, also suffering from the recession, may no longer be able to absorb the surplus labour of the second generation.

Two recent parliamentary reports have continued to highlight difficulties in the transition from school to work for pupils of Chinese origin. The Swann Report (GB. P. H of C, 1985) noted increasing resistance by young British-born Chinese to do catering work, some speaking of going to Hong Kong, although some who had left home to find other work had failed and eventually returned to the family business. Evidence suggested that ultimately children obeyed parental pressure regarding employment. The need of strong support and guidance from the school if Chinese pupils, especially girls, wanted to break out of the catering employment pattern was stressed. The Home Affairs Committee Report (GB. P. H of C. HAC, 1985) claimed that the employment of young Chinese was one of the community's most pressing problems. It claimed hidden unemployment as Chinese youth were absorbed into the family business even when uneconomic, rather than register for unemployment which was considered shameful. Although many did not wish to enter catering, there was parental pressure, especially on the first son. Records from ten schools in Liverpool in 1980–2 showed that most eldest Chinese children left school for catering, even if they had academic potential, and the second child tended to be in catering-related occupations. Girls especially were forced to work in the family business. Although there was some evidence of gradual diversification in employment, it was suggested that many young Chinese and their parents were ignorant of further education, higher education and middle-range job opportunities. Young Chinese were not being properly reached by Careers Officers and were very critical. There were hardly any examples of alleged discrimination in job searches, but there was little clear evidence of the extent of application for public sector jobs. The Committee suggested that Chinese youth experienced disadvantages in job search similar to those of black youth and reported the concern of the Chinese community that the frustration of many young Chinese would lead to delinquency and crime which would damage the community's reputation. Indeed the Unemployed Chinese Youth Project in Tower Hamlets was giving educational, vocational and welfare advice as well as organizing recreational activities.

Any assessment of the extent to which Chinese pupils' employment aspirations have been realized is thwarted by a lack of adequate information about their examination performance, their participation in further and higher education and their transition from school to work. Many pupils of Chinese origin have little or no desire to be involved in the catering trade, but there are few firm indications of the form of employment to which their aspirations are directed. From the evidence available it is as though they categorize employment in terms of the professions and the catering trade. Does this indicate a lack of awareness of the middle range of occupations? Moreover, even if there may be a trend for some more able Chinese pupils to enter further education (see pp.223–4), how does this subsequently affect their employment opportunities? The increasing involvement of Chinese professionals and overseas students in the Chinese community in the UK presents role models to the younger generation. Yet for those who cannot achieve professional positions, which offer participation in both the Chinese community and wider British society, and those who cannot attain the middle range of employment in the mainstream economy, is it just to claim that being able to fall back on family business and the catering trade is adequate compensation for failure to satisfy higher ambition? The school through the careers service has as much responsibility for guiding and supporting Chinese pupils to have a balanced assessment of occupational goals as it has to promote the development of their linguistic, educational and vocational skills which will enable them to compete for a wider and higher range of employment positions. The current economic situation calls into question the continued availability of the catering net for the employment of second-generation Chinese and acts as an additional challenge and hurdle to those young Chinese who aspire to the higher and middle range of occupations in the mainstream economy. Given the general evidence of discrimination and disproportionate unemployment amongst ethnic minority young people, it will be for future research to ascertain the extent to which young Chinese have been able to realize their aspirations or whether they have become caught up in the catering cycle.

Section 13
Teachers and Schools

Teachers' attitudes

Teachers' attitudes to pupils of Chinese origin are likely to influence their educational performance considerably. Moreover, it is important to assess the degree of congruence between teachers' perceptions of Chinese pupils and the complementary perceptions of teachers by their pupils. Fong's (1981) small-scale study in Liverpool provides such evidence as does Fitchett's more anecdotal, but none the less illuminating, monograph. By drawing on these and other accounts a broad general picture of the attitudes of teachers to their Chinese pupils can be built up. The research data focus on classroom behaviour, teacher–pupil interaction, perceived attitudes to learning, academic assessment, peer-group socialization and, in terms of home–school liaison, the effect of the evening employment of some Chinese pupils in their parents' businesses on their schooling, and the extent of teachers' knowledge of the culture and home background of their Chinese pupils.

In 1975 Garvey and Jackson concluded that pupils of Chinese origin were 'quiet, undemanding, easily overlooked' (p.29). Their decorous politeness was evidently a contrast to the boisterousness of their peers. Whilst some teachers were evidently relieved and pleased to have well-behaved children in their classrooms, others were irritated by their impassivity. Others realized the the difficulties of assessing their learning. Teachers' opinions, quoted by Fitchett (1976), were similar, some found some Chinese pupils' lack of facial expression disconcerting, and that their apparent self-sufficiency gave them a socially aloof air. Others suggested that although it took time to establish confidence between teacher and pupil, once a relationship was built up, it sometimes resulted in the teacher's perception of the pupil as friendly and having a sense of fun. Teachers of the Chinese pupils in Fong's sample in Liverpool, in three secondary schools and the Language Centre, concurred that Chinese children were well-behaved, obedient and respectful, especially compared with other ethnic minority children. Chinese pupils were seen to present fewer deviant and behavioural problems in class. For these reasons, in Fong's opinion, they sometimes attracted less then their due share of the teacher's attention. Teachers typically commented:

> She is a typical Chinese pupil. She is friendly and helpful. Always well-behaved and does her best in school.

> It is remarkable that she can be so attentive and eager to learn in view of the fact of her extreme tiredness at times. She is very bright.

> Stable, well-adjusted pupil, most staff have mentioned him as 'a pleasure to teach'. (Fong, 1981, p.17)

It is also interesting to note a study undertaken by Herman (quoted by Bagley, 1976), who collected data on the behaviour of 2,587 girls in a large number of junior and secondary schools in the London area. According to the norms of an English observer, the best behaved were the Chinese girls.

As Ladlow (1980) has observed, most Chinese children are perceived by their teachers as being quiet, well mannered and neat in their schoolwork, but because they are not demanding or disruptive, teachers may often not realize the extent of their learning difficulties or the tensions which they may experience in their schooling. For example, Fitchett and Ladlow have both suggested that, from their experience in language centres, pupils of Chinese origin often take longer to adjust to school and initially many make a less spectacular response compared with their South Asian peers. With patience and by engaging Chinese pupils in learning activities which they can enjoy and perform well in, their confidence may be established and their achievement increased. According to Lai (1975), primary teachers in London saw their Chinese pupils as diligent and competitive academically. This was confirmed at secondary level, where Fong found that nearly all teachers liked to teach Chinese pupils because they were seen as hardworking, eager to learn, attentive in class and neat and tidy in their schoolwork. A typical comment was:

> He is a particularly hardworking, intelligent person with special ability in mathematics. His oral English causes no problems, but he still has not mastered some points of grammar and so his written work is not always as good as it would otherwise be. (Fong, 1981, p.71)

Yet according to teachers' assessments on the Bristol Social Adjustment Guide, some 70 per cent of the Chinese pupils were considered to under-react. There were almost as many in the severely maladjusted under-reaction group as those who were assessed as stable (one-third). This perceived under-reaction might be attributed to the shyness, quietness and timidity of Chinese pupils which inhibits them from interacting with their teachers and peers. Moreover, the majority of the pupils said they were not keen to answer questions posed by the teacher in class. Similarly, Ng (1982) found that even in the Chinese language classes only half of the pupils said that they liked to answer questions, fewer liked to ask about what they wanted to know and only just over one-quarter about what they did not understand. Thus the evidence suggests that pupils of Chinese origin may lack the kind of skills expected by teachers for normal participation in the classroom. Since it has also been suggested that Chinese pupils lack library skills (NCC, 1984), it appears that it may take some while for them to adjust to child-centred learning and discovery methods.

Several researchers (for example, Lai, 1975; Fong, 1981; Ng, 1982) have observed that since Chinese pupils are often reserved, quiet and less conspicuous in the classroom, it may be difficult for teachers to assess how much they understand lessons. But the teachers' comments quoted by Fitchett (1976) suggest that many Chinese pupils are quick to learn despite their reluctance to interact with teachers and other pupils. Several sources indicate that Chinese pupils try hard and do their work well, even when it challenges their abilities. Whilst some have suggested that Chinese pupils prefer drill situations or rote learning to more imaginative creative work, others have said some pupils are very able, even gifted. But Wang (1981) has claimed that many teachers have said that their Chinese pupils are intelligent, but have questioned their willingness to develop their talents. On the other hand, teachers in London claimed their Chinese pupils were particularly good at mathematics and various forms of handwork (Lai, 1975), and teachers in Liverpool agreed that their pupils usually had a higher attainment in non-verbal subjects (Fong, 1981). Clough and Quarmby (1978) claimed that many Chinese pupils, concentrated in one school in London, were considered by their teachers to display considerable abilities, especially in the arts.

By contrast, there is a general recognition that Chinese children will, for the most part, experience some social isolation within the community and the school. Seven LEAs in the nation-wide study by Little and Willey in 1979 (1983) claimed Chinese pupils might have special educational needs on this account. The QCRC Conference report (1981) indicated that newly arrived Chinese pupils, in particular, tended to associate socially with other Chinese pupils. However, in Fong's study some teachers thought that some Chinese children were good mixers. Some boys, especially those who had been in a school for a few years, were said to get on well with others, particularly in sporting activities. It is disappointing to find so little evidence of teachers' perceptions about the social interaction of pupils of Chinese origin, especially in view of the lack of sociometric data.

Interpersonal interaction with teachers and peers gives rise to some concern. There are indications that, compared with other ethnic minority children, it may take longer for pupils of Chinese origin to adapt to the social context and teaching style of British classrooms, and that their quiet disposition may mask both their true emotional response and also the extent to which they are able to profit from the learning environment. But their orientation to learning does not seem to be in doubt. On the whole, teachers seem to like pupils of Chinese origin and do not encounter particular difficulties in attempting to teach them.

According to documented evidence of the views of teachers and parents, the greatest culture clash between home and school is occasioned by the fact that some pupils of Chinese origin work in the family business. Many teachers may be irritated by the effects of this on children's schooling, but remain puzzled as to their proper response. Some pupils of Chinese origin are known to work in takeaways or restaurants from time to time, but the extent of their labour and whether practices have changed in recent years are unclear. In the mid-1970s several research reports showed that boys and girls, especially those recently arrived and aged 13–15, and also younger children of junior school age, were involved in the catering trade with their parents (Lai; Cheung; Garvey and Jackson). Boys whose parents had takeaways in York handled all the business communications, which made demands upon them beyond their competence (Cheung, 1975). Indeed the recent parliamentary report suggested such involvement would increase with the introduction of VAT (GB. P. H of C. HAC, 1985). Garvey and Jackson (1975) cite many examples of children working: some returning home from school to sleep for a few hours, then to start work when a brother or sister would come off a shift, until the early hours of the morning. Sometimes children were not registered for school, and, if enquiries were made, they were sometimes moved on to another area or business. Chinese parents traditionally expect their children to help them in their work and do not consider it to be harmful. The children should accept this without question as a contribution to the good of the family unit as a whole. Child labour in the family business may be seen by parents as necessary in their attempt to make a living, or to succeed financially.

Though it may be difficult for teachers to teach a sleepy child who may have been working until one o'clock in the morning in the family business, there may be little they can do to prevent this. But when working leads to absence from school, this may be a different matter. Lai (1975) reported that the attendance records of some Chinese girls in London schools gave rise to concern, and Jones (1980) noted that the attendance of some recently arrived 14–16 year olds, again predominantly girls, was sporadic, due to their assistance with running catering establishments. Lynn (1982) cites the view of a welfare officer with experience with Chinese families that absence from school was usually due to family commitment rather than the child playing truant; he attempted to compromise between the legal requirement that the child should attend school, the educational view that he should be permitted to do so, in order to maximize his potential by experiencing the opportunities offered within the education system, and the parents' cultural expectations that the child would assist in the family business. A lenient view was taken if a child were in the last year of schooling and attended four out of five days a week, but he attempted to enforce the law with children below this age. In many ways this position is ambiguous because one of the aims of ensuring the child's attendance at school is to increase the chance of obtaining a job subsequently, yet these Chinese already had employment. Explaining to Chinese parents the importance of their children attending school may be to no avail and, in a minority of extreme cases, may result in some prosecutions brought in connection with younger children.

It is more likely, however, that pupils of Chinese origin will be helping in family businesses during the evenings after school. However, in the CRE survey (Tsow, 1984), according to both parents and children, only four per cent of children were said to work in this way. Even so, working involvement, whether as great as three-and-a-half hours on average per evening (Garvey and Jackson, 1975) may seriously interfere with homework and studying for those who are taking O- and A-level examinations. Some teachers may thus see the child's future to be sacrificed to present necessity. A *fortiori* some able pupils are sometimes required by their parents to leave school at the earliest opportunity, or are subsequently removed from a sixth-form course if their assistance is needed in the family business (Garvey and Jackson; Lynn). The working commitments of some Chinese pupils may result in tiredness during the school day and may cause them to oversleep and be late for school. But being late for school may be a way of minimizing the risk of bullying and being harassed on the way to school and in the playground (Garvey and Jackson, 1975). Some Chinese children may be left alone in their homes in the evening whilst their parents are working, or live with minimal parental supervision, which because of late-night business commitments, may not extend to seeing that the child is up in time for school or has breakfast (Lai, 1975; Garvey and Jackson, 1975; Tan, 1982). The Swann Report suggested 'parent education' might help parents to appreciate the possible effects of work pressures on their children's education and that teachers need to take working pressures into account in their response to pastoral needs (GB. P. H of C, 1985).

Another cause of absence from school for pupils of Chinese origin may be occasional visits back to Hong Kong, sometimes for an extended period. Some teachers may be concerned about such visits because of the perceived break in continuity of schooling and the need to readjust to different cultural and linguistic contexts. Yet such visits are of great significance to many pupils of Chinese origin, even those who see their future to be in the UK (Fong, Ng). Moreover, as their parents' orientation is increasingly towards settlement in this country, visits may become increasingly infrequent. In any case, surely such visits may be regarded as a first-hand educational experience for the Chinese child, and, at a little remove, also for his classmates. The teacher can use the opportunity to introduce into the classroom aspects of Chinese culture and to compare the way of life in Hong Kong with that of pupils of Chinese origin in the UK. Preparation before the child's visit and discussion upon his return may be used both to boost the confidence of the Chinese pupil and to encourage a greater awareness by other pupils.

Indeed there is a consensus throughout the literature to suggest that teachers of pupils of Chinese origin often lack an awareness of their cultural background, language and home life in Britain. Teachers may themselves admit that they do not know enough about Chinese culture, and even depend on Chinese pupils for this information (Lynn, 1982). In interviews with teachers in two primary and three secondary schools, in London, Lai (1975) found that the majority lacked knowledge about the background of Chinese pupils. Much depended on the initiative of individual teachers, but she felt that, on the whole, they lacked curiosity about the facts of life for Chinese pupils in school and at home. On the other hand, teachers in language centres seemed to know much more about pupils of Chinese origin, and to have a better relationship with them. Cheung (1975) confirmed these findings in York and, like Lynn, cited examples of teachers exhorting children to speak English at home, not understanding that parents could not communicate in English. Ladlow (1980) has suggested that this shows a lack of awareness that a failure to develop any real fluency in Chinese may mean that after a number of years children will lose the means of communication with their parents. Garvey and Jackson (1975) alleged, moreover, that it was rare for teachers to know which Chinese dialects children spoke. In the case of recently arrived pupils, teachers also need to know something of the child's previous experiences of schooling. This may lead on to an exploration of aspects of upbringing and values inherent in Chinese culture.

Teachers may be assisted in school administration if they understand more about Chinese customs with respect to naming or the assessment of ages. For example, teachers may not realize that parents may consider the naming of a child important for his future prospects (Jackson, 1979). Confusion may arise concerning the names of pupils of Chinese origin since the Chinese custom is to put the surname (usually one of around 100 family names) first, followed by one or two given or personal names, the first of which may be shared by brothers or sisters (Fitchett, 1976; Hill, 1976). It would be appropriate for a teacher to address a Chinese boy or girl by the whole name, though it may be difficult to be sure from the name itself which belongs to a boy and which to a girl. Some Chinese in this country may have Anglicized the order of their names (Mackillop, 1980). Chin and Simsova (1981) provide a helpful list of common Chinese family names. Confusion may also arise over the age of Chinese pupils, since a pupil may give it as one or even two years older than the teacher expects (Fitchett, 1976). According to Chinese tradition, a child is one year old at birth and becomes two years old the following Chinese New Year (Hill; Fitchett).

If teachers can spend some time talking individually to pupils of Chinese origin by taking an interest in the child's life and culture they will not only gain insights useful in teaching, but also help in establishing the child's confidence in the teacher and his schooling (Ladlow, 1980). But perhaps the most useful way in which teachers can acquire knowledge of their Chinese pupils is by undertaking visits to their homes, as Ladlow and Fong have advocated. The area of home–school liaison is ripe for evaluation. If greater home–school liaison with the involvement of teachers in visiting children's homes is to be seriously promoted it will involve a reconceptualization both of the role of the teacher and the working schedule. But this could do much to assist mutual understanding, particularly in respect of the cultural background of ethnic minority pupils and may, in turn, influence parents to attend school (Ladlow, 1980; Tsow, personal communication).

When Garvey and Jackson concluded their research in 1975, they claimed that teachers tended to ignore the one or two pupils of Chinese origin whom they might encounter in their own classes, or within the school as a whole. They tended to see them as 'a small temporary and insoluble problem which (if ignored firmly enough) will go away' (p.2). Garvey and Jackson alleged that least of all for Chinese pupils did the teaching profession possess the insights, knowledge, relationships and specialist pedagogic techniques necessary to maximize the educational potential and opportunities of such pupils. Many teachers, especially those in inner urban schools, with other ethnic minority pupils, were too hard-pressed to inquire into the background of pupils of Chinese origin, their language, their culture and their adaptation to life in the UK. It is now over a decade since such observations were made. But in view of the lack of large-scale research investigations into the education of pupils of Chinese origin, it would appear that Garvey and Jackson's conclusion with respect to the lack of knowledge of teachers about Chinese pupils largely holds. Whilst there are undoubtedly some teachers who have considerable experience of teaching Chinese children and an appreciation of the way in which cultural influences in their home backgrounds affect their education, others, with little contact with pupils of Chinese origin, may lack knowledge and insights to assist their educational development. Just as the educational system has not properly appreciated or made provision for the many thousands of pupils of Chinese origin in British schools, so teachers who have only encountered a few Chinese pupils will not have realized that the particular position of a pupil of Chinese origin in their own school can be multiplied many times across the country. How often when the needs or performance of ethnic minority pupils are considered are pupils of Chinese origin uppermost in the thinking of teachers or educational administrators? Some would argue that the very lack of attention which such pupils have received is in itself an example of covert racism. However, it would appear that, despite their lack of knowledge, many teachers have on the whole a positive attitude towards pupils of Chinese origin. Hence it is important to assess teacher training opportunities to acquire knowledge of the needs of pupils of Chinese origin, whether the materials and resources exist for introducing aspects of Chinese culture into the school curriculum or teachers can expect to derive any support from the first-hand experience of Chinese teachers themselves.

Multicultural education – the Chinese dimension
It should be clear from this review of research on Chinese families and the education of their children in the UK, that their common, deep cultural heritage links the Chinese through their diversity of origin, language and experience. But what account of this ancient Chinese culture and modifications to its traditions by Chinese living in the UK has been taken in the curriculum of British schools? Some commentators on the Chinese in the UK have claimed that they feel their own culture is infinitely superior to that of British culture (see Watson, 1977a, for example). Speakers at the QCRC Conference (1981) outlined the breadth, richness and tenacity of Chinese culture, but it was doubted whether it could survive through the second and third generations in the UK. Apart from an appreciation of Chinese cuisine, some popular interest in Kung Fu and awareness of an occasional special Chinese festival or celebration, there is little or no general consciousness of Chinese culture in the UK. Chan (1983) has suggested that there should be a greater awareness of the distinctively Chinese contribution to ethnic arts through calligraphy, fine art, handicraft, music, literature and dance (see also Khan, 1976). If this lack of attention to Chinese culture is true of society at large, is it also the case with respect to the curriculum of British schools? Wang (1981) has argued that although children may be able to learn about British, American and European civilizations, they cannot, for the most part, learn about Chinese paintings, calligraphy, theatre, music or a Chinese language. Tsow (in CAG & QCRC, 1979; and see 1980a) has consistently argued for a greater permeation of aspects of Chinese culture throughout the curriculum at all levels of the education system from pre-school to teacher training courses.

Research evidence suggests that with respect to ethnic minority pupils in general, and specifically in connection with pupils of Chinese origin, much more attention has been paid to developing English skills through E2L teaching than incorporating elements of Chinese culture, especially the Chinese language, into the school curriculum. This is not the place to undertake a thorough conceptual analysis of the meaning of multicultural education, its aims and objectives, though this largely remains to be done. An earlier review (Taylor with Hegarty, 1985) has attempted an overview of objectives and policy with respect to multicultural education up to the end of 1984, highlighting the absence of any clear, consistent lead by the DES and a diversity in LEA and school policies and practices, the range of teachers' views, variability in resources and inadequate teacher training provision. The account given here relates specifically to an assessment of the education system's attempt to make provision for the inclusion of Chinese culture across the curriculum and in the life of the school. It assumes much of the discussion about multicultural education in the earlier publication. However, this is a rapidly developing and confused area of argument and practice with which it is difficult to keep abreast in a research review, especially as there is a great need for evaluation and monitoring. For further general information on the contemporary debate about multicultural and anti-racist education, with its greater stress on attitudes countering prejudice and developing an awareness of power structures, and LEA developments, see, for example, Dorn (1984), Ashrif (1985), Johnson and Corner (1984), Troyna and Ball (1985) and *Journal of Moral Education* (special issue on Race Culture and Moral Education, Vol. 15, No. 1, January 1986).

In general, multicultural education attempts to promote an awareness of equality through diversity and appreciation of, and respect for, other cultures. A number of objectives have been proposed for multicultural education apropos of Chinese culture. First, multicultural education would aim to build upon, and give status to, awareness of Chinese traditions, attitudes and values which pupils of Chinese origin have as a result of their family upbringing. It might, moreover, serve to develop a natural aptitude, ability and interest in aspects of Chinese culture such as proficiency in speaking Chinese, or Chinese arts. A further objective would be to develop a greater awareness and appreciation of Chinese culture and of the contemporary lifestyles of Chinese pupils by their peers in schools. Indeed sources suggest a latent interest in Chinese civilization and language amongst British schoolchildren (Wright, 1985) and university students (Chinnery, 1975). Moreover, the Swann Report (GB. P. H of C, 1985) acknowledged a need for businessmen and industrialists to know more about the economic importance of Hong Kong and that 'the importance of China in the world and the fact that it is one of the world's historic civilizations argue a powerful case for all children knowing something of it' (p.659).

Within the school context the Chinese child is usually very much in a minority. This isolation is reflected in the lack of opportunities he is likely to have of seeing himself pictured in a school text or hearing aspects of his home and cultural life referred to in the classroom. Though in recent years there has been a much greater awareness of the need to take account of the cultural backgrounds of ethnic minority pupils, the extent to which Chinese culture has permeated the curriculum and school life may be questioned. Ladlow (1981), for example, has argued that, if aspects of Chinese culture can be mentioned quite casually as an opportunity arises in teaching, then both Chinese pupils and the whole class will benefit. Chinese pupils may sometimes seem ignorant of their cultural background, although this may be more because they simply do not have sufficient English vocabulary to discuss it and do not recognize Chinese words in their English form (Ladlow, n.d.2). Both Ladlow (1980) and Wong (in NCC, 1984) have argued for more sensitive teaching in so far as teachers should not assume that Chinese pupils necessarily know about aspects of Chinese culture, or even, for example, about life in Hong Kong. Each family is likely to have adapted to a different extent – and in different ways – in the course of living in the UK, and it is important to Chinese pupils that they should not be seen to lose face by being caused any embarrassment if some have little to contribute to lessons on Chinese culture or when allusions are made to it in the course of teaching. Others, however, may have much to contribute. The Swann Report (GB. P. H of C, 1985) noted that Chinese parents and pupils appreciated the permeation of elements of their cultural background in the curriculum and saw it as enhancing their culture in the eyes of the rest of the community, especially when it could be done by a Chinese teacher and not just as a token gesture.

Explicit and consistent attempts may be made to increase an awareness of Chinese culture throughout the curriculum at all age levels, and it may be helpful to give some examples here in illustration. For the youngest age range the BBC schools TV series *You and Me* has included stories for four-and five-year-olds in Chinese, available on audio cassette with a printed text (see Twitchin and Demuth, 1981) which may be particularly welcome, especially in view of the oral tradition (see also p.238). An acknowledgement of Chinese festivals, particularly the Chinese New Year, makes an easy and stimulating introduction to aspects of Chinese culture, which will be much appreciated by Chinese pupils. Ladlow (n.d.2) provides a helpful résumé of such festivals for teachers, and Fitchett's monograph (1976) contains an interesting paper on the way in which observance of Chinese festivals, particularly New Year celebrations and customs, has been modified in the UK. The school environment may also reflect Chinese culture by hanging Chinese calendars in the school. Interest, too, may be developed by giving pupils an opportunity to inspect Chinese cards and calligraphy, and through mention of Chinese inventions and achievements in science or history. Godfrey (1983) describes how these features can be incorporated into project work on China for lower juniors.

At the secondary level history courses have been developed which explicitly include the study of both imperial and modern China, building on the Schools Council Integrated Studies Project material (see Twitchin and Demuth, 1981). The opium wars, which led to the British colonization of Hong Kong, look very different interpreted from a Chinese viewpoint. Wainwright (1978) has described how Chinese music can be used as an inspiration for creative dance, and how a first-year secondary course enables Chinese music to be studied through recorders and singing. He reported that some schools in Manchester had been devising CSE Mode 3 syllabuses in Chinese music. Khan's review (1976) suggests that Chinese music is likely to appeal to many Chinese pupils. Some Chinese pupils, as in an example quoted by Twitchin and Demuth (1981), may be keen and knowledgeable about Chinese poetry and literature, and this can be used to stimulate access to a wealth of literature from other cultures which may be represented in the class. Tsow (1980a) has argued that Chinese literature in translation, from Tang poetry through to 20th century novels, can provide much scope for exploration of human experience, themes and techniques. If Chinese literature and that from other cultures represented by pupils in school could be given the same status as other school subjects, this would open up a new perspective for pupils. However, the absence of Chinese from schools' language options minimizes any opportunity for the exploration of Chinese literature in the original Mandarin. Moreover, examination syllabuses act as particular constraints at this level. The Schools Council Assessment in a Multicultural Society Project made some progress in this area, but the examination boards have been noticeably reluctant.

The examples above are only some of the many ways in which Chinese culture could be incorporated into the school curriculum. But what resources are available, and are they adequate for teachers' needs? The SCSCRC Conference (1976) noted a shortage of teaching materials based specifically on the linguistic and cultural background of Chinese pupils. It is possible, however, that the publication of the Nuffield Foundation materials (1981) may have gone some way to meet a linguistic need. In the CAG & QCRC Report (1979) Tsow (also 1980a) noted the need for resource material which could be used for the whole class or for independent learning for one or two Chinese children in the classroom. The QCRC Report (1981) suggested that there should be a booklet outlining Chinese values which could be given to young Chinese growing up without a proper awareness of them. It appears that although there is much available published material on all aspects of traditional Chinese culture, there is an almost complete lack of material suitable for use in schools which portrays the modification of Chinese culture in the UK as it is experienced by pupils of Chinese origin. But in school, above all, there is just such a need for Chinese pupils to be able to see themselves, and their home background, in a UK context.

Materials which may be of assistance to teachers may be mentioned briefly here. Ladlow's monograph (n.d.2) provides a useful outline of the periods and dynasties of Chinese history. Some of the great Chinese achievements and inventions such as the Great Wall, printing and fireworks can be introduced into a consideration of Chinese history. Ladlow also provides succinct summaries of different Chinese religions and philosophies, a guide to festivals and a bibliography of further reading in these areas. Another publication by Ladlow (1980), which has been drawn upon heavily in this review, contains useful suggestions for teachers based on experience with Chinese pupils and shows how misunderstandings can arise because teachers and parents have different concepts of education and social life. The ILEA booklet *Some Lifestyles of Chinese People from Hong Kong and Singapore* (1975), written and compiled by a working party of teachers, including some Chinese teachers, is useful for the case studies on living in Singapore, Hong Kong and London. One of the few books written with Chinese pupils in Britain and their peers in mind is Tsow's *A Day with Ling* (1982), a book suitable for junior-age pupils in which a white British girl spends a day with her Chinese friend. A useful bibliography by Evans (1981), compiled largely as a resources list for teachers of Vietnamese pupils, demonstrates that resources in Chinese, or about Chinese culture, may also be relevant to Vietnamese pupils. The bibliography also includes several books on Chinese history, language, calligraphy, various cultural activities, cookery and religion. Books on Chinese pottery, textiles, printing, embroidery and paper cutting are worth exploration, especially since some Chinese pupils have been said to be talented in craftwork.

The Schools Council project report *Education for a Multiracial Society: Curriculum and Context 5–13* (1981) lists a few books with Chinese settings, but gives noticeably less attention to Chinese literature than literature relating to South Asian and African pupils in its bibliography, and makes very little textual reference to aspects of Chinese culture in the case-studies illustrating the development of a multicultural curriculum in British schools. Interestingly, the report's introduction acknowledges that although the project team wanted to accord more attention to Chinese culture, their brief was largely determined by the definition of race in British society, namely, the relationship between white British society and the children of families it defines as racially different, of African, Asian and Caribbean descent. The omission of the cultural background of pupils of Chinese origin from multicultural texts appears all too common, as, for example, in the case of an otherwise useful collection edited by Lynch (1981). However, a kit called *Chinese Conundrum*, developed as a result of a multicultural education project sponsored by Lothian CRC in 1976 (1978), for 9–12-year-olds may be of assistance to teachers. The kit includes an explanation of the topics chosen linked to a philosophy of multicultural education. The work centres around the themes of festivals, food, family life, homes, religion, folk-tales and legends, using visual and audio aids. Children learn a few Chinese characters and play a single language game, which serves to illustrate the learning problems involved with a language whose written and spoken forms are different and the difficulties a Chinese pupil needs to overcome to acquire a fluency in English. A section on the Chinese New Year, for example, provides information about the festival and instructions for several associated practical activities. The kit may be used in a variety of ways: to help a class understand their classmates from Hong Kong; as a comparative study of social structures, i.e. China, Russia, and America; as a study of festivals, community life and celebrations; and as a class project. A teacher who had used the kit cannily observed: 'Children were able to get through the project in general as soon as they learned the difference between "inferior" and "different".'

Moving to the secondary level, a useful source for teachers in schools and colleges is Howe's *Studying China* (1979). At this level perhaps the most accessible insights are those of two recent novels: *Sour Sweet* by Mo (1982), about a Chinese family attempting to establish a takeaway business in Britain, and Kingston's short stories, *The Woman Warrior: Memories of a Girlhood among Ghosts* (1981), relating her upbringing in an overseas Chinese community in America. The latter book features many illuminating descriptions of home life, the attitudes of Chinese to non-Chinese (ghosts), and nicely observed contrasting behaviour at mainstream and Chinese language schools. Appendix 3 and 4 of Simsova and Chin's report (1982) list 30 popular Chinese books and selected English translations from Chinese poetry, plays and literature. A Schools Council Project at Nottingham University has produced *Lifestyles* packs, providing teachers with information on family backgrounds, including one Chinese family, which are designed to stimulate discussion and a revision of stereotypical ideas (Thomas *et al.*, 1984).

Besides books and teaching materials it is worth mentioning other useful sources for teachers. The Hong Kong Government Office and its cultural centre provide helpful digests of information about Hong Kong which could be used in a study of contemporary background as well as some material about the Chinese in the UK. Other institutional sources and Chinese magazines are mentioned by Wright (1985) and CILT (1986). Research investigations into the library needs of the Chinese in the UK include information on bookshops in London selling Chinese materials (Clough and Quarmby, 1978) and in major provincial centres (Chin and Simsova, 1982). According to Simsova and Chin, although 22 London boroughs had no Chinese book collection in their libraries in 1981, Chinese collections existed in Bexley, Brent, Camden, Hackney, Hammersmith, Kensington, Lambeth, Southwark and Westminster. Apparently there has been some increase in demand in recent years. In 1979 Cooke found that only six local authorities nation-wide provided children's books in Chinese. Clearly there is a need for greater liaison between teachers and public libraries, so that children's books in Chinese and appropriate materials for study of the cultural backgrounds and life in the UK of Chinese pupils may be obtained. To date on this front library-based research is ahead of educational research. However, the Swann Report has referred to one LEA's plan to produce TV programmes and materials which could be used by any teacher to introduce elements of Chinese culture into teaching for the benefit of all pupils.

Clough and Quarmby (1978) pointed to the importance of music in establishing a bridge between cultures and that the Chinese should be able to borrow their own music. Simsova and Chin (1982) found that some 59 per cent of their sample claimed to buy Chinese music, although they suggested that most cassettes and records available in Chinese bookshops are of poor quality, with only a two-year life (Chin and Simsova, 1981). Since the overwhelming majority (91 per cent) of their sample had access to cassette recorders, given the need for oral communication (see p.132) this facility could be exploited to promote home–school communication and to enable Chinese pupils to hear stories told in their own dialect. But, above all, as Garvey and Jackson (1975) recognized, teachers should capitalize with sensitivity on the resources of the pupil when attention is given to aspects of Chinese culture in the school curriculum. Millward (1977) has described how adolescent Chinese pupils can be particularly helpful in selecting Chinese books for library stock. Moreover, members of the local Chinese community can be invited to address schoolchildren on some aspects of Chinese culture (Jones, I., 1979).

In such ways teachers may draw on available resources to integrate Chinese culture into the school's multicultural curriculum, thereby enabling Chinese pupils to develop a greater awareness of and pride in themselves as Chinese in Britain and also extending the cultural horizons and sympathetic understanding of non-Chinese pupils. Compared with some South Asian materials, however, there are fewer resources for teachers wanting to introduce a Chinese element into the multicultural curriculum. Indeed the recent parliamentary inquiry (GB. P. H of C. HAC, 1985) recommended that the DES should take steps to see that suitable materials were more readily available. A complete absence of educational research in this area does not enable any conclusions to be drawn as to how widespread a Chinese dimension in curricular innovations may be. The impression gained is of piecemeal initiatives by individual teachers, either those with particular experience, especial commitment and long-term interest, often at language centres, or by those teachers who have particular awareness of the needs of ethnic minority pupils. However, there is no evidence – as there is with respect to pupils of South Asian and West Indian origin – about teachers' views on the inclusion of aspects of Chinese culture into the curriculum for pupils of Chinese origin, white British pupils or other ethnic minority pupils. There is a need here for a consciousness-raising exercise, both in respect of teaching practice and educational research.

Research generally (see, for example, Craft, 1981; Watson, 1984; Singh, 1984) shows that to date little attention has been paid to incorporating a systematic multicultural or multiracial perspective into teacher training, either at initial or in-service levels. In this context it is dismaying to note that, in 1977, Hopkins claimed that 40 per cent of probationary teachers in Liverpool, a city with one of the largest Chinese populations, had no previous training in multiracial education. It had only been mentioned briefly in the courses of a further 35 per cent. Only two per cent of these teachers had attended courses where multiracial education had full coverage. Since teacher training often fails to take account of the needs and interests of ethnic minority pupils, how much the less is it likely to take account of the special needs and interests of pupils of Chinese origin? The recent parliamentary inquiry drew attention to the need for the DES and relevant validating bodies to ensure that *all* teacher training institutions offer tuition relevant to a multiracial curriculum *including* Chinese culture (GB. P. H of C. HAC, 1985).

Moreover, as Tsow (1980a) demands, how is it possible for a true multicultural education to be promulgated if ethnic minority pupils are not represented by teachers from their own group? As in the case of other ethnic minority teachers, there are no accurate records of the numbers of Chinese teachers working in mainstream schools despite a recommendation of a CRC report (1975) that a register should be compiled. According to the recent parliamentary inquiry, there is a Chinese headmistress in Manchester, but no Chinese school governors. However, very few Chinese teachers feature in educational research inquiries (see, for example, CRC, 1977). Hence nothing is known of the professional circumstances of Chinese teachers, for example, whether they tend to teach pupils of Chinese origin or if they have a special role in multiracial schools. In passing it may be of some interest to note that a study of personality variables and attitudes of 277 Chinese and Indian Malay students and 83 British students in teacher training in the UK (Bate, 1970) found the student teachers of Chinese ethnic origin obtained the highest scores for conscientiousness on Cattell's 16 PF questionnaire, showing that such a teacher was more likely to be 'a protector of manners and morals, one who plans, concentrates and perseveres, shows energy and persists'. Bate attributed the high scores of the Chinese to their religious attitudes, ability and the need to ensure that they would qualify. Other results on the tests indicated wide cultural, linguistic and ideological differences in the approach to teaching of the Chinese and British student teachers. More explicit policies and practices need to be developed to encourage young Chinese to enter the teaching profession and other posts in the education service. There appears to be no specific information on their involvement in training or special access courses.

Over the years recommendations have frequently been made that bilingual and bicultural Chinese teachers should be employed to work together with British teachers, for example, in helping Chinese pupils to adjust with confidence to a new school environment, and to provide role models with which such children could identify (for example, CAG & QCRC, 1979). Some authorities with relatively large numbers of Chinese children may employ some Chinese teachers, as in the case of the English Language and Multiracial Education Centre in Liverpool, which boasts an E2L teacher, pastoral worker and home–school liaison officer of Chinese origin. Even so, there is a need for Chinese teachers in the education welfare service and as outreach workers in the local parent support project (Lynn, 1982). Chinese teachers have a peculiarly advantageous position, enabling them to liaise directly between the schools with Chinese pupils and their families to enhance understanding between parents and teachers and facilitate the adjustment of pupils of Chinese origin between these two social life worlds. On the one hand, Chinese teachers may act as role models for both parents and pupils and may be able to develop confidence and trust in the school. On the other, the school may come to have a better understanding of the needs and interests of its Chinese pupils. In Liverpool the Chinese Home–School Liaison Officer advises parents on subject choice, school transfer and social welfare benefits (GB. P. H of C. HAC, 1985). Fong (1981) found that most teachers interviewed in three secondary schools and the Language Centre in Liverpool agreed that a Chinese teacher could promote a better understanding by Chinese parents of the social and cultural values and the workings of the educational system, and on the part of schools, of the home life of Chinese pupils and their parents' expectations for their schooling.

There is, moreover, a particular need for bilingual Chinese nursery staff and playgroup supervisors to encourage participation of young Chinese at a pre-school level (Wong in NCC, 1984). A study of the use and training of bilingual nursery assistants in 1981–3 revealed that only a quarter of LEAs had such assistants and that there were very few Cantonese-speaking bilingual adults involved in nurseries visited in the West Midlands area, and none in colleges on training courses (Rathbone and Graham, 1983). Indeed there is a need for local authorities generally to ensure that Chinese children are included in pre-school provision. The Pagoda in Liverpool, for example, offers nursery classes but only for a very few Chinese (GB. P. H of C. HAC, 1985).

A potential reservoir of assistance with, and support for, pupils of Chinese origin and their families amongst Chinese teachers in the voluntary, part-time Chinese language classes remains largely untapped. In the CRE survey (Tsow, 1984) 57 out of 69 Chinese teachers in these classes claimed that they had no contact with teachers in mainstream schools. Any contact is likely to be informal and incidental since there is no structure to facilitate such interaction. Yet surely this could be of great mutual benefit: beneficial to the Chinese language teachers since many want to know more about teaching methodology, and beneficial to mainstream teachers in obtaining direct insight about their pupils' performance in a complementary educational context. Given the considerable significance of the language classes in Chinese community life (see pp.198–9) and the lack of mainstream provision, liaison between these two parallel educational networks would seem vital in the long-term development of the education of pupils of Chinese origin. In Liverpool Fong and Lynn have advocated that the local authority and Merseyside Chinese Society should work together to provide an information centre for Chinese parents which might also include playgroup activities for children, English language tuition for parents and teacher training programmes. These Chinese researchers have argued that only if such positive steps are taken towards liaison will the educational needs of Chinese children be fully recognized and the possibility of their social integration in the wider community be realized.

In her book Lynn (1982) strongly implies that British schools are guilty of racism with respect to the education of pupils of Chinese origin. Even with the general lack of substantive high-quality educational research – a gap which is in itself indicative – there are trends to support this charge. For notwithstanding notable individual initiatives on the part of dedicated hard-pressed teachers, many, on their own admission, have little knowledge about the social and cultural backgrounds of their Chinese pupils in the UK; little attention has been given to the inclusion of a Chinese element in the multicultural curriculum; teachers generally lack training and awareness of the specific educational and learning needs of their Chinese pupils; and there are few Chinese teachers to act as role models for pupils and figures of authority for their parents, and who may be available to mediate between home and school. When there is added to these omissions the reputation of pupils of Chinese origin as quiet, unassertive and easily overlooked, the lack of demands made by Chinese parents with respect to their children's education, and non-participation in school activities, it is difficult to have anything but a fairly low-key and possibly even negative impression of the education system's response to the schooling of pupils of Chinese origin.

Overview

Ignored, isolated, inscrutable – thus pupils of Chinese origin, and indeed the Chinese as a whole in the UK, might be characterized according to a review of the research literature. That pupils of Chinese origin, especially when compared with pupils of South Asian or West Indian origin, have been largely ignored within the education system, and by educational research, just as the Chinese as an ethnic group have largely been ignored in British society, is clear from the relative lack and poor quality of research information. That they have been ignored is in no small part due to the fact that they are geographically, socially and economically isolated. Moreover, the Chinese have been perceived as 'inscrutable' since as a group they have deliberately kept a low profile, not drawing attention to themselves. These factors, in combination, have made it easy for them to be overlooked. This has been no less the case with respect to pupils of Chinese origin within the education system since educational provision is often made on a quantitative basis. Thus the needs and interests of pupils of Chinese origin may not have received proper assessment or their due share of attention. Although in individual schools practice may demonstrate a greater degree of knowledge, insight and concern, the trend of research evidence belies such a position. The very fact that Chinese pupils have less often been the focus of or explicitly included in research indicates that they have been ignored by default, and may have suffered accordingly.

In the concluding section of this review of research it is necessary, given the educational context of the inquiry, to focus on educational research and the conclusions which can be drawn from it. But it is important that any assessment of the educational performance of pupils of Chinese origin should be evaluated against the background of inter-community perceptions and attitudes, and the socioeconomic position of the Chinese in Britain. Moreover, any evaluation of the research on pupils of Chinese origin and their families in the UK must take full account of the methodological difficulties experienced in research into this group. Recommendations for provision for pupils of Chinese origin and future research must depend on community, educational and research factors.

Quality of the research evidence

This review of research represents a comprehensive search of published research reports up until the end of 1985, of conference statements and more ephemeral literature on the education of pupils of Chinese origin. Some difficulty was experienced in tracing some materials identified in various bibliographical citations but which did not appear to exist. Chinese name order could have complicated the search. Although the literature on pupils of Chinese origin and their families is relatively slight, it has been considerably augmented in the early 1980s, apparently in parallel with the greater involvement of Chinese professionals in the Chinese community. Even so, research reports do not always keep pace with current practice and provision. The relative lack of educational research on pupils of Chinese origin has been a continuous refrain throughout this review. It would seem that not only has less attention been paid to Chinese pupils, compared with other numerous ethnic minority pupils, but that there is less *educational* research than socioanthropological research on the Chinese as an ethnic group. Yet the omission has been known for a decade (CRE, 1975; Watson, 1977a). But apart from notable research on library provision for the Chinese (Simsova and Chin, 1982) and some initiatives on the part of Chinese professionals (Fong, 1981; Ng, 1982; Lynn, 1982), and a larger survey by the Commission for Racial Equality (CRE) (Tsow, 1984), this lack has not been rectified. So it becomes necessary to pose the question: why, since the omission was known? Does this reflect an attitude on the part of the educational community, or on the part of the Chinese community? Or have mutual perceptions failed, by default, to encourage a climate propitious to research?

Furthermore, the quality of the educational research which exists must, for the most part, be impugned. Even allowing for the notorious difficulties in conducting research on the education of ethnic minority pupils, the status of some of the research evidence here is less than what would normally be accepted as reliable. Many studies are dubious because they have an unsound data base due to inadequate sampling rigour. Most are small scale. Many lack an obvious research design and some designs have been modified significantly on an *ad hoc* basis when difficulties have been encountered in execution. In some researches interpretations appear to go beyond the evidence given and are often little more than subjective impressions. Some studies are poorly grounded in a theoretical or interdisciplinary context and, in some cases, there has been a naïve use of sociological concepts such as 'adjustment', 'accommodation' and 'integration'. Whilst in-depth studies in the genre of illuminative evaluation can offer insights which larger surveys cannot provide because of their quantitative and statistical emphasis, it would have been advantageous to have been able to draw upon both types of material in the compilation of this review. However, much of the research falls into the former category of descriptive, sometimes largely anecdotal, accounts. Nevertheless, some of the research undertaken in connection with higher-degree studies, particularly that of Cheung (1975), who lived and worked amongst his subjects, are of particular value, and often serve to illuminate more general statements. Moreover, it must be noted that the conference reports which have been drawn upon in this review, whilst complementing research investigations, largely present unsubstantiated assertions, although the perspectives of those involved in such meetings are grounded in practical experience.

It is no doubt too easy to be sceptical about both the lack of educational research involving pupils of Chinese origin and the inferior quality of much of that which does exist. Researchers' comments indicate particular methodological difficulties in undertaking research on the Chinese community over and above those normally experienced in educational research and with ethnic minority pupils. Some of these difficulties may be outlined as a salutary reminder of the problems which should be taken account of in any evaluation of research evidence. These may also guide intending researchers in the future.

A first difficulty is that of access to the Chinese population itself. Due to the geographical dispersal of the Chinese in Britain and the fact that they are represented in large numbers only in London, Liverpool and a few other urban areas, it should not be surprising to find that over the years most research has been confined to these areas. There has been little research into the Chinese scattered in the provinces. It is, therefore, unclear whether the inclusion of more far-flung Chinese families would seriously affect the trend of research findings. Moreover, some aspects of the Chinese community, for example, Chinese associations and clubs, as Ng (1968) and Watson (1977a) have pointed out, would be virtually impenetrable for a non-Chinese socioanthropologist. In addition, there may sometimes be difficulties of access to schools. This occurred both in the mainstream, as O'Neill (1972) reported that access to a school in Liverpool with the largest concentration of Chinese pupils was refused, and amongst Chinese language schools, as Ng (1982) was not able to gain the co-operation of 25 schools chosen to be representative in size and geographical distribution, and had to modify the research design to visit only ten schools.

Secondly, considerable difficulties have been encountered in sampling the Chinese population. O'Neill (1972) was unable to obtain a random sample of Chinese families in Liverpool as no list existed and it was a fruitless task to attempt to extract names from the electoral roll as many Chinese did not register for voting. For similar reasons, Tan (1982) was not able to obtain a random sample of families in London; contacts had to be made through hospitals reported to have high numbers of Chinese attenders, clinics, voluntary service agencies and social workers. Simsova and Chin (1982) searched the list of telephone subscribers in London, Glasgow and Liverpool to use in a postal survey (see Chin and Simsova, 1981). Moreover, as Ng's (1982) experience shows, samples tend to be self-selected, and therefore not representative. In the case of the CRE survey (Tsow, 1984) there were difficulties in contacting sufficient parents of children who did not attend Chinese language classes. A list of subscribers to the Hong Kong *Reader's Digest* formed the basis of the sampling-frame, yet it was necessary to supplement the sample as most subscribers were students, or businesses, rather than families. The Chinese interviewers were asked to augment the original addresses with those of other Chinese families, provided that they were not personal friends. Even so, the interviewers had to make contact with an average of seven Chinese households before discovering a family qualified to participate in this part of the study. Whether this means most Chinese families have a child attending Chinese language classes, or that the Chinese interviewers tended to be associated with other Chinese whose children attended Chinese language classes, is not clear. But evidently the sample could not be called random and might not be representative.

The 30 families whom O'Neill (1972) interviewed and observed were those with whom she had informal contacts, though their evidence was supplemented by the opinions of at least 150 other Chinese known to the researcher. Tan's (1982) study also included personal friends in order to obtain a sufficiently large sample. Neither was it possible to obtain, in the time available, a sample of second-generation Chinese mothers with children under five to compare dietary behaviour. Thus, many samples are biased. O'Neill's sample included a large proportion of families with Chinese fathers, who had entered the UK either prior to or during the Second World War, and white British mothers, whose second-generation children tended to be better educated. Simsova and Chin's (1982) sample of library users consisted predominantly of Chinese professionals, students and nurses, rather than those in the catering trade. On the other hand, the samples involved in the research by Lai, Cheung and Tan were almost exclusively connected with catering. Moreover, apart from research by Clough and Quarmby (1978) and Simsova and Chin (1982), Chinese from Malaysia or Singapore have not been distinguished from the focus on Chinese from Hong Kong and the People's Republic of China, though there are pupils of Chinese origin with origins in Malaysia or Singapore (Jackson, 1979; ILEA, 1975; Twitchin and Demuth, 1981). So the extent to which such backgrounds make a difference in social and educational terms is not clear. The Linguistic Minorities Project (LMP) also experienced sampling difficulties when they intended to interview Cantonese speakers in Bradford but the interviewees turned out to be Vietnamese, only some of whom spoke Cantonese (see pp.132–3).

Many attempts to undertake research have been greeted with considerable suspicion by members of the Chinese population who have sometimes displayed marked initial reluctance to co-operate, although as they have come to understand the nature of the inquiry and a rapport has been established with the researcher, confidence and trust have been built up. For example, both Ng (1968) and Cheung (1975) reported that they were checked out by the Chinese they attempted to study in case they had any connection with a government agency. Other reports (for example, Nuffield Foundation, 1981) have noted the traditional reluctance of some Chinese to interact in any way with government organizations such as the Hong Kong Government Office (HKGO). O'Neill (1972) encountered considerable suspicion and continued to find access a problem until she was accepted as a teacher of English to a family. Cheung, who claimed that it would have been impossible for him to have carried out his research had he not worked amongst the Chinese in the restaurant trade in York, noted that, as he became more accepted, his status as a teacher was also helpful, as was that of his wife as a social worker. Lai (1975) mentioned the considerable suspicion of the older women from the New Territories in the homes of London families. Tan (1982) also records that Chinese mothers, being reserved and humble, found it difficult to understand the objectives of her project, and were suspicious of its intentions, since they considered that had little knowledge to share about their food beliefs and dietary pattern, and feared to commit themselves. However, after an initial breakthrough and agreement to participate, many subsequently gained confidence and began to talk freely. In other cases, however, as in the Commission for Racial Equality (CRE) survey, some individual teachers refused to be interviewed. As usual, data loss increases with distance and without personal intervention, as the CRE postal questionnaire to organizers of Chinese language schools only attained a 36 per cent response rate (Tsow, 1984).

Even though agreement may be obtained, other difficulties occur. Lai, for example, found that where housing facilities were shared sometimes other families were present in the room during the interview. Although interaction seemed friendly, Lai suggested that there might have been some inhibition in response. Tan found that when the fathers were at home during the interview they were much more talkative, trying to convince the researcher that they were more knowledgeable than their wives about food beliefs and practices. Men also preferred speaking for their wives in Cheung's (1975) study. Moreover, the secondary-age children whom he interviewed spoke more freely in school than at home. But once confidence has been established, as O'Neill discovered, the Chinese may be keen to enlighten the non-Chinese researcher about their culture and their attitudes to and interpretations of British life. So Garvey and Jackson (1975) reported that after initial reservations many Chinese parents were delighted at the interest shown in their children. Fitchett (1976) observed that all the Chinese children whom he interviewed seemed excited that someone was taking an interest in them; and Simsova and Chin (1982) recorded that the students they encountered were enthusiastic subjects for interview.

Not surprisingly, it would appear to be easier for a Chinese dialect speaker to undertake research with Chinese families. But it is important in establishing rapport that the dialect spoken by the interviewer is the same as that of the interviewee (Lai, 1975; Fong, 1981). Ng (1968) was greeted with some suspicion because he spoke Cantonese, as spoken in Singapore. Moreover, the fact that the interviewer spoke a Malaysian Chinese dialect might have influenced those agreeing to participate in Simsova and Chin's (1982) study. It would, therefore, seem important for research to involve bilingual interviewers with the appropriate dialect. The CAG & QCRC report (1979) claimed that such people were difficult to find, but this does not seem to have been the case in the CRE or LMP surveys.

Origin, status and gender may also be significant factors affecting research. The social and educational differences between researcher and researched may often be considerable and readily perceived by research subjects. But Ng (1982) has claimed that it is difficult to assess the socioeconomic status of the Chinese based on the father's occupation or on residential area. Many Chinese researchers have been overseas students researching for higher degrees. Cheung's fellow catering workers easily identified him as a student of urban origin and there were difficulties with his status, until he was no longer perceived as a business threat, but a teacher. Although O'Neill (1972) claimed not to find being British or only English speaking a handicap to research, both Lai and Fong have claimed that being Chinese is an advantage. O'Neill thought being female was helpful in gaining access to discussions with Chinese women. As it happens, the majority of researchers into the Chinese community have been women of Chinese origin.

Participant observation appears to be one of the most illuminating ways of researching into the Chinese. Cheung (1975) claimed that he needed to work in the catering trade to gain the trust of the community. His experience subsequently helped him to identify many aspects of lifestyle and behaviour which would otherwise have been missed, and to phrase questions correctly. However, in interviews, questionnaires may make Chinese parents and pupils anxious. This caused both Lai and Fong to adopt a more informal approach. Tan (1982) employed a lengthy questionnaire during five visits to 50 families, which may have been one of the factors influencing the fall-off in participation to three-fifths of the sample by the fourth visit.

A further major difficulty in undertaking research with linguistic minorities, especially when the researchers' language differs from that of research subjects, is the interpretation that is to be given to the meaning of statements. O'Neill (1972), who interviewed only English-speaking Chinese, found a considerable data interpretation problem because she felt that the central meaning was often implied but left unsaid, embedded in the cultural context. Although Lai (1975) thought it was helpful to be a Chinese researcher, she wondered whether it might have made her over-identify with some of her subjects. But it would seem more likely that the perceptions of

Chinese researchers would be at some remove from those of the majority of poorly educated Chinese parents in the catering trade. Indeed the extent to which Chinese professionals as researchers and conference participants represent the views of the Chinese community, since they are likely to be considerably distanced from the adult majority by virtue of their origin, education, occupation, orientation and outlook may be questioned. On the other hand, their insights into the community are more keenly observed and nicely related to cultural background in a way which is unavailable to some non-Chinese researchers.

These, then, are some of the methodological difficulties encountered by those who have attempted to undertake research of all kinds and at all levels within the Chinese community in the UK. Though not all of these difficulties are peculiar to the Chinese as a group, nor to ethnic minority groups as such, there are special and characteristic difficulties which should be recalled when assessing findings and instituting further research.

Conclusions

Research on the education of pupils of Chinese origin may be roughly divided, as in the procedure followed in the text, into that on educational performance and attainment and that concerned with attitudes. Over a decade ago Garvey and Jackson (1975) undertook the first and what, in many ways, remains the only wide-ranging research on the education of Chinese pupils. Although their report has been described as 'over-emotive and factually inaccurate' (Nuffield Foundation, 1981), and is regarded as dubious and exaggerated by some Chinese professionals, these researchers' observations as a result of a 12-week cross-country survey nevertheless served to warn against complacency with respect to the educational performance of Chinese pupils and their adaptation within the school environment. Research still faintly echoes their earlier contentions. More recent research has provided new insights and evidence of changes, but it is impossible to get a proper picture in view of the absence of hard, quantitative data. Thus, whilst Lai (1975) might have been correct in failing to share Garvey and Jackson's pessimism, believing that Chinese children were coping relatively well in the schools, and that their linguistic and social difficulties would disappear with time, it would be naïve, given the lack of research data on the performance of pupils of Chinese origin, to assert this position has as yet been reached. Some might argue that the absence of information would augur well. But it seems much more likely that the dispersal of pupils of Chinese origin, their small numbers in schools throughout the country and the general lack of monitoring of ethnic minority pupils are the reasons why they have rarely figured specifically in publicly available evidence on educational attainment. Until quantitative data – especially on examination performance – are available, a comparison of their achievement with that of other ethnic minority pupils, peers in local schools and peers nationally is simply impossible. A range of performance may be indicated. As Ladlow's (1980) figures for pupils of Chinese origin who have attended the Language Centre in Liverpool show (see pp.219–21), some do manage to attain sufficient proficiency in English to obtain some examination passes. As an increasing number of pupils of Chinese origin are British-born and experience all their schooling in the UK, performance levels may more clearly reflect ability rather than language facility. But there is also a consistent trend for those Chinese pupils who arrive from Hong Kong during their schooling, especially at secondary level, to experience severe difficulties in both adjusting to a different educational system and in acquiring a sufficient command of English to be able to benefit from study in other areas of the curriculum. For these pupils there must continue to be considerable concern.

Not surprisingly, as with other linguistic minority pupils for whom English is not a first language the greater part of educational attention has focussed on their acquisition of English. Like their South Asian peers, pupils of Chinese origin often operate in both their mother tongue and English. Although they are most likely to enter school with little or no knowledge of English, during the early years of schooling some fluency in spoken English is acquired fairly rapidly. Some English is usually spoken with siblings, though not necessarily, or even at all, with parents in the home. But at some point, probably prior to secondary age, English becomes the dominant language for the child. However, concern is beginning to be expressed by some E2L teachers that Chinese pupils should be encouraged to develop Chinese language skills in parallel to English skills, partly so as to enhance their command of language as such but also to preserve the means of communication with their parents and other members of the Chinese community (see Ladlow, 1980). Chinese pupils have a positive attitude to both their mother tongue and English. But many Chinese parents have limited fluency in English and so, in addition to the usual intergenerational difficulties in communication compounded when pupils are living between two social life worlds with different cultural influences, relationships are put under even greater stress when the linguistic means of expression in a common language are restricted.

Advances have been made in recent years in understanding the particular difficulties of pupils of Chinese origin in learning English as a second language (Nuffield Foundation, 1981; Ladlow, n.d.1; Jones, I., 1979) which may be over and above those experienced, for example, by their South Asian peers. But there is still no research evidence on whether the acquisition of English may be facilitated by first establishing a greater command of Chinese. Nor is there any indication of the extent to which participation in mother-tongue teaching classes, with their contrasting learning environments and teaching styles, may affect attitudes to learning in mainstream schooling and, in particular, to the acquisition of English. It is clear, however, that Chinese parents, in increasing numbers, strongly desire that their children should continue to develop their Chinese language skills and have an understanding of Chinese culture and values. To this end parents are prepared, often at some inconvenience, to enable them to attend part-time Chinese language classes, usually on a weekly basis. To date little provision has been made within the mainstream for pupils of Chinese origin, and others, to have the opportunity of learning Chinese. Research evidence suggests that parents would welcome this particularly because of the status which it would accord the language and to pupils of Chinese origin. But others, such as Tsow (1984), have argued that Chinese should be offered in after-school hours rather than as part of the mainstream curriculum. The Chinese language classes organized by the Chinese community are the most significant community development, providing a community focus, a means of encouraging the development of Chinese language skills amongst the second generation and of facilitating interaction between Chinese parents and with Chinese professionals. So it is likely that the community would prefer to see voluntary provision as complementary rather than supplementary to any which might be made within mainstream schooling.

Just as the Chinese language has not been incorporated into the school curriculum, so it would appear that, on the whole, little attention has been paid to incorporating aspects of Chinese culture into mainstream education. Yet, in the absence of systematic research evidence, it is only possible to speculate about the likely effect on the attitudes of pupils of Chinese origin to their schooling and learning. On their own admission teachers often have little knowledge about the cultural background and contemporary family lifestyle in the UK of their Chinese pupils. They have received little preparation for teaching such pupils, either in terms of assisting them with English across the curriculum or incorporating their culture into the curriculum. Finally, teachers only rarely can be helped to have a greater understanding of Chinese pupils by Chinese teachers in the school. To an even greater extent than for other ethnic minority pupils, the educational enhancement for both Chinese and other pupils which would be engendered by the systematic inclusion of aspects of Chinese culture and the Chinese language in the curriculum has yet to be widely recognized.

Where Chinese culture is acknowledged, it is usually to recognize the different values of home and school, for example, in the especially contentious matter of pupils of Chinese origin assisting their parents in the family business during the evenings and weekend. Although this may not now occur to nearly the same extent as Garvey and Jackson (1975) suggested, some teachers become aware of their Chinese pupils' work experience assisting their parents because of absences from school, late arrival at school and weariness during the day. Some proper educational concern may be expressed for the effect which such work involvement may have on the ability of Chinese pupils to benefit from their schooling. But it is also important the teachers, educational welfare officers and social workers should appreciate the cultural basis of the expectations of some Chinese parents that their children will assist them in their work. This would seem to be the most serious area of culture conflict between home and school as far as pupils of Chinese origin are concerned. Greater home–school liaison, through the mediation of Chinese teachers, would assist in developing more sensitive perceptions and greater mutual understanding on the part of teachers and parents on this and other matters of cultural significance.

Chinese parents have positive attitudes towards the education of their children and high expectations for them to succeed. Owing to a combination of factors, such as traditional non-interference, respect for the authority of the teacher, non-assertion of demand, and low participation in school activities, due to lack of English and long working hours, the views of Chinese parents about their children's schooling have generally not been well represented. Superficially it might appear that, compared with South Asian parents, they have few complaints about mainstream schooling, though they dislike what they perceive as a lack of discipline in school organization and teaching styles, particularly in so far as they expect homework for their children at a very young age. They may also have objections to the kind of food available for their children to consume in school meals. Yet, as Tan's (1982) research indicates, their response may be seen as symbolizing their reaction to the lack of recognition of Chinese culture as a whole in the school environment and curriculum – namely, for they themselves to supplement what they perceive to be necessary in cultural terms. This is evidently the case with respect to the provision of Chinese language classes. These serve both a linguistic function and to communicate the values and orientation inherent in the social structure, particularly in the family, in traditional Chinese society. It is the perceived omission of social ethics in the school curriculum which causes Chinese parents anxiety. Unlike some South Asian parents, Chinese parents are unable to claim the validation of a religious philosophy for a justification of their value orientation, but they may nevertheless perceive what is to them a fundamental mismatch between the cultural values inherent in the schooling of their children and those which they promulgate in daily life at home. Though it may appear ambivalent that they should want their children to learn English, have a good education and aspire to professional employment and a satisfying career, it is not necessarily inconsistent that they should also want their children to retain their essentially Chinese characteristics, values and dispositions.

Chinese pupils do not often seem to participate in extra-curricular activities, either school-based or in youth clubs, despite their involvement in Chinese language classes. But whether their limited participation is due to parental restriction or their own wishes is unclear. However, at least some pupils of Chinese origin want to have more social interaction and more friends, both other Chinese and their peers generally. Various factors, however, including their probable involvement in the family business, the need to help in the home, plus communication difficulties for those with less fluency in English, may however combine to militate against this. But the school itself does not seem to promote social interaction between pupils of Chinese origin and their peers. Rather the evidence suggests it may be the context for racial harassment, varying from name-calling to severe bullying. Yet surely the school has a special responsibility to actively encourage harmonious and fair relationships between pupils. This may be particularly significant for pupils of Chinese origin, as school may be the only context in which they do encounter their peers. Yet in this, as in other respects, because of their quiet disposition and disciplined behaviour, pupils of Chinese origin may be overlooked, both by their peers and teachers.

Research evidence suggests that many pupils of Chinese origin suffer various degrees of psychological tension in the school environment. This may be due to difficulties of adjusting to different teaching methods and a new educational environment if they are newly arrived from Hong Kong; frustration at their inability to express themselves in English; irritation at the more disruptive, or outgoing behaviour of their peers, particularly if they are placed in remedial streams; or to difficulties in reconciling the diverse cultural values in their home and school lives. Nevertheless, it appears that many pupils of Chinese origin have a genuinely favourable attitude to their schooling and, in particular, to their teachers. Since on the whole this would appear to be reciprocated, there are grounds for optimism for positive teacher–pupil relationships that may facilitate more accurate mutual perceptions and understandings. Many teachers, on their own admission, lack particular knowledge or understanding of their Chinese pupils and their cultural background and may require more preparation to meet their educational needs. Yet teachers are concerned to maximize the educational potential of their Chinese pupils just as much as it would appear pupils of Chinese origin are anxious so to do. For the evidence is unambiguous in this respect, namely, that they have high educational aspirations and employment expectations, desiring to escape from the catering trade. It is doubtless the extent to which they are able to realize these expectations and enter a wider job market, according to their ability, that the education system will be judged for the way it has served pupils of Chinese origin, notwithstanding the need for even greater determination and acumen in the current climate of employment.

During the last decade there have been many changes within the Chinese community as it has grown and become more established. Such changes and British perceptions of the Chinese population in the UK are likely to affect the aspirations of both Chinese parents and their children for their education and their future working lives. During these years there has been a change of orientation among many Chinese families in the UK; whereas when they had first arrived they continued to look towards their home community in Hong Kong for their main source of inspiration and identity, the evidence indicates that, even though many still retain strong family ties there, with the emergence of a second generation in the UK another phase of settlement has been established which anchors the Chinese more firmly in a British context. Yet different families in various locations throughout the UK are adapting at differential rates to a social context which in many respects contrasts significantly with that of their traditional cultural background. The orientation of many Chinese families within the UK is most likely to be still towards the local Chinese community rather than towards British society as such.

Indeed the Chinese 'community', if such it may be called, does not comprise a well-integrated group. Several sub-groups may be distinguished: the older early migrants, some now very elderly, who may have married into the local white population in areas such as Liverpool, Cardiff and the East End of London; their mixed-race children; Chinese professionals with an urban educated background; students of Chinese ethnic origin who may take a passing interest in the Chinese community during their temporary residence in the UK; and (by far the majority) Chinese adults who have immigrated during the last 20 years, and their children, many UK-born. The needs, perceptions and interests of these groups within the Chinese population are likely to be diverse. Social divisions are likely along the lines of these groupings. For example, Chinese professionals and students are taking a benevolent interest in the Chinese community in the UK in organizing mother-tongue classes for the teaching of Chinese. These are becoming a social meeting-ground for many Chinese parents as well as their children. But the parents meeting professionals in this context will still largely interact with them in their perceived role of teachers, and hence traditional attitudes are likely to come into play. Differences in spoken language reinforce community divisions, so that some Chinese may not be able to communicate orally and may also be limited by their degree of literacy. The Chinese are also often geographically separated, for although there are some substantial concentrations of Chinese in London, Liverpool, Manchester, Edinburgh and Glasgow, it is common to find a few Chinese families in almost every provincial town and a single family in even the larger villages. The need to make a living and economic competition have both brought about dispersal and reinforced it. Given these factors, it is not surprising that the traditional virtue of family loyalty has been reasserted.

But how have developments within the Chinese community in the UK affected attitudes towards British society and interaction with it? And how, in turn, has British society perceived the Chinese? Assessments of inter-community perceptions are always notoriously difficult, particularly since the research documentation is inadequate and dated. Clearly there are differences in orientation, perception and attitude on the part of Chinese families in the UK according to their place and length of residence, experience of interaction with the wider society and perhaps, especially, according to whether they have borne children who are being brought up in the UK. Though O'Neill (1972) reported that Chinese parents seemed to accept their children, irrespective of whether they became more orientated towards British social life and values or retained strong Chinese allegiances, later studies such as those by Lai (1975) and Cheung (1975) indicated that family loyalties were still regarded as paramount. Indeed the recent rapid increase in the number of Chinese language classes might be interpreted as a concerted attempt by Chinese parents to preserve Chinese values through the second generation. Though parents' desires seem sincere and genuine in this respect, it is not clear to what extent the growth in Chinese language classes marks a response towards a perceived lack of orientation towards Chinese culture in the mainstream curriculum or in British society as a whole. It would certainly appear that Chinese parents do not regard their own culture as inferior to that of British culture, even though, as some have suggested (for example, Chan, 1983), the Chinese may regard themselves as in an inferior position with respect to British society as a whole, and may see this as in some ways justifying discriminatory behaviour. Chan indicates that these Chinese generally feel that the only way to increase their status is financially through economic achievements.

The majority of Chinese in the UK have typically failed to assert their needs and rights but these are increasingly being taken up and advocated on their behalf by Chinese professionals (for example, CAG & QCRC, 1979; QCRC, 1981). They are often joined by young Chinese who have experienced most of their schooling in the UK, are fluent in English and have a greater awareness of the workings of British society and its institutions. In recent years they have articulated the needs of the Chinese in housing, social services (Lai, 1975; Lynn, 1982), dietary requirements (Tan, 1982) and education (Tsow, 1984; Lynn, 1982; Fong, 1981). These statements serve a dual function: to alert government and local authority institutions to the needs of the Chinese population and to exhort other Chinese to claim their due. For example, the need of Chinese families for advice about their social welfare rights has been reiterated constantly over the last decade. In the absence of evidence to the contrary it would seem that this is still needed or that traditional reluctance to claim welfare benefit, assert housing need or request Chinese language tuition in schools, for example, has prevailed in the apparent lack of take-up. On the other hand, the assertions of Chinese professionals attempting to increase the Chinese community's awareness of rights and also bringing to the attention of a wider public the existence of the Chinese community may be in advance of the majority's desire to draw attention to themselves or to establish closer relationships with the wider society.

It is important that the Chinese should be seen to participate more in British society as a whole, for example, by revealing aspects of their culture, both in traditional and modern forms adapted within a UK context, as some other ethnic minority groups have done. For the Chinese to become more outgoing it is necessary for there to be greater confidence and respect between the communities. The school as a meeting-point for the second generation may have a special function in this regard. For too long the Chinese community have been ignored. The Chinese have been thought of in terms of restaurants and takeaways and seen as an homogeneous group with disregard of their differences of origin (urban and rural), experiences of migration (one- or two-hop) and language (different dialects). Unlike peoples of South Asian origin, rarely are the Chinese distinguished according to their country of origin (Hong Kong, China, Malaysia, Singapore, etc.) or according to their language (Cantonese, Hakka, Hokklo or Mandarin). Generally the Chinese community, with some exceptions (see Watson, 1977a), have been perceived as law-abiding. If any particular consideration has been given to them, it is generally to suggest that adults should learn English. But do Chinese adults perceive this need? It is difficult to avoid the conclusion that there is a lack of mutual knowledge and understanding on the part of the British and the Chinese and, indeed, that both groups might be content for this situation to endure. Moreover, there is a lack of institutional frameworks in which the views of the Chinese community can be represented and difficulties within the community itself in the selection and recognition of those with the right to speak on its behalf.

Does this ignorance on the part of British society of the Chinese in its midst constitute some form of institutional racism? There appears to be very little evidence, at least in recent years, of instances of discrimination claimed by the Chinese. Typically, of course it is not the Chinese way to cause a fuss even if discrimination has occurred, for example, within the restaurant trade (see Cheung, 1975). The response of Chinese parents whose children may be consistently bullied is to remove them from that particular school, typically a response of withdrawal rather than assertion. O'Neill (1972), for instance, suggested that the Chinese in Liverpool deliberately encouraged the view that they did not have problems. However, this made it difficult for local people to see that they might have housing and social welfare needs. Thus, in the early 1970s she felt the Chinese were beginning to assume an uncaring response from British institutions. Similarly, in the mid-1970s Lai (1975) discovered that in London the Chinese were not seen by health visitors, the police or social workers as a group needing special help, and that little was known about them. Yet, according to general living standards, many Chinese families whom she studied suffered severe disadvantages, particularly in terms of housing. These had a serious effect on their family lives, although the Chinese families did not consider themselves to be deprived. They were reluctant to seek help from the state, and social service professionals had reservations about intervening for fear that this might be resented as intrusion and rejected. Thus an impasse may be reached in which both sides have false impressions, real hardship is experienced and communication, compounded by linguistic difficulties and cultural differences, does not take place. But does this mean that rights and obligations fail to exist?

Furthermore, to what extent is the extreme segregation of the Chinese in the catering trade a matter of choice, or a response to the perceived attitude or potential attitude of the wider society? Is concentration in the catering industry itself an example of institutional racism? Many Chinese parents and their children themselves have aspirations to enter into the wider employment market. So the acid test will be whether the second generation can break the cycle of involvement in the catering trade. If this should not prove possible, the degree of frustration between the generations, as well as between the Chinese and wider British society, may be considerable. The educational problem, therefore, is to ensure that pupils of Chinese origin maximize their potential through their experience of school, so that they may have the educational qualifications to be able to break away from catering if they so wish.

But is the educational system itself immune from any charges of institutional racism, such as Lynn has suggested? Some pupils of Chinese origin apparently suffer various forms of racial harassment at the hands of some of their peers, but there is little evidence that teachers have anything but a positive attitude towards their Chinese pupils, though they may be irritated by their impassive appearance and lack of overt participation in class. Yet, as has been said, many teachers on their own admission are ignorant of the specific learning needs of their Chinese pupils. Their quiet behaviour makes them liable to be overlooked by hard-pressed teachers in a multiracial classroom. There is, moreover, little appreciation of the kinds of psychological stresses which pupils of Chinese origin may experience in school and, according to the research literature, no attempts have been made to offer counselling services as has been reported for their South Asian peers. There is evidence, too, that in addition to Chinese pupils' need to improve their language and learning skills, they may also have social needs; thus it is an important function of the school to develop social and life skills. Furthermore, just as the school curriculum has largely ignored aspects of traditional Chinese culture and the Chinese language, teacher training has not set out, either at initial or in-service levels, to provide an awareness of the needs and interests of Chinese pupils, or to promote the recruitment of Chinese as teachers and home–school liaison officers. In all these respects, therefore, there may well be some grounds for claiming that in various degrees the educational system is guilty of covert institutional racism, through omission, with respect to pupils of Chinese origin. In this it is reflecting the attitudes prevalent in British society as a whole.

It may be further argued that the education service has a particular responsibility: it has a special opportunity to affect the mutual perceptions and understanding of pupils from ethnic and cultural minorities, and of their peers, and, thereby, a chance to influence not only the present but the future state of race relations in Britain. But before perceptions can be enhanced, a proper assessment of the distinctive needs of pupils of each ethnic minority group has to be made. Research literature shows that this has yet to be attempted for pupils of Chinese origin. It is customary for perceived needs to be met mainly on the basis of a quantitative allocation of resources. The larger numbers and local concentrations of pupils of Asian or West Indian origin fit with such a principle. However, even though pupils of Chinese origin are more numerous than generally realized, and continue to increase, provision for their needs on this basis is inadequate. The geographical dispersal of pupils of Chinese origin as a whole, hence their low profile, compounded by their self-disciplined behaviour, and their parents' non-participation and non-assertiveness, may in individual cases and for the group of Chinese pupils as a whole have meant a failure to benefit from available resources or to have had their specific needs and interests taken fully into account. For these reasons it is necessary for there to be reconceptualization of educational provision for pupils of Chinese origin. To date, both the degree and the specific nature of their need has been largely ignored. Although Little and Willey's survey (1983) indicated that some LEAs have an awareness of the special needs of some Chinese pupils on account of their social isolation, it would appear that apart from the attention of E2L specialists little further consideration has generally been given to the interests of pupils of Chinese origin. Here educational research has a part to play.

Recent research to establish the library needs of the Chinese in the UK may be taken as an example, since there are many parallels between the library and education service with respect to problems of provision and access for such a group (see Simsova and Chin, 1982). Like the education service, the library service experiences a tension between its need to provide an efficient service for all readers, both the majority and cultural and linguistic minorities, and within limited means. As in the education service, librarians have found that the Chinese are a particularly difficult group to serve, partly because of their reticence in making their needs known, and also because of their linguistic, social and geographical diversity. This is compounded by the lack of expertise amongst existing staff. Such well-known difficulties are particularly challenged within the education service by the need to give consideration to possible provision for teaching Chinese within the mainstream. The research librarians' approach of adopting a collaborative model involving the assistance of Chinese professionals and others in the community with bilingual and bi-cultural expertise is one which could be explored more fully with respect to this and other areas of the education of pupils of Chinese origin. For, in addition to Chinese teachers' evident expertise, which would be useful in advising on Chinese language teaching, the important community network provided by the Chinese language classes might be examined for its possibilities for establishing more effective home–school liaison with mainstream schooling.

The area of home–school relationships is a particularly significant aspect of the education of pupils of Chinese origin, which requires greater attention. More initiatives need to be made between schools and Chinese parents. More research is also required to examine the attitudes of Chinese parents to their children's education, whether they perceive value differences or whether this causes anxiety, their reasons for non-participation in school activities, and so on. It is only through more systematic, extensive and detailed research on pupils of Chinese origin and their parents in different locations across the country that an evaluation can be made of the extent to which the attitudes, aspirations and expectations which they bring to their schooling are matched with those of their teachers, and the provision made for their specific needs and interests within the school system. Other specific areas worthy of particular attention are the need to obtain examination performance data for pupils of Chinese origin, so that an accurate comparison can be made with the performance at this level of other ethnic minority and white British pupils; an investigation of the particular study and social skills required by pupils of Chinese origin; and a study of the effects of learning Chinese either in voluntary or mainstream schools, on attitudes towards Chinese and English and the development of proficiency in English. Only through mounting such research can detailed knowledge become more widely available about the specific needs and interests of pupils of Chinese origin and the capacity of the educational system to meet them.

The education service is in a special position, both because of the compulsory nature of its interaction with the Chinese population, otherwise largely economically and socially isolated, and because Chinese parents naturally focus their hopes and fears on their children and how their education may influence their future lives. The prolonged contact with the Chinese community which is ensured through the second generation gives the education service a unique opportunity to promote greater interaction and understanding between the Chinese and the British in the UK. At present the stereotype of the Chinese as inscrutable and isolated remains largely unquestioned, partly because of the ignorance of the British about the Chinese, but partly because of the lack of participation by the Chinese in British society as such. Only through a concerted attempt by both British society as a whole and the Chinese community in particular can greater mutual understanding be developed. Given its special position, the education service has a peculiarly vital and urgent role to play.

REFERENCES

ASHRIF, S. (1985). 'An anti-racist in place of a multi-cultural education', *Education Journal*, January, 14–16.

ATKINS, M. (1985). 'Minority community languages: problems, strategies and issues for teacher educators', *Brit. J. Educ. Studs*, **XXXIII**, 1, 57–69.

BAGLEY, C. (1976). 'Behavioural deviance in ethnic minority children. A review of published studies', *New Community*, **V**, 3, 230–8.

BAGLEY, C. and VERMA, G.K. (1975). 'Inter-ethnic attitudes and behaviour in English multi-racial schools.' In: VERMA, G.K. and BAGLEY, C. (Eds) *Race and Education across Cultures*. London: Heinemann, pp.236–62.

BAINBRIDGE, C. (1968). 'The lonely Chinese in London', *The Times*, 18.4.68.

BAKER, H.D.R. and HONEY, P.J. (1981). 'Background to the Chinese in Britain.' In: NUFFIELD FOUNDATION *Teaching Chinese Children. A Teacher's Guide*. London: Centre for Information on Language Teaching.

BARNES, D. (1978). 'The language of instruction in Chinese communities', *Int. Rev. Educ.*, **XXIV**, 3, 371–4.

BARR, B. (1983). 'Chinese.' In: MCCLURE, J.D. (Ed) *Minority Languages in Central Scotland*. Aberdeen: Association for Scottish Literary Studies, University of Aberdeen.

BATE, W. (1970). An examination of personality variables and teacher attitude amongst British, Malay, Chinese and Indian student teachers. Unpublished MEd. thesis, University of Bristol.

BISHOP, P. and ENGELHARD, S. (1979). 'UK Chinese help Boat People', *Observer*, 12.8.79.

BLACK PEOPLE'S PROGRESSIVE ASSOCIATION and REDBRIDGE COMMUNITY RELATIONS COUNCIL (BPPA & RCRC) (1978). *Cause for Concern: West Indian Pupils in Redbridge*. BPPA and Redbridge CRC.

BOYSON, R. (1983). 'Parliamentary digest: qualified support for mother-tongue teaching', *Where*, June, 20 (Hansard, Vol. 41, Col. 725, 26 April).

BROADBENT, J. (1984). 'Towards a programme of in-service teacher training for community language teachers.' In: REID, E. (Ed) *Minority Community Languages in School*. NCLE Papers and Reports 4. London: CILT.

BROADY, M. (1952). The Chinese family in Liverpool: some aspects of acculturation. Unpublished BA thesis, University of Liverpool.

BROADY, M. (1955). 'The social adjustment of Chinese immigrants in Liverpool', *Social Review*, **3**, 65–75.

BROWN, J. (1970). *The Un-melting Pot. An English Town and its Immigrants*. London: Macmillan.

BURGIN, T. and EDSON, P. (1967). *Spring Grove: The Education of Immigrant Children*. London: Oxford University Press/Institute of Race Relations.

CAMPBELL-PLATT, K. (1978). 'Linguistic minorities in Britain.' Runnymede Trust Briefing Paper (rev., S. NICHOLAS). London: Runnymede Trust.
CENTRE FOR INFORMATION ON LANGUAGE TEACHING (CILT) (1975). *CILT Reports and Papers No. 12. Less Commonly Taught Languages: Resources and Problems.* London: CILT.
CENTRE FOR INFORMATION ON LANGUAGE TEACHING (1986). *Chinese.* Language and Culture Guide 4. London: CILT.
CENTRE FOR URBAN EDUCATIONAL STUDIES (1982). *The World in a City.* Bilingual Education Project. London: CUES.
CHAN, A. (1983).Further information to the Sub-committee on Race Relations and Immigration.
CHAN, L. W.-L. (1981). Nutrition survey of immigrant Chinese children in London. BSc. project, Polytechnic of North London.
CHANN, V.Y.F. (1976). 'The social and educational background of Hong Kong immigrants in Britain.' Report of a talk to NAME Conference, Glasgow, 31.1.1976.
CHANN, V.Y.F. (1982). Chinese mother-tongue teaching in the United Kingdom. Unpublished paper, Hong Kong Government Office.
CHANN, V.Y.F. (1984). Paper to National Conference on Chinese Families in Britain. In: NATIONAL CHILDREN'S CENTRE The Silent Minority. The Report of the Fourth National Conference on the Chinese Community in Great Britain, November 1982. Huddersfield: NCC.
CHEN, T. (1939). *Emigrant Communities in South China: A Study of Overseas Migration and its Influence on Standards of Living and Social Change.* London: Oxford University Press.
CHEUNG, W.C.-H. (1975). The Chinese way. A social study of the Hong Kong Chinese community in a Yorkshire city. M.Phil. thesis, University of York, Department of Social Administration and Social Work.
CHIN, W.T. and SIMSOVA, S. (1981). Information Sheets on Chinese Readers, School of Librarianship and Information Studies, Polytechnic of North London.
CHINESE ACTION GROUP AND QUAKER COMMUNITY RELATIONS COMMITTEE (CAG & QCRC) (1979). *The Chinese in the UK. Conference (London) December 1978. A Report of the Proceedings of the Conference with Additional Papers on Nationality, Education, Bibliography and Statistics.* London: Commission for Racial Equality.
CHINNERY, J.D. (1975). 'Chinese at Edinburgh.' In: CENTRE FOR INFORMATION ON LANGUAGE TEACHING *Less Commonly Taught Languages: Resources and Problems.* London: CILT.
CHOW, C.-C. (1974). Report on the fieldwork placement at Check Rights Centre Liverpool University Settlement. Unpublished fieldwork report for the degree of Diploma in Applied Social Studies, University of Hull.
CLOUGH, H.E. and QUARMBY, J. (1978). *A Public Library Service for Ethnic Minorities in Great Britain.* London: The Library Association.
COLLINS, S. (1957). *Coloured Minorities in Britain.* London: Lutterworth Press.
COMMISSION FOR RACIAL EQUALITY (CRE) (1980). *Mother Tongue Teaching Conference Report.* Bradford College, 9–11 September. London: CRE.
COMMISSION FOR RACIAL EQUALITY (1981). *Race Relations in 1981: An Attitude Survey.* London: CRE.
COMMISSION FOR RACIAL EQUALITY (1982a). *Ethnic Minority Community Languages: A Statement.* London: CRE.
COMMISSION FOR RACIAL EQUALITY (1982b). *Further Education in a Multi-racial Society.* London: CRE.

318   *Chinese Pupils in Britain*

COMMISSION FOR RACIAL EQUALITY (1985). Evidence to the Home Affairs Committee. In: GREAT BRITAIN. PARLIAMENT. HOUSE OF COMMONS. HOME AFFAIRS COMMITTEE. *Chinese Community in Britain.* Vol. III Appendix 17, pp. 24–5. London: HMSO.

COMMUNITY RELATIONS COMMISSION (CRC) (1975). Report of the Meeting of Representatives of the Chinese Community in the UK held at the Community Relations Commission, 24 June.

COMMUNITY RELATIONS COMMISSION (1977). *The Education of Ethnic Minority Children from the Perspectives of Parents, Teachers and Education Authorities.* London: CRC.

COOKE, M. (1979). *Public Library Provision for Ethnic Minorities in the UK.* The report of an investigation carried out on behalf of the British National Bibliography Research Fund, Leicestershire Library and Information Service.

COUILLAUD, X. and TASKER, J. (1983). *The Schools Language Survey. Summary of Findings from Five Local Education Authorities.* May 1983. LMP/LINC Working Paper No. 3.

CRAFT, M. (Ed) (1981). *Teaching in a Multicultural Society. The Task for Teacher Education.* Lewes: Falmer Press.

CRAFT, M. and ATKINS, M. (1983). 'Training teachers of ethnic minority community languages.' Nottingham University, School of Education.

CRANE, A. (1975). 'Practical needs.' In: CENTRE FOR INFORMATION ON LANGUAGE TEACHING *Less Commonly Taught Languages: Resources and Problems.* London: CILT.

DAVIES, H. (1983). 'Making the Chinese scrutable', *Sunday Times,* 23.1.83.

DERRICK, J. (1977). *Language Needs of Minority Group Children.* Slough: NFER.

DORN, A. (1984). 'LEA policies on multi-racial education', *Education Journal,* April, 8–10.

ELLIOTT, P. (1981). *Library Needs of Mother-Tongue Schools in London. Research Report No. 6.* London: School of Librarianship, Polytechnic of North London.

EVANS, I. (1981). *Vietnam – a Resources List.* Bransgore, Dorset: Sopley Education Centre.

FEELEY, M.R. (1965). An investigation of the social integration of coloured immigrant children in selected secondary schools. Diploma in Secondary Education thesis, University of Liverpool.

FITCHETT, N. (1976). *Chinese Children in Derby.* NAME.

FONG, L.K.W. (1981). Chinese children in Liverpool. Diploma in Special Education thesis, University of Liverpool.

FONG, V. (1975). 'Planning for and development of the Chinese community in London' Department of Architecture, University of California, Berkeley.

FREEBERNE, M. (1978). 'Heirs to a proud culture', *The Times,* 29.9.78.

FRU, F. (1980). Housing Conditions among Chinese Households in Liverpool. Unpublished study, quoted by LYNN, I.L. (1982), op.cit.

FURTHER EDUCATION UNIT (FEU) (1983). Curriculum Development for a Multicultural Society: An Initial Policy Statement. London: FEU.

GARVEY, A. and JACKSON, B. (1975). *Chinese Children. Research and Action Project into the Needs of Chinese Children.* National Education Research Development Trust, Cambridge, England.

GENERAL REGISTER OFFICE (GRO) (1956). *Census 1951. England and Wales. Birthplace and Nationality Tables.* London: HMSO.

GENERAL REGISTER OFFICE (GRO) (1964). *Census 1961. England and Wales. Birthplace and Nationality Tables.* London: HMSO.

GIBBONS, J. (1982). 'The issue of the language of instruction in the lower forms of Hong Kong secondary schools', *J. Multiling. Multicult. Develop.*, **3**, 2, 117–28.
GODFREY, J. (1983). 'A slow boat to China', *Junior Education*, August, 27.
GREAT BRITAIN. DEPARTMENT OF EDUCATION AND SCIENCE (1968). *Statistics of Education 1967.* Vol.1, Schools. London: HMSO.
GREAT BRITAIN. DEPARTMENT OF EDUCATION AND SCIENCE (1971). *Statistics of Education 1970.* Vol.1, Schools. London: HMSO.
GREAT BRITAIN. DEPARTMENT OF EDUCATION AND SCIENCE (1973). *Statistics of Education. 1972.* Vol.1, Schools. London: HMSO.
GREAT BRITAIN. DEPARTMENT OF EDUCATION AND SCIENCE (1984). Mother Tongue Teaching in School and Community. An HMI Inquiry in Four LEAs. London: HMSO.
GREAT BRITAIN. PARLIAMENT. HOUSE OF COMMONS (1981). *Fifth Report from the Home Affairs Committee. Session 1980–81. Racial Disadvantage. Vol. I, Report with Minutes of Proceedings.* London: HMSO.
GREAT BRITAIN. PARLIAMENT. HOUSE OF COMMONS (1985). *Education for All.* The Report of the Committee of Inquiry into the Education of Children from Ethnic Minority Groups (Swann Report). Cmnd 9453. London: HMSO.
GREAT BRITAIN. PARLIAMENT. HOUSE OF COMMONS. HOME AFFAIRS COMMITTEE (1985). *Chinese Community in Britain.* Vol.I, Report, together with Proceedings of the Committee. Vol.II, Minutes of Evidence. Vol.III, Appendices. Second Report HAC, Session 1984–5. London: HMSO.
GROOCOCK, V. (1983). 'Cutting the tongue ties', *Education Guardian*, 15.2.83, p.11.
HARRIS, D. (1980). 'Integrating Britain's independent Chinese', *The Times*, 6.8.1980.
HESTER, H., WAINWRIGHT, C. and FRASER, M. (1977). *English as a Second Language in Multiracial Schools.* London: National Book League.
HILL, D. (1976). *Teaching in Multiracial Schools.* London: Methuen, p.76–81.
HONG KONG GOVERNMENT (HKG) (1984). *Hong Kong 1984: A Review of 1983.* London: HMSO.
HONG KONG GOVERNMENT INFORMATION SERVICES (HKGIS) (1982). *Hong Kong: The Facts. Social Welfare.* Hong Kong: Government Printer.
HONG KONG GOVERNMENT INFORMATION SERVICES (1984a). *Hong Kong: The Facts. Religion and Custom.* Hong Kong: Government Printer.
HONG KONG GOVERNMENT INFORMATION SERVICES (1984b). *Hong Kong: The Facts. Education.* Hong Kong: Government Printer.
HONG KONG GOVERNMENT OFFICE (HKGO) (n.d., late 1970s). *An Introduction to Hong Kong.* Hong Kong: Government Printer.
HONG KONG GOVERNMENT OFFICE (1982, 1984). *List of Chinese Schools/Classes in the United Kingdom.* London: HKGO.
HOPKINS, A. (1977). 'If it doesn't happen in Liverpool . . .', *Times Educ. Suppl.*, 3235, 3 June, pp. 18–19.
HOULTON, D. (1985). *All our Languages.* London: E. Arnold.
HOULTON, D. and WILLEY, R. (1983). *Supporting Children's Bilingualism.* London: Longman for Schools Council.
HOWE, C. (1979). *Studying China: A Source Book for Teachers in Schools and Colleges.* School of Oriental and African Studies, University of London.
INNER LONDON EDUCATION AUTHORITY (ILEA) (1975). *Some Lifestyles of Chinese People from Hong Kong and Singapore.* London: ILEA.
INNER LONDON EDUCATION AUTHORITY (1979). Report on the 1978 Census of those ILEA Pupils for whom English was not a First Language. ILEA Report 9484.

320   *Chinese Pupils in Britain*

INNER LONDON EDUCATION AUTHORITY (1981). Ethnic Census of School Support Centres and Educational Guidance Centres. Research and Statistics Report. London: ILEA.
INNER LONDON EDUCATION AUTHORITY (1982). 1981 Language Census. ILEA Report RS 811/82.
INNER LONDON EDUCATION AUTHORITY (1983). 1983 Language Census. ILEA Report RS 916/83.
INNER LONDON EDUCATION AUTHORITY (1986). 1985 Language Census. ILEA Report RS 1026/86.
INNER LONDON EDUCATION AUTHORITY: ENGLISH CENTRE (1979). *Our Lives: Young People's Autobiographies.* ILEA: English Centre.
JACKSON, B. (1979). *Starting School.* London: Croom Helm.
JACKSON, B. and GARVEY, A. (1974). 'The Chinese children of Britain', *New Society,* **30**, 9–12.
JAMES, H. and TENEN, C. (1950). 'How adolescents think of people', *Brit. J. Psychol.,* **41**, 145–72.
JEFFCOATE, R. (1984). *Ethnic Minorities and Education.* London: Harper and Row.
JOHNSON, A. and CORNER, T. (1984). 'Issues in multicultural and anti-racist education in Scotland.' Glasgow: SERA and NAME.
JONES, D. (1979). 'The Chinese in Britain: origins and development of a community', *New Community,* **VII**, 3, 397–402.
JONES, D. (1980). 'Chinese schools in Britain: a minority's response to its own needs', *Trends in Education,* Spring, 15–18.
JONES, I. (1979). 'Some cultural and linguistic considerations affecting the learning of English by Chinese in Britain', *Engl. Lang. Teach. J.,* **34**, 1, 55–61.
KHAN, N. (1976). *The Arts Britain Ignores: The Arts of Ethnic Minorities in Britain.* London: Commission for Racial Equality.
KINGSTON, M.H. (1981). *The Woman Warrior, Memories of a Girlhood among Ghosts.* London: Picador.
LADLOW, D.E. (1980). 'Suggestions and background information for teachers of Chinese children.' Mimeograph.
LADLOW, D.E. (n.d.[1]). English language difficulties for Chinese speakers – Résumé. Crown Street Language Centre, Liverpool 7.
LADLOW, D.E. (n.d.[2]). 'Aspects of Chinese culture'. Mimeograph. Crown Street Language Centre, Liverpool 7.
LAI, K. (1972). Problems facing Chinese immigrants in Liverpool. Unpublished fieldwork report for the degree of Diploma in Applied Social Studies, University of Hull.
LAI, L. (1975). Chinese families in London: a study into their social needs. Unpublished MA thesis, Brunel University.
LANGTON, P. (1979). *Chinese Children in British Schools.* London: CUES.
LAU, W.H. (1964). Attitudes towards family, race, teaching and self among Malayan and English students. Unpublished Ph.D thesis. University of Birmingham.
LINGUISTIC MINORITIES PROJECT (LMP) (1982a). Coventry Mother-Tongue Teaching Directory Survey 1981. Findings. First Report. University of London Institute of Education.
LINGUISTIC MINORITIES PROJECT (1982b). Bradford Mother-Tongue Teaching Directory Survey 1981. Findings. First Report. University of London Institute of Education.

LINGUISTIC MINORITIES PROJECT (1983a). *Linguistic Minorities in England.* A report by the Linguistic Minorities Project for the Department of Education and Science. London: ULIE and Heinemann Educational Books.

LINGUISTIC MINORITIES PROJECT (1983b). Mother-Tongue Teaching in Haringey. A First Report on the Findings of the Mother-Tongue Teaching Directory Survey in 1982. LMP and LINC, University of London Institute of Education.

LINGUISTIC MINORITIES PROJECT (1985). *The Other Languages of England.* London: Routledge and Kegan Paul.

LITTLE, A. and WILLEY, R. (1983). *Studies in the Multi-ethnic Curriculum.* Full Report from the Schools Council Project on Studies in the Multi-ethnic Curriculum based at Goldsmiths' College, University of London (1978–80). London: Schools Council.

LITTLEWOOD, R. and LIPSEDGE, M. (1982). *Aliens and Alienists: Ethnic Minorities and Psychiatry.* Harmondsworth: Penguin.

LOBO, E. DE H. (1978). *Children of Immigrants to Britain: Their Health and Social Problems.* Sevenoaks: Hodder and Stoughton.

LOTHIAN CRC (1978). 'Lothian CRC tackles curriculum', *Education,* **I**, 3, 2–3.

LUE, A.S.T. (1982). 'The Overseas Chinese Education Centre', *NCMTT Newsletter,* Spring.

LYNCH, J. (Ed) (1981). *Teaching in the Multi-cultural School.* London: Ward Lock Educational.

LYNN, I.L. (1982). *The Chinese Community in Liverpool: Their Unmet Needs with Respect to Education, Social Welfare and Housing.* Liverpool: Merseyside Area Profile Group.

MACKILLOP, J. (1980). Ethnic Minorities in Sheffield. Sheffield: Sheffield Metropolitan District Education Committee.

MARTIN-JONES, M. (1984). 'The newer minorities: literacy and educational issues'. In: TRUDGILL, P. *Language in the British Isles.* Cambridge: Cambridge University Press.

MAY, J.P. (1978). 'The Chinese in Britain, 1860–1914.' In: HOLMES, C. (Ed) *Immigrants and Minorities in British Society.* London: Allen and Unwin.

MILLWARD, R. (1977). Library services to the Chinese community: seminar on services to immigrant groups. Westminster City Libraries, p.10.

MO, T. (1982). *Sour Sweet.* London: Deutsch.

MOBBS, M.C. (1977). *Meeting their Needs – an Account of Language Tuition Schemes for Ethnic Minority Women.* London: Commission for Racial Equality.

MURRAY, A. (1984). 'Curriculum development for a multi-cultural society: an FEU perspective', *Educational Journal,* September, 9, 10, 22.

NATIONAL CHILDREN'S CENTRE (NCC) (1979). Report on the Third National Conference on Chinese Children in Britain, held April 1979. Huddersfield: NCC.

NATIONAL CHILDREN'S CENTRE (1984). The Silent Minority. The Report of the Fourth National Conference on the Chinese Community in Great Britain, November, 1982. Huddersfield: NCC.

NATIONAL EDUCATIONAL RESEARCH AND DEVELOPMENT TRUST (1977). First National Conference on Chinese Children in Britain. Huddersfield: NCC.

NATIONAL EDUCATIONAL RESEARCH AND DEVELOPMENT TRUST (1978). Report of the Second National Conference on Chinese Children in Britain. Huddersfield: NCC.

NG, A.K.T. (1982). Learning of Chinese by Chinese immigrant children. Unpublished B. Phil. thesis, University of Newcastle-upon-Tyne.

NG, K.C. (1968). *The Chinese in London.* London: Oxford University Press.

NORTHAMPTONSHIRE LEA (1980). *Report of LEA/Name Working Party on Mother Tongue Teaching and Mother Culture Maintenance in Northamptonshire.*

NUFFIELD FOUNDATION (1981). *Teaching Chinese Children. A Teacher's Guide.* London: CILT.

OFFICE OF POPULATION CENSUSES AND SURVEYS (OPCS) (1974). *Census 1971. Great Britain, Country of Birth Tables.* London: HMSO.

OFFICE OF POPULATION CENSUSES AND SURVEYS (1982a). 'Labour force survey 1981', *OPCS Monitor,* 11.5.82.

OFFICE OF POPULATION CENSUSES AND SURVEYS (1982b). *Labour Force Survey 1979.* London: HMSO.

OFFICE OF POPULATION CENSUSES AND SURVEYS (1983a). *Census 1981: Country of Birth.* London: HMSO.

OFFICE OF POPULATION CENSUSES AND SURVEYS (1983b). 'Labour Force Survey 1981: country of birth and ethnic origin', *OPCS Monitor,* 22.2.83.

OFFICE OF POPULATION CENSUSES AND SURVEYS (1984). 'Labour Force Survey 1983. Country of birth and ethnic origin, nationality and year of entry', *OPCS Monitor,* 18.12.84.

O'NEILL, J.A. (1972). The role of family and community in the social adjustment of the Chinese in Liverpool. MA thesis, University of Liverpool.

PERREN, G.E. (1975). 'Introduction.' In: CENTRE FOR INFORMATION ON LANGUAGE TEACHING *Less Commonly Taught Languages: Resources and Problems.* London: CILT.

POWELL, R. (1982). 'Dragon dancing in Manchester', *New Society,* 21.1.82, pp.105–6.

PRAGER, P. (1977). 'Minority languages', *Times Educ. Suppl.,* 3233, 20.5.77, p.27.

QUAKER COMMUNITY RELATIONS COMMITTEE (QCRC) (1981). The Chinese in Britain Today. Weekend Conference 30 January/1 February, 1981.

RATHBONE, M. and GRAHAM, N. (1983). *Bilingual Nursery Assistants: Their Use and Training.* London: Schools Council.

REID, E. (1984). 'Public examinations in ethnic minority languages: availability and currency.' In: REID, E. (Ed) *Minority Community Languages in School.* NCLE Papers and Reports 4. London: CILT.

ROSEN, H. and BURGESS, T. (1980). Linguistic Diversity in London Schools: An Investigation Carried out in the English Department of the University of London, Institute of Education. Mimeograph. Also: *Languages and Dialects of London School Children. An Investigation.* London: Ward Lock Educational.

SAIFULLAH KHAN, V. (1976). 'Provision by minorities for language maintenance.' In: CILT *Bilingualism and British Education: the Dimensions of Diversity.* CILT Reports and Papers 14. London: Centre for Information on Language Teaching and Research.

SAIFULLAH KHAN, V. (1977). 'Bilingualism and linguistic minorities in Britain, developments, perspectives. A briefing paper.' London: Runnymede Trust.

SAIFULLAH KHAN, V. (1980). 'Linguistic Minorities Project.' In: COMMISSION FOR RACIAL EQUALITY *Mother Tongue Teaching Conference Report.* Bradford College, 9–11 September. London: CRE.

SCHOOLS COUNCIL (1981). *Education for a Multiracial Society, Curriculum and Context 5–13.* London: Schools Council.

SHANG, A. (1984). *The Chinese in Britain.* Communities in Britain Series. London: Batsford Academic and Educational.
SILBERMAN, L. and SPICE, B. (1950). *Colour and Class in Six Liverpool Schools.* Liverpool: Liverpool University Press.
SIMSOVA, S. and CHIN, W.T. (1982). *Library Needs of Chinese in London.* School of Librarianship and Information Studies, Polytechnic of North London.
SINGH, B.R. (1984). 'Multicultural education: a study of the impact of the CNAA on a B.Ed. degree', *Educ. Studs,* **10**, 3, 227–36.
SING TAO NEWSPAPERS LTD (1980). *Chinese in Britain Handbook.* Uxbridge: Sing Tao Newspapers.
SLOSS, R.P. (1975). 'The Chinese language project – a model?' In: CENTRE FOR INFORMATION ON LANGUAGE TEACHING. *Less Commonly Taught Languages: Resources and Problems.* London: CILT.
STANDING COMMITTEE OF SCOTTISH COMMUNITY RELATIONS COUNCILS (SCSCRC) (1976). Report on the Chinese in Scotland Conference, Edinburgh, 23.5.1976.
TAN, S.P. (1982). Food Ideology and Food Habits of the Chinese Immigrants in London, and the Growth of their Young Children – Report of a Survey. London School of Hygiene and Tropical Medicine, Department of Human Nutrition.
TANSLEY, P. and CRAFT, A. (1984). 'Mother tongue teaching and support: a Schools Council inquiry', *J.Multiling. Multicult. Dev.,* **5**, 5, 367–84.
TAYLOR, M.J. (1981). *Caught Between. A Review of Research into the Education of Pupils of West Indian Origin.* Windsor: NFER-NELSON.
TAYLOR, M.J. with HEGARTY, S. (1985). *The Best of Both Worlds . . . ? A Review of Research into the Education of Pupils of South Asian Origin.* Windsor: NFER-NELSON.
TAYLOR, M.J. with HEGARTY, S. (1987). *Britain's Other Ethnic Minority Pupils – a Review of Research into their Education* (provisional title). Windsor: NFER-NELSON.
TAYLOR-FITZGIBBON, C. (1983). 'Peer tutoring: a possible method for multi-ethnic education', *New Community,* **XI**, 1–2, 160–6.
THOMAS, K.C., GIBSON, T., ATKIN, J. and CRAFT, M. (1984). *Lifestyles Pack.* Nottingham: Schools Council Development Unit in Multi-Ethnic Education. School of Education, University of Nottingham.
THOMSON, N. (1983). 'The Community Directive 77/486/EEC: origins and implementation', *J, Multiling. Multicult. Dev.,* **4**, 6, 437–58.
TIZARD, J., HEWISON, J. and SCHOFIELD, W.N. (1982). 'Collaboration between teachers and parents in assisting children's reading', *Brit. J. Educ. Psy.,* **52**, 1, 1–15.
TOWNSEND, H.E.R. (1971). *Immigrant Pupils in England: the LEA Response.* Slough: NFER.
TOWNSEND, H.E.R. and BRITTAN, E.M. (1972). *Organization in Multiracial Schools.* Slough: NFER.
TROYNA, B. and BALL, W. (1985). 'Styles of LEA policy intervention in multicultural/antiracist education', *Educational Review,* **37**, 2, 165–73.
TSANG, J. (1983). 'Forfeiting tradition to fit in with Western ways', *Daily Telegraph,* 18.2.1983, p.15.
TSOW, M. (1977). 'The Chinese – a community profile', Seminar on services to immigrant groups. Westminster City Libraries, p.9.
TSOW, M. (1980a). 'Chinese children and multi-cultural education', *Education Journal,* **II**, 2, 6.

324   *Chinese Pupils in Britain*

TSOW, M. (1980b). 'A Tower of Babel? Mother tongue? Issues related to mother-tongue teaching: clarification and framework.' In: COMMISSION FOR RACIAL EQUALITY *Mother Tongue Teaching Conference Report.* Bradford College, 9–11 September. London: CRE.

TSOW, M. (1982). *A Day with Ling.* London: Hamish Hamilton.

TSOW, M. (1983a). 'Community education: the unknown perspective – Chinese mother tongue classes', *J. Community Education,* **2**, 1, 38–44.

TSOW, M. (1983b). 'Analysis of responses to a national survey on mother tongue teaching in local education authorities 1980–82', *Educ. Res.,* **25**, 3, 202–8.

TSOW, M. (1984). *Mother-tongue Maintenance. A Survey of Part-time Chinese Language Classes.* London: CRE.

TWITCHIN, J. and DEMUTH, C. (1981). *Multi-cultural Education.* London: British Broadcasting Corporation.

VERMA, G. and ASHWORTH, B. (1981). 'Educational and occupational aspirations of young South Asians in Britain.' In: MEGARRY, J., NISBET, S. and HOYLE, E. (Eds) *World Yearbook of Education 1981. Education of Minorities.* London: Kogan Page.

VERMA, M.K. (1975). 'Hindi, Chinese and Swahili at York.' In: CENTRE FOR INFORMATION ON LANGUAGE TEACHING *Less Commonly Taught Languages: Resources and Problems.* London: CILT.

WAINWRIGHT, D.F. (1978). 'Ethnic minorities: music for the multi-cultural school', *Music in Education,* **42**, 392, 158–60.

WANG, B. (1981). 'Chinese children.' In: LIVERPOOL TEACHERS' ASSOCIATION *Before the Fire.* Liverpool: LTA.

WARD, B.G. (1977/8). 'Chinese migrants in Hong Kong and London.' (Review of WATSON, J.L., 1975). *Emigration and the Chinese Lineage: The Mans in Hong Kong and London.* (Berkeley, CA: University of California Press.) *New Community,* **VI**, 1–2, 172–5.

WATSON, J.L. (1977a). 'The Chinese: Hong Kong villagers in the British catering trade.' In: WATSON, J.L. (Ed) *Between two Cultures: Migrants and Minorities in Britain.* Oxford: Blackwell, pp.181–213.

WATSON, J.L. (1977b). 'Chinese emigrant ties to the home community', *New Community,* **V**, 4, 343–52.

WATSON, K. (1984). 'Training teachers in the United Kingdom, for a multicultural society – the rhetoric and reality', *J. Multilingual and Multicultural Development,* **5**, 5, 385–400.

WILSON, A. (1977). 'The desolate lives of some Chinese women in Britain', *Guardian,* 3.5.77.

WRIGHT, D. (1985). 'Teaching Chinese in a comprehensive school', *Modern Languages,* **LXVI**, 2, 109–13.

WRIGHT, J. (1980). 'The World in a City: ILEA Bilingual Education Project.' In: COMMISSION FOR RACIAL EQUALITY *Mother Tongue Teaching Conference Report.* Bradford College, 9–11 September. London: CRE.

Index

Swann Committee
Community Associations, 117–19,
198–9
community mutual aid, 107, 110–112,
118–9, 177
community perceptions, 102–5, 309–
10
self-perception, 102–3
of British and British culture,
112–16, 310–11
British perceptions of Chinese,
119–20, 312
Community Relations Commission
(CRC), 1, 85, 91, 96, 99, 111,
125, 274, 296
Cooke, M., 149, 294
Corner, T., 290
Cornwall, 101
Couillaud, X., 135
Council of Service for Chinese Workers,
99
Coventry, 100, 130, 131, 132, 133, 135,
139, 146, 181, 182, 187, 192, 199
Craft, A., 133, 179, 203
Craft, M., 173, 206, 295
Crane, A., 128
Crosby, 34
Croydon, London Borough of, 47
CSEs *see* examinations
culture and traditions, 76–7, 79, 81, 83
89, 94, 98–9, 101, 104–5, 106–7
115, 155–6, 166, 174, 175–6, 178,
191, 198, 200, 206, 209, 210, 229,
230, 233, 234, 239, 242, 243, 250,
255, 266, 276–7, 287–9, 306
see also social behaviour
cultural activities, 105–112, 117
cultural identity, 79, 155, 157, 176,
187, 210, 235, 243, 267–8, 277,
309–10
conflict, 115, 249–50, 253–4, 258,
267–8, 306, 307–8
curriculum, 171–2, 198, 203, 208–9,
236, 239, 243, 274–5, 289–93, 307,
308

Davies, H. 128
demography, *see* settlement and
demography
Demuth, C., 172, 258, 279, 291, 292,
302
Department of Education and Science
(DES), 123, 134, 154, 173, 195,
204, 207, 214, 277, 289, 295
Department of the Environment, 91
Department of Health and Social
Security, 91, 93
see also social services
Derby, 49, 52, 65, 123, 161, 223, 230,
269
English Language Centre, 170
Derbyshire, 181
Derrick, J., 209
Devon, 101
diet, 84–6, 88, 89, 93, 96–7, 239, 240,
243, 275–6
discipline, 97, 240, 243, 251, 272, 308
Doncaster, 181
Dorn, A., 290
drama, 176, 245, 275
dress, 242, 260–1
drugs, 32, 33, 253
Dublin, 100
Dummett, A., 35
Dundee, 181
Dunfermline, 181

Ealing, London Borough of, 44, 47,
190, 204
Edinburgh, 43, 44, 46, 47, 89, 100, 111,
178, 180, 207, 310
Edinburgh, University of, 205
Edinburgh Chinese Association, 108
Edson, P., 123
Elgin, 181
Elliott, P., 151, 178, 192, 195, 204
emigration from Hong Kong, *see* Hong
Kong
employment, 57
catering trade, post-war development of, 59–64, 65–6, 72
children in family business, 70–2,

264, 271, 273, 278
Leeds, 24, 100, 108, 109, 177, 178, 180
Leicester, 100, 181
Lewisham, London Borough of, 140
library service, *see* social services
linguistic difficulties, *see* language,
  English
Linguistic Minorities Project, 51, 52,
  69, 130, 179, 181, 190, 202, 302
  Adult Language Use Survey
    (ALUS), 130–2, 138, 139
  Mother-Tongue Teaching
    Directory Survey (MTTDS),
    130, 199–200
  Schools Language Survey (SLS),
    130, 135
  Secondary Pupils' Survey (SPS),
    130, 208
Lipsedge, M., 89
Little, A., 163, 173, 179, 198, 203, 204,
  215, 223, 232, 284, 314
Littlewood, R., 89
Liverpool, 1, 23, 31, 32, 33, 34, 43, 44,
  46, 47, 48, 49, 51, 52, 53, 54, 55,
  58, 66, 67, 68, 70, 73, 74, 76, 77,
  80, 81, 82, 86, 87, 91, 93, 95, 98,
  99, 100, 102, 103, 104, 106, 107,
  108, 109, 110, 111, 112, 113, 115,
  116, 118, 122, 123, 130, 137, 143,
  145, 150, 154, 162, 163, 164, 165,
  177, 179, 180, 185, 202, 211, 212,
  213, 217, 218, 222, 231, 232, 234,
  237, 239, 243, 244, 246, 247, 248,
  249, 251, 254, 260, 261, 262, 264,
  266, 278, 280, 282, 284, 295, 296,
  297, 301, 310, 312
  English Language Centre, 123,
    161–2, 164–6, 170, 211, 217–221,
    233, 244, 296, 297, 306
Lobo, E. de H., 78, 80, 85, 88, 157,
  250, 264
London, 1, 23, 24, 25, 31, 32, 33, 34,
  43, 44, 46, 47, 49, 50, 52, 53, 64,
  65, 66, 67, 68, 79, 83, 84, 86, 91,
  95, 100, 102, 106, 107, 108, 110,
  112, 117, 119, 122, 123, 129, 130,

131, 132, 133, 137, 138, 139, 140,
  146, 147, 148, 149, 150, 154, 164,
  176, 177, 178, 179, 180, 181, 183,
  184, 185, 187, 188, 189, 192, 195,
  199, 213, 223, 224, 229, 232, 234,
  239, 247, 253, 258, 264, 275, 284,
  285, 287, 294, 301, 303, 310, 312
  (*see also* individual London
  Boroughs)
London, University of, 205
London Association of Chinese Youth
  and Students, 117
Lothian Community Relations Council,
  293
Lue, A.S.T., 126, 152, 194, 203, 208,
  209
Luton, 180
Lynch, J., 293
Lynn, I.L., 33, 34, 38, 43, 49, 52, 54,
  55, 59, 60, 66, 69, 81, 86, 87, 88,
  89, 90, 93, 94, 98, 111, 112, 118,
  123, 129, 130, 137, 143, 150, 151,
  160, 161, 162, 164, 165, 169, 170,
  173, 213, 214, 217, 223, 225, 233,
  237, 238, 239, 240, 244, 245, 246,
  250, 254, 259, 263, 264, 268, 275,
  285, 286, 287, 297, 298, 300, 303,
  311

Mackillop, J., 52, 66, 100, 108, 112,
  116, 178, 222, 223, 234, 279, 287
Malaysia, 3, 6, 31, 35, 44, 45, 47, 75,
  86, 92, 99, 128, 190, 192, 222, 223,
  302
Manchester, 24, 43, 44, 46, 47, 93, 100,
  107, 108, 109, 112, 118, 145, 154,
  179, 180, 185, 204, 207, 218, 247,
  296, 310
Manchester Chinese Education Culture
  and Community Centre, 118,
  181, 183, 206, 207
Manpower Services Commission
  (MSC), 118
marriage, 36, 75, 77–8
  mixed, 32, 34, 73–5, 95, 115, 122,
    228, 266